CH00647836

Accounting for Tastes
Australian Everyday Cultures

Accounting for Tastes is the most systematic and substantial study of Australian cultural tastes, preferences and activities ever published. Taking its inspiration from Pierre Bourdieu's work, this book examines the relationships between the patterns of participation in the different fields of cultural practice in Australia, and analyses trends of consumption and choice that Australians make in their everyday lives. The book contains detailed examinations of people's cultural choices through a large-scale survey and interviews. It also examines the influence of American culture on Australian choices, and the way work cultures and cultures of friendship affect how Australians choose to spend their leisure time. *Accounting for Tastes* makes a substantial contribution to empirical and policy-oriented social inquiry into questions of cultural practices and preferences.

Tony Bennett is Professor of Sociology at the Open University. His publications include *Outside Literature* (1990) and *Culture: A Reformer's Science* (1998).
Michael Emmison is a senior lecturer in the Department of Anthropology and Sociology at the University of Queensland and is the co-author of *Class Analysis and Contemporary Australia* (1991).
John Frow is the Darnell Professor of English at the University of Queensland, whose most recent book *Time and Commodity Culture* was published in 1997.

Accounting for Tastes

Australian Everyday Cultures

Tony Bennett
Open University

Michael Emmison
University of Queensland

John Frow
University of Queensland

CAMBRIDGE
UNIVERSITY PRESS

PUBLISHED BY THE PRESS SYNDICATE OF THE UNIVERSITY OF CAMBRIDGE
The Pitt Building, Trumpington Street, Cambridge, United Kingdom

CAMBRIDGE UNIVERSITY PRESS
The Edinburgh Building, Cambridge CB2 2RU, UK   www.cup.cam.ac.uk
40 West 20th Street, New York, NY 10011-4211, USA   www.cup.org
10 Stamford Road, Oakleigh, Melbourne 3166, Australia
Ruiz de Alarcón 13, 28014, Madrid, Spain

© Cambridge University Press 1999

This book is in copyright. Subject to statutory exception
and to the provisions of relevant collective licensing agreements,
no reproduction of any part may take place without
the written permission of Cambridge University Press.

First published 1999

Printed in Australia by Brown Prior Anderson

Typeface New Aster 9/12 pt *System* Penta [MT]

A catalogue record for this book is available from the British Library

National Library of Australia Cataloguing in Publication data
Bennett, Tony, 1947– .
Accounting for tastes : Australian everyday cultures.
Bibliography
Includes index.
ISBN 0 521 63234 X.
ISBN 0 521 63504 7 (pbk).
1. Social surveys – Australia. 2. Popular culture –
Australia – American influences. 3. Australia – Social
life and customs – 1990– . 4. Australia – Social
conditions – 1990– . I. Emmison, Michael. II. Frow, John,
1948– . III. Title
306.08924

Library of Congress Cataloguing in Publication data
Bennett, Tony.
Accounting for tastes : Australian everyday cultures / Tony
Bennett, Michael Emmison, John Frow.
p.   cm.
Includes bibliographical references and index.
ISBN 0-521-63234-X (hc. : alk. paper). — ISBN 0-521-63504-7 (pbk. : alk. paper)
1. Popular culture — Australia. 2. Lifestyles — Australia.
3. Consumer behaviour — Australia. 4. Leisure — Australia. 5. Social
surveys — Australia. 6. Australia — Social life and customs — 20th
century. I. Emmison, Michael, 1948– . II. Frow, John, 1948– .
III. Title
HN843.5.B45   1999
306'.0994 — dc21   99-31121
                                           CIP

ISBN 0 521 63234 X hardback
ISBN 0 521 63504 7 paperback

Contents

v

Figures

Figures

Tables

Note: Unless noted otherwise on the table, the unit or measure for numbers in the table is per cent.

Acknowledgements

We are grateful, first, to the Australian Research Council (ARC) for the award of a Large Grant which enabled us to conduct the research on which the findings we report here are based. We are similarly grateful to the University of Queensland for the award of an ARC Small Grant which allowed us to conduct a pilot project which proved invaluable in refining our methodology.

Although three names appear on the cover of this book, others have, at various times, been members of the research team and contributed to the development of the project. We thank David Chant, Georgina Murray, and Judyth Sachs for their inputs in this respect, and David Chant for his advice at a later stage when the project was nearing completion. We also thank Mark Western for his willingness to share his statistical expertise with us and Terry Shaw, the Senior Research Officer of the Statistical Consultancy Unit in the Brisbane office of the Australian Bureau of Statistics, for his assistance in drawing the sample for the survey.

Although the responsibility for designing the *Australian Everyday Cultures* survey on which our findings rest and for the schedule of questions that were explored with a selection of our respondents at a later date was ours, many other people have helped in putting these two components of the inquiry into effect. We thank Barbara Johnstone for her initiative, efficiency and unfailing good humour in organising the focus discussion groups whose conversations helped us immeasurably in designing our pilot survey. We owe

Andrea Lanyon a similar debt for her thoroughness and patience in introducing two of us to the unforgiving literalism of the SAS program which, eventually, we learned to live with and even to enjoy.

Before we got to that stage, however, our data needed to be coded and entered. We thank Sean Smith, Andrew Peake, Susan Luckman and James Lette whose expert knowledge of contemporary Australian popular culture made a significant contribution to this process.

At a later stage, when all the numbers were in, we relied substantially on Eduardo de la Fuente to organise a team of interviewers to conduct home-based interviews with a selection of our respondents. We thank Eduardo for this work as well as for the clarity of the report he prepared to guide us through the interview transcripts. We are also grateful to the interviewers for the skill, tact and engagement with which they approached their task. Thanks, then, to Annelise Mellor, Gil Woodley, Linda Campbell and to Barbara Johnstone again. And a big thanks to Glenda Donovan for her prompt and expert translation of the interview tapes into printed transcripts, and to Bev Jeppesen and Monique Hudson for their help in preparing the final typescript.

We also benefited from the critical but helpful comments of the friends and colleagues who looked through the early drafts of different parts of this book. Our special thanks here to Christine Alavi, Patrick Buckridge, Jim McKay, and Graeme Turner for their insightful criticisms.

The final and greatest debt we need to acknowledge, however, is that which we owe the 2756 respondents who completed our survey, especially those who agreed to a follow-up interview. We thank them for their interest in the project, for the time they spared to share with us – whether anonymously or in person – the details of their cultural interests and activities. We have no way of knowing what any of them would make of this book. But we would like to think that, however little or however much they might agree with our arguments, they would recognise that we have sought to make good and productive use of the information they placed in our hands.

We would like to thank Penguin Books Australia for permission to reproduce the cover of Albert Facey's *A Fortunate Life* on the front cover of this book.

Introduction

To say that 'there is no accounting for tastes' is usually a way of expressing an easy-going tolerance for the 'strange' tastes of other people. It can also, however, be a way of suggesting that tastes are so individual and idiosyncratic as to be unaccountable in the sense of being beyond the reach of reasoned understanding. We start out, in this book, from the premise that this is not so. Indeed, our main purpose is to show how the tastes that are evident in the cultural choices and preferences of contemporary Australians are pre-eminently social in their organisation and character. Our likes and dislikes have a definite pattern, one which emerges from the roles played by social class, age, gender, education, and ethnicity in distributing cultural interests and abilities differentially across the population. We also argue that the social pattern of cultural tastes in contemporary Australia is enmeshed within complexly interacting forms of social and cultural power by means of which differences in cultural preference are used as markers of social position and, in some circumstances, as a way of unequally distributing cultural life-chances.

The main basis for our arguments on these matters is the statistical evidence provided by a national survey of the cultural practices and preferences of 2756 adult Australians that we conducted in late 1994/early 1995. We had three main aims in view in designing the *Australian Everyday Cultures* survey. First, in order to map as comprehensively as possible a range of cultural practices, we asked questions about everything we could think of that counted as 'culture', including home-based leisure activities, fashion, the ownership of cars and electronic equipment, eating habits, friendships, holidays, outdoor activities, gambling, sport, reading, artistic pursuits, watching

1

television, cinema-going, and the use of libraries, museums and art galleries. Second, as a way of understanding the principles underlying particular patterns of cultural activity and their accompanying likes and dislikes, we asked some questions designed to explore attitudes to aesthetic and cultural matters – views about art and suitable objects for photography, for example. Third, we explored the social backgrounds of our respondents in considerable detail, asking about their educational histories, occupations, incomes, place of residence, religion, political affiliations and views, gender, and ethnicity – as well as related questions concerning their parents' backgrounds and their plans for their children. Our purpose here was to provide the means of mapping the social backgrounds of our respondents in as much detail as their cultural tastes and interests so that, by correlating the two, we might produce a richly textured *social* cartography of cultural tastes.

This survey (reproduced as Appendix 2) is not the only basis of our discussion in what follows. As a prelude to the national survey, we carried out a pilot study centred on Brisbane and its neighbouring postal districts. Administered in late 1993, the questions we asked in this initial survey owed a good deal to a dozen or so focus-group discussions we organised earlier that year to find out at first hand the main cultural interests and involvements of Australians from different social backgrounds. We then, in late 1996 through into early 1997, conducted home-based interviews with 34 of the respondents who filled in the *Australian Everyday Cultures* survey. As with the membership of our earlier focus groups, our purpose, in deciding who to interview, was to encompass a range of different social backgrounds aiming for a rough balance of men and women, a range of ages and class positions, varying levels of educational achievement as well as a diversity of locations including rural contexts, provincial cities, two capital cities (Brisbane and Sydney) and their immediate environs. The resulting oral testimony of the cultural interests and activities of specific individuals and, as often as not, their families is a resource we draw on frequently to help make sense of the statistical patterns arising out of the *Australian Everyday Cultures* survey and to give a more vivid sense of the lived texture of the cultural practices underlying the more abstract and disembodied nature of our statistical findings.

Some of the particular areas of cultural activity we consider have been examined in earlier studies – some of them academic, others prepared for or by organisations like the Australia Council or the National Culture/Leisure Statistics Unit of the Australian Bureau of Statistics. What hasn't been attempted before, however, is a study of the *relationships* between the patterns of participation in the different fields of cultural practice that we encompass in this study. We have therefore, in designing this book, aimed to look in close detail at the main fields of cultural practice that our survey encompasses as well as considering the similarities and differences between them.

We start by taking our theoretical bearings from the work of the French sociologist Pierre Bourdieu whose *Distinction: A Social Critique of the Judgement of Taste* has been our main source of inspiration and, like all sources of inspiration, our main object of critique too. In chapter 1, we accordingly indicate what we have taken from the work of Bourdieu, especially his account of the role played by particular kinds of cultural skill – what Bourdieu calls 'cultural capital' – in organising social distinctions, and where we have judged it necessary to part company with him on either theoretical grounds or – taking account of the differences between Australia in the 1990s and France in the 1960s – empirical ones. We also discuss the respects in which our study has been shaped by the perspectives of cultural studies and the issues that are posed by work situated on the interdisciplinary borderlands between sociology and cultural studies. These include a consideration of what cultural studies has to gain from the quantitative research methods of sociology and an appreciation of the dangers which attend such methods unless their use is accompanied by a self-reflexive awareness of the constructive role they play within the research process in organising their objects of study into being. We conclude this chapter by briefly reviewing the main demographic characteristics of the sample for the *Australian Everyday Cultures* survey.

In chapter 2, our concerns are, loosely speaking, ethnographic as we consider the light our interview material throws on the social factors informing the cultural choices that individuals make in and about the house. In looking closely at what men and women from a range of different class and educational backgrounds tell us about their home-based leisure activities, their preferences in furnishings and decoration, their preferred styles of entertaining, and their collections of paintings, china or books, we show how these can be related to their socially rooted experiences and aspirations. We then locate these individual preferences and activities in a broader context by showing how, in statistical terms, attitudes towards the home and participation in home-based activities are profoundly differentiated in terms of gender, class, and education.

Chapter 3 also focuses on the home, but from a different perspective; we concentrate on the patterns of ownership of the range of media and communications technologies that are typically found in the home: telephone, television, radio, VCRs, personal computers, CDs, and so on. We also look at the uses to which these different technologies are put, and how these uses vary in accordance with gender, place of residence, class, and the age composition of households. In moving on to consider the television-viewing, radio-listening and – moving outside the home – cinema-going activities and preferences of our sample, we lend support to the now considerable body of evidence stressing the widely varied ways in which media are used by men and women, by different age groups, and by the members of different social classes.

The home, of course, is often defined in opposition to places of work. Culture, too, especially in its close association with the concept of leisure, is often separated from the world of work. In chapter 4, we counter the impression that work is a 'culture-free' zone by showing that work has its own cultures and that these are closely connected with all other aspects of cultural life. In doing so we consider the respects in which involvement in work of various kinds (full-time, part-time; employed, self-employed) and the positions that individuals occupy in work-based relations of power and authority and in the varied cultures of work are affected by a historically distinctive division of labour in which the effects of gender, class, education, region and ethnicity are prominent. We also show how these relations to work spill over into other aspects of cultural life, including cultures of friendship for example. This leads to a discussion of leisure activities associated with a range of contexts outside the home – going to the theatre, musicals, pubs or clubs; holidays; camping and bush-walking; and gambling, in all its forms – and the tendency for participation in these to be sharply polarised along the lines of conventional 'high'/'popular' distinctions.

The salience of such distinctions is a matter that we return to at various points in later chapters. They are taken into account when we consider, in chapter 5, the part played by different forms of diet, exercise and sport in organising distinctive relationships to the body – ways of working on and with the body that are, at the same time, ways of shaping a distinctive self. Our interest in these matters has to do with the role of such practices of the body in the processes of gendering, racialisation and classing through which we are formed as particular kinds of persons. Again, our evidence suggests that the roles which practices of the body play in relation to processes of person formation are closely bound up with distinctive hierarchies of body cultures articulated, in complex ways, with relations of class, gender, and ethnicity.

The concerns of chapter 6 centre on the social organisation of reading practices, including how much people read, the kinds of reading (books, magazines, and newspapers) they prefer, their favourite authors, the books they buy, and so forth. Gender proves to be the most significantly differentiating factor here. Although there is a good deal of shared ground between women's and men's reading, other aspects of their reading are markedly polarised into what are virtually entirely separate feminised and masculinised domains. Our interests in this chapter focus on the relationships between this gendered organisation of reading practices and conventional hierarchies of literary value. While women's preferences are often for genres which are held in low esteem, it is also true that women are much more likely than men – who prefer scientific and factual genres – to read canonical literary works. This picture is complicated, however, when the effects of class are taken into account.

Chapter 7 looks at music, where differences of taste have served as an unusually sensitive measure of the relations between 'high' and 'low' culture and of the role which such relations play in distinguishing different social classes from each other. How far is this true in Australia? To answer this question, we look at the evidence regarding our respondents' musical likes and dislikes as represented by their favourite and least-favourite musical genres, performers and composers. We also look at the evidence we gathered about musical knowledge and the extent to which this varies with social position. This proves important in assessing those arguments which contend that musical tastes, rather than reflecting a distinction between 'elite' and 'mass' taste cultures, correspond to a division between cultural 'omnivores' and 'univores': that is, between the wide-ranging and inclusive tastes of those with high levels of education and the more restricted tastes of less-educated groups. We argue that such views, although not without merit, fail to distinguish properly between the distribution of knowledge about music and the distribution of musical likes and dislikes. On the larger question the chapter addresses, however, we conclude that music does indeed remain one of the most sensitive measures of cultural capital and of its relationships to class.

One of our strongest reservations regarding Bourdieu's *Distinction* concerns its insularity in discussing French culture as a hermetically closed system. In view of the degree to which, historically, Australian culture has been shaped by the cultural flows of different phases of European and Asian migration, this has never been a viable option here. It is even less so today when the boundaries between different national cultures are becoming more porous as a result of increasingly globalised patterns of cultural production and distribution. How do these factors affect the cultural interests and preferences of Australians? This is the central question guiding our discussion in chapter 8 where we take another look at our evidence relating to film, television and music preferences, but from the perspective of considering the extent to which age affects an interest in Australian compared with American materials. The conclusions we draw are mixed. Young people are the most likely to prefer American music and television over Australian material, yet – and it is here that we are critical of simplified accounts of globalisation as 'media imperialism' – this does not seem to imperil young Australians' sense of their national identity. Equally, when viewed in the light of the strong government support the Australian film industry has enjoyed since the 1970s, the strong interest of young Australians in Australian films suggests the positive role that cultural industry policies can play in building national audiences.

Policy questions are to the fore of our concerns in chapter 9. Written at a time when the role that governments should play in supporting cultural activities is very much in question, this chapter examines the extent to which government support for cultural activities increases their accessibility to a broad cross-section of the population. This involves a consideration of the composition of the audiences for public broadcasting, for the institutions of public culture (museums, libraries, art galleries), and for publicly subsidised cultural forms – opera and the theatre, for example. These are considered in relation to the operation of private cultural markets. Our findings suggest that, while there is little doubt that public broadcasting and the institutions of public culture do not recruit their audiences evenly from across all sections of the population, they are more successful in this respect than are private cultural markets or the 'flagship' institutions of theatre, opera, and the like which operate on a hybrid public/private funding basis. We accordingly argue that current tendencies leading towards the increased privatisation of both culture and education are likely to result in a more unequal distribution of cultural life-chances – or opportunities to participate in cultural life – than is at present the case.

We return, in chapter 10, to the questions from which we take our initial bearings in chapter 1: how are relations of class and culture organised in Australia? how do these intersect with relations of gender, age, ethnicity, and culture? what are the connections between these forms of cultural power and the exercise of social power? In order to answer these questions, we first draw together a series of summary profiles of the different demographic groups discussed in the earlier chapters, paying particular attention to age cohorts, genders, and social classes. In looking at the specific configurations of these variables that are evident in different fields of cultural practice, we argue that they do not give rise to a simple 'high'/'popular' dichotomisation of cultural practices that can be mapped on to relations of social power in a singular fashion. The result, rather, is a number of competing cultural dichotomisations articulated to different social divisions, suggesting a relatively plural and diffused set of connections between the social and cultural forms in which power is organised and exercised.

We have, then, cast our net widely in mapping the distribution of Australian cultural practices. Inevitably, though, there are significant aspects of Australian cultural life that we have not been able to include in our statistical portrait. We are aware, in retrospect, of many other questions we could usefully have asked in the *Australian Everyday Cultures* survey, and of some that we should have asked. Our discussion of class, for example, would have benefited if we had asked about the ownership of shares and other assets. That said, it is notoriously difficult to obtain statistically reliable information about the cultural practices of the richest and most economically powerful classes, and we remain unsure whether asking questions of this kind would have thrown much light on the cultural preferences of the high bourgeoisie who, in our study as in most forms of social inquiry, remain more or less invisible. We should have liked, too, to have explored the sexualities and sexual practices of our respondents in view of their evident cultural significance in their own right and in their implications for other areas of cultural choice and practice. It was clear, however, that including questions on these matters would have significantly affected the response rates and the validity of our findings. Some important voices are also missing from the interviews we conducted. These would have been more representative had we worked harder to ensure that an adequate complement of 18 to 25 year olds was included in the interview sample.

No doubt there are other shortcomings, but we leave these for our readers to identify. Whatever the merits of our findings, however, we have, in working together on this project, become strongly convinced of the need for debates concerned with questions of cultural theory, policy and practice to be conducted in relation to the kinds of empirical evidence we have gathered during this inquiry. We have found the different methods we have used enormously fruitful in giving us a detailed sense of the richness and complexity of people's cultural activities, and we hope this book conveys something of the fascination and pleasure we have found in thinking and writing about them.

Chapter 1

Theorising Cultures

Culture and Classification

The American sociologist Howard Becker once wrote that 'people do not experience their aesthetic beliefs as merely arbitrary and conventional; they feel that they are natural, proper and moral'.[1] That feeling is at the heart of the phenomenon that this book explores: the making of cultural choices, in every dimension of daily life, which differ in relatively systematic ways according to the kind of person you are – or rather the *kinds* of person, because these differences occur along a number of different axes of social being. We all have a sense that these choices – preferring yum cha to McDonald's, or living in the city rather than living in the suburbs, or wearing silver instead of gold, or listening to Bach rather than Wagner or Pearl Jam rather than Elton John – are significant; they go to the core of who we are, and we are likely to feel that anyone who is blind enough to make the opposite choices is in some sense deficient or even downright strange.

Cultural choice positions us: it tells us and others who we are, and it defines for us and for others who we are not. It sorts us into 'kinds' of people. Although these kinds come to seem 'natural', they have everything to do with the organisation of the social. By this we mean, not that some ineluctable force channels us into the taste-cultures that 'correspond' to the different modes of our social being, or that a mysterious logic matches up our 'choices' with a social destiny, but rather that the sorting, the grouping, is done by us as we shape and elaborate a social place that is partly given and partly chosen in the open-ended formation of our lives. The choices are always constrained by the hard realities that structure life-chances, but culture is a matter of our formation of ourselves, under specific circumstances and in specific relations to others, as members of a group – indeed of a multiplicity of intersecting and overlapping groups.

These questions of cultural choice and practice have been central to those strands of sociology running from Thorstein Veblen and Max Weber (and, at a later time, from Erving Goffman) that have been concerned with how symbolic material is put to use in the processes of social differentiation; they have also been important issues in contemporary cultural studies. The model from which we have drawn our inspiration in this book is the work of Pierre Bourdieu, who has explored the social complexities of the French cultural system in a number of books over the last thirty years. In particular, we have closely followed the example of *Distinction*, first published in 1979 and translated into English in 1984, which remains the most ambitious and most comprehensive analysis of the social functions of taste, and which has developed the most rigorous theoretical vocabulary currently available as a basis for this analysis.

Based on two major surveys, undertaken in 1963 and 1967–8, of a sample of 1217 people in Paris, Lille and a small provincial town, Bourdieu's research seeks to investigate in a systematic manner one of the most simple yet most fundamental questions about culture: how is it differentially distributed, and what statistical regularities can be observed in this distribution? This question supposes that the distribution is not random, and that its regularities will correspond to other dimensions of human activity and of social structure. It is a matter, that is to say, both of social differences, and of social differentiation; and it assumes that the meanings of culture have more to do with the uses to which it is put (uses that Bourdieu summarises in the word 'distinction') than with any intrinsic value of aesthetic and cultural materials. If culture distinguishes people and groups of people both in the sense of setting them apart and in the sense of raising some above others, it follows that it has to do not only with social difference but also with social inequality; the exercise of taste puts culture to the use of sorting out the distinguished from the vulgar, the socially 'high' from the socially 'low', across a potentially infinite number of scales.

In Bourdieu's model, the major dimension of social inequality involved in these uses of cultural materials is social class; class and culture form parallel and mutually overdetermining worlds. Erickson (1996: 217) summarises his position in this manner:

> class and culture are both vertically ranked in mutually reinforcing ways. The culture of the highest classes becomes the most distinguished culture, apparently because it is innately superior but really because it is the culture of those who rule. In its turn, culture is a class signal that helps to maintain class domination and to shape individual life chances, much as economic capital does.

What is at stake in cultural choices, then, is not simply differences in taste but the ability of the dominant class to impose the value attributed to those differences, in such a way that some choices count as 'legitimate' and others lack legitimacy. Rather than obeying a purely aesthetic logic, aesthetic judgements transpose distinctions of class into distinctions of taste, and vice versa, and thereby strengthen the boundaries between classes. But they also assert the legitimacy of the dominance of the ruling class. Bourdieu argues this through an economic metaphor: competence in 'legitimate' cultural codes constitutes a 'cultural capital' which is unequally distributed among the social classes, although it has the appearance of an innate talent, a 'natural gift'.

The concept of cultural capital performs two complementary tasks. The first is to explain how advantages of birth or wealth are translated into social prestige by a displacement of these primary indicators of social power into partly autonomous systems of aesthetic and cultural values. The second is to elucidate the mechanisms by which patterns of social advantage are reproduced in and through the schooling system despite the fact that modern centralised state education systems were designed specifically to provide equality of opportunity for children of all classes. An alternative explanation would involve making the double assumption (a) that natural talent is the basis of social advantage, and (b) that talent or intelligence is genetically transmitted; but these assumptions hardly explain why it is, as Bourdieu and Passeron (1964: 12) put it, that – in the France of the time – a child of upper-class parents had 80 times the chance of entering tertiary education as the child of an agricultural labourer, 40 times that of the child of a worker, and twice that of the child of middle-class parents.

The notion of cultural capital is of course a metaphor. In his most precise treatment of the concept Bourdieu (1986: 241–2) defines capital as

> accumulated labour (in its materialised form or its 'incorporated,' embodied form) which, when appropriated on a private, i.e., exclusive basis by agents or groups of agents, enables them to appropriate social energy in the form of reified or living labour;

the distribution of capitals among individuals and classes determines 'the chances of success for practices'. By 'capital' Bourdieu does not, however, mean solely financial wealth; rather he distinguishes between three forms in which the crystallisation or reification of 'social energy' is manifested:

> as *economic capital*, which is immediately and directly convertible into money and may be institutionalised in the form of property rights; as *cultural capital*, which is convertible, on certain conditions, into economic capital and may be institutionalised in the

form of educational qualifications; and as *social capital*, made up of social obligations ('connections'), which is convertible, in certain conditions, into economic capital and may be institutionalised in the form of a title of nobility. (Bourdieu 1986: 243)

Like the other two forms, cultural capital is unequally distributed among social groups – or, to put this more precisely, it is differentially formed in accordance with the different experiences and conditions of existence of the different social classes. These experiences and common conditions, however diverse they may be for individuals, are integrated in what Bourdieu calls the *habitus*, a 'system of durable, transposable *dispositions*' (Bourdieu 1977: 72) which produces ways of looking at the world and of operating in it which are relatively common to the members of any particular social class and which is something like a 'class unconscious'. Within the schooling system, the differences between habitus are reinforced and intensified, and are thus translated into differences both in modes of learning, and in the kinds of knowledge that are acquired; the school rewards certain kinds of attitude and competence, and disfavours others (Bourdieu & Passeron 1970: 25). This is to say that there is an 'affinity' (which is of course in no way accidental) between the cultural and cognitive habits of the higher social classes and the criteria of acceptance and success in the school system, and it is this affinity, rather than innate ability *by itself*, which explains the relatively greater success rates of students from those classes (Bourdieu & Passeron 1964: 37). The habitus, and the cultural capital that flows from it, thus provide the cultural and cognitive *resources* for scholastic success (or, alternatively, set in place the conditions for scholastic failure). Within the cultural domain, differences between habitus are manifested both as variable competences in judgement, and as series of rough homologies between the choices one makes and the positions one occupies in very different fields. Here, too, these structural differences resting upon elective affinities are consequential. To make cultural choices, even at the most trivial level, is at once to position oneself and to be positioned in the game of social distinction; cultural capital may complement or supplement or displace or even oppose economic capital, but it is always a force within a field of forces.

Bourdieu's specific investigation of a range of domains of cultural practice is immensely rich, and his theorisation is a good deal more complex than we can do justice to here; we refer to a number of aspects of his analysis in the subsequent chapters. At the same time, we have some major theoretical differences with him, which we briefly outline here (for a fuller discussion see Frow 1987).

The first of our arguments with Bourdieu has to do with the scope of his analysis, and this in part reflects no more than the changing of the world since the 1960s, as well as the specificity of his analysis to the strongly hierarchised social and cultural structures of France. *Distinction* pays little attention to popular culture, and particularly not to mass-mediated culture: television, for example, is barely discussed. More generally, Bourdieu has been criticised (e.g. Garnham 1986: 432) for his failure to theorise institutional structures, such as the culture industries. The other major gaps in his work – and these tend to be constant throughout his oeuvre – have to do with his lack of interest in questions of gender and of race and ethnicity. The primary category through which he analyses the differential structure of social relations is class; as we indicate in a later section of this chapter, however, his account of class oscillates between a conventional ranking according to relation to economic capital (bourgeoisie/employers, petit bourgeoisie/middle class, working class), and a stratification by occupation. It is never clear how these two very different models of class translate into each other – and indeed we believe that they cannot, since they are built on incompatible conceptual bases. One of the major ambitions of our study is to put into practice a more adequately theorised model of social class.

A second problem that we identify in Bourdieu's work is the tension between, on the one hand, the theorisation of practice (especially in his more anthropologically oriented writings) as fluid, interactive, strategic, relational, and, on the other hand, the construction, in his sociological analyses, of conceptual oppositions which tend to be static and substantial. Much of his statistical charting of correspondences between taste cultures and socioeconomic groupings depends upon such reified dichotomies. The tension is evident in the very structure of his sentences, which, with their layering of clauses and their often convoluted attempt to grasp reciprocal or interactive modes of causality, nevertheless ground these dialectical movements in structures of simple dichotomy to which they constantly return.

A third problem has to do with the concept of habitus, which depends upon precisely such a dichotomy – between the inside and the outside, the social and the individual – in order to posit its transcendence in the notion of a 'structured and structuring structure' (Bourdieu 1994: 170), the practical sense embedded in the body which allows for the repeated generation of relatively constant choices and actions across time and in the face of changed conditions. Yet – as Bourdieu himself somewhat uncomfortably recognises (Bourdieu & Wacquant 1992: 129) – the concept comes dangerously close to being a tautology (one makes petit-bourgeois choices because one has a petit-bourgeois habitus); and as Jenkins (1992) argues, in its emphasis on the integration of social agents into predetermined positions, it may be little more than a sophisticated form of structural functionalism.

The final problem that we identify is that Bourdieu's account of a world organised by parallel and mutually reinforcing hierarchies of class and taste may reflect a 'modernist' structure of social power which is no longer fully applicable to the mass-mediated, weakly taxonomised social formations of the end of the twentieth century. Drawing on a number of historical studies, DiMaggio (1987) has argued that it was only in the late nineteenth century that the distinction between high and popular culture was fully formed and institutionalised. Based in 'the construction of ritual and organisational boundaries separating artist from audience, culture from commerce, the tasteful from the tasteless' (446), these vertical classificatory systems had the effect of conveying 'a moral content that reflects credit onto the social constituencies of highly ranked genres' (447). The boundary strength of the classifications is a function of the sharpness of the break between social classes, and of their internal consistency. A high degree of structural consolidation, and thus of congruence between different dimensions of status (wealth, family standing, education, ethnicity, political influence), is therefore a precondition of strong vertical hierarchies of the kind that Bourdieu describes. With the advent of the widespread commodification of culture, and thus of mass markets in which producers and distributors seek extensive and weakly differentiated audiences in order to achieve economies of scale, the ritual differentiations between status groups tend to decline. We are entering, DiMaggio suggests (452), a period of 'cultural declassification'. It may be that DiMaggio is describing in part the difference not just between nineteenth- and late twentieth-century America, but also between the kinds of society that France and the United States, with their very different structures of social mobility, represent. Whether or not this is the case, it seems likely that this account of the weakening of taxonomic boundaries is equally applicable to contemporary Australia, and we have used it as a possible model in our exploration of cultural practices and preferences.

Questions of Method and Discipline

A further difference between our work and that of Bourdieu consists in the disciplinary protocols which have shaped our inquiry. Bourdieu, of course, has always written as a sociologist; indeed, militantly so in his unremitting advocacy of the virtues of an empirically grounded, theoretically reflexive sociology over the more philosophical and, in his eyes, fanciful intellectual styles which have characterised the work of many other leading French intellectuals. In Anglophone countries, questions concerning the relations of culture, class, gender and ethnicity have been equally to the fore in debates within cultural studies – debates which, supposing we had an inclination to do so, have been too influential to be ignored. We have, however, had no such inclination. To the contrary, our purpose in working together on this project has been to learn from the different disciplinary perspectives we have been able to contribute as a team whose members include one whose career and professional identity has always been within sociology, a second who has moved from a disciplinary training in comparative literature to locate his work mainly within cultural studies, and a third who has moved between sociology and cultural studies at different points in his career. Given this, the question of opting for either sociology or cultural studies simply never arose; the issue was always one of how to effect a productive imbrication of the concerns and procedures of both.

The most important theoretical and practical considerations this raised for us concerned our relationship to the quantitative methods of sociology. On the one hand, we wanted to make an empirical contribution to the concerns of cultural studies which often suffer from the lack of an appropriately disciplined engagement with 'the real'. On the other, we were painfully aware of the ethical and theoretical difficulties that can accompany the uncritical application of quantitative methodologies. Others also reminded us of these.

When making a preliminary presentation of our findings at a cultural studies conference, for example, we were asked whether, in deciding to conduct a national statistical survey of Australian cultural practices, we had been mindful of the role that statistical surveys had played in the development of modern forms of social surveillance. Our answer was that, yes, it had concerned us considerably. The connections, in the mid to late nineteenth century, between the first social surveys to concern themselves with mapping the tastes and cultures of the working classes and the development of administrative forms aimed at effecting, in Mary Poovey's words, the 'surveillance and ocular penetration of poor neighbourhoods' (Poovey 1995: 35) are perfectly clear. As parts of a distinctive strategy of government, their purpose was to make the ways of life of the poor visible and, thereby, amenable to statist forms of administrative regulation. There is equally no doubt that the cultural statistics that are collected in contemporary societies are significant components in the organisation of power relations through which ways of life and the relationships between them are subjected to administrative regulation. This leads critics like John Hartley to dismiss statistical research into media audiences as a form of 'clipboard empiricism' which, in providing knowledge which allows agents of various kinds to act on audiences with a range of ends in view, has to be seen as part of a 'technology of control' that is inimical to the real activities and interests of audiences themselves (Hartley 1996: 64–5).

There is, in our view, a more complex politics of visibility that has to be worked through in relation to matters of this kind. There is, for example, no means, in the absence of sophisticated cultural statistics, of pursuing cultural diversity or access and equity policies in anything other than a purely gestural fashion. Such policies are precisely about managing ways of life and their interrelations and, as such, they require detailed forms of statistical monitoring if they are to be pursued with vigour and commitment. It is arguable that the absence of an appropriately detailed and holistic statistical map of Australian cultural practices and their participants has been a serious impediment to the ability of governments, supposing they have had the will, to pursue cultural diversity and access and equity policies with anything like the kind of 'bite' required to make such policies truly effective. For our part, then, the *Australian Everyday Cultures* survey has been conceived, in part, as a way of making good this gap and so contributing to the concerns of those political and administrative tendencies which favour cultural policies committed to the pursuit of social equity and justice.

This does not, however, address our theoretical reservations regarding quantitative survey methods. These mainly concern how the results of such methods are represented. We said earlier that our interest in such methods was prompted partly by a wish to subject cultural studies to a disciplined form of engagement with 'the real'. The danger, though, is that, if interpreted in the light of the positivist assumptions which often accompany them, the results of quantitative methodologies can often be mistaken for reality itself. The perspectives of cultural studies are a safeguard against this tendency – clearly identified by Theodor Adorno in his engagements with American sociology (see Jay 1973) – towards the reification of technique, for they provide a constant reminder that the application of statistical methods of inquiry gives rise to specific ways of representing 'the real' which, as is true of the results of other forms of inquiry, have distinctive rhetorical properties. The categories that organise our survey are constructs, artifices of a method which frames the questions in a certain way, chooses a particular form of the independent variables, weights the data to conform to the national census figures, and subjects them to complex statistical manipulations (each with its inbuilt assumptions) to produce the 'findings' which then form the raw material for theoretical interpretation. Statistical analysis, in Mary Poovey's words, 'both depends on and produces that which lies beyond representation': it '*depends* on the unfigured in the sense that its characteristic tables always include the uncounted; the figures imply, if they do not in fact record, not exact counts but *estimates*', from which a fiction of totality is then extrapolated; and it *produces* an excess in so far as it constructs in advance the categories which determine what is to be counted and which then govern the forms of implication that can be drawn from the tables (1993: 275). But – we must immediately add – these constructs do not cease to be valid because they are the outcome of methodological fictions: on the contrary, they have an existence which is independent of our will; they produce regularities, patterns of repetition which are indicative of the 'hardness', the resistance, of social fact; and they have the capacity, crucial to empirical research, to take us by surprise.

The sorts of interpretive issues that are at stake here, and which have been long and extensively debated in the social sciences, are lucidly formulated in an early essay of Bourdieu's on opinion polls. In this essay

Bourdieu (1979) put forward a formulation that goes to the heart of our concerns when he maintained that public opinion does not exist but that its effects are, nonetheless, real. What did he mean by this? His purpose was to take issue with the claims of opinion pollsters who confuse the representations of opinion they have produced for a really existing entity. For Bourdieu, there is no such thing as a public opinion on any set of matters that is already there, waiting to be discovered, prior to and independently of the application of particular techniques for organising and expressing an opinion. And those techniques always rest on and presuppose particular sets of social relations just as they give a particular shape to the opinions they purport simply to reflect. The opinions people express, that is to say, are brought into being by the contexts in which they are solicited and are given a determinate form by the way in which the questions are posed. The circumstances in which opinion polling takes place and the social relations they involve (telephone interviews, random-intercept interviews, in-depth face-to-face interviews, interviews involving anonymous or known interviewers) make a difference to the opinion one has and, indeed, to whether or not one has one at all. Equally, the way in which questions about opinion are posed (simple yes/no options, multiple choice questions, open-ended questions) makes a difference to the form in which it is possible for interviewees to give their opinions a public expression. When Bourdieu says that public opinion does not exist, then, he means that it does not exist in any other form than as a set of representations which has been arrived at in the context of particular social processes involving discursive forms through which opinions are shaped in particular ways. When he goes on to say that the effects of public opinion are real, he means that, as a set of representations, any statement about public opinion has real effects in the contribution it makes to shaping social or political processes: the role played by opinion polls in influencing voter behaviour at elections is a case in point.

Our own survey and the results it has generated are inescapably subject to the same limitations. Administered postally and accompanied by a personal letter on university letterhead in which we distinguished our purposes from those of commercial surveys, it invited our respondents to join with us in particular relations of knowledge production. In structuring the options for those respondents in a variety of ways throughout the survey, we shaped the form in which it was possible for cultural tastes and interests to be expressed. And in reporting our findings, we have opted for ways of representing them that have visually dramatised those distributions of taste that are most relevant to our concerns. In all these ways, then, this book needs to be read not as a simple reflection of the cultural tastes and interests our respondents already had before we asked them but as, in important respects, the outcome of a process through which those tastes and interests have been shaped into particular forms by the form of our questions and by our subsequent conversion of the raw material of our respondents' answers into this text.

Social Class

A central component of our inquiry has been the construction of an appropriate model of social class. Perhaps the most crucial consideration for us was the need to develop a non-reductionist account of the relations between class and culture such that cultural practice and preference would be constructed as a *constitutive* dimension of class position. As with many other aspects of his work we found that there is much we could take from Bourdieu for this purpose, but also much that is wanting. Most importantly, despite his resolutely empirical credentials, Bourdieu provides no obvious guidelines as to how his conception of class can be replicated.

There are at least two different analytical levels to be found in Bourdieu's discussions of social class: the first, an abstract conceptual level in which classes are constituted by their unequal relations to various forms of capital; the second, an ultra-empirical typology of ad hoc class fractions without any sustained theoretical basis, which he takes over directly from the typology used by the French national statistical institute, INSEE. Classes in the former sense are seen by Bourdieu (1987) as 'agents' in a 'multi-dimensional social space' which are engaged in a struggle for the appropriation of scarce goods using as resources various types of capital – economic, cultural, social and symbolic. Classes can thus be differentiated in terms of the overall *volume* of capital they possess, by the *composition* of their capital (the relative proportions of economic and cultural capital, in particular), and according to their movement or *trajectory* through social space as the amount and type of capital they accumulate vary (Bourdieu 1987: 4). Those richest in economic capital are designated the dominant fraction of the dominant class; those most endowed with cultural capital represent the dominated fraction of this class. Significantly, the most salient struggles for cultural supremacy are seen by Bourdieu as taking place *between* these two fractions of the dominant class.

However, in *Distinction* (1984), when he offers analyses of specific instances of class tastes, Bourdieu resorts to a sixteen-level typology of class fractions. These are derived by differentiating his three core classes – dominant, middle and working[2] – on the basis of the level of educational capital of their constituent fractions. The resulting typology, reflecting as it does the occupational structure of French society in the 1960s (it includes 'domestic servants', for example), is of little value to Australia in the 1990s.

Of necessity, then, we turned to the two most influential existing empirical conceptions of class, those of Erik Olin Wright and John Goldthorpe.[3] Our model combines aspects of both of these schemes. From Wright's neo-Marxist model we retain the assumption that relationship to the means of production – being an employer or an employee, for example – is of central importance to class location. We have not retained Wright's broader analytical framework which allocates people to class positions, initially on the basis of their 'contradictory' class interests and subsequently on the basis of the combination of 'assets' they can potentially exploit. Wright's employee categories – 'expert managers', 'non-managerial experts', 'expert workers', and so on – are not intuitively obvious and do not easily translate to alternative conceptual frameworks.

Goldthorpe's model, in contrast, is built upon a Weberian foundation and pays closer attention to shared work- and market-situations as determinants of class position. Unlike Wright, Goldthorpe does not distinguish between employers or owners of business enterprises and the senior managerial and administrative employees of these enterprises, amalgamating them all within his single category of the 'service class'. For Goldthorpe, occupations are aggregated into classes on the basis, on the one hand, of comparable sources and levels of income, degree of security and chances of advancement; and, on the other hand, of the degree of autonomy which attaches to the content of the work role. From Goldthorpe we retain an important distinction between white- and blue-collar work, as well as the importance of supervisory status as a factor internally differentiating the working class. In addition, we have added an assumption of our own concerning the use of education to mark a distinction between professionals and para-professionals which is central to the Australian status system.

To operationalise the *Australian Everyday Cultures Project* (AECP) class model, we collected information about our respondents' current occupation in sufficient detail to determine their employment status as well as whether they exercised a managerial or supervisory function.[4] On these initial filters we superimposed a measure of the occupation's skill level based on the eight groups of the Australian Standard Classification of Occupations (ASCO) devised by the Australian Bureau of Statistics. Our resulting class model consists of nine categories. The first – although one that is marginal to our model – is that of the *never employed*. This category draws together many different categories of unemployment: the chronically ill and disabled, housewives, sole carers, students, and those who have not yet begun employment. Seven per cent of women and 5.1% of men belong to this category. Because of its heterogeneity we make virtually no reference to the cultural preferences and practices of this group in our later analyses.

We then distinguish two classes of owners of the means of production: *employers* and the *self-employed*. The difference here is, in the first instance, quantitative, with the former operationally defined as having three or more employees, the latter made up of people who work on their own account or who employ up to two others. Both classes are widely distributed in terms of industry sector and occupation. Twenty-nine per cent of *employers* are classed as 'managers' of businesses which presumably they own, including 4.3% farmers and 17.2% in retailing, restaurants, and hotels; a further 15.1% are in professional occupations, including 4.6% who are health practitioners, 3.4% in accounting, public relations and other business services, and 3% in the culture industries; 6.8% are in para-professional occupations; 20.8% are in trades, including 8.3% in the building trades and 4.3% in food trades; 12.1% are classed as in clerical work and 8.9% in sales work; there are 3.8% in manual occupations.

The class of the *self-employed* also covers the whole spectrum of occupational groupings (and in both cases our model assumes that the fact of autonomy of employment is of greater significance than this heterogeneity): 30.6% of the self-employed are classed as managers of their businesses, including 18.2% farmers and 11.1% in retailing, restaurants, hotels, etc.; 12.7% are in professional occupations, including 2.2% health practitioners; 1.9% are in para-professional occupations; by far the largest proportion (29.7%) of the self-employed are tradespeople, including 12.6% in the building trades; 7.6% are clerical workers and 8.9% sales and service workers; 4.2% are plant operators; and 4.8% are in manual occupations.

Managers are those who exercise full managerial functions in their job and whose occupational titles qualify them for inclusion in ASCO major group 1. The majority (56.8%) are classified as 'specialist managers' and work in finance, production, personnel and distribution; 29.7% are sales and service managers employed in retailing, restaurants and hotels; 9.1% are farm managers.

Professionals and *para-professionals* are employees with occupations in ASCO major group 2 and 3 respectively. *Professional* occupations include natural scientists (1.5%), building and engineering professionals (13.7%), doctors and other health practitioners (4.6%), primary and secondary school teachers (26.5%) and tertiary level teachers (7.9%), social workers, lawyers, and ministers of religion (4.1%), accountants and other business professionals (17.0%), artists and other cultural producers (5.7%) (journalists, directors, musicians, etc.), and finally a miscellaneous group (8.1%) which includes social scientists and librarians. The category of *para-professionals* comprises occupations such as registered nurses (36.8%), police officers (12.7%), engineering and building technicians (14.2%), medical and scientific technicians (2.2%), transport technical workers (7.0%), and a large miscellaneous group (18.2%) which includes welfare workers, ambulance and prison officers, inspectors and regulatory officers and sportspersons.

Supervisors are those whose job entails a supervisory or managerial function and who are employed in occupations falling into ASCO major groups 4, 5, 6, 7 and 8. Essentially they fall into two categories: supervisors of

blue-collar labour (46.4%) such as tradespeople, plant and machine operators and other manual labourers; and supervisors of white-collar workers
(53.6%) such as clerical, sales, and personal service workers. *Sales and clerical workers* are those without supervisory status in these same white-collar
ASCO major group 5 and 6 occupations. The occupational breakdown is:
49.0% doing clerical work (accounting, filing and recording clerks, typists,
receptionists, data processors, and so on) and 51.0% doing sales work (insurance, real estate, sales assistants – the largest group at 26.7% – tellers and
cashiers, and personal service workers including childcare workers, home
companions, etc.). Finally we distinguish *manual workers*, those without any
supervisory functions in the blue-collar occupations in ASCO major groups
4, 7 and 8. These groups cover the following occupations: 37.7% in trades
(metal, electrical, building, printing, vehicle, food, and horticultural trades);
20.4% plant and machine operators (including quite large numbers of truck
drivers and textile workers); and 41.9% labourers (trades assistants, factory
hands, agricultural labourers, cleaners, construction workers, and a range
of miscellaneous occupations).

The breakdown of the full class model is set out in figure 1.1.

A class schema such as the one in figure 1.1 is, of course, a one-dimen-
sional construct to the extent that it fails to indicate the processes and
relations – principally those of gender, age, and education – which collectively influence the recruitment of agents to these locations. To give some
sense of this – to show that class structures are profoundly relational – we
present in table 1.1 a composite demographic portrait of our sample by class
according to gender, age, and educational level.

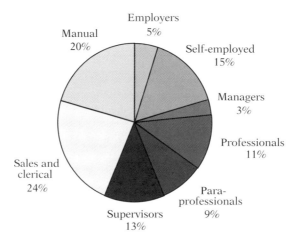

Figure 1.1 Distribution of respondents into AECP class categories

Table 1.1   AECP class categories by gender, age and education

	Female	Male	18–25	26–35	36–45	46–59	60+	Comp. sec.	Voc. & part tert.	Comp. tert.
Emp.	34.8	65.2	0.0	12.0	36.2	24.1	27.7	54.5	24.8	20.7
Self-emp.	38.7	61.3	6.2	22.9	22.2	25.7	23.0	57.1	32.1	10.8
Mgr	25.5	74.5	3.6	17.4	21.2	28.8	29.1	45.7	17.7	36.6
Prof.	49.0	51.0	8.0	21.0	27.4	29.6	14.0	13.2	19.9	67.1
Para-prof.	53.9	46.1	10.7	23.9	24.1	16.8	24.5	42.7	37.2	20.2
Supv.	42.4	57.6	13.6	24.1	24.8	20.9	16.7	52.9	33.8	13.4
Sales/cler.	80.7	19.3	29.6	23.1	15.9	14.5	16.9	61.1	30.5	8.3
Manual	35.0	65.0	23.8	18.6	19.2	18.3	20.1	64.7	31.1	4.3

Each of these factors noted in table 1.1 has a determining influence on the allocation or recruitment of people to classes. The two owner classes, managers (most significantly of all), supervisors, and the working class are predominantly male locations. Women constitute 80.7% of sales and clerical workers, and the gender balance in the remaining professional and para-professional classes is approximately equal. Younger people are found to a greater extent in the two core sections of the working class, sales and clerical work and manual labour, than in other class locations. There are no employers under 25 and fewer than 10 per cent of the self-employed, managers, and professionals are this age. Managers and employers are more likely to be aged 60 and over than others, and professionals the least; no doubt this has to do with the coupling of professional occupations with tertiary education. Two-thirds (67.1%) of professionals have completed tertiary level training, nearly double that of the next highest class (managers, with 36.6% tertiary trained). Overall, the differences between the class locations appear most marked when considering the proportions of each class who have experienced tertiary education. Just over a fifth of employers and para-professionals are tertiary trained, as are 13 per cent of supervisors and 10 per cent of the self-employed. This proportion drops below one in ten for the working classes, with manual labourers having the lowest proportion (4.3%) of all.

The affinity between class and education is, of course, one of the most enduring features of the stratification systems of the advanced societies and the relationships we have identified should come as no surprise. Overall, however, the information is of value, for if, as Bourdieu suggests, educational capital is strongly linked to cultural capital, then some idea of how

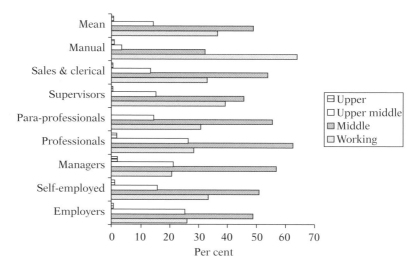

Figure 1.2 Class position by self-assigned class placement (AECP class categories)

educational differences are constitutive of class positions is of central importance for our forthcoming analyses.

We will consider now one final aspect of our class model which also has a potential bearing on our later deliberations. The analytical categories we have adopted are in part descriptive, in part technical, and in part vernacular. The categories through which people experience their class belonging – to the extent that they are aware of this at all – are generally speaking different. The lay discourses of class work with a sense of position within a hierarchy: we are in the middle, at the bottom, upwardly mobile, or at the top. Is there any evidence that our structurally assigned class actors have a sense of class belonging which is commensurate with their assigned position?

We can report first that an overwhelming majority of our sample (89%) agreed that there was a class structure in Australia. Sixty-eight per cent were able to place themselves in a class without hesitation, and of the remaining 32 per cent, a further 29 per cent were able to do so when prompted. The self-assigned class placements made by our sample are compared with their structural position in figure 1.2 and table 1.2.

These self-placements substantially confirm the findings of earlier studies (Baxter, Emmison, Western, M., & Western, J. 1991; Chamberlain 1983) which reported that about a third of the Australian population claim a working-class identity, about half choose the category of middle class, with the remainder selecting upper-middle or upper-class identities. By far the most conspicuous feature of this table is the rejection of a working-class

Table 1.2 Class position by self-assigned class placement (AECP class categories) (row percentages)

	'Working'	'Middle'	'Upper middle'	'Upper'
Employers	25.9	48.5	25.1	0.5
Self-employed	33.1	50.6	15.5	0.8
Managers	20.7	56.5	21.0	1.8
Professionals	10.0	62.3	26.2	1.5
Para-professionals	30.5	55.2	14.3	0.0
Supervisors	39.1	45.4	15.2	0.3
Sales & clerical	32.7	53.9	13.1	0.3
Manual	63.9	32.0	3.3	0.8
Mean	*36.4*	*48.8*	*14.2*	*0.6*

identity by professionals (the figure of 10 per cent is virtually only a quarter of the sample average), and a corresponding tendency among manual workers to claim this as their preferred class location. It is tempting to conclude that the educational differences between the classes are of most importance here. Yet if education and cultural involvement are as strongly linked as our research suggests, then our tastes and preferences may well be influential factors in their own right in determining not only our identity – the kind of person we think we are – but also our sense of where we belong in a stratified social order.

Chapter 2

Cultural Choice and the Home

What does it mean to prefer one colour scheme to another? What values and significance are attached to the paintings that people choose for their homes? How do people spend their time at home? What kind of home would they most like to have? In what style do people like to entertain their friends and visitors? What food do they like to serve, and in what setting?

In this chapter we concern ourselves with such questions in order to identify some of the social logics which underlie the cultural choices that are involved in the day-to-day decisions we make involving judgements of taste. Yet there are limits to how far these questions can be pursued on the basis of statistics. Although they can tell us a good deal about the social distribution of tastes, they do not tell us much about the principles which connect particular tastes to particular social positions or about the role which such judgements of taste play in the social strategies and trajectories of those who make them. We shall, then, as a way of generating a set of interpretative principles that will allow us to identify the underlying social logics governing judgements of taste, look first at the relationships between cultural choice and the home through a set of case-histories of the actual choices of specific individuals.

These case-histories are divided into three groups. In the first, we look at how two middle-class women, both well educated and with demanding and responsible jobs, talk about their homes. We do so with a view to illustrating how closely their cultural choices in domestic decor are related to the cultivation of specific kinds of distinction which play an important role in forming their identities as women and as the occupants of particular class positions. With the second group, we look at the quite different values which inform the preferences of two working-class women with only primary or secondary levels of education as well as those of a full-time housewife whose class position, in part influenced by her husband's para-professional occupation, is somewhat more ambivalent. Finally, we examine the attitudes towards home and domestic leisure of two men – one a manual worker with little formal education, and the other a university-educated senior manager with a large international company. Taken together, these case-histories will allow us to see how the factors of gender, class and education interact with one another both in the choices people make about their homes, and in how they speak about those choices. We shall then, when we look at the statistical distribution of our sample's preferences on these matters, be able to interpret them in ways which show how the principles of taste underlying the cultural choices of individuals are shaped by the complex and often contradictory values, identities, and strategies of distinction associated with the different social groups to which they belong.

Home Improvements

Let us go back to our opening question concerning what might be involved in the choice of a colour scheme. The answer, in the case of Gillian, is: quite a lot. Indeed, the colours Gillian wants for her new home are a way of both stating and resolving some of the tensions – personal, familial and social – that she has worked her way through in defining her own social trajectory as a young woman (29 years old) holding a senior and responsible position in health management. Like her husband, also in a management position (giving them an annual household income of between $80 000 and $90 000), Gillian's work involves significant supervisory responsibilities. She sees these as distinguishing her own position and its obligations (long hours and a responsibility to make sure that what needs to be done is done) from those of award workers. The influence of her professional responsibilities is also evident in her strongly negative views of trade unions which she regards as impeding her ability, as a manager, to organise productive patterns of team-work while also diminishing individual workers' sense of responsibility for determining their own futures.

For her own part, Gillian is clear that her future – and her children's future – is very much in her own hands. She sees education as having a crucial role to play here. Having arrived at her present station in life by virtue of the mobility conferred through education – her parents had only varying degrees of secondary education but, on a shop assistant's salary, had supported her through university – she has clear views about her children's education. Although their first child was only 7 months old when Gillian answered the questionnaire, she and her husband had already decided to send her children to a private school, seeing this as the key to future generational mobility, and preferably to one that placed a strong emphasis on art and music. This reflects Gillian's own cultural interests. She owns a number of original artworks and has a considerable ceramics collection, while also owning art books, classical literary texts, works of poetry, biographies and historical books. Her artistic interests, however, while broad ranging, are mostly of a conventional kind: she prefers realistic art but is open to abstract art if she can find the right place for it.

Describing herself as middle class, Gillian's main concern is 'getting on in life', and she is keen to pass these values on to her children (she had had a second child by the time we interviewed her):

> I guess, (that's) the culture that we've instilled in our kids – to strive for the best.

How does this manifest itself in the cultural choices she makes in and about the home? That these choices are hers is something that Gillian is very clear about. Although there are some areas in which decisions are shared – her husband, Malcolm, has more contemporary tastes than Gillian, but would sometimes compromise in reaching joint decisions about what furniture to buy – her views prevail when it comes to choosing colour schemes:

> **INTERVIEWER** And your husband is happy for you just to have the house exactly the way you want it.
> **GILLIAN** Yeh. Yeh. Doesn't mind at all. Been very good that way.

This proves to be important to the significance that Gillian invests in the colour scheme she plans for her new home as a means of establishing an appropriate distance between her present social status and aspirations, and her social and family origins. Having recently moved to a provincial Queensland city and set up home in a relatively new house, Gillian sees her new home as – for the moment – the co-ordinating centre of her life. *Home Beautiful* and *Home and Garden* are her favourite magazines. Although going out occasionally to the cinema, to musical performances or to art galleries and museums, most of her leisure activities are centred on the home. Eating out only rarely and then mainly for practical purposes (a weekly trip to KFC or McDonald's on the night they shop), Gillian and her husband prefer to do their own entertaining:

> . . . we prefer to entertain at home or to go to friends' homes, and I guess it's more relaxing in that sense. Nicer atmosphere. You're not being rushed through a meal, or noise and 'carry-on' all around you.

Most of this entertaining involves work colleagues. Since they have recently moved interstate away from their families of origin, entertaining is no longer a family-centred activity. For this reason, Gillian prefers that her guests not bring their children with them, just as, when eating out, she prefers child-free restaurants.

Although she says she likes to serve an informal buffet-style meal, this seems less and less informal the more she describes it. Serving, always, entrées, a main course and dessert, Gillian's pride and joy is to do so in a dining-room setting with a 14-seater table which functions as a crucial *mise-en-scène* for the display of her persona to the social and professional peers she invites to dinner.

> **INTERVIEWER** You go to such an effort to do the menu when you do have your dinner parties, (do) you set the table out formally?
> **GILLIAN** Love doing that . . . Love collecting china. Eight dinner sets . . . I've got two antique dinner sets – one was my grandmother's, it was her wedding present and I've got that now. And the rest tends to be very 'everyday' Johnson & Johnson type stuff . . . Most of it is Royal Albert . . . That kind of thing. And I love that sort of stuff. I like crystals. I just like nice things. Nice cutlery . . . Love placemats. That's another quirk. I love placemats and I love clocks . . .

When choosing the three terms from the survey which come closest to describing her ideal home, Gillian opts, in order of preference, for 'well-designed', 'spacious' and 'easy-to-maintain'. Her three least-preferred qualities for a home are, again in order, that it should be 'traditional', 'lived-in' or 'imaginative'. The significance that she invests in the contrast between these two sets of values becomes clear when Gillian talks about her preferred colour scheme in view of the role this plays in establishing a social distance between the traditional, lived-in and imaginative decor of the parental home she has left and the kind of home she aspires eventually to live in. When asked to describe her new home, Gillian talks about little else but the colours: 'the whole theme of the house, to me anyway, tends to be pinkish which I find a little bit hot'. She wants something completely different:

> **GILLIAN** If I were to choose a colour scheme, I tend more towards the cool, towards blues and green and that sort of thing . . .
> **INTERVIEWER** Right. So, why would you choose cool colours?
> **GILLIAN** I simply have a preference for them. And apart from the fact that even in weather such as this, the temperature hits up to 37, 38 and you feel cool. Definitely the colours that I prefer. So, where I've been able to in rooms where I could have an influence, then I'll put curtains that have got blues and greens in them and that sort of thing. Mostly tapestries, that sort of thing. And, certainly the curtains in the formal area, the creams, the sage. When I had them made they said: 'Oh goodness, I really would advise against it'. And I said: 'Look, truly, I know what I want'.

Gillian does indeed know her own tastes: too well, in fact, for us to believe her account that she just happens to like cool colours or likes them solely for practical reasons. Later in the interview, she draws a sharp distinction between her tastes in colour and Malcolm's in terms which make clear the social and familial issues at stake for Gillian in her preference for cool colours. It also becomes clear why it is so important to her that her husband should let her have the pick of colours in the home. Malcolm's preferences are for reds and blacks, for sharp and bright colours. So were his mother's:

> **GILLIAN** His mother loved black, red and chrome and red, red and bright things! Everything's very dominant. If she was going to put a tablecloth on the table, it would be red. If she was going to go and choose a suit, it would probably be either red or bright pink . . . Everything's bright. Nothing wrong with bright colours. I like some bright colours but I couldn't live with that heavy colour all the time.

Malcolm's parents, like Gillian's, were working class. As the conversation unfolds, it becomes clear that Gillian is unable to live with strong and sharply contrasting colours because she associates them with her husband's background and her own in a 'two-bedroom, fibro Housing Commission house' that she describes as 'disgusting by anybody's standards'. The gaudy veneer and laminex surfaces of a 1970s working-class decor are something she wants 'to get away from'. Nor is this just a matter of escaping her parental past: Gillian accounts for her colour preferences in terms which suggest that these also serve as a means of measuring her distance from a present that might have been her own but for the route out that her education has given her. Gillian's sister did not go to university but had chosen, like their mother, to be a 'stay-at-home mum' supplementing her husband's salary with bits of part-time work as a shop assistant or as a casual worker with the local council. Unlike Gillian, however, her sister still likes reds, blacks, and chrome, tastes which, in Gillian's mind, reflect her sister's subservience to her husband who, like both Malcolm and Gillian's father, likes bold and strongly contrasting colours. Still trapped in her class background, Gillian's sister also embodies a pattern of gender relations that Gillian associates with the familial and class origins she has herself escaped – and yet is still always escaping. Being able to make the choices about how to decorate her home is, for Gillian, a way of marking her distance from a background of domestic violence in which her father's abuse of her mother is strongly connected, in her recollection, to her mother's subservience to him in all matters of domestic cultural choice – a pattern which she sees being repeated in her sister's choice of partner and, symbolically, of colours.

As we can see, then, a good deal is invested in Gillian's colour-scheme preferences. Her passion for light, cool, subdued colours is an elaborate statement which helps her to organise a clear distinction between where she has come from and where, in both class and familial terms, she is headed. It is not surprising, then, that her tastes in clothes rest on the same principles, particularly since, when dressing for work, these help her in fashioning the kind of professional self she wants to 'wear' in her work settings. Expressing her preference for 'a nice cut with clothes rather than frilly, tizzy things', Gillian, echoing her colour scheme for the home, likes 'light blues and greens', neutral rather than pastel colours, recalling her dislike for red, black and chrome in her rejection of 'very bright things'.

Barbara is like Gillian in many ways, but her 'home improvement' projects have a different slant. A registered nurse, Barbara works in a military hospital where she supervises the operating theatres. She received her nursing training in the British navy – aged 45 at the time of interview, she was too old to have entered the nursing profession via a Bachelor of Nursing – and, having worked for a number of years in a major public hospital, had recently left it because of the declining standards brought about by reduced funding. Although Barbara is sad to see the public health system being run down, the reasons she gives for leaving it do not reflect any sense of political protest on her part. As a National Party supporter she does not think that governments should provide universal health care, seeing this as a responsibility for individuals to take care of themselves. She gives, as her main reason for leaving, her belief that her own high professional standards of health care would have been seriously compromised had she continued to work in a public hospital where sterilisation procedures had deteriorated to the point of approaching 'third world standards' and where she felt that personal initiative was stifled by a cumbersome bureaucracy.

Like Gillian, Barbara describes her husband as a financial controller, but also as a works and property manager. Between them, they earn over $100 000 a year and this is reflected in their lifestyle and habitat: they live in a fashionably old house in one of the better suburbs close to the centre of Brisbane. Describing herself as upper middle class, Barbara views hard work as the most important attribute for getting on in life and, matching her views about public health care, holds to a vigorously individualistic ethic in her political views. She believes that governments should play as small a role as possible in managing the economy and that social-welfare provisions should be kept to a minimum – matters on which Gillian, a Liberal Party supporter, holds more mixed, middle-of-the-road views.

Like Gillian, Barbara's home is important to her: her favourite magazines, a little bit more upmarket than Gillian's, are *House and Garden*, *Belle Design and Decoration*, and *Vogue Living*, while she also includes *Our House* among her favourite television programs. She, too, thinks of home as a place which has constantly to be improved (renovation is her passion) if it is to play its part in testifying – to herself and to guests – the distinctive social and professional personas she and her husband have cultivated. For Barbara, however, this is very much a joint project – she speaks of her husband as her 'best friend' and proudly insists that they always reach a joint and ami- cable decision on everything to do with their home – and one that is differ- ently organised from Gillian's in that, in Barbara's description, the function of home is to attest to signs of distinction which stress the values of a life spent mainly away from home. Neither Barbara nor her husband is a home- body. Both have full-time professional commitments which keep them out of the house for most of the week, and their social life – participating in various health and sports clubs, Barbara is also an active member of a charity trust – is also centred outside the home. They eat at restaurants regularly – usually once, and sometimes twice a week – and prefer to meet their friends there rather than entertain them at home. When cooking herself, Barbara has a strong preference for exotic and innovative cuisine and, when entertaining, does so simply but stylishly – she prefers eating alfresco to anything more formal – in a domestic environment that has been carefully planned in accordance with two overlapping principles.

The first of these is that the home should be efficiently streamlined, a place of clean lines and no clutter. Like Gillian, Barbara includes 'well-designed' and 'easy-to-maintain' among her preferred attributes for an ideal home but, unlike Gillian, for whom it is a negative factor, she also wants a home to look imag- inative. On the negative side, Barbara doesn't want a traditional home or an elegant one, and least of all does she want a house that looks lived-in. This had played a significant role in her decision not to have children:

> Yes, clean lines no clutter. I hate clutter. That's why I don't have children. I don't like things particularly out of place. Again that probably comes from my nursing background. But my husband is the same. He likes things just so.

This fondness for clean and clinical lines, and a rejection of clutter or intri- cate design, informs all aspects of Barbara's tastes. It is evident in her description of her renovated kitchen:

> The timber is Tasmanian oak timber in the kitchen cupboards. That is limed, not in white but in yellow, which is the colour of the walls, yellow. The tiles and the splash-back – the angle of the tiles – mirror the leadlights in the windows, the three leadlight windows in the kitchen and that's very Mediterranean again. Very clean lines, I don't like clutter and we have a big walk-in pantry at the other end of the kitchen and a big double refrigerator, pretty much hidden as well. Pretty simple lines.

The second principle, and it is a complementary one, consists in her con- ception of the home as a place for displaying a cultured cosmopolitanism acquired by way of extensive travel, both in Australia and overseas. This is evident in her architectural renovation of her home in accordance with Mediterranean principles of design, transforming a traditional Queenslander style into one that is both cosmopolitan and modern. It provides the background for displaying the memorabilia of her, and her husband's, travels. These include an expensive plate collection as well as a fair number of original works of art and signed limited editions which, as often as not, have been selected less for any definite set of aesthetic principles than because they 'fitted in with the decor'. Nearly all of the art in the house has been bought to remind Barbara and her husband of somewhere they have been and these personal associations matter more to her – even though she has some art training, can speak knowledgeably about art and has clear likes (landscape painting) and dislikes (abstract art) – than any significance the paintings might have in art-historical or painterly terms. Asserting the rights of the collector, Barbara is unequivocal in stating what art means to her as a visible symbol of the money invested in it:

> Yes there is something else behind the painting that is on the wall and what the artist has put into it. It is what we have put into it as well by purchasing it.

For Barbara, then, choices about the house are essentially choices about how to shape the home into a place which testifies to a tasteful cosmopolitanism whose markers have been acquired principally through a touristic relationship to a number of overseas and Australian cultural sites. Home is a setting for signs of a life centred elsewhere.

Home Sweet Home

Dorothy, Mary and Elizabeth differ from Gillian and Barbara in the degree to which their lives revolve around their homes as the centres of locally based networks of family, friends and neighbours. Taking little part in cultural activities outside the home, they speak of it more as a place to *be* and *do* in rather than as a stage that has to be prepared to support a set of performances directed to audiences outside the immediate networks of kith and kin. This is reflected in the terms from the survey that they select to describe their ideal home. 'Comfortable', 'lived-in' and 'uncluttered' – all terms expressing a conception of home as being primarily for the benefit of those who live there – rank highly in their choices, while terms suggesting that a home should be valued for how it might appear to outsiders are rejected. 'Elegant', 'modern' and 'distinctive' are the values that both Elizabeth and Dorothy least associate with their ideal homes while Mary shares the last two of these and adds 'uncluttered'. These evaluations are clearly rooted in ways of life which, compared with Gillian's and Barbara's, are more firmly anchored in a particular place. As we have seen, both Gillian and Barbara had moved away from their parental homes and the world of their childhood. Elizabeth and Dorothy, by contrast, still live in or near the places where they were born, while Mary lives in the neighbourhood where her husband grew up.

These views about home also reflect the different class positions and class trajectories of this group of women. Dorothy's cultural choices provide perhaps the best route into these questions even though her class location is somewhat ambiguous. Working part-time as a cook in a local childcare centre, Dorothy, who did not complete her secondary schooling, counts as working class in terms of her own position within the labour market. She does not, however, see herself in these terms. Lacking a strong sense of class identity, she sees herself as middle class if pressed to define herself in class terms, and her material circumstances, assessed at the level of the household, are also objectively middle class. Her husband, Tim, who has an engineering degree, holds a management position which, with Dorothy's part-time earnings, yields an annual household income of between \$32 000 and \$40 000. They own their own home (unusual for a 46 year old) and the land on which it is set: they live on acreage, which had been passed down to her husband from his father, in a rural setting close to Brisbane. They are, then, comfortably off but not ostentatiously so – they own two oldish Volvos and a Camry – in a manner which reflects the combined economic benefits of credentialism, in the form of the role played by a university education in enabling Tim to obtain a management position, and inherited capital in the form of land. Most of this, however, had been sold earlier in their marriage to help pay for their daughters' education, reflecting a decision to invest in education as the best means of securing the continuing middle-class trajectory that Tim and Dorothy plan for their children. With two daughters already at university and a third about to apply for admission, Dorothy recognises that she and Tim would be 'paying for education for some time yet' to ensure their children's future prospects:

> Yes, they do have to, to get anywhere, well particularly nowadays, they need to have something behind them to get a good position somewhere. They can't just leave school at 15 and go in and become a lawyer.

However, this investment is not just monetary in form. Indeed, the single greatest investment in the children's education is that of Dorothy herself in the decision – made at the time they were married – that she would be a full-time homemaker. This is central to her conception of herself and her positive conviction that her always being there when her daughters came home from school has been her main contribution, and a vital one, to her children's educational advancement:

> Yes. I hate not being here. There's been a couple of times when I've had a doctor's appointment or something and I haven't been here and I really don't like it. I really want to be here for when they walk in the door. I think it's important to them. And I think we're seeing that now. But they're turning out respectable young ladies.

There is, however, no sense of loss or sacrifice in any of this. A positive love for the home as the organising hub of a full and rich family life is evident in the way Dorothy describes all aspects of her home life. Here, for example, is how she responds when asked to elaborate on her fondness for board games:

> Well, most weekends, at least one night of the weekend, we'll play *Pictionary, Trivial Pursuit* or . . . sometimes, cards . . . The whole family plus hangers-on that are here. Friends. The girls' friends – they all come too. So. Yeh, at least, at least, every fortnight we do and we have friends come over too, they fix a meal, something like that. Lots of laughs and fun.

The sense of the home as a place for doing things in is evident in Dorothy's answers to the question we asked about domestic leisure. These show an active involvement in a wide range of activities centred on the home: gardening, making clothes, playing cards and board games, reading, listening to the radio and music, home repairs, DIY, drawing, and craft. Doing things outside the home is not seen as important unless it is a matter of supporting another member of the family – attending a theatrical production in which one of her daughters is performing, for example – and is governed by the simple principle that if they can't afford to take all members of the family out for a meal, say, or away on holidays, they stay at home.

The consequences of this relationship to the home are evident in Dorothy's approach to questions of domestic design and decor. Her views on these matters differ sharply from those of both Gillian and Barbara in the stress she places on making home a place that can accommodate a multiplicity of different family-based activities:

> **INTERVIEWER** And the rest of the house is painted beige as well?
> **DOROTHY** That sort of a comfortable creamy colour.
> **INTERVIEWER** With a lot of brown furniture?
> **DOROTHY** Yeh. Brown dining-room suite, lounge-room suite. The timber dining-room suite with fabric chairs that are solid timber.

INTERVIEWER Very nice. Why did you choose that?

DOROTHY We liked it. And we wanted an extending table. We wanted one that we could sit a lot of people round.

INTERVIEWER Is that where you sit and do your games, the board games?

DOROTHY Yes. Yes, and we have dinner there every night. Every night we eat in there with whoever's home. And, at the moment with the girls and their part-time work, we, some are there, some are not. But everyone'll eat there. The only meal we eat here in the kitchen is breakfast.

INTERVIEWER And then you built a double garage?

. . .

DOROTHY Converted it into a pool room. My husband plays pool and snooker with some of his mates every weekend. If they don't come, that's when we play *Trivia* and *Scrabble*. But I still play with the girls if he's not there. But the girls play pool with him too. I do, but not very often. If he's out there with the girls, I usually do the ironing or something like that.

Although she received some art education as a part of her schooling and has an interest in drawing, Dorothy's tastes in art are conventional and, more important to our point here, do not exist for her as a separate realm of autonomous judgement. There is no sense that she thinks of art as something that has to be valued for its own sake and that this might require the cultivation of a special set of skills. The question of what to *like* in a painting is very much connected to that of what to *do* with it in a family context:

INTERVIEWER And, still on the line of art. Can you define your taste in art?

DOROTHY Things that are real. I don't like any things that are sort of like Picassos or something like that. I don't like them because you don't look at them and see something real.

INTERVIEWER What about Van Gogh? . . . Like the *Sunflowers*?

DOROTHY Yes, that's okay. But it's still not . . . it's always just a little bit off 'real'. And I like things to look as they really look. The *Sunflowers* are just a bit sort of garish or just not as you see it in the garden. I just like things that really look real.

. . .

DOROTHY . . . I know that Graham would like paintings of draughthorses and if I was looking at paintings, I'd especially look at draughthorse ones, because he had that when he was a boy.

INTERVIEWER Because he's from a farming background . . . isn't he?

> DOROTHY Yes. And he has had draughthorses all his life when he was growing up. And he would dearly love one with a big draught-horse and I'll just keep looking until I find one and I'll eventually get him one.

At an earlier point in the discussion Dorothy makes it clear that she has little interest in art galleries and would 'much rather go and see a cake decorating display or something'. This is not a casual contrast as she has a real passion for cake icing which is, for her, a genuinely creative aesthetic activity but one whose creativity is defined in terms of its role in family life. Having described the cake she iced for her father, a keen card player, on his seventieth birthday – 'I actually made the cards as cards with the King and the Queen and everything flooded in floodwork on them and peanuts and a little tray, a score pad and things like that' – Dorothy goes on to say that she sees cake decorating as an art rather than a craft because it demands a capacity for originality:

> DOROTHY I think that craft to me seems like you have to start with something. Like you start with weaving stuff or knitting needles or you have to have something to start with. Whereas an art starts from nothing and makes something from nothing. As in starting off with just a packet of icing sugar and away you go.
>
> INTERVIEWER And also what about the originality and inno-vativeness?
>
> DOROTHY That's important because, I mean, when you make like the cake I did for my Dad – I've never seen one like it before and I haven't seen one since – and it was just something I made up in my head because I knew Dad likes cards.

We can see in Dorothy's preferences, then, as well as in the views she holds, a set of cultural choices centred strongly on a particular gendered pattern of investment in the home as the primary scene of family life. Her relations to home form a part of the support role she plays in a familial class trajectory which aims to secure a middle-class position for her children by converting inherited capital into educational capital. It is clear from her views on art, however, that this does not involve any particular stress on the importance of acquiring distinctively aesthetic or cultural forms of capital.

Mary has much in common with Dorothy. She is also in her late forties and, having recently retired from a job-share position as a meals-on-wheels co-ordinator, is unambiguously working class in terms of her own occupational location. She and her husband own their own home and enjoy a comfortable joint income of between $50 000 and $60 000 a year. Although she did not complete her Catholic secondary education – she was orphaned at an early age and spent much of her adolescence being moved from home to home – Mary and her husband have supported their two sons through university and into safely middle-class occupations: one is a lawyer and the other a health instructor. Where Mary most obviously differs from Dorothy is, first, that her husband's class position – as a spare-parts salesman in a two-person business in which he is the employee – is also clearly working class and, second, in her strong identification with that class position and the values most typically associated with it. As we have seen, although Dorothy does not identify herself strongly in class terms, she inclines to think of herself as middle class. As a Liberal Party supporter, her values are highly individualistic reflecting her belief that people get out of life what they put into it and she is concerned that her children should continue to improve their middle-class position through their own efforts. Mary, by contrast, both sees herself as working class and holds strongly to a collectivist set of values: she believes that governments have significant responsibilities in the provision of health, welfare and educational opportunities, for example, and votes Labor.

Although she is clearly proud of her children and pleased that they have done well, Mary shows no signs of being dissatisfied with her own class position or of wanting to follow the middle-class trajectories of her sons. While she admits that their children have introduced her to new tastes (she never had smoked salmon until given some by her daughter-in-law but it now forms a part of her weekly shopping list), there is no sense that she is at all at odds with her class destiny. This is reflected in her attitude to home. In marked contrast to the home improvement projects of Gillian and Barbara, home, for Mary, is a place for a family to be in and, as such, its paramount value is that of comfort:

> Some people just have an in-built knack of what looks nice and what goes with something to make it look nice. Me, I just buy what I like. If it matches something, it's good luck more than good management, but I do try to make it a house, so when you come into it you feel comfortable and at home . . . And you know it's not a house that's starchy, that you think, I won't sit there, I'll crush the cushion or I should take my shoes off because everyone's shoes are at the front door, you know. Yeah, it's never been that sort of a home, that's what I like . . . And homey, I'm a Cancerian and we like our home and we like our family to like our home. My family are very comfortable coming here. They visit very often and they come in the door and they don't mind helping themselves to whatever's in the fridge or the cupboard. They feel at ease, they feel like it is still their home, they can just make themselves comfortable.

When asked why she doesn't like a house to be 'distinctive' and 'modern', and why she likes clutter, Mary articulates her refusal to be modernised in terms which express her commitment to a set of working-class family and communal values:

> **MARY** No, because I'm a bugger for bits and pieces. If you look in there on the piano and that I've got – all the family gives me photos because they know I like to sit the photos around and lots of the family give me frogs because I'm a frog fanatic and everywhere you look in the house there's little frogs . . . My china I really love but I use it all the time. My husband started it off years ago, bought me a cup, saucer and plate and I've sort of built it right up and then, when we had our china wedding, we ended up buying the dinner plates and things so that in the Royal Albert we've got our complete dinner service and inside we've got lots of bits and pieces for it. So they're my treasures, but we use them all the time, even with my little grandson. I put them out for him as well.
>
> **INTERVIEWER** . . . So what do you particularly like about that type of china, why do you think you like that rather than your Ikea plain white plates?
>
> **MARY** I think that's because I'm old-fashioned, I'm an old type of person that likes those type of things, straight modern lines are not my thing.
>
> **INTERVIEWER** One of the other things you mentioned that were least important to you was distinctive style in housing, what does that mean?
>
> **MARY** Well way-out, I class distinctive as way-out.
>
> **INTERVIEWER** And I suppose also in this area you'd really stand out if your house was different because they are quite similar.
>
> **MARY** Yes, they were all built by one builder basically. They were all project homes, they were cheap at the time. They've stood the test of time, they're quite good, now you see people are adding tops and doing things to them and they look nice. But they're still in keeping with the neighbourhood, like nobody's got any really way-out type houses around here.

Elizabeth, in her early thirties, is younger than Mary but shares her strong identification with the working class as a part of her family background – her father was a sheet metal worker – and has a similarly strong commitment to the collectivist and welfarist social and political values of a regular Labor voter. Her material circumstances are considerably more constrained, however. Her household income – she works part-time as a sandwich lady and her partner, Dennis, is employed as a painter – is in the $22 000 to

$24 000 range. With three children all attending state schools and rent to pay on a housing commission home in inner Sydney, this means that there is relatively little disposable income after the costs of running their one car – a 1989 Nissan – have been met. Elizabeth accordingly reports little involvement in any cultural activities outside the home, except for the odd family visits to a McDonald's or KFC. Even this is seen as costly, however, and something she does only rarely:

> Even to take them to McDonald's for five of us and the dogs will have a cheeseburger brought back for them as a treat, we are mainly looking at $30 just for that and I said to Dennis, I'd rather go out and buy a nice roast or some seafood for that and have a really nice meal at home here that I can cook up with garlic bread and a nice piece of fish.

Although it is not something she aspires to for herself, Elizabeth's main aim in life is to provide her two daughters and a son with a route out of the economic grind of working-class life, but only if they wish to take it:

> I don't – like Jacki says – nothing against me – but she just doesn't want to sit at home all day, get some big thrills out of watching a couple of hours of TV a day and cooking tea. She wants a career and I'm rubbing my hands together thinking, this is great. I love the attitude 'cause I want more for my kids, much much more than what I had. But at the same time I've got to realise that I can't fulfil what I want for myself through them. They've got to have this them-selves. They've got to make their own decisions in life and I think that I will still give them the best home life that I can give them. I'll still give them the things they need in life to get through and it's up to them . . . It's got to be their choice in life but, yeah, it would break my heart for them to come home and say, well we're leaving school and going to work full-time at McDonald's when they're capable of doing so much more with their lives. Like I said to Jacki . . . you earn $20 000 a year, forget the big house on the water with the BMW convertible sitting in the drive because it's just not going to happen . . . You can't have a job at McDonald's and have the BMW car. The two just don't go together, you'll end up with the good old Datsun at McDonald's . . .

When asked to give her views on good and bad taste, Elizabeth stresses her own lack of the refinement and skills – of etiquette and self-presentation – she believes her children will need if they are to be socially mobile. 'I don't think I fit in the social sector of Lady Susan Renouf', is how she puts it. 'I think I'd be a little over the top for them sort of people.

I don't think I'd mix very well with them sort, I haven't got the plum in the mouth.' However, while unable or unwilling to acquire them for herself, she is equally adamant that her children need to learn some social graces:

> Jacki's tutor was here and I think her mum drops her off in the BMW and I'll be on the phone to my sister and I'll turn around and say 'Oh well, Stanley's nothing but an effing bastard' and Dennis will say 'Do you have to? That doesn't look good for Jacki.' I said but I'm in my own home if she doesn't bloody like it that's just bloody bad luck. He said a bit of decorum wouldn't hurt. You know I'm not out to impress anybody, either they like me or they don't and I'm not asking her, she can tutor Jacki somewhere else if she doesn't like coming into my home. I said if I can't be myself in my own home, I never had the etiquette training when I was a young girl, I don't, I won't put on false pretences and try and be something that I'm not. I can't do that. Even though I do try and tell the kids well, manners here wouldn't hurt. And I do try so very very hard to practise what I preach, I really do.

Elizabeth's fierce commitment to her children's future and her sense of the distances they have to travel if they are to be socially mobile are reflected in her attitudes towards her home. Two issues stand out here. The first is the stress she places on cleanliness as a way of distancing herself, her home and her family from the taint of living on the brink of necessity:

> It doesn't mean just because you live in a Housing Commission home at good old Doonside that you've got to fit the image. You keep yourself well-presented. Your home clean.

For Elizabeth, accordingly, the most important aspect of entertaining – given that Dennis usually does the cooking – is that of presenting an image of complete cleanliness and tidiness:

> As far as table decoration goes, everything's got to be clean, ironed. Presentation to me in that area is very important. Everything you, yeah the kitchen area's got to be clean. I always regularly wash my curtains and windows every three or four months . . . I just like clean windows, I like things to be clean . . . And that's the same with my table setting and my dinner ware. It doesn't have to be expensive but if you care for it it's clean, it looks fine.

Equally noticeable, and a significant point of contrast with Mary, is the value Elizabeth places on the home being uncluttered. That this is an ideal rather than an actually achieved state is clear from the way Elizabeth complains that her children mess up the bookcase – meant, in Elizabeth's eyes, solely for the encyclopedias she has invested in – by leaving their videos there. Rather more important, however, are the underlying reasons for this preference which has to do with the home's role as a place for both Elizabeth and her children to play their respective roles in furthering the educational careers that will serve as their tickets to economic advancement. The home is, in Elizabeth's account, uncluttered by any decoration – no paintings, posters or art objects of any kind – and is, for her, primarily a place that needs to be kept cleared for her own constant action in support of her family:

> Because Jacki wants the nice big house down at Kogarah and to have the nice car and the house-cleaner that comes in once a week, and she's not domesticated at all. Just getting her to make her bed, the only reason why she does that is because she'll lose two bucks off her pocket money, otherwise she wouldn't do it. And my mum's still absolutely horrified to this day that I still do her ironing for her. And I said but to me that's part of being mum, that's my job. She said, but she's nearly sixteen. I said but she could be flogging the books, instead of standing there ironing. Why iron when you've got mum there willing to do it for you when she could do extra book work? So to me that's silly. So to me I do the incidentals of the ironing and she'll get the books out which I'm happy having it like that.

Men About the House

Like most of the women who were interviewed, Elizabeth talks animatedly and at length about her home, what it means to her and its relationship to other aspects of her life. This is not true of many men. Whereas women often claim either the sole or major responsibility for decisions about domestic decor or furnishing, few men do and many concede that they usually leave such matters to their wives. While this results in a certain degree of taciturnity when men are asked about the qualities they look for in a home and what they do about the house, this very taciturnity is revealing – indeed, eloquent – in what it tells us about the gendered patterns of involvement in, and attitudes towards, the domestic space.

John is a case in point. A trained carpenter who works as a stevedore, he lives with his wife Wendy in a beach-side suburb of a capital city to which they moved some years earlier – he was 54 when he filled in the questionnaire – because of his interest in surfing. A committed trade unionist, John's social and political values are similar to those of Mary and Elizabeth. Spending a good deal of his life outdoors – he is an active member of the local surf club and plays golf and a number of other sports quite regularly – home is not, for him, a place that he either spends much time in or wants to spend much effort on:

> **INTERVIEWER** I noticed that probably one of the things that you seem to get to do a bit of is home repairs and some home improvements. Is that totally out of necessity or do you get some relaxation from it?
>
> **JOHN** No, it's probably necessity more than anything, you know. When things start to fall apart they have got to be fixed.
>
> **INTERVIEWER** And having been a carpenter has that ever extended to you making things at home?
>
> **JOHN** No, not really, I haven't bothered a great deal, you know.
>
> **INTERVIEWER** And the thing that you do the most, you said at the time for relaxation was listening to the radio.
>
> **JOHN** Yeah, well I lay in bed and listen to the radio or read if there isn't much on TV. I like all the sports, races. I listen to the races on the radio.
>
> **INTERVIEWER** And there are lots of things that you do hardly ever, gardening?
>
> **JOHN** Yeah, I never do it. I'm flat out mowing the lawn sometimes. It has got to be about ten inches long before I think about it. No, I have no burning desire to be a champion gardener.

Similarly, when asked about the various memorabilia and ornaments on display in the house, John typically refers these to his wife as a part of her domain:

> **INTERVIEWER** Now I was going to ask you about one of the things that you said that you had in your home was pottery and ceramics. And I can also see that you have got some tapestry.
>
> **JOHN** Yeah a little tapestry. Wendy used to do a little ceramic work, you know, but there are a couple of things up there, the jugs and plates and . . . some of them were left to Wendy from an aunty years ago, you know. She likes them.

For John, home is a place to escape to from work and a place for relaxation. This is reflected in his preferred value for his ideal home, namely that it should be 'easy-to-maintain' and, his second and third choices, that it should be 'comfortable' and 'clean-and-tidy'. On the negative side, he is least interested in a 'modern' home and does not want a home that might be described as either 'elegant' or 'uncluttered'. While these values are similar to some of those held by the women whose preferences we have already discussed, John invests them with a distinctively male form of minimalism:

JOHN Well, we were talking about if we won the Lotto or something like that last night, well, I'd still look for the same sort of things. But, only of course, they'd be on a larger scale. A unit to me is ideal because it's basically self-contained and you don't have to really do anything other than just vacuum the carpet every now and again, have a bit of a clean up plus your own washing and that's it. You don't have to worry about the exterior of the place and you don't have to worry about the grounds or anything like that.

. . .

INTERVIEWER You don't look for a house that's distinctive or elegant. Can you elaborate on what you mean by that?

. . .

JOHN Well, some of the Queensland homes. Not the traditional Queensland homes but some of the ones that they sort of produce, they've got gables all over the place. They're still a modern home but they've got gables in just about every direction and columns here and there. It's just an overly produced type of dwelling where everything just sort of stands out too much. And also, I always look at it from a painter's point of view. Terrible type of places to maintain.

Grant's relationship to his home is, in some ways, similar. When asked about home furnishings or decor, for example, he constantly passes the question off as one that really concerns his wife:

Yeah, my wife tends to pick the furniture. I go along. In real terms she picks the furniture, yeah, I agree, no, why don't you do this. Will it fit? I tend to walk around with a measuring tape. She picks the furniture.

As an active sports fan, most of his leisure is centred outside the home. He rarely does things about the house and very many of the activities we asked about under this heading he had never done.

Beyond these points of similarity, however, Grant and John have very little in common; their shared masculine traits in relation to the home are inflected differently by their different class positions. A British migrant with a university diploma in engineering, Grant holds a national management position with an engineering company. His annual household income, based mainly on his salary, although his wife does some telemarketing, is in the $90 000 to $100 000 range. He is, however, a Labor Party supporter but with a fairly mixed set of social and political views: he is opposed to government intervention in the economy and to universal health care, and strongly opposed to Aboriginal land rights. He also identifies himself strongly in class terms. Describing himself as middle class – and with the fine distinction only an Englishman could make that he sees himself as lower-middle class in a British context but as upper-middle class in Australia – he attributes his class position mainly to his education. A life member of his local Masonic lodge, he shows, in this and other ways, a highly developed sense of social distinction: he and his wife have stopped going to the cinema as they don't know 'who had sat in the chair before'.

These differences in class position are reflected in the fact that, for Grant, the separation of work and home is less distinct than in John's case. Since he regularly works a 60-hour week, his major say in the home has been to ensure that it is sufficiently equipped with office and communications technologies to be able to operate as, so to speak, an office away from the office. Perhaps more important, he can see very little difference between his ideal home and the house he actually lives in, a closure reflecting the degree to which he interprets his home as a sign of a mobility trajectory that has, essentially, been completed: Grant has arrived at wherever he had been heading. Preferring a home to be 'clean-and-tidy', 'comfortable', and 'spacious', he feels that his present home – a two-storey house in a quiet Sydney cul-de-sac and bordering on parkland – largely fulfils all three criteria, and over-fulfils the last:

> It's probably a little bit too big but, yeah, it meets all of those criteria . . . Yeah, I guess compared to where I grew up, if we are talking house versus house, my house now would be classified as probably nearly a mansion compared with what we had. My mother has just returned home and she says, this is a mansion. So yeah, I know where I came from, I know what I've got now.

These differences, essentially differences in class ethos, are carried over into how John and Grant see the relationship between home and entertaining. For John and Wendy, home entertaining is mainly a matter of a few friends and neighbours from the surf club coming by for a casual meal and serving their usual cooking, something simple but tasty:

> Yeah, generally baked dinners mainly if friends come. Wendy will cook a baked dinner and we will have a couple of bottles of wine with it. Sit down and just have a talk and just mainly, not really fancy food.

For Grant, by contrast, entertaining means serving something special with the accent placed on formality with a very clear division of domestic labour:

GRANT Yes, it wouldn't be just come over sit down and chat, you know. It would be sit down to a proper dinner and things like that.
INTERVIEWER And you and your wife, would you both be involved in deciding what to have or setting up or who to have?
GRANT Yeah, we would both be involved in that, although what to have would be Mrs Marks and I would get to set the table, I guess.

Mapping Tastes

Our purpose so far has been to account for some aspects of the lived texture and social dynamics of taste by showing how the values that individuals invest in their homes can be illuminated when considered in the light of their social characteristics. We have, for this purpose, focused on gender, class position, and education, and on the ways in which these interact in the context of specific social trajectories. We now turn to lend some statistical support to the forms of argument and analysis which have underlain the discussion so far. In doing so, we shall continue to limit our attention to the roles of gender, class, and education in organising cultural tastes. This is not to discount the significance of other factors – especially age and ethnicity – which we consider in detail in later chapters. Here, however, our concern is not to give a complete account of tastes in and about the house but rather to illustrate some of the statistical patterns we shall be exploring more fully as the book progresses.

We look, first, at gender. It is clear that men and women hold very different views about their ideal homes. Table 2.1 gives, in the first two columns, the percentages of women and men who, whether as their first, second or third choice, indicate a preference for the attribute indicated. The third column then gives the ratio of male to female choices. The gendered logic at work in this pattern of choices seems reasonably clear. Women's preferences, when ranked according to how they most differ from men's, reflect an orientation that centres inward on the home and its relationship to its family members. The stress is on practicality ('uncluttered', 'easy-to-maintain', 'clean-and-tidy') and, most importantly, on the home as a place to be lived in. The attributes which men prefer more strongly than women, by contrast, mostly relate to the display functions of the home – its role in presenting an image of the self and of the family to the outside world. At their polarised extremes, if women's most distinctive preference when measured against men's is for a home to have a lived-in feel about it, men differ from women most in their wish that home should be distinctive, that is, that it should make a public statement about the distinguishing style of its owners or occupants.

The home is similarly very much a gendered space in terms of what people do in and around the house. We can see, in table 2.2, that there is a

Table 2.1   Ideal home by gender

	Female	Male	Male as % of female
Mainly female			
Lived-in	16.1	12.1	75
Uncluttered	11.4	8.5	75
Elegant	6.4	5.1	80
Imaginative	8.2	6.7	82
Easy-to-maintain	48.6	41.5	85
Clean-and-tidy	50.6	47.7	94
Comfortable	59.4	55.6	94
Mainly male			
Spacious	24.8	27.1	109
Traditional	7.7	8.6	112
Well-designed	31.1	35.9	115
Modern	8.5	11.9	140
Distinctive	3.1	6.1	197

Table 2.2   Participation in domestic leisure (often and sometimes) by gender

	Female	Male	Male as % of female
Mainly female			
Clothes making	43.4	2.9	7
Craft activity	61.3	15.1	25
Creative writing	18.9	9.3	49
Board games	41.7	32.4	75
Drawing or sketching	17.2	13.4	78
Photography	52.1	43.7	84
Playing cards or chess	45.6	43.9	96
Mainly male			
Gardening	77.5	77.8	100
Fantasy/role-playing games	7.7	9.5	123
Playing a musical instrument	14.5	20.4	141
DIY home improvements	39.9	61.6	154
Home repairs	47.7	77.2	162
Computer or video games	19.0	32.9	173

considerable degree of difference in men's and women's participation in different forms of domestic leisure. While gardening is a more or less equally shared activity, other activities directed towards the maintenance of the home and family are significantly differentiated, with women focusing on family activities (making clothes, craft activities) while men are more engaged in maintaining the physical infrastructure of the home (DIY and home repairs).

If this is not surprising, the distribution of other activities is somewhat more notable, with women – except for playing a musical instrument – more likely to engage in creative activities (writing, drawing, photography) than men while also preferring more traditional games (board games, cards, chess) which typically involve the whole family. Men, by contrast, have higher rates of preference for role-playing games and especially for computer and video games which, in pitting one or two players against either the machine or one another, are often less successful in involving the family as a family.

There are also marked differences in the kinds of things men and women collect in the home. As we have seen, men tend to defer to women – just as much as women claim this as their area of decision – in the choice of domestic ornaments and decorations. It is not surprising, then, that women are more likely than men to own collections having a domestic or decorative function: figurines, ornaments, plates, teaspoons (see table 2.3). Men's interests, by contrast, focus on collections having no obvious connection to the home. Indeed, their association with a larger world outside the home, as well as their evocation of a lost childhood, is evidently a part of their attraction for Kenneth:

> Ever since I was a boy, I've always had a great interest in aircraft and I suppose, being a kid during the war, and living up north and seeing squadrons of planes flying over, that sort of thing. Being indoctrinated by magazines and all that sort of thing with it. But . . . I'm interested in architectural drawings. So, I'm interested in just studying a drawing of a model aircraft and all the details. Understanding the difficulty the draughtsman had in producing a thing as detailed as a scaled-down aircraft. But I also like the demand of the very detailed work in building a model. That appeals to me.

However, gender does not play as strong a role in relation to all aspects of cultural choice associated with the home. There is, for example, little significant difference in men's and women's choices about styles of entertaining or the kinds of food they prefer to serve when cooking for guests. Men prefer barbecuing, but only by a relatively modest margin of 4%, while women are about 5% more likely to choose buffets than men. For the rest, men's and women's preferred styles of entertaining are very similar, as are their patterns of eating out, reflecting the fact these are activities that couples tend to do together on the basis of joint decisions, negotiations and compromises. The same is true, and probably for much the same reasons, of choice of cars. Within the top twenty cars according to first car owned per household, only eight models show an association with one gender that is 1% or more greater than its association with the other gender: Holdens (excluding the Statesman), Toyotas and – except for the Fairlane – Fords for men; Mazdas, Mitsubishi, Nissans, Hondas and – most markedly – Subarus

Table 2.3   Collections by gender (first, second and third preferences for collections recording a total of ten or more preferences)

	Female	Male	Male as % of female
Mainly female			
Plates	1.4	0.1	7
Teaspoons	1.3	0.1	8
Ornaments	1.2	0.1	8
Figurines	1.8	0.3	17
Cards/postcards	1.6	0.9	56
Themed collection	3.9	2.7	69
Magazines	1.0	0.7	70
Shells	1.3	1.0	77
Mainly male			
Stamps	17.0	19.5	115
Coins	13.3	18.7	141
Gemstones	0.6	1.3	217

for women. When it comes to the cars they would like to own, however, men's and women's tastes – freed from the constraint imposed by the need to reach a joint decision within a limited budget – are more clearly differentiated (see figure 2.1). While a good number of men remain faithful to their Holdens, others, giving their fantasies free rein, are more likely to opt for sports cars (Ferrari, Lamborghini, Porsche) and elite European cars (Jaguar, Mercedes). Women's preferences, by contrast, tend more towards the lower end of the market (Ford, Toyota, Nissan, Datsun, Mitsubishi) or, where they include European cars, towards makes with a reputation for safety, reliability and durability (Volvo and SAAB, for example).

Perhaps the most striking aspect of this figure, however, is BMW's leadership of the fantasy car market for both men and women followed, a close second, by Mercedes. Jaguar and Rolls-Royce, by contrast, come some way down the list. It is possible that this is related to the ways in which many of our interviewees, when asked whether they think of Australia as a class society, are keen to distinguish Australia from Britain. Michael, a socialist with a very strong working-class identification, insists that Australia is a class-conscious society:

> people who live in St Ives immediately think they're better than somebody who lives in Burwood or people who live in Burwood think they're better than somebody who lives in Surry Hills.

However, he is equally at pains to characterise this class consciousness as primarily concerning wealth and therefore different from those forms of

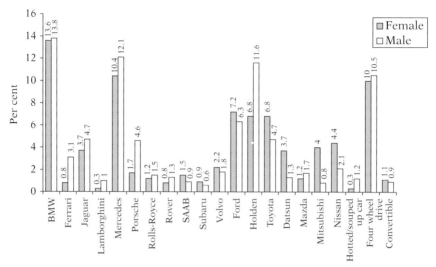

Figure 2.1 Cars most like to own by gender

social snobbery which he sees as the historical legacy of the forms of aristocratic distinction developed in Britain and (improbably) America. For Patricia, too, 'there's probably class here but definitely not, I mean, there's definitely not like it is in London for instance'. Similarly, in talking about cars, a number of people explicitly reject a Rolls-Royce as too ostentatious a symbol of social exclusivity: Frank doesn't want a Rolls because he thinks they are 'just great lumbering tanks' but also because he doesn't like their image, while Colin maintains he would be embarrassed to drive a Rolls as too evidently a status object. The BMW, by contrast, represents a happy compromise for many of those we interviewed in being European but not British (only Grant, an English migrant, expresses a wish for a Jaguar because it is British), comfortable rather than sporty (clearly a major issue for the women who liked BMWs), and stylish without being overstated. The statistical patterns suggest that BMWs are also, together with Mercedes, a happy compromise for those who see themselves as members of either the upper or upper-middle classes, with Mercedes recruiting the favour of 26.6% and BMWs 20.4% of those who identify themselves in these terms.

Social class also proves to be important in other areas of cultural choice connected to the home, often ones in which the effects of gender are muted. Styles of entertaining, for example, exhibit some appreciable class differences, with managers, professionals, employers and para-professionals having a strong commitment to serving formal dinners compared to the other classes, particularly manual workers for whom, at only 6.2%, this is not a popular activity. Employers, professionals and para-professionals also stand out as liking to entertain alfresco, while professionals are distinguished from all other classes in their markedly low rate of preference for barbecuing (see table 2.4).

In other areas, however, class clearly has less marked effects than gender. This is true of the patterns of involvement in different forms of domestic leisure, few of which show any overwhelming signs of belonging to a particular class. Nonetheless, some trends are worth noting. Sales and clerical workers and manual workers are the least inclined to be actively involved in home maintenance activities, reflecting the reluctance, evident in the interviews, for those with trade skills to use them at home, as well as a greater tendency for the members of these classes to live in rented accommodation: this is true of around close to 27% for both classes compared with an average for the other classes of just under 16%. Sales and clerical workers are the most involved in craft activities and clothes making, reflecting a mixture of economic circumstances and the overwhelmingly female composition of this class. We might also note, finally, that professionals are the most likely to engage in creative writing and to play a musical instrument, and by a factor which distinguishes them significantly from all other social classes. With 35% of professionals playing a musical instrument, this is more or less twice the rate of the class next in line on this activity (sales and clerical workers) and nearly two-and-a-half times the average of 14.4% for all other classes (including sales and clerical workers). It is also noteworthy that employers are significantly more likely than the members of other classes to want their homes to be 'distinctive' while manual workers are the most likely to want a home to be clean, 'uncluttered' and 'modern'.

Class also proves modest in its measurable effects so far as attitudes to art are concerned. This is mainly because the question we asked exploring preferences between realistic, abstract and experimental art resulted in an overwhelming preference for realistic art and a more or less random distribution of the preferences for other kinds of art. The same trend is evident in the interviews, where it is clear that most people buy art for highly specific reasons – usually because of their associations with particular places or persons – or for particular occasions. In the case of Patricia, for example, the painting her husband gave her for her wedding present had established a family ritual:

> it's sort of like what you call a Black & Decker present in a way, in that, it's sort of my birthday and we thought well, this is a nice time to get another painting.

Table 2.4 Preferred way of presenting a meal by class (column percentages)

	Emp.	Self-emp.	Mgr	Prof.	Para-prof.	Supv.	Sales/cler.	Manual	*Mean*
Formal dinner	22.0	13.8	27.7	22.1	21.2	16.8	13.4	6.2	*14.8*
BBQ	18.6	19.0	14.1	9.4	17.2	15.5	16.9	19.6	*15.6*
Casual family meal	52.2	59.4	53.7	57.1	49.4	60.2	57.2	68.8	*61.1*
Buffet	2.7	5.1	3.7	7.2	7.6	6.1	9.2	3.9	*5.9*
Brunch	0.0	0.1	0.0	0.0	0.0	0.0	1.6	1.2	*0.5*
Alfresco	4.5	2.6	0.9	4.3	4.5	1.5	1.8	0.3	*2.1*

Considerations of this kind, then, are usually more important than a commitment to any particular aesthetic style. That said, few would disagree with John when he says:

> Well, I like to be able to just look at something, you know, just walk in and say: well, I like that, rather than going all around it and getting someone to explain what it is supposed to be. I like to be able to see what it is without people telling you what it is.

Carol is of a similar persuasion:

> I like things that I understand. I don't like things created out of metal and put together and say that's a work of art. I cannot understand that work of art. It has to be something that I understand, that I look at and think, perhaps that it's true, it's real.

These views are echoed, statistically, in the high rates of preference for realistic art – from 57.2% for manual workers to 78.6% for managers – that are expressed by all classes. A preference for abstract art is highest among para-professionals (10.8%), a good number of whom are practising artists, followed, more surprisingly, by sales and clerical workers (9%). Preference for experimental art is highest among the self-employed and professionals at close to 5% each.

However, class exerts more systematic effects when it comes to the ownership of art. With the exception of the column relating to rock posters, Table 2.5 displays a common class pattern for the ownership of different kinds of art objects. High levels of ownership are established by employers; there is then, a slight dip in ownership on the part of the self-employed

Table 2.5 Ownership of works of art by class

	Emp.	Self-emp.	Mgr	Prof.	Para-prof.	Supv.	Sales/cler.	Manual	*Mean*
Original artworks	64.3	58.4	71.5	72.2	58.3	52.9	50.0	34.5	*50.9*
Pottery/ceramics	71.4	65.8	68.5	68.3	66.1	62.0	72.8	54.0	*64.2*
Limited edition prints	21.0	14.7	22.4	26.2	23.7	13.8	13.5	7.9	*14.5*
Sculptures	16.0	15.8	17.6	22.4	16.9	13.6	14.7	9.8	*13.9*
Rock music posters	20.6	17.4	17.9	15.6	11.7	21.0	22.2	19.7	*20.8*
Nature posters	26.6	18.8	26.8	31.8	24.8	25.4	27.0	23.9	*25.6*
Art posters	22.0	16.6	22.4	33.0	22.9	18.3	19.6	13.2	*19.5*
Political posters	0.8	0.7	2.0	6.9	1.2	1.9	0.9	0.2	*1.49*

which picks up again with managers to peak with professionals. Para-professionals retain reasonably high levels of ownership – on average, a little above those for the self-employed – but these begin to fall again with supervisors and sales and clerical workers to reach what are consistently their lowest levels with manual workers.

Differences of this kind are, in part, a reflection of the differences of income associated with different class positions. Mary articulates the logic at work here with characteristic economy when she is asked about the role of art in her childhood:

> **INTERVIEWER** So what did you have in your home when you were a child growing up?
>
> **MARY** Art-wise?
>
> **INTERVIEWER** Yes.
>
> **MARY** Nothing.
>
> **INTERVIEWER** Nothing?
>
> **MARY** No.
>
> **INTERVIEWER** So, why was that if he (Mary's father) really liked it?
>
> **MARY** Cost. We wouldn't have had the money.

Household income, then, does make a difference: around 63% of those with more than $80 000 per year own original paintings compared with a little more than 58% of those with incomes in the $15 000 to $26 000 range. However, the role of income in this respect is less significant than that of education. This touches on a topic that will occupy our attention at a number of points in the following chapters, for it is the importance of education in shaping tastes that usually accounts for the tendency for professionals and managers to exhibit the highest levels of involvement in aesthetic culture. For the moment, though, table 2.6 will suffice as an illustration of the relative influence of income and education in these matters. The figures here express the rates of ownership of art objects associated with the highest levels of education (completed tertiary) as a ratio of those associated with the lowest (primary). Those with a tertiary education are 240% more likely to own original paintings or drawings than those with only primary schooling. Likewise, the figures for income express the rates of ownership for the highest band of household income (more than $80 000 per annum) as a ratio of those associated with the lowest income level (less than $15 000). In all cases, the range of difference associated with education is significantly greater than that associated with income and is especially pronounced in the case of art posters and signed limited editions. Here, the range of effect of education is two-and-a-half to three times that of income.

The effects of education can also be seen in the more qualitative aspects of people's aesthetic choices. The question we designed to explore these issues asked respondents to decide how to classify a series of topics we had proposed as possible subjects for a photograph, a device used to great effect by Bourdieu in *Distinction* and, in more detail, in an earlier (1965) study (see Bourdieu, 1990). Did they find the topics beautiful, interesting, clichéd or unattractive? The results of this question are of interest here less because of the pattern of responses in relation to particular topics than for what the overall distribution of responses between the different categories tells us about how people from different social backgrounds interpret and use these categories. Here, again, class is not the decisive factor. Table 2.7 gives the class distribution for the use of the different categories of response across all the topics respondents were asked to consider. This shows relatively little difference in the rates at which members of different classes draw on different categories in answering this question. The rates of usage of the categories 'beautiful' and 'clichéd' show only 1 or 2% variation. The largest variation is in the use of 'interesting', and even here there is only a modest difference of about 6% between the low use of this category by manual workers at around 29% and the high use by professionals at a little over 35%.

By contrast, gender gives rise to a systematic set of effects in the much greater tendency of women to opt for the more straightforwardly aesthetic

Table 2.6 Ownership of art objects – education and income compared

	Completed tertiary as % of primary	Highest as % of lowest income level
Original works of art	240	145
Pottery/ceramics	183	159
Signed limited editions	927	294
Sculptures	481	246
Art posters	708	277

Table 2.7 Subjects for photographs – class distribution of categories (column percentages)

	Emp.	Self-emp.	Mgr	Prof.	Para-prof.	Supv.	Sales/cler.	Manual
Beautiful	22.5	22.9	23.7	22.5	23.6	20.9	25.8	23.6
Interesting	35.2	32.2	35.5	35.2	31.8	31.7	29.7	28.9
Clichéd	15.3	15.8	14.4	15.3	16.3	17.6	15.3	15.1
Unattractive	26.9	29.2	26.5	26.9	27.8	29.8	29.1	32.4

term 'beautiful' compared to men who, in a pattern of response we shall encounter in more detail in later chapters, prefer to use the more documentary category of 'interesting' when reacting positively to the photographic interest of a particular topic (see figure 2.2). Men use the category 'beautiful' less than women in relation to eight topics, while the reverse is true only in relation to four topics (a car crash, a tackle in a football match, a demolition site and a halved onion). The category 'interesting', by contrast, is used more frequently by men in relation to all categories except for three: Aboriginal dancers, a halved onion and Sydney Opera House.

If we turn now to the role of education, the most interesting effect by far consists in the tendency for those with lower levels of education to opt for bipolar aesthetic responses, either designating a topic beautiful or going to the opposite extreme and labelling it unattractive. To put this another way: the higher the level of education, the greater the tendency to opt for the more nuanced and qualified judgements embodied in the categories of 'interesting' and 'clichéd'. Thus 72.6% of those with only primary schooling classify a landscape as beautiful, 26.6% as interesting, only 0.8% as unattractive, and none at all as clichéd, whereas the responses of the tertiary-educated are more evenly spread across the full range of possibilities, with 58.3% opting for beautiful, 33.2% for interesting, 7.3% for clichéd and 1.3% for unattractive. Similarly, those with primary schooling strongly reject a car

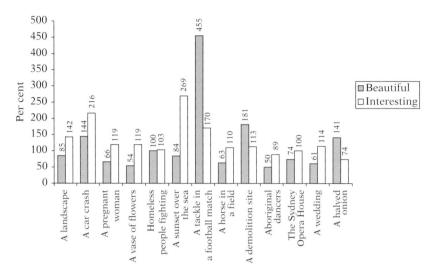

Figure 2.2 Subjects for photographs – male as percentage of female

crash as a suitable subject for a photograph, 91% classifying it as unattractive, 1.1% as clichéd, 6.4% as interesting and 1.6% as beautiful. The tertiary-educated, by contrast, while no more likely to consider the topic beautiful (less, in fact, at 0.2%), make greater use of the intermediate categories – 18.7% see it as a possibly interesting subject, while 6.6% view it as clichéd – leaving only 74.5% applying the harsher negative assessment of being unattractive. The extreme bipolarity of these responses on the part of those with lower levels of education is not matched in relation to all the topics we asked about. What is salient, however, is the tendency for broader use to be made of the full range of possible responses at the higher levels of education. This is evident from figure 2.3 which tallies the responses for the two bipolar aesthetic responses (beautiful as the positive pole and unattractive as the negative pole) for three educational cohorts and shows that, without exception, the tendency for responses to be limited to these two options decreases with level of education.

These questions begin to open up one of the central issues we shall be concerned with in following chapters: the role of the education system in distributing those forms of cultural competence which distinguish those who are easily able to answer questions exploring cultural tastes and values from those for whom such questions are more difficult to handle and often threatening. Either/or choices between sharply polarised options are likely to be easier to cope with for those with relatively low resources of cultural capital. Another sign of this is the marked tendency for the no-response rates to increase significantly with lower levels of education for those questions

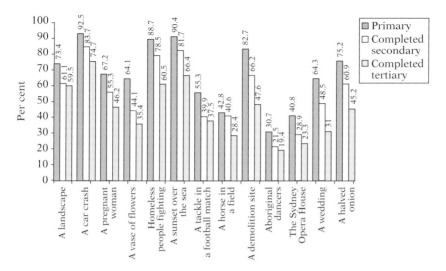

Figure 2.3 Subjects for photographs by education – combined 'Beautiful' and 'Unattractive' responses

exploring the qualitative and attitudinal aspects of cultural taste. Our question concerning preferences between realistic, abstract and experimental art, for example, gave rise to a 24.4% no-response rate on the part of those with only primary schooling compared with 10.6% for those who had completed secondary school and 4.7% for those who had completed a tertiary education.

These questions, however, will not be pursued further here. Our purpose in this chapter has been simply to place such questions on the agenda, rather than to explore their intricacies. We have also wanted to relate these issues to the ways in which, in the admittedly somewhat artificial context of an interview with a visiting researcher, real people talk about their cultural lives. It will therefore be fitting to conclude by looking at an exchange between one of our respondents, Carol, a woman in her sixties who had relatively little formal education, and the interviewing researcher who, although clearly 'leading the witness', makes Carol a party to the theoretical debates concerning the relations between education and cultural capital:

> INTERVIEWER Just a little question. Just a link that might tie up. You said 'I don't like things I can't understand'. Do you think that may be because at school you only did art once a month. You think maybe there is something there? If you had some knowledge that would have helped you understand the sculpture or painting, you would have felt more comfortable?

CAROL Yes, definitely. It's a lack of understanding that is what it is about. I look at a painting and I think that my grandchildren could do that. But it is a work of art and my grandchildren do squiggles. But I cannot understand it.

INTERVIEWER You have no knowledge of the school of thought that it comes from and that then is a contributing factor to why you don't go. Do you feel uncomfortable?

CAROL Yes, yes. I can't understand it so therefore I pass it by. It goes back to why I like to do flowers. But then I've been taught how to do it. I can see what I have to look for in a garden or out in the country that I can pick up to create that out of. So that is a similar sort of thing.

INTERVIEWER It is, it's the same. The knowledge you have to be taught. It's what is known as cultural capital. It's a disadvantage, it keeps you away.

CAROL Children today have that. Well to a point. I'll show you a drawing that my grandson did. He is very much into art. I was never taught. Once you are taught you then gain an appreciation. The same with the piano. I can't work out how they play the piano. But I could use an accounting machine. I could do all that with my fingers because I had been taught to do that.

This nicely places the acquisition of cultural skills on the technical level that is their proper milieu.

Chapter 3

Media Culture and the Home

Over the last decade, the home has become an increasingly important site for the proliferating technologies of the digital age. More than any other aspect of cultural life, the explosion of home-based forms of entertainment and communication has come to symbolise the rapid pace of technological change in the last decades of the twentieth century. When we started our research the vast majority of Australians only had access to the four free-to-air television channels.[1] A little over three years later, with the roll-out of cable television infrastructure completed, at least in the urban centres, Australians have the option (provided they first pay for the privilege) of viewing up to 50 additional channels. High-density television is on the horizon, with wall-sized screens set to transform the lounge- or living-room into a 'home theatre'. It is rumoured that digital video discs (DVDs) will soon make the only quite recently introduced video-recorder redundant, and there are regular forecasts of the imminent arrival of cyber commerce and gambling as we each connect to the internet through our personal computers.

It is difficult to estimate how much of this electronic brave new world is an accurate picture of the shape of things to come and how much is wishful hype from the communication companies.[2] Whatever the case, our aim in this chapter is not so much to make an assessment of these forecasts and the policy questions they raise as to examine how people use and evaluate the electronic media, focusing on their use in the home. We have two primary goals: first, to document the patterns of ownership of the main forms of domestic cultural technology and their social functions within the home – the manner in which they have become part of everyday life; and second, to look at the assessments Australians make of media content – the television and radio stations, the types of programs and films they prefer and the most salient variations in the structure of media preferences.

For a people whose cultural heritage and mythology are supposedly so strongly linked to the bush and the spirit of the pioneers, Australians have been very eager to embrace the technological products of the urban capitalist economy. The rapid uptake, first, of television and then of the video-recorder by Australian consumers (with the concomitant decline in cinema patronage)[3] has been a success story which manufacturers of more recently developed domestic technologies have sought to emulate. Australians, so the conventional wisdom goes, are 'technophiles': for example, the proportion of households – 30 per cent – which currently possesses a mobile phone is one of the highest among OECD countries.[4] What does the overall pattern of ownership of domestic media technology look like?

Three items are at virtual saturation levels in Australian homes: radios, television sets and telephones. Ninety-nine per cent of households contain at least one radio and television set and 97 per cent have a phone. Several other items are at near saturation level: video-recorders (86.6%), cassette players (90.9%), cameras (90.0%), and record players (73.7%). Two factors – age and household income – appear strongly correlated with possession of technology. Ownership rates are more or less consistent across all cohorts until the age of 60, when they fall sharply; conversely, the higher the income a household enjoys, the more likely it is to possess the various forms of technology. Ownership of certain items – the personal computer is a case in point which we examine in more detail later – is also strongly linked to the nuclear family household type. Finally, it is clear that some household technologies are more than merely domestic or recreational and reflect the linkage of the home to the wider economic sphere.

Table 3.1 shows the variation in rate of ownership for each item of technology by age of respondent. With the exception of the three technologies already at saturation, ownership levels fall dramatically among those aged 60 and over. Only a quarter of the elderly own a CD player, as against the national average of 62 per cent; video-recorders are found in only 65 per cent of their households; and fewer than one in ten of the elderly have a personal computer or an answering machine. These trends may be partly due to the fact that disposable incomes of the elderly are generally lower. But most of the disparities in ownership patterns appear to be cohort-related rather than a function of aging *per se*. It seems likely that older people simply have not felt the same urgency as other groups to replace existing record and cassette players with new CD equipment or to invest in personal computers. There is no evidence that the computer- or CD-owning cohorts of today will discard these items once they replace the current over-60s.

Not surprisingly, the level of household income is a key determinant of ownership of the non-saturation-level items of technology. As table 3.2 shows, with the exceptions of video-recorders, where ownership levels peak in households earning between $60 000 and $80 000, and videocameras,

Table 3.1   Ownership of domestic technology items by age
(percentage of respondents with at least one item)

	18–25	26–35	36–45	46–59	60+	*Mean*
Radio	98.2	98.3	98.7	97.9	97.6	*98.6*
Television	98.5	98.1	98.7	99.2	98.2	*98.6*
Video-recorder	87.7	91.7	92.8	90.5	64.7	*86.6*
Cassette player	97.0	94.5	94.6	91.4	77.3	*90.9*
Record player	73.0	70.8	79.3	79.1	61.5	*73.7*
Compact disc player	80.8	70.5	66.9	65.5	25.1	*62.4*
Camera	93.1	92.1	94.6	91.9	77.4	*90.0*
Videocamera	15.0	19.3	21.8	24.2	8.2	*17.3*
Personal computer	47.0	32.0	54.7	39.8	9.5	*36.9*
Fax machine	7.2	6.6	9.1	9.4	3.2	*6.9*
Telephone	95.8	97.7	97.6	96.5	96.0	*96.8*
Answering machine	27.5	29.9	27.5	26.8	9.9	*24.1*
Modem	5.1	6.8	6.5	5.3	1.3	*5.3*

Table 3.2   Ownership of domestic cultural technology by household income
(percentage of respondents with at least one item)

	<15K	15–26K	26–40K	40–60K	60–80K	>80K
Video-recorder	73.4	83.5	89.7	92.6	93.9	91.7
Record player	66.9	72.1	75.9	79.1	76.4	80.0
CD player	36.8	49.9	65.1	73.9	79.1	83.0
Camera	78.6	87.7	94.1	95.3	96.6	97.0
Videocamera	10.7	16.0	19.4	22.6	20.6	24.4
Computer	19.9	26.7	33.2	47.2	52.2	64.8
Fax machine	3.5	5.6	5.9	6.6	11.0	18.3
Answering machine	14.4	18.3	22.6	26.7	34.4	46.5
Modem	2.2	3.5	4.4	4.7	8.3	11.3

where ownership levels dip slightly in these same households, ownership levels of all non-saturation domestic technologies steadily increase as household income increases.

Multiple ownership of domestic media technology is widespread. Radios are the most common items, with over two-thirds of households having at least two radios and nearly 30 per cent reporting owning four or more. A clear majority of households contain two or more television sets (58%), and nearly 40 per cent have at least two telephones, cassette players and cameras. Ownership of the remaining forms of technology is generally restricted to one item, although close to one in five homes (18%) has two video-recorders. Family size – specifically the presence of children at home – is the most likely determinant of the ownership of two items, but for multiple possession of any technology, household income is more important.

We can begin to get a clearer understanding of how this wealth of domestic technology is woven into the fabric of everyday life by looking first at how ownership patterns vary across social classes. Table 3.3 presents the rank order of ownership by class location for the six less commonly occurring forms of technology ranging from CD players, which are found on average in just over 60 per cent of Australian homes, to modems which had only 5 per cent penetration at the time of our survey.

The two technologies most relevant for everyday communication – telephone answering equipment and fax machines – are most likely to be found among those with business responsibilities or commitments: employers and the self-employed. Nearly 40 per cent of the self-employed have an answering machine, as do close to a third of employers and professionals. The two business-owning classes are more than twice as likely to own a fax machine as the sample overall and they also lead the way in ownership of video-cameras, although the relevance of this equipment for business is not immediately obvious. Computer ownership is highest among professionals and employers, with majorities of each of these classes having a personal computer in their home. However, the former are nearly twice as likely to have access to on-line services and the internet through a modem. The ownership of CD players, an item with no wider economic or educational significance, more closely reflects the distribution of economic capital within households. Overall, working-class households appear to be the most excluded from ownership of the more specialised items of domestic technology.

Computers and the Home

In many respects, the personal computer within the home is the technological item emblematic of the digital revolution. There are, nevertheless, conflicting assessments about its domestic impact. Some commentators believe it is unlikely ever to become a familiar household item, and the penetration computers have currently achieved is about as far as they are likely to go; other estimates are for a steady increase in the number of computer-owning homes to a point where they will be found in the majority of households by the turn of the century.[5]

Our data indicate that by 1995 just over 36 per cent of Australian households owned a PC, and of these 12 per cent had the capacity for internet connection through a modem.[6] The most common use reported for the home computer was work or business (38.4%), followed by education (30.4%) and entertainment (26.4%), with just under 5 per cent stating their computer was mostly used for household management. We have already noted the impact which age, income and social class have on ownership levels. Other

Table 3.3 Ownership of domestic technology – rank order of possession for selected objects by class

CD player		Videocamera		Computer		Fax machine		Answering machine		Modem	
Mgr	75.1	Emp.	25.8	Prof.	53.8	Emp.	18.0	S-emp.	37.2	Prof.	11.2
Emp.	70.7	S-emp.	23.1	Emp.	52.4	S-emp.	15.1	Emp.	32.5	S-emp.	8.0
Prof.	70.4	P-prof.	17.9	Mgr	39.8	Supv.	7.4	Prof.	31.8	Mgr	7.3
Supv.	66.3	Supv.	16.6	P-prof.	37.0	Mgr	6.8	Mgr	25.9	Emp.	6.9
Sales	64.4	Sales	16.5	Sales	36.5	Prof.	6.8	P-prof.	23.7	Supv.	4.9
P-prof.	60.1	Mgr	16.5	S-emp.	35.0	P-prof.	4.6	Supv.	21.6	Sales	4.2
Man.	55.8	Prof.	15.1	Supv.	34.9	Man.	3.6	Sales	21.4	P-prof.	3.6
S-emp.	54.8	Man.	13.2	Man.	23.8	Sales	2.7	Man.	12.7	Man.	1.5
Mean	*62.4*	*Mean*	*17.3*	*Mean*	*36.4*	*Mean*	*6.9*	*Mean*	*24.1*	*Mean*	*5.3*

factors which correlate strongly with ownership are place of residence and, perhaps most significantly, the presence and age of children in the home. Inner-city dwellers are most likely to own a computer at home (46.5%), with those in small towns the least (23.1%). Rural residents use their computer for work or business more than any other group but least of all for education. Class differences in usage are also marked: the computer is overwhelmingly a work machine for those whose livelihoods depend on business. In contrast, for manual workers the computer is primarily a means of entertainment, but it is also used for education. Table 3.4 summarises the household differences in the use of computers for region and class.

By far the most significant factor in predicting whether a household owns a computer is the presence of children. In some instances this can result in near-saturation-level ownership, particularly in the case of pre-teen and teenage children. Moreover, we find in these households a notable shift in the reported use of the computer from being an adjunct to business or work to being primarily an educational device. Table 3.5 is an attempt to summarise the relevant information which connects class location and family type. The information is presented as follows: for each class location the proportion who own a PC is shown (in italic) for each of the child age subgroups. The primary use to which the computer is put in the household is then presented, although to simplify an already detailed table the minority 'household management' function has not been included.

We can observe here, even if in the somewhat broad canvas of a statistical picture, a point noted by several other commentators on home computing (e.g. Haddon 1994; Murdock, Hartmann & Gray 1994), namely the ways in which computer use appears to be intricately interwoven with the structure of the domestic household. The most conspicuous feature of the table is the almost uniform increase in the number of households owning computers as

Table 3.4   Primary household use for personal computer by region and class

	Work/business	Household management	Entertainment	Education
Region				
Inner city	38.3	6.4	17.0	38.3
Provincial city	40.0	4.6	26.2	29.2
Suburban	37.0	4.4	26.8	31.8
Small town	33.3	5.6	38.9	22.2
Semi-rural	38.2	7.3	20.0	34.5
Rural	56.3	0.0	22.9	20.8
Class				
Employers	62.0	1.2	11.3	25.4
Self-employed	66.8	2.0	9.1	22.1
Managers	47.6	4.1	20.0	28.4
Professionals	50.0	6.0	15.4	28.6
Para-prof.	25.8	4.1	36.7	33.4
Supervisors	40.5	5.5	37.8	16.3
Sales/clerical	23.3	3.6	29.4	43.8
Manual	12.9	6.7	46.0	34.4

the age of the youngest child at home increases, at least up to the end of the teenage years. For each class, and we stress this also includes the otherwise digitally reluctant manual working class, a majority of members report owning a computer during at least some of the time they have responsibility for rearing children. The key years appear to be when children are aged between 6 and 19. Ownership levels are highest for the majority of classes when the youngest child at home is aged between 6 and 12; the major exception is with para-professionals, where computer ownership peaks at a remarkable 90 per cent – the highest observed in any class – among those with teenage children. Perhaps the most interesting cases are those of manual workers and supervisors, where the increases recorded are the steepest, coming as they do from an almost insignificant base of 4 per cent in homes with infant children. Employer computer ownership also rises relatively steeply from a base level of just over a fifth among those with infants to a peak of 75 per cent in the homes of those with pre-teen children.

The increases in ownership levels are accompanied by changes in the overall patterns of reported uses for the computer. The most consistent of these is the rise in the educational function of the computer. Again, for most classes the increase is linear as the age of the child rises until the end of the teens, when it drops again. But there are some important variations between classes concerning the primary use made of the home computer, even allowing for the influence of children. In employer households the computer keeps

Table 3.5 Ownership and primary use for personal computer by class and age of youngest child at home

Class	<1 year	1–5 years	6–12 years	13–19 years	20 yrs+
Employers	*22.3*	*65.2*	*75.5*	*69.7*	*41.0*
Work	no data	84.9	47.8	52.4	57.1
Entertainment	no data	6.5	16.2	20.1	0.0
Education	no data	8.5	36.1	27.6	42.9
Self-employed	*24.7*	*48.9*	*54.7*	*55.2*	*23.1*
Work	80.0	83.3	38.7	33.4	71.1
Entertainment	0.0	0.0	17.2	17.1	0.0
Education	0.0	16.7	41.6	49.6	28.9
Managers	*30.2*	*55.2*	*66.8*	*65.6*	*26.7*
Work	100.0	43.1	39.0	19.3	0.0
Entertainment	0.0	56.9	49.5	14.7	0.0
Education	0.0	0.0	11.5	66.0	100.0
Professionals	*39.5*	*49.9*	*85.1*	*73.5*	*45.8*
Work	0.0	60.9	50.5	17.7	83.0
Entertainment	0.0	26.8	15.5	17.7	0.0
Education	57.7	9.2	27.0	61.9	0.0
Para-professionals	*55.4*	*35.6*	*72.3*	*90.5*	*44.3*
Work	44.5	11.2	29.9	7.4	38.0
Entertainment	55.4	13.9	45.8	30.9	30.2
Education	0.0	53.7	24.3	61.7	31.8
Supervisors	*4.6*	*45.4*	*57.5*	*56.9*	*22.7*
Work	0.0	51.2	44.8	15.0	55.9
Entertainment	100.0	36.1	36.8	45.5	21.3
Education	0.0	12.7	13.2	33.8	22.8
Sales/clerical	*29.4*	*23.2*	*51.1*	*58.2*	*33.7*
Work	19.3	53.2	15.0	13.6	34.1
Entertainment	24.5	15.7	36.7	31.4	30.3
Education	56.2	31.1	48.3	50.5	35.6
Manual	*4.1*	*36.2*	*51.8*	*43.6*	*24.8*
Work	0.0	0.0	18.2	5.0	10.3
Entertainment	100.0	41.9	50.1	57.7	67.6
Education	0.0	50.8	26.3	37.3	11.0

its primary work function regardless of the age of children. For professionals, leaving aside the somewhat atypical reported educational use in the homes of those with infants, it is the work function of the home computer which is also dominant until the onset of the teenage years, when educational concerns again come to the fore. The fact that a number of other classes report high educational uses in contexts where their youngest children are infants or pre-schoolers alerts us to some interpretative difficulties in the data. For example, we have assumed so far that it is the age of the youngest child at home – the benchmark feature of the variable – which is of most consequence in shaping the use to which the computer is put, an assumption which ignores the influence that older siblings might have. It is also entirely possible that parents may code their own use of the computer as 'educational'.

Perhaps the most telling gap in the data is the absence of a diachronic dimension to these reported domestic uses. We have no way of knowing whether households alter their use of computers over time as their composition changes, or whether demographically different households reach specific decisions about computer purchase and usage at particular points in their life-cycle.

We can gain some insight into these issues from comments made by our interviewees about the place of computers in their homes. For Grant, who works in senior management and who no longer faces competition for the computer now that his children have left home, the computer has become a means of telecommuting:

> GRANT My computer I link up to work so I can do work from my office in the home. So I can work at home if I wish to. Invariably in my job I do.
>
> INTERVIEWER And is it good being able to work from home given that I notice that you work a lot of hours a week in your job? Does that allow you to be at home even though you are working?
>
> GRANT Obviously I do spend a lot of hours at work, but the nature of my business is such that you tend to spend a lot of hours here, but at night times when I go home after dinner I might need to speak to Germany. I can send a fax to Germany or if I've got to speak to overseas people I can do it with the fax from my computer or if I just physically, just have to do some straight typing, I can just turn around and do that and then if I want to stop and sit down and watch a bit of TV or news things like that.
>
> INTERVIEWER And do you think that is one good thing about the advent of computers?
>
> GRANT It is definitely a good thing. For many years my wife said you are always in the office. And you know I would sit in the office on a Saturday afternoon or even a Sunday morning and just be physically typing and well, you know you can do this anywhere. It's allowed me to do that.

In the time which had elapsed between completing our survey question-naire and their interview, a number of our respondents had acquired computers. Tony provides a good example of someone who had become an enthusiastic owner – a paid-up member of the digital class:

> INTERVIEWER And looking at the list of pieces of equipment that you have in the house, the things that you didn't have at this stage (of the survey) were personal computer, fax machine, answering machine, modem. I guess that has completely changed.
>
> TONY We have everything. We are souped up, we are ready to run. We are plugged in, we have the internet available. We have two answering machines. We have a fax machine. We have a huge, super computer for business, you know, although I did buy one that was multimedia capable with the deliberate intention of having something the kids could use so it is on the counter and Ben put his games up on the computer so it is a fight for space.
>
> INTERVIEWER So you have two computers?
>
> TONY Only one, although one and a half. We have an old Apple that is not being used. So only one that everyone is fighting to use. Well, actually it's me and the kids – Laura is not interested.

Tony's comment about his wife's indifference to their computer is echoed in a number of other cases. On the whole, it appears to be men and children (of both sexes) who express the most interest in having and using a personal computer. Men never express an outright rejection of computers, whereas a number of women, including some whose job responsibilities involves using them, do. Patricia, a secretary for a local government council, and Elizabeth, who is currently a housewife, are two of these:

> INTERVIEWER Right. Now there's a list of things that you own in the house. And one of the things that you own is the computer.
>
> PATRICIA I don't own that. My husband owns that.
>
> INTERVIEWER And you've put here, 'it must be used for education'. Now, you don't use it, or –
>
> PATRICIA I hate it.
>
> INTERVIEWER You hate it?
>
> PATRICIA I work on computers all day but I don't like computers. I use it from time to time but I'm not on it every spare moment I can get. I only use it when I'm forced to.
>
> . . .
>
> INTERVIEWER There was a list of things that you had and I can see some of them, radio, television, video-recorder; now you didn't at the time have a computer or videocamera, you still don't have one?

ELIZABETH No.

INTERVIEWER Any interest in them? Do your children use them at school?

ELIZABETH Oh yeah, yeah. The kids do use them. To me it would be just like putting a maths book in front of me, the computer, even though I have used one with the charity that I was involved in.

Other women in our interview sample had a different perception of information technology. In Andrea's case it is the female members of the household who are the computer users:

INTERVIEWER I noticed that you said you had a personal computer in the house and we're keen to know who uses it the most?

ANDREA Me. And my 13-year-old daughter.

INTERVIEWER Right, is that for school work?

ANDREA School work and she likes games as well.

INTERVIEWER And what about yourself?

ANDREA Um, I was secretary at the swimming club for a couple of years and I was doing newsletters every week for that.

INTERVIEWER Right.

ANDREA And just learning, programs, spreadsheets and all those fun things like that keep us out of mischief (laughs).

For Kay, a primary school teacher, early exposure to computing together with current job responsibilities and her educational aspirations made the purchase of her own machine a rational decision:

INTERVIEWER OK, if we can move on to some of the things you have in the house. You have virtually everything except a fax machine and a modem. And you do have a personal computer which you have been using. You have it for education?

KAY Yes, for school.

INTERVIEWER And for your own studies?

KAY Yes, I bought it originally to do the work that I was doing with my Masters. I put off that decision for a long time. I was dragging one backwards and forwards from school. So I bought it to do my Masters. I knew I couldn't get away without having a computer and also I am the computer co-ordinator at school so I make the purchasing decisions at school and I do a lot of work at home on my computer.

INTERVIEWER Right. So when you bought a computer you were obviously quite influenced by the fact that at school you had been involved.

KAY Yes, I had actually learnt computer studies when I went to teachers' college in the 70s and did punch cards and that sort of stuff. I then came back and did a computer education course about ten years ago so a lot of that is totally out of date. But I have always been in charge of computers but I still feel I know nothing about the internet. The information just keeps on ballooning.

Our research suggests, then, that on the basis of current trends, the majority of Australians will at some point in their lives become home computer users. Although computer ownership tends to be concentrated in the more affluent, better-educated households, they are sufficiently widespread as to minimise the possibility of a 'digital underclass' emerging. At present only one sector of society – the elderly – remains significantly excluded from computer ownership, but we see no reason why the current high-owning middle-aged cohorts will not continue to use their computers in later life. We now turn to consider the domestic technology which the elderly embrace to a greater extent than any other adult group – television.

Television

Watching television is widely regarded as the single most common form of domestic recreation (Abercrombie 1996; Barwise & Ehrenberg 1988). After sleeping and working, it is the activity which next occupies the most time during people's days. Despite the amount of time it consumes, however, it is generally regarded as a 'low involvement' medium. As Barwise and Ehrenberg argue:

> People mainly use television to relax with and be entertained. We do not want to spend 25 hours per week worrying all the time about what we are seeing; quite the reverse. There may be two or three programs where we are rather concerned about what is happening on the screen or are highly involved with the characters, but we watch the news mainly because we do not like to be out of touch rather than because we necessarily care all that much about the stories themselves. There is usually *some* involvement in what we watch but mostly it does not go very deep. *Low* involvement but not *no* involvement. (1988: 123, emphasis in original)

Ethnographic research into family viewing habits (Morley 1986; 1992) has also demonstrated that we frequently undertake other activities in conjunction with our viewing, and that it may not even be the primary focus of our interest. We may be eating, reading, talking, or perhaps not even in the same room as the television for long periods when it is on.

The *amount* of television we watch, *when* we watch and *how* we watch are all matters which are strongly influenced by the type of household structure we have. Compare the freedom that Simon, who lives alone, has in determining his viewing habits with the situation of Elizabeth, a working-class mother who has three children of quite different ages. Simon appears to have a regular schedule of programs which he uses to mark the passing of the week:

> **INTERVIEWER** What sort of programs do you watch and how much television would you watch?
>
> **SIMON** How much? Probably too much is the answer to that. If I go through the programs . . . on Monday I religiously watch *Friends*, I religiously watch *Frontline* and currently at the moment there is an SBS series on *Hitler's Henchmen* so I'm watching that. Come 8.30 p.m. I'm going to have to change my video. Tuesday I religiously watch *The Bill*. Wednesday I don't think there is anything that I watch. Thursday *Seinfeld* and *Men Behaving Badly*. Friday *One Foot in the Grave* and there used to be a show, I can't remember what it was called, it had Amanda Burton in it . . . *Silent Witness*. Just lately it has gone back to reruns, some of the Australian early shows, *Scales of Justice* that sort of thing. So I have been watching some of that but not as religiously. Saturday *Mother and Son* I usually watch the repeats of that. I've got into *Heartbeat* but if I don't see it I'm not going to cry. *The Bill* I used to religiously watch. I used to watch *Rumpole* but, of course, that's not on any more but I have started watching this *Peak Practice* with the guy from *Inspector Morse* in it.

For Elizabeth, in contrast, television viewing is, if not quite a luxury, something which has to be fitted in with the everyday demands and responsibilities of family life. She was asked by the interviewer to elaborate on her questionnaire response that television-watching in her household was by 'mutual agreement':

> **INTERVIEWER** You said here at the time that you mostly watch television with your family and you put that by mutual agreement, that's a very liberal interpretation.
>
> **ELIZABETH** Yeah, well the only time that it's mutual is because everybody's got their own bloody set. Everybody gets to pick what they want. We've only just bought the girls their telly last October, I think and then we'd no sooner bought that, two weeks before Christmas and our main set blew up. And here I am in the bedroom a new Super Nintendo deck and games and I thought, oh my God this is going to

be lovely, this Christmas, the kids waking up thinking great, we've got Super Nintendo and we've got no bloody TV set. So we had to go out and buy that the Christmas just gone and I said to Dennis, this is ridiculous paying money for TV sets. So up until then, in the end it was whoever I picked out of the hat got to watch what they wanted on TV of a night, that way there was no arguments when it came to the three of them. Yeah, it was a draw of the hat whose name got picked out they could watch what they wanted in that hour.

INTERVIEWER The things that you put that interested you to watch were the news, current affairs and personal issues TV – the example they had was *Donahue*. Do you still watch?

ELIZABETH No, not really. It's mainly, I will watch *Home and Away* of a night. The kids all watch, now this is interesting because we have the main set out here, then my daughter has one in her room which was given as a joint birthday present for both the girls 'cause they share the same bedroom and then we've got one in our room that I bought myself years ago when the kids, when I first bought the Nintendo for the kids. Because once I bought the Nintendo that was it, I just didn't get to watch TV because they were always on it. So I thought, I'll buy myself a little second-hand one, that at least I can watch the news of a night and watch a couple programs myself and I'm up in my room resting, they know where I am if they need me. So Wayne watches *The Nanny*. But things have gotta be done before the TV comes in of a night. Tea's gotta be done, dishes have gotta be done, showers have gotta be done then, but I'm up in my room from 6.30 of a night because Dennis says, well mum cooks tea of a night, so I don't see why mum's got to be landed with the dishes. So then I have my shower and if I have to, and I go up into my room to watch TV of a night. Jacki will settle down or these days it's a hit and miss 'cause she's out flogging books of a night. So she puts about two or three hours of work into her school books. There were just so many fights with the TV of who's gonna watch what, so I thought, and Dennis said, that's ridiculous having another TV in the bloody house, we don't need it. And I said, but you don't have to try and be referee to three kids of a night, especially when they're all different age groups. I said, they're not always gonna watch, like watching what the other one watches, so it's better this way. So Jacki's usually here at the dining-room table after 6.30, Sandra's up in her room, Wayne's out here and I'm in my room. But they know where I am if they need me, even though Jacki reckons it's not a real good family unit when we're all scattered different places of a night when we've all settled down.

INTERVIEWER Well, at least you're all in the one house.

The contrast could scarcely be greater. Although they are ostensibly describing the same practice, the similarity almost ends there. For Simon, watching television is a matter of individual taste: whatever he feels like on a particular night. For Elizabeth, it is a delicate matter of negotiation and compromise to be fitted in with the already difficult daily round.

It seems clear that in the majority of households, television-watching is subject to some form of negotiation. Nearly 70 per cent of our sample reported that TV viewing was a family activity, and for the vast majority (82.8%) program choice was said to be made by mutual agreement. Viewing alone is, understandably, most likely to occur in single-occupancy households, although a quarter of those who share a household with one other person also watch television alone. Television viewing as something that involves friends rather than family appears to be the preserve of the young, with over 50 per cent of those who watch with friends aged between 18 and 25. Figure 3.1 presents the breakdown of viewing arrangements by age cohort.

In considering how much television is actually watched, our data suggest that Australians are similar to members of other advanced industrial societies in their television consumption. Just over 10 per cent (11.8%) of the population could be regarded as 'heavy' viewers, watching 30 hours or more per week, with a further 26 per cent reporting that they watch between 20 and 29 hours. The largest grouping (38.7%) watch between 10 and 19 hours every week, and just over one person in five (22.3%) watches 9 hours or less. Only 1 per cent of the population does not watch any television. Heavy television watchers tend to be older and less educated: 23 per cent of those aged 60 and over report watching more than 30 hours a week, as do 17.4 per cent of the primary-educated. Heavy television viewing is actually lowest

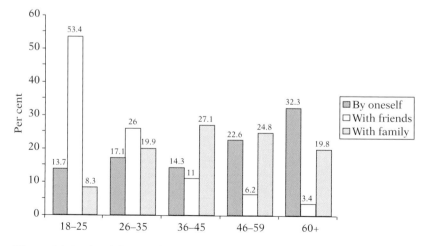

Figure 3.1 Age breakdowns of how television is normally viewed

in the cohort aged between 36–45 (6.2%), perhaps a consequence of the demands made by family and children. Of equal interest is the fact that there is no difference between male and female rates of heavy viewing for this cohort. The impact of feminism in Australian households may well be observed in this minor indicator of egalitarianism.

The time spent watching television is inversely related to educational attainment. Close to one in five (17.4%) of those with only a primary education are heavy viewers, but the figure drops to 12 per cent for those who have completed secondary education and then again by half for the tertiary-educated. Social class differences, however, are not as clear cut. Professionals – generally a well-educated stratum – are the least likely to be heavy watchers (7.3%), but they are closely followed by the self-employed (8.4%), whose educational credentials are usually far lower. The heaviest consumption of television is not found in the manual working class but rather with the para-professionals, with a figure of 17.7%. The viewing

Table 3.6 Television consumption by age, education and class (column percentages)

	'Heavy viewing': 30 hours or more	'Light viewing': 9 hours or less
Age		
18–25	6.6	24.9
26–35	9.2	24.1
36–45	6.2	22.7
46–59	9.8	23.1
60+	23.0	13.6
Educational level		
Primary	17.4	18.6
Some secondary	12.6	14.9
Comp. secondary	12.6	20.7
Vocational	7.9	23.9
Part tertiary	9.0	29.6
Comp. tertiary	6.4	26.4
Class		
Employers	9.0	17.7
Self-employed	8.4	25.8
Managers	12.9	16.4
Professionals	7.3	30.6
Para-profs	17.7	22.4
Supervisors	10.2	17.5
Sales/clerical	10.4	24.6
Manual	13.4	17.4

profile of manual workers is almost identical to that of managers, with 13 per cent of each class categorised as heavy watchers. Table 3.6 presents summary profiles of 'heavy' and 'light' viewers for age, education and class.

Despite the almost universal nature of television viewing, it was not unusual to find many of our interview sample issuing disclaimers when the subject came up. For Lilian most television is 'just dreadful . . . an insult to our intelligence . . . I'd rather read a book than watch all that drivel'. Claire's television set is 'nineteen years old' and she is 'sort of hoping that it might die . . . there's so much rubbish on and it is such a terrible time waster'. But she adds, rather self-consciously: 'If we had a lovely big television I'm sure I would absolutely vegetate'.

Irene and her husband are 'minimalist' watchers:

> **IRENE** We watch the seven o'clock news on Channel 2 purely and simply because we feel we need to know that the world is still going outside. Having said that, on the nights when he's (her husband) out I don't watch the news. I only turn it on for the weather.

Barbara had subscribed to one of the cable television providers but she is concerned to dispel any impression that having so many channels available is likely to result in an increase in her viewing hours:

> **BARBARA** Well, with the introduction of Foxtel we thought we would never bother going to the movies again but, you know, they don't have top movies on 24 hours a day, 7 days a week or when you want to sit down and watch something. I probably video tape a hell of a lot less than I used to, but maybe it's because I'm busier and I prefer to read rather than watch television. Again I allocate my time. My leisure time is pretty special like everybody else. But I like to allocate quality time and I don't like to sit down and watch television for the sake of watching television. I refuse to do that. I'm particular about what I watch, what I read. If it suits me I'll do it. I don't veg in front of the television. I'm not a 'Norm'.

Of course, there are others who speak with obvious enthusiasm about the programs they enjoy. Mary is devoted to police programs:

> **INTERVIEWER** Okay, let's talk about TV a little bit. When you said the types of programs that you liked most, first you said the news, then you said police and detective shows.
> **MARY** Ha ha, my son reckons I've got a problem because I watch every police show going.
> **INTERVIEWER** What do you like about the police shows?

MARY Well, if you believe my son, he reckons I must have an author-ity problem, ha ha. I just like them I don't know, they call me Detec-tive (name) maybe I think that's my forte.

INTERVIEWER Do you like the ones that are set in Australia, do you like shows like *The Bill* as well?

MARY *The Bill* and *Heartbeat* are my two favourites, but my husband reckons that every one that comes on I say they are my favourites, because when *Blue Heelers* came on and I get excited and say this is my favourite, he says 'you say that about every one that comes on!'.

When pressed about the reasons for liking these shows, Mary has a clear-cut response. Despite the violence which they sometimes contain – an aspect she clearly does not enjoy – it is their narrative closure that she finds most satisfying:

INTERVIEWER But you'd rather watch police shows over movies?

MARY Yes, I think a lot of the movies are really scary now and I hate those sort of really scary type shows, I don't watch things like the *X Files*, I'm not into that type of thing and I really get into the shows, I'm hopeless I get so worked up, if there are people jumping out of doorways and murdering people and things right through the show and it's all um, yeah, my heart's pumping and I'm all worked up, I turn it off and turn the video on and the next day I watch it.

INTERVIEWER Okay, well getting back to the police shows then, they don't scare you in the same way, you know sometimes if they are dealing with violence?

MARY They are dealing with violence and some of them are quite violent but mostly they're one-hour shows and I know they're going to solve the crime and it's all going to be over and done with, and I suppose basically I know how it's going to finish up, that's prob-ably the difference.

INTERVIEWER And how is that usually?

MARY The good guys win.

But it is the news that dominates the nominations for the type of television program that people most want to watch. Just over half of all first choices went to this category. 'Films' attracted 11 per cent of first preferences, with 'humour' slightly fewer and 'sport' in fourth place on 6 per cent. Four types of program, in short, account for nearly 80 per cent of all television-viewing first preferences. Given this degree of preference concentration, there may appear to be little value in considering the demographic breakdown in choices for the minority genres. But not to do so would be to overlook some valuable comparative findings. In chapter 6 we examine reading preferences

Table 3.7 Favourite types of television program by gender – first preference (column percentages)

	Female	Male	Male as % of female
Mainly female preferences			
Soap	6.3	0.4	6
Variety	0.6	0.1	17
Quiz shows	1.7	0.4	24
Family sitcoms	4.8	1.5	31
Quality drama	6.0	2.0	33
Children's shows	0.9	0.3	33
Open learning	0.2	0.1	50
Current affairs	2.5	1.6	64
Arts programs	0.6	0.4	67
Personal issues	0.6	0.4	67
Police shows	1.2	0.8	67
Reality TV	0.5	0.4	80
Mainly male preferences			
Films	10.8	11.5	106
News	49.0	52.5	107
Humour	9.4	11.4	121
Documentaries	3.0	4.3	143
Sport	1.7	11.7	688

and look at how these are significantly gendered. A similar situation obtains with the gender preferences for types of television program; indeed, in some respects the correspondence is almost absolute. Table 3.7 presents the breakdown of television program preferences by gender. The separate female and male figures show the overall distribution of preferences for each category of program, ranked in descending order from programs which appeal mainly to women to those which have mainly male audiences. The third column expresses the male figure as a percentage of the female.

The impression could be gained from the literature on television viewing that soap operas are the only type of program of interest to women. This has certainly been the genre which has attracted the most scholarly attention from feminist researchers concerned to make a 'redemptive reading' (Brunsdon 1989: 121) of it.[7] Our data suggest that although soaps are clearly coded as a female genre, they in no sense exhaust women's television viewing. If anything, men's viewing preferences seem to be much more restricted than women's. The four favourite types of program overall – news, sport, films and humour – account for 87 per cent of male first preferences, but only 70 per cent of women's. Women have a wider repertoire of program interests, showing additional liking for soap operas, drama, and family sitcoms. Male interest in soap operas expressed as a percentage of female choice is identical to that which differentiates them over the preference for reading romances. Men in turn outweigh women by a margin of nearly 700 per cent in the priority accorded to watching sport on television, which is just less than the equivalent figure for reading about sport.

It is important, however, not to regard these variations as arising simply from gender as a marker of essential difference. Ethnographic audience research has pointed not only to the existence of gendered preferences in program types, but also to different styles of watching on the part of men and women. For men, the home is a place of leisure, and watching television is something that is done attentively and as a self-contained activity. For women, even those in the workforce, watching television is more likely to be an activity which – as we have seen in Elizabeth's case – has to be fitted into all manner of domestic responsibilities, or which is done in more disengaged or sociable ways. As David Morley notes in *Family Television*, the wives he interviewed:

> feel that to just watch television without doing anything else at the same time would be an indefensible waste of time, given their sense of domestic obligations. To watch in this way is something they rarely do, except occasionally, when alone or with women friends, when they have managed to construct an 'occasion' on which to watch their favourite program, video or film. The women note that their husbands are always 'on at them' to shut up. The men can't really understand how their wives can follow the programs if they are doing something else at the same time. (Morley 1986: 150)

Abercrombie (1996) has suggested that *all* cultural objects – not just television – can be seen as subject to one of two different modes of consumption or appropriation. He calls these the 'literary mode and video mode' (1996: 182). The literary mode, modelled, as the name suggests, on the idealised way of reading a book, insists that when people engage with a cultural object they should give it their full attention; moreover, it is inappropriate to read several books at once or to violate authorial intentions in relation to plot and narrative sequence by starting at the end or re-reading favourite passages rather than reading the book as a whole. In the video mode, named after the archetypal use of the video-recorder, these relations do not hold. There is no sense of there being a correct sequence of reading; people are at liberty to start at any point they wish, and to replay selected sequences or passages. Whereas the literary mode is associated with a more serious or demanding analysis of the text, the video mode is less exacting. Abercrombie argues that these two modes work with quite different values. The literary mode is that typical of elite or 'high'-cultural consumption, the video mode is what we normally associate with popular culture. Any cultural object can in principle be appropriated by either the literary or the video mode. In the case of television-watching, the video mode would be exemplified by frequent changes of channel, even by watching several programs 'at once' or by the more distracted[8] style of viewing that Morley identifies as a female solution to the dictates of household responsibilities. He adds:

> This explains the contempt with which men frequently greet women's viewing of soap opera. It is not only the content of soaps that is derided, but the distracted way in which they are watched. Men's watching, on the other hand, is much more in literary mode, which tends to attract greater social approval. (Abercrombie 1996: 183)

Above all, a person's age more than anything else determines the content of what is viewed. Figure 3.2 shows the breakdown of age-related preferences for the eight most popular types of television program which together account for 93 per cent of all first choices. The percentage figures corresponding to figure 3.2 are given in table 3.8.

If evidence was ever needed that television serves different needs, the data in table 3.8 surely provide it. For the young, television appears overwhelmingly to be a source of multiple forms of entertainment; for older Australians – and one appears to become 'old' at about the age of 40 as far as program preference is concerned – it is a source of information. This is not to overlook arguments about the blurring of genre categories, and claims that news and current affairs programs have become hybrid forms of 'infotainment'. We cannot ignore the desires and pleasures that might accompany

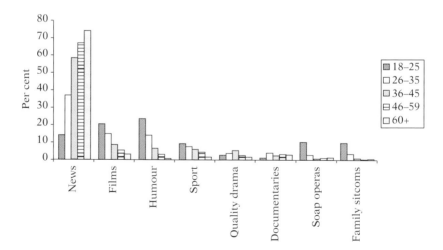

Figure 3.2 Top eight favourite types of television program by age – first preferences

Table 3.8 Top eight favourite types of television program by age – first preferences (column percentages)

Program type	18–25	26–35	36–45	46–59	60+
News	14.4	37.4	58.8	67.6	75.1
Films	21.2	15.3	9.2	6.0	3.9
Humour	24.3	14.8	7.2	3.7	1.4
Sport	9.9	8.2	6.9	5.3	2.6
Quality drama	3.3	4.6	6.3	3.4	2.5
Documentaries	1.9	4.6	3.6	4.1	4.3
Soap operas	10.7	3.2	0.9	1.2	1.7
Family sitcoms	10.4	4.2	0.9	0.3	0.5

watching the news. But the remarkably consistent increase in the proportion of each cohort which nominates the news as their first preference in program choice suggests that quite different meanings are being attached to the news, and indeed the meaning of television itself, as one ages. Moreover, these data point to something of a contradiction: the more television you are likely to consume, the narrower becomes your range of program preferences. While we do not necessarily accept all that he has to say on these matters, Roger Silverstone's (1994) arguments about the 'ontological security'[9] that television provides would seem to offer a useful framework for accounting for the attraction that the news commands. For Silverstone, the essential characteristic of television is its 'veritable dailiness' (1994: 2); to understand television is to understand how it has managed to insinuate itself into the fabric of our everyday lives. The security that television offers, he suggests, is a consequence of its regularity and sequentiality. Commenting upon a (US) finding that 'the weather' is the 'most consistently watched television program', Silverstone suggests that this is because the weather bulletin 'provides constant reassurance (even in times of bad weather) both of the ability to control the elements (albeit only through talk and graphics . . .) and to encourage or reassure the viewer that tomorrow will be (basically) all right' (Silverstone 1994: 16). He continues:

> But it is the news, I think, which holds pride of place as the genre in which it is possible to see most clearly the dialectical articulation of anxiety and security – and the creation of trust – particularly for adult viewers . . . News is addictive, the more so when the world is unsettled. News is a key institution in the mediation of our threat, risk and danger and central . . . to our understanding of our capacity to create and maintain our ontological security. And it is this, as well as (or as much as) its significance as its role as a provider of information . . . which needs to be understood if we are to recognise

> the basis for television's persistent importance in everyday life. (Silverstone 1994: 16–17)

Although ontological security may not be the appropriate term in their case, the young may exhibit similar forms of habituation in their choices of the evening comedy, soap opera or sitcom. It is worth noting that the gender inflection of viewing preferences is more pronounced in the youngest cohort than in any other. Young men are about five times as likely as young women to nominate sport as their first preference, while young women, in turn, favour family sitcoms by a similar margin. But it is the preferences for soap operas which demonstrates the gendered nature of genre preferences most clearly, with young women outnumbering young men by an extraordinary margin of 38:1.

In comparison with gender and age, the effects of education and class location appear more muted in accounting for variations in program choice. Indeed, most of the differences attributable to educational attainment turn out on closer inspection to be a function of the age composition of the educational groups or of gender. The news, for example, is of most interest to (older) primary-educated people (67.9%), and of least interest to those with only some tertiary education (34.2%). The latter record an interest in films (20.3%) and sport (11.2%) which is nearly twice that of the sample average. Employers (69%) and managers (66%) rate the news as their first preference to a greater extent than other classes, but even in the case of its lowest rating – 44 per cent for sales and clerical workers – it is easily the most popular type of program for that group. Manual workers show the most interest in sports programs (12%) followed by supervisors (10%) and employers (9%), all male-dominated locations. But employers have little interest in two of the other most popular genres: only 4 per cent choose humour as first preference, compared with a sample average of 10 per cent; and a similar proportion (3.9%) favour films against a sample average of nearly 11 per cent.

Age is also the most likely predictor of the choice of station or channel, particularly when preferences for the public broadcast system are considered. As table 3.9 shows, the proportion who choose to watch mainly the ABC rises steadily with each age cohort and there is a concomitant decline in the numbers who never watch this channel.

Exclusivity in preferred station choice does not appear to be watertight: 8 per cent of those who claim they mainly watch the ABC also state they mainly watch a commercial channel. But it is apparent that commercial television is the first preference in viewing for all cohorts, although the two middle-aged cohorts are more likely to be occasional watchers. Interest in the SBS mirrors that of the ABC, with the young about half as likely as the two oldest cohorts to watch it at least on a regular basis and twice as likely

Table 3.9   Preferred television station by age (column percentages)

	18–25	26–35	36–45	46–59	60+
ABC					
Watch mainly	3.1	9.7	18.2	20.3	30.0
Watch regularly	15.6	30.5	29.0	31.6	28.9
Watch sometimes	66.4	53.2	48.0	43.5	38.2
Do not watch	15.0	6.5	4.2	4.4	2.2
Commercial					
Watch mainly	63.8	55.9	36.2	35.5	42.9
Watch regularly	21.9	27.1	35.1	33.3	30.6
Watch sometimes	11.9	14.9	26.5	30.0	24.7
Do not watch	1.5	0.8	2.0	1.3	1.5
SBS					
Watch mainly	1.3	1.8	3.4	4.2	5.3
Watch regularly	7.5	8.4	11.1	11.7	10.9
Watch sometimes	40.4	41.1	42.3	49.4	45.5
Do not watch	32.6	26.6	21.6	15.7	16.9
Not available	18.2	22.1	21.5	18.9	21.4

not to watch it at all. Age again complicates the effect of educational attainment in relation to preferences for non-commercial television: Australians who have completed tertiary education are the most likely to watch the ABC (26.2%), but they are followed by those – mostly older people – who have only reached primary-education level (22.6%). The primary-educated are also the most likely *never* to watch the ABC (8.2%). Class differences in television station preferences, as measured by the possession of cultural or educational capital, are, however, much more transparent. As figure 3.3 shows, attachment to the public broadcast system is strongest among professionals and weakest in the case of manual workers; this situation is reversed when the commercial sector is considered.

In chapter 9 we offer a more detailed discussion of what we call the field of 'restricted culture', and raise the paradox that many of the institutions which comprise this domain should, by virtue of their public provisioning, in theory at least belong in the realm of unrestricted culture. We look at the ABC as an example of a public cultural institution whose audience is characterised by socially restricted forms of competencies attendant on class position and educational background. Here we simply note that, although table 3.3 provides some of the strongest evidence of the impact of social class on cultural taste, it remains to be seen exactly how restricted the ABC is in comparison with other forms of public and private culture.

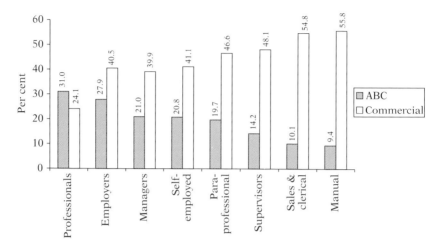

Figure 3.3 Television station preference by class

Our discussion here has focused on preferences and priorities – what people say they most like to watch out of the repertoire of material available for consumption. It has not been based on the actual audiences empirically associated with particular types of program, information which is the mainstay of the ratings figures. It is these which feature in the majority of quantitative audience studies;[10] Barwise and Ehrenberg (1988), for example, use only audience rating data in their comprehensive investigation of television-watching and, as a consequence, they are led to the view that television is 'truly a mass medium' in that the demographic profile for any type of program largely reflects the population at large. For Barwise and Ehrenberg,

> how much television an individual views is not primarily determined by age, sex, income, or any other demographic classification . . . How much we watch is largely a matter of personal taste and habit, constrained by the competing appeals and demands of other activities and pastimes. (Barwise & Ehrenberg 1988: 14–15)

In relation to the ratings data they present which show that the time spent watching different types of program is almost constant across the various demographic audience groups, Abercrombie comments that:

> this is a remarkable finding. In other fields of activity . . . one finds that different social groups have different social behaviours. For example the middle class have very different tastes and leisure pursuits from the working class; women and men tend to have very

different kinds of job. Yet all social groups watch a remarkably similar mix of types of television. (Abercrombie 1996: 148)

We cannot confirm or disprove the comments relating to the audience composition of specific programs. Our data clearly indicate, however, that, at least as far as subjectively disclosed tastes and preferences are concerned, Australians are far from uniform when it comes to the consumption of television. Age and gender in particular, and social class and education to a lesser extent, are both quantitatively and qualitatively significant in shaping our participation in this most commonplace of cultural practices. To what extent is this pattern repeated with the two other media we consider: radio and the cinema?

Radio

Radio has been described as the 'most paradoxical' (Counihan 1990: 27) of the modern media, heard everywhere and yet with almost no visible presence, 'aural wallpaper' (Molnar 1997: 201) which is ignored, for the most part, in public forums and academic debate. Any account of the recent history of transformations within Australian radio (see, for example, Miller 1997; Potts 1989; Turner 1993) cannot, of course, avoid the impact television has had on its popularity and its subsequent refashioning. As Miller, Lucy and Turner (1990) put it:

> Television gutted radio of its most popular programming – quiz shows, talent quests, situation comedy and, ultimately, soap opera. While there are residual traces of all these in Australian radio, and while certain specialised forms of programming will prevail at certain times of the week . . . Australian radio's primary response to television has been to choose one of two options: talk or music. (Miller, Lucy and Turner 1990: 158)

Although they are dramatically circumscribed in what they can offer, our data nevertheless point to radio's almost universal continued appeal. With the exception of watching television, listening to the radio ranks alongside listening to music as the most popular form of domestic cultural activity. Indeed, in the case of young people, the two activities are virtually synonymous.[11] Age does appear to be the demographic factor which offers the most potential for insight into listening habits, both in terms of time spent and type of radio station preferred. Just over three-quarters of the 18–25 year olds in our sample reported that they often listened to the radio, with a figure of about 65 per cent for each of the remaining age cohorts. For the young, radio means music; for older Australians, it is the provision of talk – news, sports commentaries, talkback, as well as more serious current affairs and discussion – that gives radio its appeal.

In chapter 7 we look in detail at music tastes and preferences; for now let us simply note that the preference structure discussed there – in particular the breakdown of tastes by age – is largely duplicated by the preferences for types of music on the radio. The easy listening format is the most popular type of music program, with 35 per cent of our sample indicating that they were regular listeners but with nearly twice as many aged 60 and over (42%) as among the young (22%). Classic hit programs attract a regular audience of 24 per cent – higher in the 26–45 nostalgia-driven demographic. Mainstream rock (MOR) and alternative rock programs command regular audiences of 19 per cent and 13 per cent respectively, but with young audiences of about 45 per cent each. But only about half of this number would listen regularly to both types of program.

Although music programs dominate the preferences of the young, paradoxically, this group is most likely to cite 'the radio' (and correspondingly least likely to use newspapers) as their main source of news: nearly 30 per cent (higher (36%) among those with tertiary qualifications) nominate the radio as against the sample average of 25 per cent. In common with television, news stands out as the program which is most listened to on a regular basis (63.6%) but current affairs (36.5%), talkback (22.6%) and sport (22.2%) each attracts large regular audiences. Preference for each of these talk-based program formats all increase – with uniform regularity – with age, but even the young will admit to listening to the radio news. Forty-one per cent are regular listeners, and only 14 per cent say they never listen.

Not surprisingly, given that the program preference structure so closely follows an age demographic, the *type* of radio station most listened to is similarly marked. As table 3.10 shows, commercial FM and, to a lesser extent, commercial AM stations together account for six out of ten station preferences. The FM station format, in particular, dominates the choice of the young, commanding 60.4 per cent of their station allegiances alone, and it is still the most favoured station for the 36–45-year-old cohort.[12] From then on its significance declines, and it is selected by only 10 per cent of the cohort aged 60 and over. In contrast, the numbers of people who prefer to listen to commercial AM, the ABC regional stations and Radio National all exhibit marked increases with age. The ABC's youth radio station, Triple J, is the second most popular with the young – it rates 15.5 per cent overall but significantly more (24.5%) for those whose highest education is vocational – but they have virtually no interest in the remaining public broadcast stations. Compared with the young, older Australians (60 and over) are 63 times more likely to be Radio National listeners.

Table 3.10 Type of radio station mostly listened to by age (column percentages)

Radio station	18–25	26–35	36–45	46–59	60+	*Mean*
Commercial FM	60.4	53.9	45.3	22.5	10.4	*39.2*
Commercial AM	14.8	15.9	23.4	25.9	30.2	*21.9*
ABC AM Radio National	0.3	4.0	7.4	13.9	18.8	*8.7*
ABC AM regional	0.5	5.7	8.8	13.4	15.0	*8.6*
ABC FM JJJ	15.5	8.4	2.2	1.1	1.6	*5.8*
ABC FM classical	0.6	1.7	4.5	6.4	7.3	*4.0*
Ethnic radio	0.0	0.6	2.0	4.5	4.4	*2.3*
Community radio	2.0	4.3	1.3	6.1	3.4	*3.4*
Other	5.7	3.6	3.1	3.8	4.9	*4.2*
Don't listen to the radio	0.2	1.8	2.1	2.4	3.9	*2.1*

The market dominance of the commercial FM format is such that it is only marginally dented by considerations of educational attainment and class. A preference for commercial FM rises with each level of educational attainment, peaking at 49 per cent among those with some tertiary education before falling to 30 per cent – still the highest for this group – for those who have completed tertiary level. Among those with only primary education, however, it is a minority preference, ranked fourth behind commercial AM, ethnic radio and the ABC regional stations. Table 3.11 presents the breakdown of radio station preferences by class. FM stations are the most popular with all classes with the exception of managers, for whom the commercial AM format ranks marginally higher. As was the case with television, a preference for the quality ABC stations – Radio National and Classic FM stations – is highest among the professional and managerial strata and lowest with manual workers.

The strong support for ethnic radio among the working class appears to be an artefact of the number of migrants from southern Europe and Asia who are employed in manual labour. Indeed, there is a clear indication that ethnicity – as indicated by country of birth – is a powerful influence on the choice of preferred radio station. Ethnic radio is easily the most popular among migrants from southern European countries, with 39 per cent of their preferences. For Asian migrants it ranks second, close behind commercial FM, with 24.7% of preferences.

A related, although somewhat different, configuration of the relations between country of origin and station preference can be observed in the proportion of migrants from northern Europe – a region from which professionals are significantly drawn – who select the ABC's classical music station as their preference. The figure of 12.8% is three times the sample average.

Table 3.11   Type of radio station mostly listened to by class (column percentages)

Radio station	Emp.	Self-emp.	Mgr	Prof.	Para-prof.	Supv.	Sales/cler.	Manual
Commercial FM	37.8	36.6	25.4	27.4	36.1	43.8	46.8	43.1
Commercial AM	21.4	20.7	27.8	8.4	31.4	25.2	21.3	20.2
ABC Radio National	6.8	13.1	18.4	20.5	6.2	9.1	5.4	3.0
ABC AM regional	18.8	11.5	10.7	15.7	6.4	7.4	8.1	3.7
ABC FM JJJ	0.0	4.7	3.7	5.5	6.1	4.7	6.8	7.8
ABC FM classical	4.7	2.7	7.8	12.8	6.7	1.3	3.0	1.1
Ethnic radio	0.0	1.3	0.0	0.6	0.3	1.9	0.5	6.2
Community radio	2.5	2.7	2.7	3.3	0.9	3.2	2.7	7.2
Other	5.4	3.8	1.8	3.1	2.7	2.9	4.2	5.3
Don't listen to the radio	2.7	2.7	1.8	2.9	3.3	0.6	1.3	2.4

Film

Finally in this initial examination of media tastes we look briefly at the case of film. Although the cinema is evidently not a domestic medium, there are strong indications that many – if not most – Australians regard films as an aspect of television culture.[13] In response to a question inquiring about where they watched films an overwhelming majority indicated that they watched them at home. Fifty-four per cent saw films when they were screened on television and a further 27 per cent watched them on video. Less than a fifth of the population (17.9%) said that film viewing was primarily a cinematic experience on the big screen; a minute proportion (0.2%) reported that they used the drive-in cinema as their primary venue. Predictably, the age of a respondent is closely related to patronage of the cinema, but place of residence is equally important.

As figure 3.4 shows, the youngest cohort are three times as likely to visit the cinema as the oldest group of Australians. They are even more likely to watch by taking out a video, a practice which drops off sharply among the aged, who are the least likely to own the necessary equipment. Inner-city residents, not surprisingly, report using the cinema to see films to a much greater extent (41%) than other groups. This figure declines uniformly as one's place of residence becomes further from the metropolitan centres, with only 4 per cent of rural dwellers using the cinema as their principal means of watching films. Professionals (29.5%) patronise the cinema to a greater extent than other classes; manual workers (10.4%) and the self-employed (11.7%) are the groups least likely to watch films in this way.

The most important factor influencing decisions about which film to watch is the plot. Nearly half of our sample nominated this as the primary

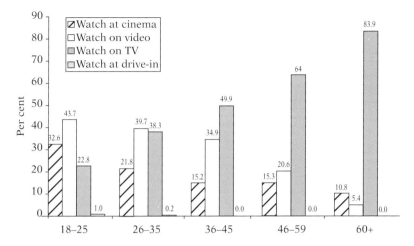

Figure 3.4 How films are watched by age

reason for choosing a film, with almost a third selecting a film on the basis of the actors involved. Fifteen per cent based their preference on the reviews a film had received, with the other respondents choosing either the special effects (2.6%) or the director (1.1%). Older people are most likely to base their decision on the actors who star in the film (43.6%), while for younger people the plot is the most important element (51.4%). Professionals and the tertiary-educated more generally are the groups most likely to be influenced by the reviews a film has gained (22.0%).

No one category of film dominates the distribution of preferences, although the top three account for over 60 per cent of first choices. 'Comedies' are the most popular type of film, with 26 per cent of first preferences, followed by 'adventure' (18.7%) and 'dramas' (16.0%). Gender is once again the most telling factor in determining film preference type. Table 3.12 shows the by now familiar distribution of gender choices using the same form of presentation we adopted earlier for television genres. Romances are easily the most feminised type of film, but dramas are the most popular type of film overall for women. In the absence of 'sport' as a conventionally recognised film genre, male preferences are most clearly marked in the case of 'war' films.

Age and gender interact in quite specific ways in determining film genre choices. Young Australians prefer comedy the most (33.2%) and this preference is common to women and men alike in the 18–25 cohort. Comedies are of least interest to the elderly (16.7%), who are twice as likely as the sample average to choose musicals (15.7%), documentaries (12.6%) and westerns (10.4%). Young men are more likely to choose adventure films than

Table 3.12   Favourite types of film by gender – first preference (column percentages)

	Female	Male	Male as % of female
Mainly female preferences			
Romance	8.7	0.3	3
Musicals	8.9	2.8	31
Dramas	25.2	8.1	32
Horror	1.5	0.9	60
Art films	1.5	1.1	73
Independent	1.5	1.1	73
Comedy	24.9	23.7	95
Mainly male preferences			
Thrillers	8.4	9.4	112
Cartoons	0.4	0.5	125
Documentaries	5.2	8.1	156
Adventure	11.0	25.3	230
Film noir	0.1	0.4	400
Westerns	1.8	9.7	539
Spectaculars	0.3	1.8	600
R or X rated	0.2	1.7	850
War	0.4	5.0	1250

men overall (31.4%); young women, however, have far less interest in musicals and romances than their elder sisters. Educational differences in preferred choice of film are significantly affected by the age composition of the various cohorts. The primary-educated strongly favour westerns (15.7%) and musicals (17.3%), but support for these genres is only about 2 per cent among the tertiary-educated.

We have concentrated in this chapter on providing a largely statistical picture of Australians' tastes in media culture. Many of the themes which have emerged here will be revisited in later chapters which deal with different aspects of cultural life. But our interest in media culture is by no means exhausted, for we have available additional, and richer, data with which to assess this issue, and we shall return to it in chapter 8.

Chapter 4

Leisure and Work

Cultures of Work

The concept of leisure is generally defined by its opposition to, and indeed its sheer difference from, the world of work: it is the 'absence' of work (Seabrook 1988: 2), or the 'reward' for work (Rojek 1989: 9); leisure time, rather than the empty and inauthentic time of work, is where our lives 'really' or most 'authentically' take place.[1] Yet to understand work and leisure as essentially incompatible activities is merely to reproduce a conceptual structure internal to the reward mechanisms of industrial capitalism. However meaningless our work might seem, it nevertheless centrally defines our social being; and the processes of leisure are a crucial *part* of the system of work, at once contrasting with it and integrally supporting it. Indeed, recreation may itself be hard work, as is argued in Staffan Linder's (1970: 3–4) thesis that, as productivity rises in work time, the yield on time in other activities also rises, thus generating a general increase in the scarcity of time.

Perhaps most importantly, we want to argue that work is not conceptually different from culture; work has its own cultures (its ways of doing things and relating to others, its forms of pride and honour); and it meshes with every other aspect of cultural life. We have not undertaken a detailed investigation into the cultures of work in this survey, but we have some basic information from which we can extrapolate many of the underlying conditions of such cultures. Let us start by looking at the simplest question: who works?

To this first question about employment (see figure 4.1), we added two further questions which allow us to gauge the extent to which people control the conditions of their employment, and the extent to which they have power within a hierarchy of authority. The question concerning independence asks if people are or were employees, self-employed, or unpaid workers in a

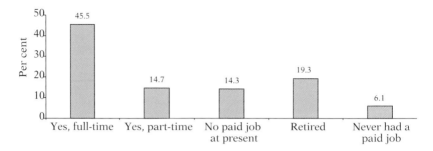

Figure 4.1 'Do you have a paid job?' (overall percentages)

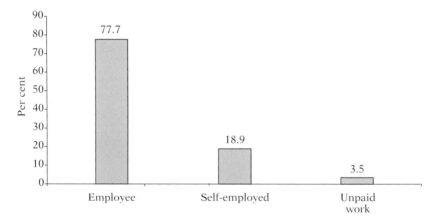

Figure 4.2 Employment status (overall percentages)

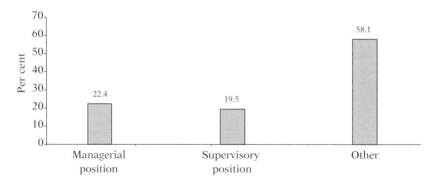

Figure 4.3 Managerial/supervisory status (overall percentages)

family business or farm (see figure 4.2). The question concerning authority asks if respondents occupied either managerial or supervisory positions at their place of work (see figure 4.3).

These data are the building blocks from which we can begin to develop a sense of different experiences of power and solidarity in the workplace. But first we must try to disaggregate these figures in order to get at the important differences that they conceal. The organisation of work is, in the first instance, markedly different for men and for women, as is shown in figure 4.4.

The key numbers in figure 4.4 are those indicating the substantial disparities in rates of full-time and part-time work; the very high level of female unemployment (although of course nothing here tells us the extent to which this is voluntary or involuntary); and – perhaps unexpectedly – the fact that almost as many men as women have never had a job. In terms of independence, women score at only half the rate of men in owning their own business; and although almost as many women are in supervisory positions as are men, their chances of being managers are only half as great.

The figures for employment by age are largely structured by two facts: that most people over 60 are retired (80.2%, with only 4.7% in full-time employment); and that many of those under 25 are in some form of tertiary education, which means that fewer of them (43.4%) have a full-time job, more have a part-time job (22.8%), and a high proportion have never had a job at all (21.2%). People in this age bracket are very unlikely to be self-employed (only 3.9%), or to be managers (6.8%) or supervisors (13.3%). Together these two facts mean that in talking about occupational structures, the truest picture is given by the groups aged from 26 to 59 years. Looking only at these, the mean figure for full-time employment would be 60.2%, for part-time employment 16.1%, and for unemployment 18%. Those who have never had a job constitute only 1.3% of the population once we discount the bias introduced by youth and the cohort effect which concentrates the chances of having never worked in a culture which now belongs to the past.

The class distribution of work is given in table 4.1. Some features of table 4.1 are definitional: our class model, which is heavily weighted to occupation, does not distribute those who have never had a job into other positions on the class spectrum (for example, by spouse's occupation); employers and the self-employed are by definition not employees, and all others by definition are; and manual workers are definitionally separated from supervisors and managers. The row for unpaid workers, similarly, catches those who work on a farm or in small family businesses, and thus aligns them with the self-employed.

Assuming that full-time work (as opposed to part-time work or unemployment) is, by and large, a valued possession, managers are the most highly rewarded group in this sense, and sales and clerical workers the least.

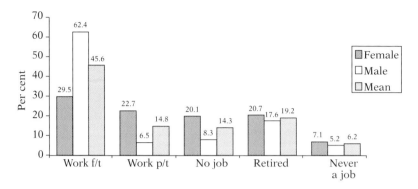

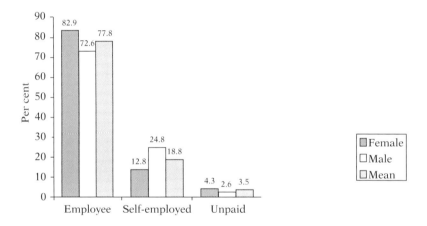

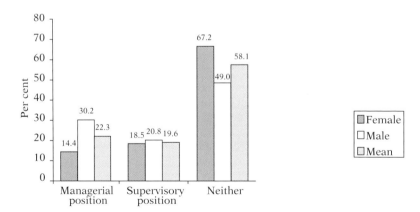

Figure 4.4 Distribution of work by gender

Table 4.1 Distribution of work by class (column percentages)

	Emp.	Self-emp.	Mgr	Prof.	Para-prof.	Supv.	Sales/cler.	Manual	Never a job	*Mean*
Work f/t	55.9	53.9	61.9	59.0	47.9	61.5	35.6	46.3	0.0	*45.5*
Work p/t	12.9	14.2	6.3	13.9	19.6	10.7	25.3	13.1	0.0	*14.7*
No job	6.4	12.8	3.8	11.3	14.6	10.0	21.1	18.5	0.0	*14.3*
Retired	24.8	19.0	28.0	15.8	17.9	17.7	18.1	22.1	0.0	*19.3*
Never a job	0.0	0.0	0.0	0.0	0.0	0.0	0.0	0.0	100.0	*0.0*
Employee	0.0	0.0	100.0	100.0	100.0	100.0	100.0	100.0	0.0	*77.7*
Self-emp.	88.0	83.5	0.0	0.0	0.0	0.0	0.0	0.0	0.0	*18.9*
Unpaid	12.0	16.5	0.0	0.0	0.0	0.0	0.0	0.0	0.0	*3.5*
Managerial	67.0	55.0	92.7	22.5	17.3	26.3	4.4	0.0	0.0	*22.4*
Supervisory	23.4	12.6	5.3	26.1	37.4	66.2	3.4	0.0	0.0	*19.5*
Neither	9.6	32.4	1.9	51.5	45.3	7.6	92.2	100.0	0.0	*58.1*

The two major working-class groups, sales and clerical workers and manual workers (who together make up just under 40% of the population), are the most vulnerable to unemployment (21.1% and 18.5% respectively), with para-professionals not far behind on 14.6%. The high incidence of part-time work among sales and clerical workers (25.3%) reflects the female character of this class, and the same is true to a lesser extent of para-professionals. If independence is reserved to the two employer classes, authority in the workplace as measured by the occupancy of managerial positions is more broadly distributed. Again, the striking figure is for managers; and it is interesting to note that the most highly educated group, professionals, scores relatively low for authority in the workplace. This is, though, doubtless offset by the greater degree of autonomy in controlling their conditions of work that is one of the distinguishing characteristics of the professions.[2]

This apparent anomaly is continued when modes of work are considered in relation to educational qualifications. The clear indication here is that the higher the level of education attained, the more likely you are to be an employee; and the two groups with the lowest educational levels are the most likely to be self-employed (see table 4.2).

Those with completed tertiary education are the most likely to be either managers or supervisors, but with that exception, educational qualifications are again largely irrelevant to the holding of a position of authority. Full-time work is distributed most strongly to those with vocational or apprenticeship qualifications (72.2%, against a mean of 45.5%); those with a tertiary degree are some way behind, on 62.7%; and those with secondary qualifications have a rate of only 48.5% in full-time work. Below this (those with primary or incomplete secondary levels) strong cohort effects again intervene: these

Table 4.2 Independent employment in each educational category (column percentages)

	Primary	Some sec.	Comp. sec.	Voc./appr.	Part tert.	Comp. tert.	*Mean*
Employee	70.8	72.6	79.7	75.0	81.4	84.3	*77.7*
Self-emp.	23.8	22.1	17.5	22.0	15.8	14.0	*18.9*
Unpaid	5.4	5.4	2.9	3.0	2.8	1.8	*3.5*

groups are much more likely to be retired (61.4% of primary, 25% of part secondary), or never to have had a job (10.5% and 16% respectively).

The returns to education in terms of full-time employment and of independence in the workplace are thus not at all straightforward. What is more clearly apparent is the direct link between a private-school education and the rewards of work: those respondents who were privately educated tend at least as strongly as the publicly educated to be in full-time work, to be self-employed, and to be managers or supervisors; and their score on workplace authority is about 10 per cent above that of those educated in the public system.

Even more direct is the correlation of work with income. The rate of full-time work rises steadily to an annual household income of $80 000, before falling away slightly with the highest income group, which is slightly more likely than the group immediately below it to work part-time or to be presently without a job. The same trend is evident in the increasing likelihood of being an employee up to the second-highest income level; at the highest level this trend is reversed, as its members are more likely (24.5% against a mean of 17.9%) to be self-employed, as well as having a strong likelihood (43.3% against a mean of 23.1%) of being managers. The most striking correlation in terms of income, however, is the negative one of retirement: retired people make up 38.5% of the lowest income group (24.4% of this group are unemployed, and 20.5% have never had a job; only 7.6% are in full-time work), and 27.9% of the second-lowest group, where there is again a high rate of unemployment (17.2%) and part-time work (16.9%).

Let us look, finally, at the regional distribution of work (see table 4.3). Perhaps the most striking set of figures here has to do with the difference between rural residents and all others – we assume that those living in rural areas are predominantly involved in farming or farm-related work. These people are markedly less likely to be employees; more than half of them (58.8%) are either self-employed or engaged in unpaid work in a family business or farm. Similarly, they are much more likely than those living elsewhere to be managers, and in general much more likely to hold positions of authority.

Table 4.3   Distribution of work by location (column percentages)

	Inner city	Prov. city	Suburban	Semi-rural	Small town	Rural	*Mean*
Work f/t	63.2	40.9	47.8	55.5	35.4	40.9	*46.2*
Work p/t	11.3	13.4	15.0	15.0	14.3	16.3	*14.6*
No job	10.3	12.2	13.3	16.1	13.8	27.9	*14.3*
Retired	11.5	19.9	19.3	12.4	24.1	13.1	*18.7*
Never a job	3.8	13.6	4.7	1.0	12.5	1.8	*6.2*
Employee	84.4	76.3	82.8	72.4	78.3	41.3	*77.8*
Self-emp.	14.8	21.4	15.0	26.3	19.5	37.3	*18.9*
Unpaid	0.8	2.3	2.2	1.3	2.3	21.5	*3.4*
Managerial	23.8	28.4	19.5	28.6	18.6	41.6	*22.6*
Supervisory	30.8	19.4	18.3	17.3	21.3	18.7	*19.4*
Neither	45.4	52.3	62.1	54.1	60.1	39.7	*58.0*

Against this authority and independence must be set the greatly increased chance of unemployment (twice the national mean), and the low proportion of rural people in full-time work. This is something that they share with people in small towns and in provincial cities; work is unevenly distributed between the major cities and the rest of the country (with the only apparent exception of the semi-rural areas, which are largely the outer suburbs of metropolitan centres). One factor intensifying this inequality is the heavy concentration of retired people and people who have never had a job in small towns and provincial cities. By contrast, people in large cities are much more likely *not* to be self-employed, although they do exercise more authority in the workplace than any other group except rural residents.

One dimension of work not picked up in the figures but for which we have evidence in our interviews concerns historical changes in the conditions of employment. A number of older interviewees recall a time when work was expected to last a lifetime, and when employers provided training through apprenticeships. Frank, who works with a private employment agency, has first-hand experience of the subsequent casualisation of work:

> Clients use us as an agency . . . They use us because they do not want people for 40 hours a week. They might want them for 20. I mean, and I did it, I'm now in the office of the agency that I worked for for about six months beforehand and previous to that I'd been in full-time work for 12 years with essentially the same employer. A lot of people that come to us they have been working for 10 years or 15 years same thing and redundancies are just happening. Companies are shedding, they are not so much even shedding the workforce, they

just don't want the workforce that they have. They still have the same requirements for labour but do not want a full-time workforce and whether this is related to a lot of the workforce legislation, I don't know. A lot of people think it is. But I don't agree, I think it runs a bit deeper than that. I think it's just that when they work for us, when the client uses an agency, to a large degree they no longer have that responsibility. We make a profit out of them but they would rather pay just single-hourly rates to have a labour force that they don't have to worry about. They don't have to keep people on tap and keep them working.

The culture of work in Australia is the outcome, then, of historical processes involving complex determinations including a marked division of labour by gender, by age, by region, by education, and by class. These divisions are formative of cultures, both immediately of cultures of work (relations of access to and of independence and authority within the workplace), and less directly of the whole assemblage of social relations, including those of 'leisure' and 'recreation', which are built around the central fact of work in Australian society. We turn now to consider the formation of friendships, and then move from there to the domains of 'leisure' more generally.

Cultures of Friendship

We asked our respondents whether their friends were mainly drawn from among work colleagues, former school friends, sporting or other leisure groups, neighbours, or some other group. Overall responses were roughly equally divided between these five categories (the 'other' group comprised varied sources, but the major ones were friends from university and church groups), and the variations have a lot to tell us about social differences.

The major division is between those whose friendships are formed away from home (at work, from among school friends, and from sport or leisure groups), and those whose friends are chosen from among their neighbours. This division corresponds quite closely to one that we draw in later chapters between inclusive and restricted forms of cultural participation, and we can perhaps make the contrast more pointed by looking only at the choice of friends from among work colleagues or from among neighbours. Table 4.4 is schematic, but it does give a sense of the extremes of a cultural spectrum in which an older, less-educated, less urban, lower-income group forms its friendships from among the resources to hand, perhaps valuing the local and the familiar over the wider world of strangers; and a higher-income, better-educated, more urban group gives work a more central place by making it continuous with social life. The latter is in one sense a more outward-looking group, and certainly these people are also more likely to form friendships among school

Table 4.4   Formation of friendships among neighbours and work colleagues

Neighbours	Work colleagues
Employers, self-employed, manual workers	Managers, para-professionals, professionals
Strong increase with age	26–59 group
Declines with education	Rises with education
Declines with income	Strongest with highest income
Inner city low, rural high	Inner city high

friends and in the sporting and leisure groups to which they belong; but in another sense it is a group more narrowly constrained by the social relations of employment.

Where do our respondents meet their friends for social occasions? Overwhelmingly (63%) in the home; the only deviations from this norm are for the under-25s (44.1%), the highest income group (54.6%), and those who live in the inner city (49.6%). The more interesting figures are for the two other major venues, pubs/clubs and restaurants. Between these two it is possible to observe a similar sort of opposition to that characterising the formation of friendships. Pubs and clubs are of course rather different kinds of venue, the former frequented by people who are young, predominantly male, and predominantly skilled and manual workers, para-professionals, and students; clubs have an older clientele, although still with a strong male and working-class base.[3] Those who meet friends at restaurants, by contrast, are strikingly more likely to be female (a three to one ratio), well educated, and to belong to one of the higher classes on our scale: managers, professionals, and employers. The self-employed are below the mean, and manual and skilled workers very substantially below it. The choice of restaurants as a meeting place is more frequent with increasing age (up to 60, when it drops away), and it rises with income, with education, and with living in the inner city.

These indications are taken up in a different way by the responses to another question that we asked about where people go if and when they eat out. We gave them three choices (not mutually exclusive): fast-food outlets which do not serve alcohol, such as McDonald's or Kentucky Fried Chicken; fast-food outlets which do serve alcohol, such as Pizza Hut or Sizzlers; and restaurants; and we asked respondents how often they ate at each of these.

The major determination of the likelihood of eating at places like McDonald's and KFC is age: the younger you are, the more likely you are to do so. There is some variation by class: sales and clerical workers and manual workers are above the mean, professionals and the two employer groups are below it. Income is not a significant determinant, and the variation by educational level (with the primary-educated scoring well below the mean and those still in tertiary education well above it) simply reflects an age effect. This effect is also evident in the second category, fast-food outlets serving alcohol, where there is a steady decline in attendance with increasing age. Again there is a small degree of variation by class, with manual workers scoring above the mean and the self-employed below it – the latter probably having to do with the lower availability of such places in country areas. Unlike the first category, where income played no role, attendance at places like Pizza Hut and Sizzlers rises with household income to a level of $60 000, before falling away with the two highest-income groups.

In the case of restaurants, class determinations are much more marked: against a mean of 28.8%, professionals score 49.3%, managers 47.1%, and employers 42.5%; manual workers, by contrast, score just a third of the rate of professionals at 16%. Age is not a major factor, with frequencies remaining constant until the age of 60. Attendance rises with educational level, with private-school education, and with income. Inner-city residents score twice the mean, small-town and rural residents score below it. The one major difference between these responses and those which have to do with meeting friends at restaurants is in gender: here the proportions of women and men are equal (29% and 28.7%). This suggests that, while men and women attend restaurants together and in equal numbers, restaurants are of much more significance to women as a way of meeting friends, whereas men have a wider range of opportunities for social contact available to them.

Entertainment

In the opposition between restaurants and pubs or clubs, on the one hand, and restaurants and fast-food outlets, on the other, we find a clear dichotomy between two very different modes of cultural practice, an opposition which in various ways (and with numerous complications) runs right through this study. It is partly a matter of class, but more importantly a difference between the cultures of the educated and the less-educated. We turn now to a set of questions about attendance at live entertainment venues, responses to which produced a similar dichotomisation of cultural practices.

The simplest way of demonstrating this is perhaps by listing, first, those venues at which attendance rises with age, and second, those in which it declines with age (see table 4.5). Only two other categories of venue, shows and exhibitions, and cultural festivals, fall outside this pattern of clear rising or declining trends.

This age-based opposition is recognisable, in almost all respects, as an opposition between 'high' and 'popular' cultural forms. And it corresponds closely to the results of a principal components factor analysis that we undertook of this set of venues.[4] A factor analysis organises sets of responses into clusters of close affinity; this analysis yielded two major clusters, one

Table 4.5 Attendance at entertainment venues – rises/declines with age

Rises with age	Declines with age
Orchestral concerts	Rock concerts
Chamber music	Movies
Ballet	Theme parks
Musicals	Night clubs
Opera	Pubs with live bands
Theatre	Film festivals
Special exhibitions	

Table 4.6 The factor pattern matrix of choices of cultural venues†

	Factor 1	Factor 2
Attend rock concerts	40	**73***
Attend orchestral concerts	**84***	30
Attend chamber music concerts	**82***	37
Attend the ballet	**85***	30
Attend musicals	**79***	26
Attend opera	**82***	31
Attend the theatre	**77***	25
Attend the movies	25	**57***
Attend special exhibitions at museums	**67***	35
Attend theme parks	52	**58***
Attend night clubs	26	**85***
Attend shows, exhibitions, expos	46	50
Attend pubs with live bands	20	**86***
Attend film festivals	**65***	**58***
Attend cultural festivals	**67***	47

† Values are multiplied by 100 and rounded to the nearest integer; the threshold value is set at 0.55.

interpretable as a high uptake of high-cultural forms, and the other as high uptake of popular-cultural forms. Table 4.6 and the scatterplot in figure 4.5 highlight the opposition between these two modes of uptake.

The associated choices clustered in the two factors are:

• *Factor 1:* orchestral concerts, chamber music concerts, ballet, musicals, opera, theatre, special exhibitions, film festivals, cultural festivals
• *Factor 2:* rock concerts, movies, theme parks, night clubs, pubs with live bands, film festivals

The similarities of these clusters with the tables of rise and decline by age are obvious. The only differences are the assignment of film festivals to both factors, and of cultural festivals, neutral in the earlier table, to factor 1. The

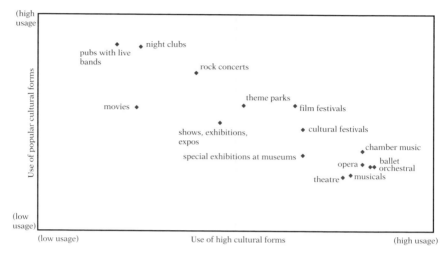

Figure 4.5 The factor pattern of choices of cultural venues

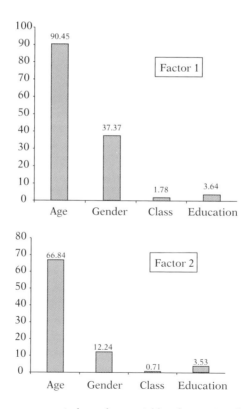

Figure 4.6 Mean squares on independent variables, factors 1 and 2

Table 4.7 Tukey-Cramer multiple range test – means for age

	High culture			Popular culture	
E	−0.62	60+	C	−0.71	<25
D	−0.29	46–59	B	−0.11	26–35
C	0.05	36–45	A	0.25	36–45
B	0.38	26–35	A	0.25	60+
A	0.59	<25	A	0.40	46–59

category of shows and exhibitions remains neutral. Again, it is clear that this is something like an opposition between 'high' and 'popular' cultural practices, and we shall henceforth designate factor 1 as 'high culture' and factor 2 as 'popular culture'.

In order to evaluate the organising principles underlying this grouping, we undertook a multivariate analysis of the two factors by four independent variables – age, gender, class, and educational level. The mean square figures for each factor (see figure 4.6), which reflect the degree of explanatory weight that can be attributed to each independent variable, indicate that the major determinant of variance is age, followed by gender. Class and educational level explain relatively little of the variation in choice of live entertainment venues.

We then undertook post-hoc testing on the Tukey-Cramer multiple range test in order to analyse the overlap and separation among the four independent variables.[5] This test assigns a letter value to the elements of each variable, in such a way that means which are significantly different carry a different letter. This is clearly and straightforwardly the case with the means for age in relation to the high-culture factor (see table 4.7). The lowest means here designate the highest degree of participation in this 'high'-cultural factor, and the separate letter values indicate a clear separation of the age ranges. Participation in this factor thus increases consistently with age. The reverse pattern is evident in relation to the popular-culture factor, where the three oldest groups (not in that order) have similarly low degrees of participation in the 'popular-culture' factor, and the practices of the two youngest groups are significantly different from each other and from that of the three oldest groups.

A graphic representation of cultural consumption by age is shown in figure 4.7, in which the vertical axis measures cultural consumption in terms of means on the two factor scores associated with the loadings in table 4.6. The scale and direction of factor scores are arbitrary, and hence have not been given on the plot; we have replaced them with the words 'high' and 'low'. However, overlap and separation of the means can still be determined statistically. Overlap is indicated in the figure by a shape containing similar

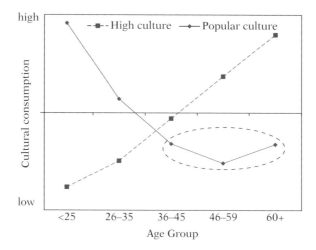

Figure 4.7 Cultural consumption by age

means; otherwise means on the same line differ significantly (at the 5% level).

The tests for variation by gender likewise produce a clear separation between men and women, with women having significantly higher participation rates than men on the high-culture factor and significantly lower rates on the popular-culture factor.

The results for class are more complex (see table 4.8). For factor 1, the five 'A' and five 'B' groups overlap significantly among themselves and differ significantly from each other. Thus managers, professionals, and the self-employed have distinctively high participation rates in high culture; manual workers, supervisors, and sales/clerical workers have significantly low rates;

Table 4.8   Tukey-Cramer multiple range test – means for class

			High culture				Popular culture	
B		−0.27	managers			C	−0.04	sales/clerical
B		−0.22	professionals			C	−0.04	manual
B		−0.20	self-employed	B		C	0.08	para-professionals
B	A	−0.09	employers	B	A	C	0.13	self-employed
B	A	−0.05	para-professionals	B	A	C	0.15	supervisors
	A	0.08	sales/clerical	B	A		0.23	employers
	A	0.08	supervisors	B	A		0.28	professionals
	A	0.13	manual		A		0.37	managers

and para-professionals and employers overlap with each of the other groups. For factor 2 the intertwinings are more intricate, with sales and clerical workers and manual workers having a distinctively high participation rate in popular culture, managers a distinctively low rate, and the other classes shading into each other along a spectrum.

The analysis of educational levels, finally, produces the configurations set out in table 4.9. Whereas in absolute terms it is the tertiary-educated who participate most fully in high-cultural activities, the predominance of the primary-educated when the education variable is varied against the other three variables is a strong indication of the overdetermination of educational level by age.

What we can draw from these analyses is a clearer sense of the relative force of each of the independent variables in determining 'high' and 'popular' modes of participation in live entertainment, and a sense too of the complex intrication of the elements of each variable in structuring these distinctive modes of practice. The traditional languages of theoretical description are not, however, particularly useful in rendering this complexity; whereas the language of statistical modelling offers a multi-dimensional probabilistic account of the interaction (covariance, implication, multiple determination) of factors within a delimited but potentially open field, its verbal translation relies on the simpler logic of the movement of 'actors' within a narrative framework. Drawing on the fundamental narrative patterns of quest and antagonism, it organises the relations between analytic elements either as a linear causality, as an unstructured aggregation, or as a dichotomy. Indeed, these are strategies to which we ourselves have, of necessity, had recourse in writing this book: in order to clarify a mass of interlocking data with fuzzy outlines, we have dramatised the most striking findings, or we have reduced a field of causal relations to the simplicity of a dichotomy, or we have enumerated the separate effects of age, of gender, of class, of education, and so on as though they could be summed to a meaningful whole. But such strategies are never adequate to the complexity of social causes, and we have tried to work towards the possibility of a model which will be truer to the

Table 4.9   Tukey-Cramer multiple range test – means for educational levels

		High culture				Popular culture	
	C	−0.49	primary	B		−0.12	part tertiary
B		−0.17	completed tertiary	B		−0.11	vocational/apprenticeship
B	A	−0.04	some secondary	B	A	0.07	completed secondary
	A	0.07	completed secondary		A	0.11	primary
	A	0.13	vocational/apprenticeship		A	0.13	some secondary
	A	0.15	part tertiary		A	0.26	completed tertiary

multiplicity and relationality of social determinations, without, however, surrendering its explanatory power.

Thus, rather than relying entirely for our account of cultural practice on a single dichotomy (that between 'high' and 'popular' culture, for example) dividing and governing the whole field, we seek to use the language of multivariate and multifactorial analysis in such a way as to stress the 'specific effectivity' of each of the elements that enters into the overall determination of a particular set of practices. In the case of the four independent variables through which we have analysed the choice of live entertainment, the predominant weighting given to age and, to a lesser degree, gender tells us little in itself. We don't know *why* age cohorts have relatively homogeneous tastes, and only a longitudinal study would tell us whether a taste structure is formed in youth and then remains constant, or conversely whether generational taste structures change over time. But this weighting of the variables starts to make sense when we consider the inflection of the dominant variables by the range of other determinations: taste cultures can then be seen as configurations with considerable specificity. In the case of the two configurations we have identified with respect to live entertainment venues, the first, the 'high-cultural' factor, would be described in terms of seniority and femaleness overdetermined by the role of managers, professionals, and the self-employed, and by the massive weighting given to age in determining the role played by educational qualifications. Factor 2, conversely, is characterised by the similarly emphatic role of the young and a strong but less distinctive separation of age groups, by maleness, by the significant role played by the two major working-class groups, and by the dominance of students and skilled workers.

These patterns are both like and unlike those to be found elsewhere in our analysis, and the difference is important precisely because it points to the specificity of each domain of cultural practice. Let us briefly contrast this pattern with those which can be found in relation to a cognate but rather differently structured domain, that of the ownership of art objects. Here again we have done a principal components factor analysis, which identifies three clusters of association (see table 4.10).

Again, we undertook a multivariate analysis of these three factors by the four key independent variables: age, gender, class, and educational level. The weightings are rather different in each case (see figure 4.8).

Post-hoc testing on the Tukey-Cramer multiple range test allows us to see that these three factors can quite readily be reduced to an opposition between a 'high'-cultural cluster and male and female variants of a 'popular'-cultural cluster. The four variables all carry considerable explanatory weight in relation to factor 1, but gender is the strongest of them: the pattern of ownership of aesthetic objects described here is strongly female, highly educated, made up of the two knowledge classes (professionals and managers),

Table 4.10   The factor pattern matrix in ownership of art objects†

	Factor 1	Factor 2	Factor 3
Original paintings/drawings	**69***	−4	3
Pottery or ceramics	**66***	29	−18
Signed limited ed. prints	**54***	−16	14
Sculptures	**58***	8	11
Rock music posters	−9	**72***	22
Nature posters	10	**72***	−11
Art posters	12	**41***	**59***
Political posters	5	−9	**84***

† Rotated factor pattern, values multiplied by 100; threshold value is set at 0.35.

and tends to exclude the young and the old. This pattern is in most respects archetypal for high-cultural practice in Australia. Of the other two factors, factor 2 is almost exclusively inflected by age, and factor 3 predominantly by gender; they both largely comprise the under-25 age group and tertiary students; and factor 2 is strongly female and shows no significant variation by class, whereas factor 3 is strongly male and gives a distinctive place to professionals (although there is overlap with managers and supervisors).

The point of this comparison is no more than to emphasise the distinctiveness of each cluster, even when it is a matter of quite closely related patterns of cultural practice and preference. We theorise this distinctiveness by means of a concept which Bennett (1983: 218) has called the reading formation, and Frow (1983, and 1995: 14–46), drawing on Bennett's work and that of Marghescou (1974) and Appadurai (1986), calls the regime of value. By regime or formation of value we understand a semiotic apparatus, an institutionally grounded set of discursive and intertextual determinations that inspire and regulate practices of valuation, connecting people to objects or processes of aesthetic practice by means of normative patterns of value

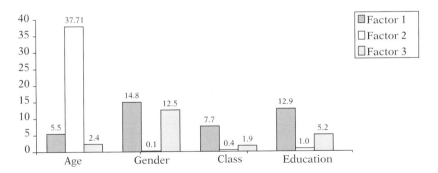

Figure 4.8 Mean squares on independent variables, factors 1–3

and disvalue (see Bennett 1985: 7). Since regimes characteristically form around evaluative practices, they do not necessarily refer to an authorised body of objects which are taken to 'fit' the regime; many regimes allow the assimilation and regulation, more or less durably, of quite heterogeneous objects. Objects and those who value them thus tend to be contingently tied together by the regime; they are not separable elements with fixed properties but 'variable functions within a discursively ordered set of relations' (Bennett 1985: 10). Similarly, the relative autonomy of regimes of value vis-à-vis the social order means that while they may recruit preferred constituencies (working-class men, all women, gay people, the tertiary-educated, and so on), they are normally not reducible to them. Yet although, unlike Herbert Gans' (1974) concept of 'taste cultures', they are not directly expressive of social groups, regimes of value nevertheless tend to be anchored in a particular infrastructure: an education system, a salon culture, a pub culture, the mass media. While it is possible to make a broad distinction between 'high' and 'popular' regimes, and thereby to assimilate rather diverse areas and modes of practice, we wish to stress here a more complex understanding of the 'space of dispersion' (to use Foucault's term) within which regimes of value operate. And let us note a final corollary: precisely because of their diversity and heterogeneity, regimes of value are not reflections of pre-existing social orders of class or gender or age, but are, on the contrary, formative of them.

Vacations and Outdoor Activities

We turn now to another major dimension of leisure activity, doubly structured by its relation to the world of work and to the home. For many Australians, holidays are formally built into their conditions of employment as paid annual leave; this arrangement discriminates full-time paid employees from the self-employed, from the unemployed and retired, and from those who work casually or part-time. In one sense, paid annual leave is a dimension of wages or salaries, but it takes the form of a gift of time (or, better, a *return* of a portion of the time expended during the working year). We are interested in who receives this gift and who does not; in the uses that are made of it; and in the social imaginary within which these uses are formed.

We asked our respondents first how often they took a holiday away from home, and we found that our sample divided roughly equally into a third who take holidays less than once a year, a third who take them once a year, and a third who take them more than once a year. The distributions by class are set out in figure 4.9. Professionals and managers stand out for the high frequency with which they take holidays; para-professionals are not far behind them. The self-employed have the lowest frequencies, but they are closely accompanied by employers and manual workers. Two rather

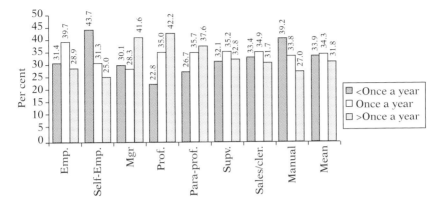

Figure 4.9 Frequency of holidays by class

different factors are at work here. In the case of the two self-employed groups, there is a clear trade-off between autonomy and free time (especially in the case of the rural self-employed, who stand out as having a particularly low rate of vacationing). In the case of manual workers there is no trade-off at all: scarcity of time and money keeps them in a position of considerable social disadvantage.

The other factors strongly correlated with frequent vacations are high educational levels, high income, living in the inner city, youth, and non-Catholic private-school education; the rate for women, too, is somewhat higher than that for men. In these respects, this configuration looks very similar to the regimes of 'high'-cultural practice that we have examined earlier in this chapter, with the marked difference, however, that this configuration is skewed to youth rather than age. Figure 4.10 shows the rates at which the different age cohorts take more than one holiday a year.

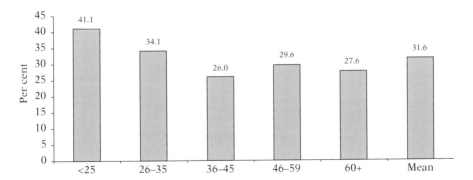

Figure 4.10 Frequency of holidays by age – more than once a year

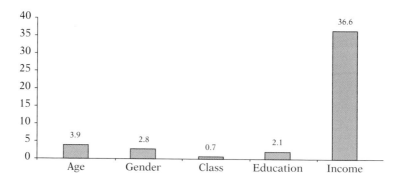

Figure 4.11 Mean squares on independent variables governing frequency of holidays

The strong correlations with age, with educational level, with location, and so on, do not, of course, necessarily indicate a causal relationship. A multivariate analysis of five key independent variables produced the mean squares shown in figure 4.11. The results give a clear indication of a conclusion to which commonsense might equally have brought us: that income is the major factor determining how often people are able to take holidays away from home. It does not fully explain the low rate for employers, but it does clarify the extent to which level of income dominates this social practice, virtually to the exclusion of all other determinations.

Income is spent in accordance with values and constraints. In order to move towards clarifying the structures of value underpinning respondents' choices, we asked what values were important to them in choosing a holiday, giving them a range of options developed in focus groups at the pilot stage of the project. We discuss this set of choices by clustering them into groups.

The first is the two choices dominated by young men: 'adventure' and 'outdoor activities'. 'Adventure' is strongly correlated with the under-25s, and managers stand out in the class profile of this activity. 'Outdoor activities' correlates most strongly with the 26–45 age group; with the self-employed, managers and professionals; and with people with vocational training and tertiary students. The second, in which young women predominate, comprises a single choice, 'good entertainment'; this choice is made most frequently by those with relatively low educational levels, and those living in small towns. The third group comprises three valued activities favoured by older people, especially those over 60. They are 'touring', which is dominated by managers and by people living in rural areas; 'intellectual stimulation'; and 'meeting new people'. The fourth, again comprising only a single choice, 'experiencing a different culture', is dominated by people with high levels of both cultural and economic capital: employers, managers and professionals; the highest income group; the highest educational level; slightly more women than men; and all ages more or less equally. This choice is strongly correlated with the inner city, and markedly *not* with rural areas. Finally, there is a group of three categories which are distributed more or less equally across class, education, age, gender and income groups. They are 'peace and quiet', 'getting away from the crowd', and 'lazing around'. Their similarity of content as well as their universality suggest that these descriptions are central to the normative understanding of what a holiday is.

In a sense, these ten choices tell us relatively little about what Australians want of their vacations: holidays are not, by and large, occasions for the use of imagination or even for high levels of activity; they are the negation of other areas of life, rather than the focus of creativity. There is, however, a certain tension evident between relatively passive and relatively active forms of holidaying, and it is clarified in the responses to our next question which asked whether respondents preferred to take organised tours or to make their own arrangements. We have schematised the answers in table 4.11. In general these groupings seem to index age and degree of cultural capital, although again we must stress the non-coincidence of this structure with other similar structures of cultural preference (anomalous here, for example, is the grouping in the 'organised tour' column of inner-city residents and women). The mean squares generated by our statistical analysis confirmed our sense that age is the dominant factor in organising this choice.

Our next question, asking about the sort of accommodation people stay in when they go on holidays away from home, merges questions of capacity (what people can afford) with questions of cultural preference; and the mean squares resulting from multivariate analysis, while giving strongest weight to income levels (65.5), also allow determinate force to age (43.6) as well as, to a lesser extent, to gender (9.1), to class (7.7), and to educational level (5.1). We found that the choice of hotels is strongly correlated with income, with employers standing out as the heaviest users. This choice is also quite strongly correlated with high levels of education, with private schooling, and with inner-city or suburban residence. Motels, by contrast, are used by all classes except employers. Use of motels declines with age, but not with income; in all other respects there are few significant variations in this option.

Employers again score high in the third category of accommodation, resorts (professionals, however, barely choose resorts at all). Money has a lot to do with this choice, as does education; it is evenly distributed across all age groups except the over-60s, and residents of all locations except rural areas. The fourth option, camping or staying in a caravan, may be a some-what ambivalent category, since camping in the bush can be a quite different thing from staying at a camp-and-caravan site. With that caution, we note that this choice is made most frequently by professionals and para-profes-sionals, but it is fairly evenly spread across all groups except employers, as

Table 4.11   Groups preferring organised tour/own arrangements

Organised tour	Own arrangements
Employers, self-employed, sales/clerical, manual workers	Managers, professionals, para-profs, supervisors
Lowest incomes	Highest incomes
Women	Men
Lowest education	Highest education
Eldest	Youngest
Inner city and suburban	Provincial and rural areas
No children at home	Children at home

it is across all income levels except the highest. Rural residents are high users, those from the inner city are very low.

The final two categories – 'self-catering units' and 'staying with friends' – are the two most frequently nominated categories. Self-catering accommodation is most popular with the self-employed, managers, and supervisors, but it is fairly evenly spread across the class continuum with the exception of manual workers, who are more likely to stay with friends or in a caravan. It is strongly chosen by all income groups, with a slight bias to the two highest, and with the middle range of educational levels; and it is markedly preferred by people from provincial cities and from semi-rural locations – but not by those from small towns and the country. Staying with friends, finally, is nominated with equal frequency by all classes, all age groups, and all educational levels (although it is somewhat lower with the primary-educated). The lower your income the more likely you are to stay with friends; and residents of all geographic areas except the semi-rural are likely to make use of this means of taking a holiday.

These questions have all asked what it is that people actually do. Our next question asks what they would like to do if money were no object, and specifically whether they would prefer to take holidays in their own state, elsewhere in Australia, or overseas. The clearest picture of the social imaginary structuring responses to this question is given if we contrast the extreme values (see table 4.12).

Although this question asks about an ideal state of affairs in which the constraints of actual income play no part, the values organising responses nevertheless reproduce in the starkest possible form the dichotomies of social privilege. One could hardly ask for a clearer demonstration of the ways in which desire and imagination are differentially shaped in relation to social position. Moreover, these columns correspond precisely to people's *actual* experience of overseas travel (the subject of our final two questions about holidays), with one major exception: that experience rises with age, whereas

Table 4.12   Preferred holiday

Own state	Overseas
Self-employed, para-profs, manual workers	Employers, managers, professionals
Over-60s	Under-25s
Primary-educated	Tertiary-educated
State and Catholic schools	Private schools
Aborigines	Non-Aborigines
Lowest incomes	Highest incomes
Provincial cities, rural, small towns	Inner city, suburbs

the desire to travel declines. Given the similarity between this regime of value and those organising the choice of 'experiencing a different culture' as a factor in choosing a holiday, and the preference for making one's own arrangements rather than using organised tours, it would probably not be inappropriate here to extrapolate from this schematic dichotomy to a more generalised structural opposition between a set of practices and preferences which is conservative and restricted, and another which is more active, more open to the unfamiliar, and more inclusive. Again, however, let us stress the contextual specificity of these regimes, and hence the instability of the configurations of social determinants which compose them.

To conclude this section, we would like to look briefly at a set of activities which are closely related to holidays and often form part of them. In considering the regimes governing outdoor leisure activities, we are concerned with a relation to the natural world other than that of work. Since these activities involve a relationship between the country and the city (including questions of access, of the use of local resources, and of escape from the built environment), we begin by looking at the distribution of these practices by location (see table 4.13).

We might underline the salient differences in this distribution by simply listing the highest scores for each activity under the relevant location (see table 4.14). But these correlations are somewhat misleading, since some activities, like walking, visiting the beach, and swimming, are quite evenly distributed, whereas others are not: in the case of activities such as bush-walking, camping, fishing, and hunting there is a clear difference between the two metropolitan locations (inner city and suburban) and the provincial and rural locations, where people engage more fully in these activities. The inhabitants of provincial cities and of semi-rural areas, however, score above the mean on almost every category, whereas people in small towns and rural areas are less inclusive in their range of outdoor activities (this is of course in part a matter of geographical necessity).

Table 4.13 Distribution of outdoor activities by location†

	Inner city	Prov. city	Suburban	Semi-rural	Small town	Rural	*Mean*
Go walking	88.1	92.4	89.2	84.4	82.4	86.4	*87.8*
Visit the							
beach	84.0	73.4	82.5	76.4	74.5	66.3	*79.0*
Swim	67.5	67.9	66.8	69.2	63.1	63.2	*66.2*
Bush-walk	46.4	61.7	41.6	59.4	52.0	56.4	*47.8*
Go camping	30.4	53.5	33.6	50.6	43.3	51.3	*39.3*
Go fishing	32.9	50.3	34.5	43.7	41.7	45.6	*38.8*
Body-surf	35.5	25.2	26.5	30.4	20.5	23.0	*25.9*
Surf	17.9	18.9	13.8	19.4	14.7	10.9	*14.9*
Go fossicking	8.0	9.0	5.8	9.9	23.6	14.6	*9.9*
Go sailing	16.2	9.6	8.0	7.9	6.8	6.1	*8.3*
Go hunting	7.0	8.7	5.3	9.3	8.3	19.3	*7.6*

† Aggregated percentages combining the responses 'often' and 'sometimes'.

Table 4.14 Highest intensity of activities by location

Inner city	Prov. city	Suburban	Semi-rural	Small town	Rural
Visit the beach	Go walking		Swim	Go fossicking	Go hunting
Body surf	Bush-walk		Surf		
Go sailing	Go camping				
	Go fishing				

Just as walking, visiting the beach, and swimming are almost universally practised, so too are they very regularly distributed by gender, by age (with the exception of the over-60s, who walk and visit the beach more or less as much as other age groups, but swim less), by class, and by income. With the age-related exception of the two lowest education groups, all levels of education are above the mean in a rising gradient. Professionals go bush-walking more than anybody else, but they go fishing, surfing, and hunting somewhat less than other classes, and go camping at the mean rate. This may have to do with the gender distinctions that mark these activities (see figure 4.12).

All of the activities shown in figure 4.12 – in contrast to bush-walking, for example – involve a more active, more interventionist relation to the natural world, and perhaps a greater exposure to it; it may be in some such terms that we can explain the class and gender differences operating here. We might observe a similar pattern in relation to educational level, too; the four most 'universal' activities – walking, visiting the beach, swimming, and bush-walking – are all strongly correlated with increasing levels of education,

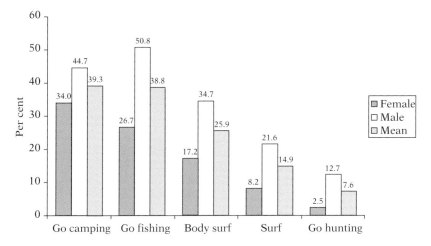

Figure 4.12 Outdoor activities strongly distinguished by gender (aggregated percentages combining the responses 'often' and 'sometimes')

whereas camping, fishing, and hunting are not. The general pattern that we find here, then, reverses the dichotomy of active/passive that seemed to operate as an important part of the value systems governing holidays: to put it in the most simplified terms, the higher the level of cultural capital, the more contemplative and less interventionist is the relation to the natural world.

Gambling

If leisure activities relate to the world of work by an inversion of the experience of time, gambling relates to the structure of waged and salaried income (or the dole) by negating its regularity and predictability. Whether or not it involves a calculation of the possibility of sudden wealth, gambling replaces routine with the open-endedness of chance.

Yet gambling is not all of a kind: different forms of gambling involve very different attitudes to winning, and very different stakes; and there are clearly older and newer cultures of gambling in Australia ('residual' and 'emergent' cultures we might call them, if these terms didn't carry too teleological a force), which to some extent reflect the social divide between the big cities and the rest of the country.

The overall frequencies for gambling are set out in figure 4.13. In order to sort out the cultural differences organising gambling, we have divided this list into four clusters: 1) lotto and scratch-its; 2) bingo and social gambling; 3) casinos, the TAB, and on-course gambling on horse racing; 4) poker machines and on-course gambling on the dogs.

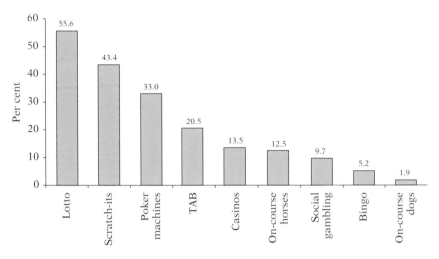

Figure 4.13 Gambling (overall frequencies)

1 Lotto and scratch-its (instant lottery tickets) are 'impersonal' forms of gambling in the sense that they involve competition within and against a system rather than face to-face betting (although this impersonality may be countered by sharing tickets in a work-syndicate or a family group). They are the two most widely diffused forms of gambling, and are unusual in that they are not dominated by young people: both show a steady rise with age to the oldest cohort, when they decline slightly but still stay above the mean. Both are regularly distributed across the social classes, with the weakest rate of participation from professionals, followed by the two employer groups. The four lowest educational groups (especially the group with vocational or apprenticeship training) are the strongest participants in both activities, and the two tertiary-educated groups the weakest; in both cases people with state or Catholic schooling score higher than those with private schooling. Both forms of gambling are weakest in the inner city; lotto is strongest in provincial cities, scratch-its in small towns. Men and women participate in both about equally, with a slight predominance of women for scratch-its (47.5% to 38.7%). And both rise regularly with income before falling away sharply at a certain point – lotto at the $80 000 household income level, scratch-its at $60 000. In short, the profiles of these two forms of gambling are strikingly similar; they are the forms preferred by people who are at the lower income and educational levels, are mostly lower class (with the exception of managers, who gamble on nearly everything), and tend not to live in the major cities.

2 Bingo and social gambling are the 'personal' counterparts of lotto and scratch-its: both are intensely social activities in which winning tends to

be subordinate in importance to the experience of the game; both are pursued most strongly in small towns. In most other respects, however, their profiles are rather different. Bingo is played most enthusiastically by those over 60, followed by those under 25; and it is played by about twice as many women as men (7.2% to 3.0%). It is a working-class pastime, in which the most dedicated participants are sales and clerical or manual workers. Its popularity declines with education and with income. Social gambling is a somewhat more masculine activity (11.2% of men as against 8.2% of women), and its strongest proponents are young people and managers; it shows an irregular and slight decline with age levels. There are no regular correlations with income; and while both the primary- and the tertiary-educated tend not to gamble socially, skilled workers and tertiary students do. Two sub-cultures within this 'social' culture of gambling, then, are distinguished most sharply by age and to some extent by gender.

3 The cluster of casinos, the TAB, and on-course gambling on horses is set apart from other forms of gambling by its distinctive class composition: employers and managers are the dominant classes in each of them, with an additional strong component of manual workers for on-course gambling on horse racing. Each has a slight bias to men, and a similar age profile in which the youngest one or two age groups are preponderant (although in the case of the TAB there is also a high rate for those aged 46–59); the oldest age group is below the mean in each case. People with vocational or apprenticeship training participate very strongly in each of these forms of gambling, although the tertiary-educated have a differential relation to them; tertiary students score very high for casinos, but below the mean for the TAB and horses; those with completed tertiary education score above the mean (and significantly so) only for the TAB. Distribution by income is variable, but in none of these forms of gambling do the lowest or the highest income groups achieve a high participation rate. The TAB and on-course gambling are exceptionally high in small towns, whereas casinos are most strongly frequented by people living in suburban and semi-rural areas. In a sense, this formation combines the rather different, and differently periodised, cultures of the casino and horse racing; it is held together above all by the coherence of the class structure that informs it.

4 The final cluster, comprised of gambling on poker machines and on greyhound racing, again combines a core of common characteristics with some clear differences. These two forms of gambling are both strongest with those under 25; people with vocational or apprenticeship training score very high, and the tertiary-educated have a low participation rate. Both forms are very high in small towns and provincial cities. Manual workers participate strongly in each, especially in betting on greyhound racing, although managers achieve the highest score for gambling on

poker machines and don't take part at all in betting on the dogs. The major difference between them is that, whereas both sexes play the poker machines in about equal proportions (34.3% of men to 31.7% of women), betting on the dogs is a thoroughly masculine pastime (2.9% to 0.7%). Although at first blush betting on the dogs might seem to be more cognate with betting on the horses, in fact the two cultures are very different: allowing for the ubiquity of managers, this is as strongly working class a cluster as social gambling.

Indeed, in terms of its class composition, gambling is largely a lower-class activity, with the exception of the third cluster comprising casinos, the TAB, and on-course gambling on horse races, which is marked by the weight of economic rather than of cultural capital. We might say that the first cluster (lotto and scratch-its) has the winning of money as its primary goal; the second (bingo and social gambling) is primarily about sociability; the fourth (poker machines and betting on the dogs) is structured by a mix of winning and sociability; and the third (casinos, the TAB, and betting on the horses) has to do with a mix of winning and a form of prestige which has less to do with the display of educated taste than with the conspicuous expenditure of wealth. Each of these four modes – and perhaps we could say that this is more generally true of all leisure activity – is organised by an *imaginary* relation to income: an inversion of the world of work, and the affirmation of an anti-world of unearned achievement and the camaraderie of risk.

Chapter 5

Care of the Body, Care of the Self

In this chapter we examine the care of the body by means of diet, exercise, and sport. By 'care' we mean not just the maintenance of health and energy but the active shaping of the self by way of attention to, training of, and pleasure in the body. We examine four ways in which bodies are imagined and formed in relation to normative patterns of social value. Dieting and exercise, we argue, can be understood as what Foucault (1988: 18) calls technologies of the self, a concept that he defines as designating forms of action 'which permit individuals to effect . . . a certain number of operations on their own bodies and souls, thoughts, conduct, and way of being, so as to transform themselves in order to attain a certain state of happiness, purity, wisdom, perfection, or immortality'.[1] Diet and exercise, that is to say, are ways of working on the body but also forms of moral exercise, intimately bound up with the shaping of the self. To a large extent this is also true of the playing of sport, which serves instrumental ends such as fitness and health, as well as generating pleasure in the use of the body and, in many cases, in its relation to other bodies. These uses and pleasures, too, have to do with the development and reinforcement of a sense of proper selfhood. The watching of sport, finally, involves a relation to the trained and often spectacular bodies of others; like all of these relations, we argue, it involves a social imaginary of the body, a set of ideals which gives us a sense of who and what we are, and what we might be.

Pierre Bourdieu (1984: 192) speaks of this social imaginary as a bodily *hexis*: a relation to the body by which 'strictly biological differences are underlined and symbolically accentuated by differences in bearing, differences in gesture, posture and behaviour which express a whole relationship to the social world'. The key values put in play here concern the body's strength, its health, and its beauty; or to put it differently, they have to do with the intersection of the axes of power and sexuality along which bodies are imagined to have effects upon the world. To the extent that the relation to the body is a matter of forming oneself not only as a physical casing but as a whole person, this relation is an ethical one, a component of the care of the self. It involves choices about the body as a component of the moral self: how can I *embody myself* in such a way that my whole person will be a good person, or a person of force, or a person radiating sexuality or physical and moral health?

As in the rest of this book, our argument is that these choices and values vary according to different dimensions of social position. Variations having to do with gender are perhaps the most salient ones in the context of diet, exercise and sport. In contemporary Australian culture the body is gendered before it is anything else, and we will examine in some detail the ways in which gendered bodies are shaped, and 'kept in shape', in accordance with widely diffused norms (even the refusal to care for the body is, of course, a socially consequential choice); and we will look at the ways in which the system of organised sport maintains a segregation of gender roles. But in many ways age is an even more fundamental dimension of variation, so obvious that at times it is almost invisible: participation in exercise and sport declines directly with increasing age; and in every age cohort these activities play a crucial role in the consolidation of peer-group cultures. Class and education are the other major variables governing the choices people make about the care and pleasures of the body; and one of our major findings – not a novel one, but one that might seem paradoxical to those who think of bodily activity as the opposite of intellectual activity – is that the care of the body is both more intensive and more extensive as one's educational level rises. This is the thesis that we have developed in relation to other areas of cultural practice in Australia: that increased education tends to go with an increased interest in a *range* of activities (and, conversely, that lower levels of education predict a narrower range in all areas); and that, in this context, it makes sense to think of the sociocultural space as being organised by a distinction between inclusive and restricted forms of practice, rather than by one between 'high' (or 'legitimate') and 'low' (or 'popular') practices.

Practices of the body (which are always intertwined with representations of the body)[2] are at once physical and cultural. To put this provocatively, we could say that bodies don't 'have' a gender or a race or a social class, but rather undergo lifelong processes of gendering, of racialisation, and of classification which make them recognisable in certain ways, figure them forth as the signs of a social status. These processes have to do in part with what Turner (1996: 38) calls the 'exterior' body (the complex interplay between ascription and display of identity that structures the body as a representational ground); and in part with what he calls the 'interior' body (my representation of my body to myself, under complex constraints). These 'inner' and 'outer' processes are never neatly separable. Rather, as Probyn (1993: 129) writes, they involve the 'folding together' of inside and outside through practices of care of the self.

These propositions are generally true about bodies in all cultures. But they are true with a particular intensity for our own, because of the shift in the last decade or so towards an understanding of the body as an individual project. Two widespread assumptions underpin this shift: first, that bodies are essentially malleable; and second, that the shaping of the body is a matter of choice of lifestyle (Shilling 1993: 129). The contemporary body, at least for certain social groups, is thus less the site of manifestation of a social or individual identity than it is the site of the *construction* of identity. This supposed plasticity of the body (Bordo 1993: 245–6) is at the heart of the cluster of practices of diet and exercise that we examine in the following sections.

Before we turn to examine diet, however, it will be useful to look at some of the patterns which underlie the socially configured choices that we make about the body – patterns that we might think of as forming a practical ethics. We can best do this by means of three sets of citations from the interview materials.

The first is taken from an interview with Susan, a nurse who is now studying in Sydney, who talks about having taken up aerobics. She says:

> The body/mind dichotomy was something that I was trying to address. If you are sitting at a desk for hours reading and early last year I was sinking in the quicksands of philosophy a bit, all that stuff to read, and I just sort of thought I needed more exercise and I started aerobics partly because of that to supplement working . . .

This is a particularly lucid statement of a position (ultimately a religious one) which regards physical activity not as an end in itself, and not as a source of pleasure or of health, but rather as a way of balancing body and mind, creating and maintaining a harmony between their contrary energies.

The second citation comes from another female para-professional, Andrea, living in regional Queensland, who says:

> Sport's a commitment and once you join a team or a club you've got to see it through. That takes up a lot of time and I think that's important for children to have that behind them, especially now when jobs are so few and they may not have a job and I think it's important that they have other interests to kill time, to be able to occupy themselves.

Her partner adds:

> Saturday's get out of bed at a quarter to 6 for swimming training,
> then come home to get ready for music at a quarter to 8, and then
> softball at 9.30, and then to a birthday party from 12 to about 3 and
> then to football training Saturday night.

This is immediately recognisable as conforming to a strong Protestant ethic:
sport is a kind of work, and it is morally virtuous because it is character-
building. It requires moral commitment and a sense of duty, and it has the
additional virtue of teaching the appropriate use of time – we can almost
hear Andrea saying 'the Devil makes work for idle hands'.

Finally, a statement from a male para-professional from Brisbane, Nigel,
who dislikes sport and what it represents culturally. He asked if he could
answer a question about sport so that he could make his feelings known,
saying:

> Too much is made of it. I think that because we base our culture
> on how well we do at sport. I mean the big news is that Jeff Kennett
> has got some sporting competition there, whereas some scientist
> might invent something more interesting but it never got on the
> news. He has to go out of the country to get any help for that.

Here, body and mind, or at least cultural representations of body and mind,
are set in opposition, as incompatible sets of values. The ethos is in a sense
the classically Christian one, transposed into intellectual rather than spiritual values, of contempt for the body and what it stands for.

The value of the interviews lies in the way they allow us to get at these
underlying ethical principles which guide the various practices of the body.
The statistical data have a different value: they allow more or less objective
sociological description of the relation between behaviours and broad social
categories. They don't in themselves guide us to the operative value systems,
but they do allow us to set up patterns of correlation between types of activity and types of social person across a wide set of axes. Let us now turn to
an analysis of dietary practices.

Diet

Management of food intake in order to increase or maintain health, to
control weight, or to negate or mortify the body, has a long and primarily
religious history. In Turner's brief sketch (1996: 39), dietary management
'emerged out of a theology of the flesh, developed through a moralistic medi-
cine and finally established itself as a science of the efficient body'. The
characteristically modern forms of dietary practice have their origins in

nineteenth-century processes of individualisation, secularisation, and ration-alisation of the disciplines of the body, in the course of which 'the idea of diet as a control of the soul in the subordination of desire gradually disap-peared' (1996: 169), to be replaced by the generalised aim of 'the preserva-tion of life to enhance the enjoyment of pleasures, the increase of sexuality and the extension of enjoyments' (171).

We distinguish between three forms of dieting in contemporary Australia: 'natural' or 'health-food' diets (to which we have added the use of vitamin supplements); special medical diets; and weight-reduction diets. We also included a question about smoking, because of its significance for contem-porary notions of bodily health.

'Health-food' or 'natural' diets

Which groups of people identify their diet as 'health-food' or 'natural'? Class is the most interesting correlation here (see table 5.1) (unless otherwise stated, figures in the following tables are column percentages designating those who answered 'yes' to the question).

The strikingly high figure for para-professionals (nurses, police, techni-cians, and so on) may be an indication less of class location than of (poten-tial or desired) class mobility and of the value placed by this class upon the kinds of 'expert' knowledge (credentialled, but not of the highest social value) that constitute its own distinctive class position. Health-foods, 'natural' or 'organic' foods, and macrobiotic diets are associated with widely diffused technical knowledges about the supposed effects of different foods upon bodily health, as well as with suspicion towards highly industrialised forms of food production. They are thus bound up with a rationalisation of the care of the body which is at once deferential to scientific knowledge, and hostile to its application in agribusiness. The very low figure for manual workers here is probably to be expected, because that class rates low on most activities involving care of the body, and on most activities which, like this one, rate relatively high for education. There is a slight but significant bias to women (8.3% against 6.4% for men); and the very low figure (3.4% against a mean of 7.3%) for workers with vocational and apprenticeship training tends to indicate that this activity is regarded as inherently 'feminine'.

The figures for variation according to location are also interesting (see table 5.2). The relatively high figure for the inner city is to be expected, since this location figures high for all relatively educated and relatively youthful activities. The high rural figure is a surprise, however, because participation rates in the country tend to be low on most counts. It's worth noting that a large number of para-professionals live in the country (about 12%, the highest figure for place of residence for this class); it could also be that country people consider themselves to have a healthy diet by virtue of their

Table 5.1 'Health-food' or 'natural' diets by class

Emp.	Self-emp.	Manager	Prof.	Para-prof.	Supervisor	Sales/cler.	Manual	*Mean*
6.3	8.1	9.1	9.4	15.5	6.4	7.4	4.4	*7.3*

Table 5.2 'Health-food' or 'natural' diets by location

Inner city	Prov. city	Suburban	Semi-rural	Small town	Rural	*Mean*
9.9	6.2	7.1	7.3	5.7	13.0	*7.3*

consumption of local produce. Aborigines also score well above the mean, and again this may indicate not so much that they consciously follow a healthy diet as that they consider their normal diet to be inherently healthy. In terms of social prestige, a health- or natural-foods diet ranks somewhat down on the scale because of the non-predominance of professionals and managers.

Use of vitamin supplements

The patterns of vitamin use are strongly akin to those for following a natural or health-food diet: professionals and para-professionals score high, again indicating their greater assumption of expertise in relation to health issues; manual workers are again below the mean. Cost does not seem to be a significant factor, since usage is constant across all income levels, with a small rise at the highest level. Two facts – that use of vitamins is more frequent among women and that skilled workers (that is, those who have been trained in a trade) score low for it – together indicate that this is a feminised practice. There is a gradual and steady, but not marked, increase with age. Again, country people score high, and this time the score is clearly not to do with their consumption of natural produce.

Special medical diet

With special medical diets, by contrast, it seems to us that material circumstances rather than cultural patterning can be seen to play a major role, since the key determinants of following a special medical diet are age and low income – two factors which, indeed, seem to go together (see tables 5.3 and 5.4). Professionals and para-professionals score high on this diet, and this seems to reflect the greater health expertise on the part of these two classes; but essentially this is a poor person's diet.

Table 5.3 Medical diet by age

<25	26–35	36–45	46–59	60+	*Mean*
0.7	1.8	2.8	7.3	9.6	*4.5*

Table 5.4 Medical diet by income

<15K	15–26	26–40	40–60	60–80	>80K	*Mean*
5.7	6.7	3.9	5.0	2.3	2.3	*4.6*

Smoking

There is some negative correlation between smoking and education, but the low figure for the primary-educated has to do above all with age (this group mainly comprises older people). The more significant correlation is the one indicating that it is only tertiary education that significantly reduces the frequency of smoking (see table 5.5). Similarly, only professionals are markedly low on the scale (see table 5.6).

There is a clear pattern of rise and then steady decline with age, with the over-60s scoring very low. Most relatively disadvantaged groups – manual workers and Aborigines, for example – smoke heavily, but not all: farmers don't, for example. Note the correlation with the inner city (see table 5.7). Age cultures may be the key factor here (the inner city is inhabited by those age groups – from 25 to 45 – which smoke most heavily), and this would suggest that frequency of smoking is more a matter of peer-group pressures than of class in the strictly economic sense.

Weight-reduction diets

We have left weight-reduction diets to the last because these are by far the most widely practised form of dieting in Australia, and are perhaps what is most immediately conveyed by the notion of 'being on a diet' or 'dieting'. What do the responses to this question tell us? First, and overwhelmingly, that it is a gendered practice, involving three times as many women as men (5.8% against 1.9% of the sample). What are we to make of this concentration of weight-reduction dieting among women? This is a question about the structure of value in which a set of practices, a set of ideal body images, a metaphorics of the body, and an 'expert' paramedical language come together in a charged relation to the gendered self. Bordo (1990: 85) suggests that the slender body's function as 'a metaphor for the correct management of desire' is directly connected with 'the figuration of female sexuality, power, and desire as *hunger*'. Both in the contemporary language of anorectics and in the dominant western religious and philosophical traditions, she

Table 5.5   Smoking by level of education

Primary	Some sec.	Comp. sec.	Voc./appr.	Part tert.	Comp. tert.	*Mean*
15.3	20.9	25.8	21.2	18.8	12.5	*19.9*

Table 5.6   Smoking by class

Emp.	Self-emp.	Manager	Prof.	Para-prof.	Supervisor	Sales/cler.	Manual	*Mean*
17.6	19.2	21.3	13.3	19.5	22.4	21.6	25.7	*19.9*

Table 5.7   Smoking by location

Inner city	Prov. city	Suburban	Semi-rural	Small town	Rural	*Mean*
25.4	20.2	19.3	17.1	23.2	18.5	*19.9*

writes, 'the "virile" capacity for self-management is decisively coded as male', whereas 'all those "bodily" spontaneities   hunger, sexuality, the emotions – seen as needful of containment and control have been culturally constructed and coded as female' (1990: 101). It is this imaginary of the female body – so strikingly different from that which governs men's relation to their bodies – that has made dieting into a powerful normalising strategy of self-surveillance and self-transformation.

This imaginary has a history. Kirk (1994: 174) writes that:

> The 'normal' body for many women in Australia and elsewhere in the West is now much more slender than it was in the 1950s, and the conjunction of representations of bodies with the consumption of products (through advertising) has created desire for corporeal normality and a consequent willingness to submit to self-imposed regulatory regimes such as dieting and exercising.

To be more precise, the contemporary 'slender body' involves the reconciliation of at times contradictory norms: thinness on the one hand, and muscularity and athleticism on the other. These two ideals, writes Bordo (1990: 90), 'though superficially different, are united in battle against a common platoon of enemies: the soft, the loose; unsolid, excess flesh'; the firm, developed body has now 'become a symbol of correct *attitude*; it means that one "cares" about oneself and how one appears to others, suggesting willpower, energy, control over infantile impulse, the ability to "make something" of oneself' (1990: 94).

Dieting is thus an 'ethical' practice in the sense that the ascetic figure of the slender body 'is designed to produce an acceptable social self, particularly a self that conveys sexual symbolism . . . The modern soul or psyche is expressed through the body, that is, through a sexually charged body image which is socially good' (Turner 1996: 23). The notion of being 'in shape' is one of conformity to a kind of Platonic ideal, and it entails a series of *moral* virtues: 'organisation, competence, and good time-management, as well as self-confidence, assertiveness, and high self-esteem' (Chapman 1997: 214, paraphrasing Spitzack 1990). Indeed, despite Turner's argument that there has been a turn from ascetic spiritual discipline towards a 'calculating hedonism' (Turner 1996: 39), it is arguable that weight-control practices continue to be informed by what we should properly call a spiritual force. At the extreme, the language used by anorectics

> includes Christian/ascetic themes, with a dualistic construction of mind/matter and spirit/appetite coded in terms of purity/contamination, and the ultimate goal of cleansing the soul of desire/hunger. Thus, certain foods are seen by the anorectic at times as tainted, contaminating, and dangerous, while the practice of self-denial and, at times, self-mortification, is seen as purifying. (Bordo 1990: 110, n. 25)

But these extreme values are, in a more subdued form, identical to the routine understandings of those who struggle with a body seen as other than the self, as recalcitrant to control, and as subject to outbursts of hunger.

If the norm of the slender body is initially coded as female, it is nevertheless the case that practices of weight control are different, and differently valued, across the social spectrum. Weight-dieters are richer than most, and they are neither old nor young, being concentrated between 25 and 59. Employers score very high indeed, followed by managers, supervisors and – because of the gendering of this diet – sales and clerical workers. Manual workers and skilled workers score very low, probably because weight-reduction diets are perceived as feminine. Because of the association of this diet with wealth and with office workers, it is tempting to see it as reflecting an unhealthy lifestyle; but this is probably too simple, and it might be more appropriate to locate it at the intersection of gender and social and economic power. The low score for professionals means that it does not correlate highly with educational level, and it may be that – as with 'health' dieting – the key explanatory factor here is social mobility (or more precisely, a desire for social mobility). Bordo provides a negative form of this explanation when she writes that, when associations of fat and lower-class status exist, they are usually mediated by qualities of attitude or 'soul' – fat being perceived as indicative of laziness, lack of discipline, unwillingness to conform, and absence of all those 'managerial' abilities that, according to the dominant ideology, confer upward mobility. (Bordo 1990: 95)

As examples of the 'positive' form taken by successful upward aspiration she cites popular teen movies like *Flashdance* and *Vision Quest* which 'render the hero's and heroine's commitment, will, and spiritual integrity through the metaphors of weight loss, exercise, and tolerance of and ability to conquer physical pain and exhaustion' (Bordo 1990: 95). In a familiar pattern, social distinction is the victory promised by the mortification of the flesh.

Exercise

Like weight-control diets, exercise has become an increasingly formalised and institutionalised activity in the last few decades, underpinned by an industry which expanded dramatically during the 1980s (see Glassner 1989: 180). Among the conditions for this transformation of exercise were shifts in the nature of work towards more sedentary forms of occupation; the development of a discourse which turns this change into a *problem*, and proposes as its remedy a systematised program of activities anchored in a 'lifestyle'; and finally, the sorts of change in ways of understanding the body that we examined in relation to diet, and especially a new sense of the malleability of the body and of its subordination to the will.

Exercise is a way of transforming the body by repetition of a series of actions which develop particular groups of muscles and burn energy. It ranges from relatively informal activities like walking through to highly disciplined ones like aerobics and gymnastics. In its modern form its origins lie in the eighteenth-century development of Swedish gymnastics as a scientific form of drill, with an initially military application later extended to the education system, as a part of that great movement of rationalisation of the disciplines of the body that Foucault describes in *Discipline and Punish*.

Exercise has been a central element of the Australian education system since the early 1900s. Introduced as a means of preparation for military service and for the improvement of the national physique, it has moved through three major stages (we follow here Kirk's (1994) account). An initial militarist regime of discipline is followed, at the end of the Second World War, by a shift to a looser form of training where the emphasis is displaced from dealing with large groups performing identical activities to dealing with individual fitness, and from the imposition of a disciplinary structure to the development of enjoyment and a motivation to lifelong participation (Kirk 1994: 173). Since the 1970s a further regime begins to render this relaxed yet still recognisably 'modernist' program obsolete, as the shrinking resource base of the public school system combines with the power of commodified and spectacular sport and the associated cult of the malleable body to push the discipline of the body out of the schools and into the realm of commercial popular culture.[3]

Our respondents have been formed by all three of these regimes, but predominantly by the second. We shall give a brief account of walking, cycling, jogging, power-walking, weight-training, and membership of health or sporting organisations, and then a more extended account of aerobics.

Walking
Walking, like aerobics, appears twice in our survey: as an 'activity' about which respondents were asked, and as one of the sports, designated by them rather than us, in which they said they took part. Not surprisingly, there are differences between the two sets of answers – not significant ones, but sufficient to serve as a warning about the need to take questionnaire responses in context; there is a much higher mean for participation, for example, when the name of the activity is prompted. In both sets of responses, however, it is evident that walking is remarkably evenly distributed across the population. Slightly more women than men engage in it, but all of the social classes walk extensively, and it is constant for all ages and all income groups. The same goes for level of educational achievement, with the exception that those with a completed tertiary education are significantly above the mean. It is, in short, perhaps the most widely shared of all the activities in this survey.

Cycling
The class distribution for cycling is set out in table 5.8. The results are anomalous in a number of ways, particularly the high score for manual workers on a scale on which para-professionals, managers, and professionals all score high. Complicating the interpretation of these figures may be an ambiguity about the word 'cycling', which can designate either an activity designed for exercise or competitive sport, or an instrumental means of transport. But it may also be that there are two different structures of prestige operating here: one in which cycling is a relatively fashionable activity attracting the more highly educated classes (professionals and managers), and another in which its values of physical strength and endurance are attractive to a working-class constituency. In other respects, the variations for this sport are more predictable: it is a young person's sport, peaking in

Table 5.8 Cycling by class (combined responses 'often' and 'sometimes')

Emp.	Self-emp.	Manager	Prof.	Para-prof.	Supervisor	Sales/cler.	Manual	*Mean*
19.5	28.0	32.7	31.7	37.7	24.3	29.1	33.8	*29.3*

the 26–35 age group; participation rises with educational level up to partial tertiary; there is no regular correlation with income; and cyclists live in the inner city (which correlates with 'fashionableness') and, especially, in provincial cities (which correlates with the practical use for transport).

Jogging
Jogging is a lower-middle-class activity, strongly correlated with youth, with middle to upper-middle income levels, and with secondary education or with being a tertiary student; para-professionals score high, employers (as usual) score very low. It is a strongly gendered activity, with men outnumbering women in a ratio of 30.8% to 18.2% – indeed, in almost all demographic respects it can be considered the male counterpart to aerobics. Participation is above the mean only in provincial cities, and it is well below the mean in rural areas.

Power-walking
This is the only one of these exercise activities in which employers exceed the mean; they are mirrored, lower down the class scale, by supervisors and exceeded by sales and clerical workers – that is, by white-collar workers at the working-class end of the scale. But sales and clerical workers score high for another reason, or another reason as well: this is a female activity (27.7% as against 15.1%), which is why managers, a very male class, score low. The rejection of power-walking by workers with vocational or apprenticeship training similarly reflects its feminisation. It is correlated with high income and very high education, but it is not a high-cultural activity, because of the low participation by professionals and managers. Its interest lies in the strong intersection here of the axes of power and gender: power-walking (there is nothing random about the name) is an exercise for those who wish to assert their possession of power.

Weight training
Young men predominate here (23.7%), but we are particularly interested in how many young women also do weight training (14.7%): like power-walking and perhaps like exercise in general, this is one of the areas in which women are able to assert a form of strength. There is a steep and regular decline with age, and a steady rise with income level. This form of exercise is low in prestige, as indicated by the high scores for manual workers.

Membership of health or sports organisations

This category gives us something like a standard profile of that portion of the population which exercises. There are two significantly low figures, for those whose country of birth is not Australia, and for Aborigines. Otherwise the scores conform to a familiar pattern: membership of health and sporting organisations declines, but not sharply, with age; it is fairly constant across all classes, but professionals are significantly above the mean (26.8% against a mean of 20.7%); men outnumber women by a ratio of 23% to 18.8%; membership is highest among the tertiary-educated and among the two highest income groups; and provincial cities (which are above the mean for most outdoor activities not involving water) score significantly higher than other locations.

Aerobics

Like weight-reduction dieting, and in direct contrast to jogging (which in many other ways it closely resembles), aerobic exercise is an almost entirely female activity: 26.8% of women take part in it, as against only 4.6% of men. Its class distribution is set out in table 5.9. The distribution clearly follows that of gender among the social classes, with the high score for sales and clerical workers reflecting the domination of that class by women, and the low scores for employers, managers and manual workers reflecting the predominance of men in those groups. There is a regular decline in participation by age, and – with the exception of a higher level of participation by university students, and a lower level by those (mainly men) with vocational or apprenticeship training – a regular correlation with educational level. Participation rises with income; it is concentrated in metropolitan (inner-city or suburban) areas; migrants participate almost as much as those born in Australia; and Aboriginal participation is significantly lower than the mean.

The analogy between aerobics and weight-reduction dieting is a revealing one: both are contributors to that new combination of beauty and strength ('curvaceous muscularity') which, in the early 1980s, replaced the ideal of thinness that had been dominant since the 1960s. Like dieting, it works 'from the inside out, requiring an assertion of will over the body' (Morse 1987/8: 24). But Morse makes the distinction that, 'while dieting shrinks the body and its power both literally and metaphorically, exercise prepares

Table 5.9 Aerobics by class (combined responses 'often' and 'sometimes')

Emp.	Self-emp.	Manager	Prof.	Para-prof.	Supervisor	Sales/cler.	Manual	*Mean*
5.3	12.0	9.0	16.9	18.2	14.7	27.7	12.7	*16.0*

a freely-moving subjectivity which can be active in the world. As such it contradicts long-prevailing notions of feminine passivity and stasis' (24). More generally, dieting and exercise are forms of secular ascesis, working by means of the repetitive imitation of an ideal body form which can never be completely or finally achieved. Both of them collapse the distinction between work and leisure:

> At the postmodern health club – filled with glimmering machines which disaffirm their modernism by being labour-*making* devices ... leisure is work, impulses are harnessed into repetitions-per-minute, and the conscience [is] now of the body as much as it is of the soul. (Glassner 1989: 187)

Both are highly rational and rationalised activities which require a faith in the possibility of deferred benefits (a faith based in a 'technical' knowledge about kilojoules and the expenditure of energy) and of the upward mobility that accompanies such a deferral (Bourdieu 1978: 839). Both depend upon an ethos of purification in which the shaping of the body is a means of combating the excesses of the flesh. And both are crucial components of an imaginary of the body which segregates and defines the genders, revalues and restructures the aging process, and turns the body into an instrument of social achievement.

Sports Played

Dieting and exercise are largely individual practices, and they are instrumental in the sense that the body's pleasures in eating and in releasing its energies are rigorously subordinated to an exercise of will. In turning to the playing of sport, we move to a set of practices which are sociable and in which bodily skill and control are the means for achieving a pleasure which (together with the pleasure of winning) is envisaged as an end in itself.

We asked our respondents to list up to three sports that they play regularly and three sports that they play sometimes. In our analysis we combined the figures for regular and occasional use, both in order to give more reliable numbers and because we are more interested in general, non-specialised participation in sport than in the narrower spectrum of sports played by enthusiasts.

Figure 5.1 presents the ten most popular sports, expressed in descending order.[4] Only ten sports are played with any regularity: all other sports listed (58 of them in all) were played by such small numbers of people that they yielded no reliable figures. There is a significant difference between the popularity of sports watched live and the popularity of sports that people

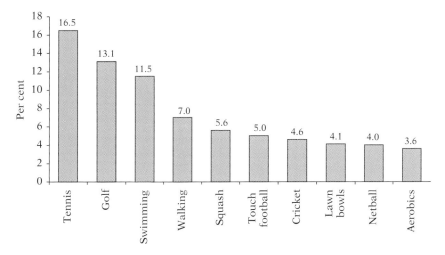

Figure 5.1 Sports played in order of popularity (combined responses 'regularly' and 'sometimes' as percentage of whole sample)

themselves play: none of the four major football codes, for example, is played to any significant extent by our respondents (who are, of course, all over 18), and of the top ten sports watched live only tennis, golf, swimming and cricket are common to both lists.[5]

There is one other figure of great significance that needs to be added to this list: more than a third of our sample (36.6%) told us that they never play sport. This figure is of course greater than any other single mean, and we shall return to it later.

For the moment, let us consider how to make sense of the responses we received to this question by looking for the patterns by which they are organised. We begin by drawing schematic 'profiles' for four of the ten most popular sports in order to establish salient contrasts.

Tennis is the most popular of all sports played by respondents either regularly or occasionally, and it is quite evenly distributed across the class spectrum (see table 5.10). The one significant deviation is for professionals, who score well above the mean (unless otherwise indicated, the figures in the following tables of participation in sport are column percentages combining the responses 'regularly' and 'sometimes').

Tennis is played equally by women (16.5%) and men (16.6%),[6] and is constant for all age groups up to 60. Participation rises regularly as the level of education attained rises, and it rises similarly with income level. It is higher for those who have attended private schools, and for those who were born in Australia. It is played everywhere, but somewhat more in the country and in small towns and provincial cities than in large cities.

Table 5.10 Tennis by class

Emp.	Self-emp.	Manager	Prof.	Para-prof.	Supervisor	Sales/cler.	Manual	*Mean*
14.0	18.4	18.8	29.4	17.3	16.5	16.2	14.2	*16.4*

Aborigines do not play it much. On these indicators, tennis is a prestigious sport; but it is one, paradoxically, that is played by all classes, including manual workers, who in general participate very little in sporting activity.

One way of explaining this apparent paradox would be to take seriously Bourdieu's stricture that 'the nominal unity ... registered by statistics ... masks a dispersal, greater or less depending on the sports, of the ways of playing them'. The example he gives is precisely that of the diversity of ways of playing tennis:

> the tennis played in small municipal clubs, in jeans and Adidas shoes on hard courts, doesn't have a great deal in common with tennis in whites and pleated skirts which was the rule some twenty years ago and which is kept up in select clubs. (Bourdieu 1990: 158)

Yet, although we agree fully with this caution, it is not clear from our data that our tabulations are in fact registering a contrast between two different ways of playing the sport, one which would be regular and formal, the other which would be irregular and informal. We would have expected that, were this the case, we would find significant variation between the disaggregated figures for regular and occasional participation. This is not the case, suggesting that there may be two distinct modes of *regular* participation, one 'formal' and one 'informal'. Tennis is, in either case, a sport that carries at once a high cultural value and a broad appeal across the generations, the sexes and the social classes.

Touch football, by contrast, is played by the young, by men rather than women, and by people with secondary or part-tertiary qualifications, most strongly by the most masculine educational group, workers with vocational or apprenticeship training. It is the one sport in which manual workers score significantly above the mean (10.7% as against a mean of 5.4%; cricket is the only other sport in which they score higher than the mean). Migrants do not play it much, and it is played everywhere, but somewhat more frequently in small towns. There is some correlation with rising income, which means that it is not a poor person's sport. But then no sport is: it is only in the category of 'never playing sport' that the lowest-income groups outscore all others (it is worth remembering here that the lowest incomes are typically those of aged and other pensioners).

Touch football is the opposite of an elite sport, then, and the contrast between these two sports sets up a dichotomy between, on the one hand, a highly rule-governed game, perhaps somewhat old-fashioned and somewhat formal, with no gender bias and with a constituency which is democratic but in which the professional class predominates; and, on the other, a sport marked by its spontaneity and its lack of complex rules, its bodily contact, and its working-class male constituency. This distinction corresponds quite closely to the distinction Bourdieu makes between two distinct forms of bodily *hexis*: the instrumental relation to the body and the stress on the openness of bodies to each other which characterises the working class, and what he describes as 'the tendency of the privileged classes to treat the body as an *end in itself*' (Bourdieu 1978: 838). In terms of these oppositions, then, tennis is prestigious but relatively inclusive, whereas touch football is the closest thing on our scales to a 'popular' form of sporting activity. To be 'popular', however, is not the same thing as to be inclusive: touch football is quite strongly exclusive of women, of middle-aged and old people, of migrants, and of Aborigines.

Golf shows a clear bias to the two employer groups and managers, especially the latter, who score double the mean (see table 5.11). This pattern gives support to the view that golf is important in Australian business culture as an occasion for networking. Professionals score below the mean for participation in golf, as do the two main unskilled working-class groups, sales and clerical workers and manual workers. Like most other sports, golf is strongly gendered, played by 20.9% of men as against 5.8% of women. Participation rises steadily to the age of 60, and even then the decline is not, as it often is, a sharp one. Although level of education is a clear factor in determining who plays, there are two anomalies: the high participation rate for skilled workers with vocational or apprenticeship training indicates that the game is not restricted to the higher socioeconomic classes (skilled workers do not make up a large proportion of either the employer or self-employed group), as well as reinforcing its masculinity; the low rate for tertiary students (or those who have never finished a degree) (see table 5.12) reinforces the observation that, unusually, the game is not dominated by (and is probably not fashionable among) young people.

Private schooling is not a significant factor in whether one plays golf; income is (see table 5.13). But note again that the two lowest-income groups are not far below the mean: unlike the situation in many, perhaps most other countries, golf in Australia is not the sole preserve of the wealthy. Finally, the playing of golf is uniform across most regions (inner city and suburban, rural and semi-rural, small towns); but it is massively higher (25.5% against a mean of 13.1%) in provincial cities. Migrants play it significantly less than those born in Australia, as do Aborigines; in this

Table 5.11   Golf by class

Emp.	Self-emp.	Manager	Prof.	Para-prof.	Supervisor	Sales/cler.	Manual	*Mean*
17.7	18.0	28.3	12.0	14.4	13.8	8.4	10.3	*13.1*

Table 5.12   Golf by level of education

Primary	Some sec.	Comp. sec.	Voc./appr.	Part tert.	Comp. tert.	*Mean*
5.4	13.9	13.8	18.3	8.3	15.8	*13.1*

Table 5.13   Golf by income

<15K	15–26	26–40	40–60	60–80	>80K	*Mean*
12.7	11.4	13.6	15.7	16.5	15.7	*13.1*

and many other respects golf is close to touch football on the spectrum of sports commonly played.

Lawn bowls, finally, is the one sport that is dominated by the elderly: 11.3% against a mean of 3.5%. Managers are the single largest group, followed by the self-employed, supervisors, and sales and clerical workers. Employers, professionals and para-professionals, and manual workers all fall below the mean, probably for rather different reasons: employers and manual workers as part of their generally low participation rate, professionals and para-professionals because of the relatively low cultural prestige of lawn bowls. Men (4.3%) play it somewhat more than women (2.8%), but this difference is not as marked as for most other sports. There are a number of other ways in which lawn bowls is anomalous: it is the only sport in which those with only a primary education predominate (this is directly correlated with age, reflecting the different educational values of an earlier historical time); and there is a regular *decline* in participation with rising levels of educational attainment (see table 5.14).

Likewise, participation is *negatively* correlated with income. The game is not played at all in the inner city, and is strongest in provincial cities and, especially, small towns (which score almost double the mean). Migrants play it much less than those born in Australia, Aborigines do not play it at all.

Our last and by far the largest category is that of those who declare that they *never play sport* at all. Perhaps the most striking aspect of this group is the strong negative correlation with level of education (see table 5.15).

Table 5.14 Lawn bowls by level of education

Primary	Some sec.	Comp. sec.	Voc./appr.	Part tert.	Comp. tert.	*Mean*
8.2	5.2	3.6	3.0	1.7	0.9	*3.5*

Table 5.15 Non-participation in sport by level of education

Primary	Some sec.	Comp. sec.	Voc./appr.	Part tert.	Comp. tert.	*Mean*
57.4	47.5	33.7	36.0	28.3	25.3	*36.6*

To put this in positive terms, the more educated you are, the more likely you are to participate in sports. In class terms, employers and manual workers are the strongest non-players, while managers are at the opposite end of the scale, followed by professionals (see table 5.16).

Women score higher on this negative scale than men (40.3% to 32.8%). As might be expected, there is a regular correlation between non-participation and increasing age, and those with no children at home are much less likely to play a sport. People without formal education and those who attended state schools are above the mean for non-participation, and those from private schools are well below it. The poorer you are, the less likely you are to play a sport. Those from the suburbs and the country play less sport than those who live elsewhere, and migrants and Aborigines play less than the Australian-born and non-Aborigines. As McKay (1991: 11) summarises it, 'sport is participated in by predominantly young, affluent and relatively well-educated male Australians'.

Let us now try to extrapolate some more general conclusions from these descriptions, and in the first place from what we know about those who do not play any sport. We can say that participation in sporting activity tends to *rise* steadily with level of education, with income, and with attendance at private schools. It tends to *decline* with increasing age, with being a migrant or an Aborigine, and with having no children at home. Managers and professionals have the highest participation rates; employers and manual workers the lowest (employers perhaps because they have the highest average age of all class groups, and because they are not particularly well educated; manual workers because they are the least-educated class).

Perhaps the clearest pattern to emerge is the division between male and female sports. There are only two exceptions to this pattern: lawn bowls, and (in particular) tennis. Of the other sports, golf, squash, touch football and cricket are all strongly male sports; and swimming, walking, netball and aerobics are all strongly female. As Morse (1987/8: 22) argues,

Table 5.16 Non-participation in sport by class

Emp.	Self-emp.	Manager	Prof.	Para-prof.	Supervisor	Sales/cler.	Manual	*Mean*
42.6	33.0	18.3	28.7	33.4	33.7	34.0	41.4	*36.6*

'Sport plays an important role in gender maintenance; indeed, sport is the last major social institution segregated by gender, and in its hierarchy of value, male performances are favoured'.

The second pattern concerns the correlation between increasing participation in sport and increasing levels of educational attainment. We can identify two variants in this pattern. In the first, exemplified by tennis, swimming and walking, there is an unambiguous correlation all along the scale. In the second, exemplified by golf, squash, touch football, cricket, netball and aerobics, there is a regular increase in participation up to the level either of vocational/apprenticeship training or of partially completed tertiary education, and then a decline (although never below the mean) in the group of tertiary-educated respondents. These two variants give us models of sports which correspond to possession of high and of medium cultural capital. Finally, the case of lawn bowls reverses the usual pattern, with a *negative* correlation between participation and increased educational level. This reversal complicates the general rule, but is unusual enough that it works to confirm rather than disprove it.

The third pattern involves the predominance of a particular class, or a small cluster of classes, in the playing of a sport. Table 5.17 is the full table of participation by class.

We have identified the clusters of predominance set out in table 5.18. The salient feature of this list is the absolute predominance of the two most highly educated classes, professionals and managers, in five sports, and their shared predominance in three others. These are clear indicators of the formative role of cultural capital in guiding participation in sport. One final pattern is a negative one: the class with the highest degree of cultural capital, that of professionals, scores below the mean on four sports: golf, touch football, netball, and lawn bowls. This datum allows us to construct the upper and lower extremes of a hierarchy of cultural value ranging from tennis and swimming at the top to touch football and netball at the bottom. However, the complexity of the relations between class and culture do not allow any simple categorisation of the intermediate sports.

We received some insight into the meaning of these patterns from a question that we asked about what respondents enjoyed most about the sports they played. There are limits, of course, to how deeply a survey

Table 5.17   Participation in sports by class (aggregated column percentages)

	Emp.	Self-emp.	Mgr	Prof.	Para-prof.	Supv.	Sales/cler.	Manual	*Mean*
Tennis	14.0	18.4	18.8	29.4	17.3	16.5	16.2	14.2	*16.4*
Golf	17.7	18.0	28.3	12.0	14.4	13.8	8.4	10.3	*13.1*
Swimming	7.6	9.2	9.7	20.2	14.5	11.6	14.3	7.8	*11.3*
Walking	6.0	6.7	8.4	9.4	7.0	4.8	10.6	4.6	*6.7*
Squash	4.4	5.1	9.3	6.6	9.0	9.9	5.3	5.1	*5.7*
Touch football	3.7	3.9	1.7	4.8	7.7	4.4	3.6	10.7	*5.4*
Cricket	3.1	4.9	8.7	6.7	5.2	6.7	3.4	6.0	*4.9*
Netball	0.0	1.6	2.3	3.0	5.3	2.3	12.6	3.0	*4.7*
Aerobics	1.9	2.5	1.4	6.3	3.4	1.5	7.6	2.2	*3.7*
Lawn bowls	2.4	4.9	8.6	1.9	1.2	4.7	4.1	2.7	*3.5*

Table 5.18   Clusters of predominance

Professionals: tennis, swimming
Sales/clerical workers and professionals: aerobics
Managers: golf, cricket, lawn bowls
Managers, para-professionals and supervisors: squash
Sales/clerical workers: netball
Sales/clerical, professionals and managers: walking

question can go in seeking to explore the multiplicity of meanings that people attach to social activities. Nevertheless, the four most salient categories of response – 'fitness', 'health', 'relaxation', and 'competition' – give us, with all their banality, a sense of the differences between the pleasures that different social groups take in the playing of sport.

The first three all involve the care of the body. *Fitness* is the most definite and active form of such care, a shaping of the body according to a model of physical perfection. It is heavily occupied by the two youngest groups and by those with a partial or completed tertiary education; and it is managers and sales and clerical workers who most fully espouse it. *Health*, by contrast, is a more general form of care, involving less an active moulding of the body than a preservation, a kind of defence. Here, the key group is the professionals, and the nomination of this category declines with increasing age and rises with education and income. The category of *relaxation* foregrounds the contrast between work and leisure (whereas 'fitness', as we saw earlier, turns leisure into a kind of work). Again, it is correlated with the three best-educated classes (professionals, managers, and para-professionals), as well as with the self-employed; but unlike 'health' and 'fitness', it is a somewhat more masculine category, and it is of little interest to the young. The last major category, *competition*, is dominated by the two employer classes and, very strongly (11.8% against a mean of 5.4%), by managers; it is markedly more male than female (8.5% to 2.5%), and it declines steadily with age. It rises regularly with educational level as far as part-tertiary, but then falls away sharply, to below the mean, with the group who have completed tertiary education. All of this tells us a good deal about the classes with most education and the classes with most organisational capital; it also tells us a lot about youth and about masculinity. It tells us less, however, except in a negative sense, about the lower social groups, those who participate less in sport, and those who are socially marginal.

Suppose, finally, that we were to try to correlate our findings with an analysis of some of the structural characteristics of the different sports: would this tell us something either about the sports themselves or about the way different social groups imagine their relation to game-playing and to the uses and pleasures of their bodies? We identified four structural characteristics that seemed particularly pertinent: is the sport played competitively or not, and how is competition organised? does it involve physical contact between players? does the amateur version of the game have a counterpart in a major professional sport? and how expensive is it – to what extent does it involve more than minimal physical equipment? The resulting distribution of sports is set out in table 5.19.

We can distinguish a number of patterns in table 5.19 which give us some rather interesting information about the ethos of different social groups. First, the scale of competitiveness pits a cluster of team-based competitive sports with strong lower-class participation against clusters of upper-class sports where competition is a matter of an individual striving against another individual, or against him- or herself, or – as in the case of the three strongly 'female' sports – where there is no competition. Second, the criterion of physical contact opposes the sport which is most strongly working class and male to all the others. Third, the four sports which have a major professional counterpart (which happen to be the ones that overlap with the list of sports watched at live venues) constitute four of the five sports dominated by professionals and managers. Finally, the distinction between a requirement for elaborate and for minimal or no equipment sets professional and managerial sports which are competitive in nature against sports which are either played predominantly by professionals and non-competitive, or which are working class. We can summarise these patterns in terms of two gross simplifications. The first is that 'lower-class' forms of sport tend to be played in teams and are more

Table 5.19   Distribution of sports

1 nature of competition			
team against team	**one on one**	**individual**	**not competitive**
touch football	tennis	golf	swimming
cricket	squash		walking
netball			aerobics
lawn bowls			

2 nature of interaction	
physical contact	**little or no physical contact**
touch football	all others

3 relation to sports industry	
professional counterpart	**no major professional counterpart**
tennis	squash
golf	walking
cricket	aerobics
swimming	lawn bowls
	touch football
	netball

4 physical apparatus required	
equipment	**minimal or no equipment**
cricket	netball
golf	swimming
tennis	walking
squash	touch football
lawn bowls	aerobics

likely to involve physical contact, whereas 'upper-class' sports tend to be played individualistically and without bodily contact, and to have a counterpart professional form of the sport. The second is that a distinction between male and female sports correlates with a distinction between competitive and non-competitive forms of game-playing. These are – in very schematic outline – the parameters that structure the 'everyday' experience of participant sport in Australia.

Sports Watched

As we indicated before, there is a considerable discrepancy between the sports that people play and the sports they watch. Table 5.20 presents the mean percentages for sports which are watched regularly at live venues by our respondents. This table gives an absolute measure of the relative popularity of the various spectator sports across the whole population, and an indication of the clear difference between participation and spectatorship:

Table 5.20 Sports watched
regularly at live venues
(percentages of total sample)

1	Australian rules	12.1
2	Cricket	12.0
3	Rugby league	9.4
4	Tennis	8.8
5	Swimming	7.4
6	Motor car racing	6.3
7	Basketball	6.1
8	Soccer	6.1
9	Golf	5.2
10	Horse racing	5.0
11	Motorcycle racing	4.8
12	Track/field	4.2
13	Gymnastics	4.1
14	Ironman comps	4.0
15	Rugby union	3.9
16	Netball	3.9
17	Speedway racing	3.5
18	Surf carnivals	3.4
19	Boxing	3.3
20	Stockcar racing	2.2
21	Hockey	1.6
22	Wrestling	1.6
23	Volleyball	1.4
24	Water polo	0.6

only cricket, tennis, swimming, and golf are common to this list and the list of the ten most frequently played sports.

But an even greater difference between the playing and the watching of sports emerges when these absolute figures are broken down into an analysis of particular variables. Consider, for example, the breakdown of the overall spectatorship of sports by the different social classes, as shown in table 5.21.

Table 5.21 Watch sports regularly at live venues, by class (means for all sports)

Emp.	Self-emp.	Manager	Prof.	Para-prof.	Supervisor	Sales/cler.	Manual	*Mean*
4.4	4.5	5.1	3.1	3.9	6.2	4.9	6.6	*5.0*

Table 5.21 represents almost a reversal of the corresponding pattern for *participation* in sport, at least at the outer limits. If we take the corresponding percentage means for all sports played, the comparative rank order of classes for participation and for spectatorship is as set out in figure 5.2.

Those classes like the professionals and para-professionals which had scored very high on the playing of sport score very low on watching it, whereas manual workers, who play little sport, watch it a great deal. The reversal is not, of course, complete: employers neither play nor watch much sport, and managers, supervisors, and sales and clerical workers retain a relatively strong

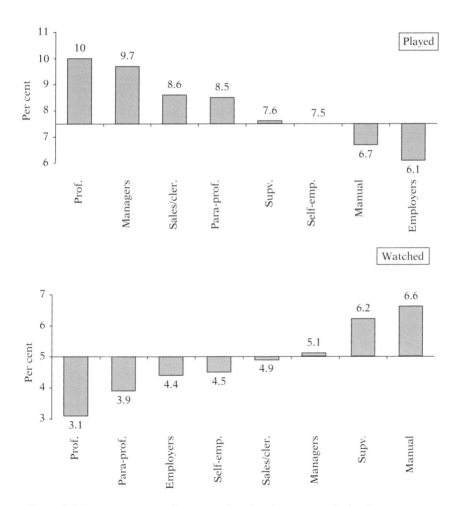

Figure 5.2 Percentage means for sports played and sports watched at live venues, by class (relations to the overall mean)

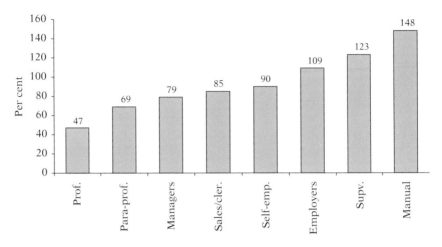

Figure 5.3 Percentage relation between relations to means for sports played and sports watched, by class

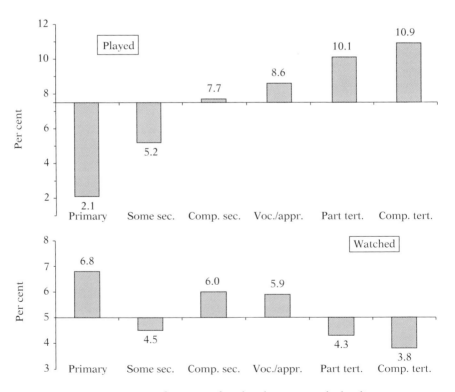

Figure 5.4 Percentage means for sports played and sports watched at live venues, by educational level

position on both scales. But the value hierarchy which led from the most-educated to the least-educated classes has been substantially reversed, and the real shift in the class composition of the playing and watching of sport is evident if we relate deviations from the mean on each scale. Figure 5.3 charts the movement from participation to spectatorship, expressing it as a percentage relation between relations to the mean. This is a measure of difference between the two scales, and it corresponds to a clear hierarchy of cultural capital.

This hierarchy is confirmed if we turn to look at the scores for watching sport cross-tabulated by level of education. Here the group of respondents with only a primary education, who had participated in the playing of sport to such a low extent, scores substantially above the mean, whereas the tertiary-educated groups score well below it. Figure 5.4 gives the percentage means for sports played and sports watched by educational level, while figure 5.5 shows the percentage relation between these different modes of involvement in sport.

Perhaps the most dramatic demonstration of this reversal between participation and spectatorship is given in the relative figures for Aborigines, expressed as a percentage relation to the mean (see table 5.22).

Could we perhaps posit that there is a kind of compensation mechanism operating here, such that those who are unable or unwilling to play sport make up for it by a greater interest in the watching of sport?[7] Certainly the playing and the watching of sport seem to tend towards being exclusive rather than complementary activities. The figures for spectatorship by age would complicate such an assumption, however. The figures for participation and

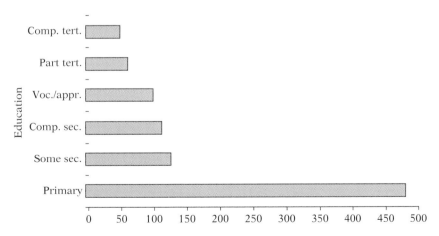

Figure 5.5 Percentage relation between relations to the mean for sports played and sports watched, by educational level

Table 5.22 Aboriginal participation and spectatorship in sports (percentage relations to the mean, and percentage relation of relations)

	Participation	Spectatorship	% relation
Non-Aborigines	102	96	94%
Aborigines	58	204	352%

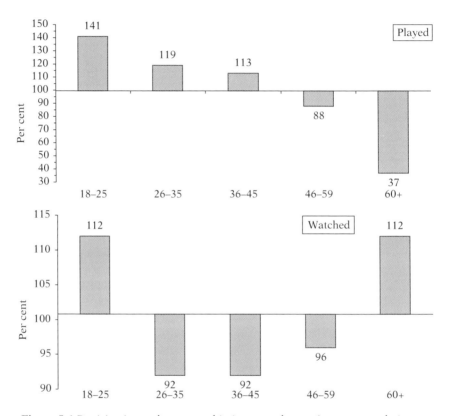

Figure 5.6 Participation and spectatorship in sports, by age (percentage relations to the mean)

spectatorship varied by age and expressed as a percentage relation to the mean in each case are set out in figure 5.6.

The really dramatic shift here, of course, is with those who are 60 and older. For other age groups the distance between their levels of participation and of spectatorship is less great. What we can observe is that this distance narrows with age, with participation declining somewhat more rapidly than spectatorship; and that it is then reversed from the age of 45, as the emphasis shifts towards the watching of sport.

A further variable that we should consider is that for income. Here the figures show the same sort of movement as those for educational level: the two poorest groups go from scoring low on participation to scoring just below or just above the mean on spectatorship; the two middle groups go from scoring slightly above the mean on participation to scoring slightly below the mean on spectatorship; and the two wealthiest groups go from well above the mean on participation to being on or somewhat above the mean on spectatorship. High income, that is to say, makes one a more inclusive player as well as an average to above-average watcher of sport, whereas low income makes one a restricted player and an average to below-average spectator.

Two further sets of determinations may have a bearing on overall levels of watching and playing sport: location and gender. Figures for location show little variation between rates for participation and spectatorship in each area of residence, indicating that regionality has little bearing on the differential relation between the playing and the watching of sports. Finally, the figures for respondents' gender (the first figure is a percentage mean for all sports, the second is a percentage relation to the overall mean) are set out in table 5.23.

As was already evident from the relatively high position of sales and clerical workers in the comparison between the two scales by class, the hierarchy of cultural value which applies to sport is deeply inflected by gender. The widening of the gap between men and women in the case of spectatorship indicates that being female combines with high levels of education and income to construct a chain in which two opposed sets of values cohere around participation and spectatorship. This opposition is, again, that polarity of inclusiveness of interest and restrictedness of interest that informs cultural consumption in Australia.

In registering this shift in value from the playing to the watching of sport, we move towards an imaginary of the body which relies upon projection on to the bodies of others rather than on a sense of one's own bodily skills. The recognition of biological limits that comes with increasing age is certainly an important factor in this, but a role is perhaps also played

Table 5.23   Participation and spectatorship in sports by gender (means of column percentages, and percentage relations to the mean)

	Participation		Spectatorship	
Female	7.1	(95)	3.9	(78)
Male	8.2	(109)	6.2	(124)
Mean	*7.5*		*5.0*	

by the pleasures and rewards of vicarious achievement. Spectator sports are primarily competitive; Elias and Dunning (1986: 42 and passim) speak of sport as a form of mimetic violence, a displacement into the controlled space of game-playing of the dangers, risks, and invested emotions of the social world. In this sense, the shift of the value structure associated with spectator sports down the class scale, the educational scale, and the scale of income, as well as the shift towards a more strongly masculine value structure, may have something or even much to do with a learned disposition towards vicarious success.

There are two further things that need to be said about spectator sport, although we do not explore them any further here. The first is that the tendency over the last two decades has been towards the staging of increasingly spectacular mass sporting events. Sport at live venues tends to involve large crowds (and is partly an *experience* of losing oneself within the mass body of the crowd); and it tends to put on display, and systematically to circulate, men and women who are stars, with all the affective charge that a star-system carries with it. Second, and concomitantly, spectator sport is now more than ever a commodified system (McKay and Miller 1991; Lawrence and Rowe 1986), and its values increasingly approximate to those of the entertainment industries. In this, too, it differs substantially from the value systems of participant sport, and the forms of embodied selfhood that they entail.

Chapter 6

Reading by Numbers

In reporting the findings of an oral history project concerned with Australian reading practices over the period 1890 to 1933, Martyn Lyons and Lucy Taksa highlight a strong tendency for women readers to devalue their own literary tastes and preferences. While the detailed evidence of the testimony they had collected suggested that women had been 'keen and selective readers', most of the interviewees, when asked about their own or their mothers' reading, tended 'to write it off as of no value or consequence' (Lyons & Taksa 1992: 39). Women, in these rememberings, condemned themselves as frivolous readers, both for reading idly, as a diversion, rather than, as the terms in which they typically contrasted men's reading with their own, for a particular purpose; and for their preference for romance fiction over more factual and educational kinds of material. Lyons and Taksa's concern is to restore to women's reading a sense of its historical richness, diversity and complexity, and thereby to reprieve it from the forms of self-condemnation which organised these memories. As such, their work parallels those feminist inquiries which, in rebuttal of masculinised hierarchies of literary value, have examined the varied, and often critical, ways in which women use and interpret such feminised genres as romance and soap opera.[1]

Yet, however much these new accounts of reading may have revalued the status of both women readers and women's genres, many women clearly still hold the genres they like in low regard. This is clear from the way in which the women in our interview sample react when asked whether they like romance fiction. Only one of them expresses an unambiguous preference for romance fiction and outlines her reasons in a manner that is not apologetic, *explaining* her reading habits without feeling any need to *explain them away*. Mary, an older reader formed in the working-class culture of Sydney's western suburbs, thus accounts for her liking for romance fiction in terms of how it fits into the rhythms of her life:

> What do I like about reading romances? Probably, I read romance stories in between other stories because it's something you can just read, you can pick up and put down, it's light and it doesn't take you a lot of involvement, that's probably what I like about them . . . When you're busy – it's all right when you've got a couple of hours and you can sit down and read and have a good time – but when you're busy you can pick it up and put it down and you don't sort of get lost in the story, where you're up to and that. So every time I go to the library I always bring home, as well as the other books, I always bring home a few Mills and Boon you can just read in between when you haven't got much time.

Other women readers, however, actively, if often ambivalently, disavow an interest in romance fiction. For Sheila, also in her 60s and a fan of the *Poldark* novels, reading romances can only be legitimated if tempered by an enlightening burden of historical fact.[2] Her condemnation of romance fiction for lacking this dimension serves as a means of drawing an important boundary line between her own reading and that of other women readers:

> Well a lot of that [historical romance] is based on fact but it's got the bit of romance and everything too. But just a plain, soppy, I call them soppy, unreal romance. They may be great for old ladies who that's all they can manage and maybe they like to relive their past or imagine that their past was like this. I think they have their place. But I'm not ready for that yet.

Dorothy reacts similarly in making it clear how important it is to her sense of self that she not be classified as a Mills and Boon reader. A keen reader, she initially tells the interviewer that she will read whatever she can get her hands on. 'Fiction, non-fiction, the lot . . . I'll pick up anything and read anything.' Testing the ground, the interviewer asks:

> **INTERVIEWER** Well, would you read a Mills and Boon?
> **DOROTHY** No.
> **INTERVIEWER** You wouldn't read a Mills and Boon?
> **DOROTHY** I don't know why. I just don't . . . I've got . . . I think they'd be . . . I like getting into a decent book that doesn't just take a couple of hours to read. I like something that goes on. But no, I've never read one and . . . no particular reason why. I know a few women who do read Mills and Boon regularly and sort of devour them, always seem to be quite silly women. I don't know. Maybe that sounds silly. I don't want to be thought of as a silly lady.

INTERVIEWER That's interesting. So, what do you expect to get out of the story then? Like Mills and Boon is pure fantasy.

DOROTHY I think I get a lot out of books because playing *Trivial Pursuit*, there must be just so much stuff tucked up in the brain that you don't know that's there. And someone asks you a question and it's quite easy to get the answers because somewhere around you've tucked the answers there – 'I've read that somewhere' – and I think that's important, reading to just expand your knowledge.

Here, then, a disavowal of romance fiction is a way for Dorothy to invest her reading with significance by connecting it to her fondness for board games which she sees as both a family activity and fun and yet still improving.

Statistically, however, despite these disavowals, romance fiction remains high in women's reading preferences. In the *Australian Everyday Cultures* survey, it is the third most popular genre with women readers, with 26.2% of women including it among their favourite books after 28.2% for thrillers and adventure books and 27.4% for crime, murder and mystery books. A rather more telling point, however, is that romance fiction is, by and large, read only by women, whereas both thrillers and crime fiction recruit a substantial cross-gender readership. There is, however, another side to this statistical picture. For if women's association with romance fiction – the most frequently disparaged and despised of genres within conventional literary hierarchies – is a strong one, so also is their association with the most valued genres in those hierarchies. We shall look at the details later. For now, suffice it to note that women are much more likely than men to read the literary forms which conventionally enjoy the highest aesthetic esteem – poetry, classical authors and contemporary novels – just as they are also considerably more likely to own those kinds of books which suggest a deep involvement in literary and aesthetic culture. However, these are unlikely to be the same women. When we look more closely at women's genre preferences, we find that the preferences for both romance fiction and for aesthetic literature have strongly marked class locations. Only 13.3% of professional women include romances among their favourite books, compared with 34.9% of women sales and clerical workers, whereas these ratios are reversed in the case of classical authors who are read by 19.2% of professional women but by only 5.7% of women sales and clerical workers.

While these interconnections between different social factors and their influence on the organisation of reading preferences are the main issues that concern us in this chapter, we have chosen gender as our route into these questions for two reasons. First, whether we are concerned with questions of class or education, the role of these factors in the social organisation of reading is often less immediately significant than that of gender which, in some areas, dramatically polarises the field of reading into what are virtually separate and gender-exclusive domains. Second, compared with many other areas of cultural choice – cinema, television, and some aspects of musical preferences, for example – the effects of gender on the organisation of reading practices are often clearer and more pronounced. This is perhaps because reading is a more individualised activity and so an area in which the different choices and preferences of men and women are likely to prevail over the more shared decisions, whether of the family or the couple, which characterise watching television, going to the movies or listening to the radio. Certainly, this sense of 'a book of one's own' and of its importance in securing, especially for women readers, a space of one's own is as clear in our discussions with readers as it has been in other recent studies.[3] Just as important, however, is the fact that the operations of publishing markets are often strongly segregated along gender lines. For these reasons, then, it will repay our attention to look more closely at how men and women differ from one another in what they read, how much they read, and in their attitudes to reading before considering how gender interacts with other social variables to produce a complex social patterning of reading in which the role that reading plays in articulating distinctions of class is closely connected to its gendered associations.

Reading as Gendered Practice

'Reading surveys', Lyons and Taksa state, 'show that, in any English-speaking country, at any point in the twentieth century, girls read more than boys' (Lyons & Taksa 1992: 45). They also, in our case and in most of the other survey data that are available, show that this differentiation persists into adulthood, with women reporting that they read more than men and more often.[4] In the *Australian Everyday Cultures* sample, 69.7% of women read often compared with 48.9% of men, 12.8% of whom say that they hardly ever read whereas this is true of only 4% of women. Similarly, when asked whether they read books, 13.8% of men say no compared with 4.8% of women. The only area in which this pattern of emphasis is reversed is that of newspaper reading with men, at 49.9%, more likely to read a newspaper daily than women at 38.1%. Women are also more likely than men to own significant numbers of books. Whereas 20.8% of women own between 100 and 200 books, and a further 20.2% own between 200 and 500, the comparable figures for men are 17.1% and 13.2%. However, rates of ownership are more or less equalised around the 10 per cent mark for both men and women in relation to larger collections of over 500 titles. This is probably related to the fact that, although they read books less than women, men are more likely to buy the books they do read while women – in a pattern which confirms a recent national survey of library users[5] – are more likely to borrow books from friends or from libraries: 27% of women indicated that they mostly obtain books in this way whereas this is true for only 19.5% of men. Perhaps more important than the number of books owned, however, is the fact that women are significantly more likely than men to own books which have high-cultural associations. As Figure 6.1 shows, this difference is especially pronounced in the case of books that are aesthetically coded (literary classics, art books, and poetry) while diminishing in the case of books which have a predominantly factual or documentary orientation (history books, biographies).

This difference between women's preferences for literary or aesthetic forms of reading and men's interest in factual and documentary reading carries over into the genre preferences of men and women readers. Table 6.1 presents the results of our inquiries into favourite kinds of reading in a form which reveals how far, at their extremes, men's and women's genre preferences are polarised. The figures for the first two columns represent the percentages of women and men indicating a preference – whether first, second or third – for the genre specified. The right-hand column then provides a measure of the gender-specificity of particular genres by showing how likely it is that men will choose the genre in question compared with women. The resulting hierarchy of reading preferences indicates not which are the most popular genres with women and men respectively; rather, it tells us – in descending order – which genres are most strongly preferred by women relative to men, and those for which men's relative preferences are highest. Thus, the placing of romances at the top of this hierarchy does not mean that this is the most popular genre with women – this, for women as for men, is the thriller – but that it is the most feminised form of reading to the degree that men are less likely to

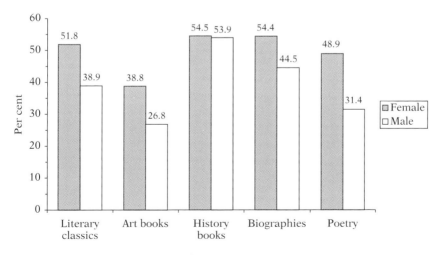

Figure 6.1 Book ownership by gender

Table 6.1   Favourite books (total preferences) by gender

	Female	Male	Male as % of female
Mainly female preferences			
Romances	26.2	1.8	7
Historical romances	15.4	1.1	7
Cooking	21.3	5.3	25
Contemporary novels	18.2	5.2	29
Poetry	5.9	2.0	34
Classical authors	6.8	3.0	44
Craft/hobbies	14.8	8.2	55
Biographies	22.5	12.8	57
Crime/murder/mystery	27.4	21.6	79
Occult	1.8	1.7	94
Educational	11.7	11.5	98
Mainly male preferences			
Thriller/adventure	28.2	32.5	115
Gardening	11.4	13.2	116
Horror	5.0	6.3	126
Humour/comedy	14.5	19.2	132
Travel, exploration	9.2	15.9	173
Historical	8.2	14.4	176
Science fiction	5.2	14.5	279
Erotica	1.4	5.8	414
Political	1.1	4.6	418
Scientific	1.1	6.5	591
Sport & leisure	2.7	22.0	815

read romances than they are all other forms of reading for which women have higher rates of preferences than men. Conversely, the more the figure in the right-hand column rises above the matching ratio of 100%, the more strongly and exclusively male is the genre concerned, peaking with sport which men are over eight times more likely to include in their favourite reading than women.

The pattern of preferences for choice of favourite author offers a closer picture of these gender differences. In Table 6.2 the ten most frequently nominated first-choice authors have been arranged in rank order, with Stephen King at the top of the list with 133 nominations, and Tom Clancy coming in tenth with 28 nominations. Jeffrey Archer and Agatha Christie are the only authors who recruit a reasonably balanced cross-gender readership, although thriller writers like Stephen King and Wilbur Smith do attract a substantial female readership. What is perhaps most noticeable, however, is the almost total absence of male interest in the best-selling

Table 6.2 Favourite authors according to gender, first preferences only (column percentages)

	Female	Male
Stephen King	17.5	35.9
Wilbur Smith	8.0	28.5
Agatha Christie	11.0	7.2
Danielle Steel	13.0	0.3
Jeffrey Archer	8.1	9.1
Virginia Andrews	11.9	0.8
Catherine Cookson	11.0	0.9
Sidney Sheldon	8.7	3.1
Bryce Courtenay	8.2	2.7
Tom Clancy	1.5	11.6

Note: the percentages in this table relate only to the men and women who included these ten authors in their first preferences.

authors of romance fiction: Catherine Cookson and Danielle Steel, for example. Nominations of favourite authors also include a selection of classical literary authors: Jane Austen, Emily Brontë, William Shakespeare, Thomas Hardy, Ernest Hemingway, D.H. Lawrence and Leo Tolstoy are the most common. In all cases except one, a larger percentage of women than men include these authors in their full range of preferences for favourite authors. The exception to the rule here is Hemingway, hardly surprising in view of the stress his fictions place on male self-discovery through a challenging encounter with nature, solitude or a threatening adversary.

The division of reading interests along gender lines, then, is quite sharp. Women's strongest relative interest in the popular fiction genres of romance and historical romance is paralleled by men's interest (although by no means to the same degree) in science fiction. A liking for crime fiction, thrillers, horror and comedy genres is more evenly shared, while erotica is primarily a male genre.[6] It would be a mistake, however, to infer from this that women's reading lacks a sexual interest and motivation, as this has, for women, traditionally been expressed through romance fiction and is an aspect of the genre's associations that is strongly foregrounded in contemporary cover design and promotional literature. Account must also be taken of the similar role of crime fiction whose now strong and growing female readership is clearly related to the increasing feminisation of the genre through the influence of women writers and their leading female characters – Sara Paretsky's Victoria Warshawski and Patricia Cornwell's Kay Scarpetta, for example – as well as of the new forms of erotic writing directed specifically at women: Tobsha Learner's *Quiver*, for example, or Linda Jaivin's *Eat Me*. It is perhaps in relation to the higher literary genres, however, that men's and women's reading differ most. Women's dominance of the aesthetic genres is clear: men's preferences for classical authors is 44% of women's and considerably less for poetry and contemporary novels. Conversely, men have far higher rates of preference for genres with a factual or documentary orientation: historical, scientific and political writing, for example.

Some aspects of these differences are illuminated by the interview material. Daniel, a retired 75 year old, explains his fondness for biographies in terms which, in accenting the role of 'world-historical individuals', contrast significantly with those used by women readers to describe their liking for historical genres:

> **INTERVIEWER** I noticed that you like biographies in particular. Is that because they're essentially real life? They're real reports as opposed to being fantastic or sensational, do you think?
>
> **DANIEL** Yes. I'd say, I go for biographies of lives that have always interested me. Whether that's the Winston Churchill type of person, the General Wavell or war people and of course today's politicians. Bob Hawke is a very, very interesting man to read about . . . And of course, . . . Gough Whitlam and . . . Malcolm Fraser . . . To me they're interesting because they're, well, they're important people. They've covered some aspects of their lives which we only just take part in as constituents.

For Lilian, also retired – she is in her mid-60s – and an avid reader of history of all kinds, historical writing which melds fact and fiction is valued for its ability to provide an empathic form of access to the past.

> Yeah. And, I've just been to Norfolk Island. So, all the history involved in that, you know, it was just wonderful. I just love to read about it. I've read a book on the beginning of Australia. The Australian Theory. I forget the writer. It's a woman who writes it. And . . . there's ten books in the series right from when they're convicted in England and they come out here and it's every aspect of Australia's history it goes through. And it's true facts in it. Even though it's written as novels. And they are fantastic. I read the whole ten of them. I could read them again just like that. They were so good. But, it's all history.

A similar set of differences is evident in the pattern of men's and women's preferences for magazines. These are summarised in table 6.3, the most striking – although unsurprising – aspect of which is the marked polarisation between the various categories of women's magazines, whose

Table 6.3 First preference magazines by gender

	Female	Male	Male as % of female
Mainly female preferences			
Women's (young)	7.5	0.2	3
Women's (fashion)	1.9	0.1	5
Women's (home)	36.2	3.7	10
Home and garden	6.4	1.3	20
Health	1.1	0.3	27
Craft	0.6	0.3	50
Tabloid magazines	9.3	9.1	98
Mainly male preferences			
Arts	0.7	1.0	143
News magazines	3.1	4.6	148
Young avant-garde	0.2	0.3	150
Scientific & nature	2.5	5.5	220
Food/cuisine	0.3	0.7	233
Collecting/hobbies	0.4	1.5	375
Men's magazines	0.1	0.4	400
Music	0.4	2.2	550
Computers	0.3	2.1	700
Wheels	0.4	6.8	1700
Sports	0.7	13.8	1971

readership is almost entirely female, and car and sports magazines whose readership is just as exclusively male.

It is worth noting that, in the estimation of many readers, women's magazines enjoy a low status on a par with romance. Only one interviewee – Elizabeth, a working-class mother who had little formal education – speaks unselfconsciously about her reasons for liking women's magazines:

> I think they're very easy to read because I have a lot of trouble with reading, writing. I think they're very plain, they're not complicated for me. I think they don't seem to be cluttered with too much in them. I like looking at the recipes. I like the short stories . . . because at the moment I couldn't even concentrate. Even though I can read and write, and there might be words that I honestly don't know but I know roughly what the meaning of that word is even though I might not be able to pronounce that word. But I roughly know what the meaning is of that word. So my education leaves a lot to be desired, it's not very good. I think the *Woman's Day* is more plainer to read, I can read it easy.[7]

For many women, however, owning up to reading women's magazines is a semi-cathartic confessional act. 'I'm a sneak reader of women's magazines', is how a participant in one of our focus-group discussions puts it. 'I've never admitted this before – I read women's magazines.' For others, reading women's magazines falls in the same category as reading romances – something to be disavowed. For Dorothy, women's magazines are, quite literally, untouchable: 'Don't touch them. I just feel they are garbage . . . I will never buy one! Everything you see advertised on the TV appears to me to be trash! So, I'm not interested in them.'

When, as they occasionally do, men confess to reading women's magazines they are eager to contextualise that activity in ways that would retrieve it from any appearance of being, so to speak, the literary equivalent of cross-dressing. Philip, who includes *Women's Weekly* with *New Scientist* and *Time* as his three favourite magazines, accounts for his interest in *Women's Weekly* in terms which align it with the factual and documentary orientation which characterises his reading interests generally. When asked what he likes about *Women's Weekly*, Philip replies:

> Well again, it wasn't so much the stories. Again, it was more information. I'll tell you one of the things that I was quite interested in was gardening and plants. Things to do with, you know, fertilisation and proper maintenance of plants and gardens, that sort of thing. They used to have a good section on that. They had good sections on cooking. Not that I was a cook. But I used to draw my wife's attention to these. Because she was a good cook.

The gendering of this interest in information – of reading to find out things, to put time to good use, to keep abreast of current affairs – is very clear from the statistical distribution of magazine preferences. Apart from the women's magazines we have already discussed, women's interests – which also include an informational component – centre on magazines relating to the home and home-based activities, such as crafts, while also including magazines concerned with the body as an object of health and nutritional care. Men's interests, by contrast, centre on informational magazines – arts, news, scientific and nature magazines – which, except for those that focus on hobbies, are overwhelmingly concerned with the world outside the home. Sport and pornography, of course, also address the body, but in quite different ways from health and nutritional magazines in their construction of, in the first case, usually male bodies in competitive struggle and, in the second case, usually female bodies laid bare before a dominating male gaze.

Some aspects of these differences come through in how men describe their magazine reading as well as in how their reading is described by their wives. Grant typifies, although in an extreme form, the documentary and pragmatic approach to reading of many men when he describes his interest in the *Australian Business Monthly*:

> Again we get it at work. I have a bit of a skip through. I have a bit of a look, again you pick out the articles that you are interested in. I get engineering magazines, packaging magazines. Again it's have a look at the index, nothing in it this month. Chuck it away.

Dorothy gives us a nicely distanced anthropological perspective on the strange reading habits of the male – described by Kate Legge as obsessively centred on '"how to" manuals' (Legge 1997: 5) – in speaking of the singular passion of her husband, an electrical engineer, for electronic magazines: 'But he's probably never read a complete book, I'm sure. But all he's interested in is electronic stuff. The kids call it his books of numbers because that's all it appears to be – lots of little numbers.'

Again, there are exceptions here. Nigel and his wife, Muriel, who reverse the usual division of household responsibilities with Nigel doing the cooking and looking after the house while Muriel maintains the car and does all the mechanical and electrical repairs about the house, practise a similar reversal of reading interests. Nigel, an avid reader with a strong preference for fiction of various kinds, when asked whether reading was a joint interest, replies: 'Muriel doesn't read. She only reads things like manuals and things like that.' As a general tendency, however, it is clear both that what we read and the kinds of cultural values and interests invested in our reading are significantly influenced by our gendered formation. This situation becomes more complicated when we take other factors into account, but rarely in a manner which entirely overrides the role of gender. This will become clear when, having looked – as we do next – at the role of class and education in organising and differentiating reading practices, we return to consider how questions of gender interact with class and education in the social patterning of reading preferences.

Social Class, Education and Literary Culture

In his biography of Paul Keating, John Edwards recalls a conversation in which Keating, while indicating that he 'enjoyed books' and thought that 'writing was fine', placed painting and music on an altogether different aesthetic level. 'They are up here, he said, his hand moving right up in the air' (Edwards 1996: 428). This reflects a fairly typical masculine hierarchy of artistic forms, particularly in the status it accords music as an activity which – witness the almost exclusively male readership for music magazines recorded in table 6.3 – recruits high levels of male involvement. But this is not to say that books and reading play an unimportant role in relation to

social processes of distinction. To the contrary, reading of any kind is frequently regarded as having a higher value than many other cultural activities: watching television, for example. Describing television as mostly an
'insult to our intelligence', Lilian is clear that she would 'rather read a book
than watch all that drivel', while Barbara also stresses that she would rather
read than 'veg in front of the television'. It is clear, however, that we need
to pay close attention to the feminisation of literary culture when considering the role education plays in the acquisition and transmission of literary
forms of cultural capital as well as the role which such capital plays in processes of class formation.

That said, the role of education in organising reading practices is both clear
and marked. Level of education significantly affects the extent to which reading
is a regular activity. Of those who have completed a tertiary education, 72.8%
read often, compared with 50% of those who have only some secondary education. While this disparity is not as marked in relation to newspaper
reading – indeed, at roughly 50% each, those with only primary education are
just as likely to read a newspaper on a daily basis as are those with tertiary
qualifications – the effects of education are clear in relation to newspaper
choice. As table 6.4 shows, except for a slight dip in the case of those with
post-secondary vocational qualifications, a preference for national daily
broadsheets rises consistently with level of education. Equally, preferences for
daily tabloids and Sunday papers as well as for local, regional and provincial
city papers tend to be highest for those with only primary and secondary
education or those whose post-secondary education has been mainly vocational. Metropolitan dailies, by contrast, recruit their readership much more
evenly from across the full range of educational cohorts, while readers of the
ethnic press are noticeably concentrated among those with low levels of formal
schooling, accounting for 6.7% of those with only a primary education.

Level of education also gives rise to significantly different relationships to
book culture as manifested by book-buying and book-collecting habits. The
tendency to acquire books mainly by purchasing rather than borrowing them
from a library or from friends increases consistently with level of education
from 32.3% of those with only primary schooling to 51.1% of those who
have completed their tertiary education. It is equally clear that those with
higher levels of education are more likely to own significant book collections. Whereas 6.5% and 5.1% of those with primary schooling and incomplete secondary schooling report owning book collections of between 100
and 200 titles, the comparable figures for those who have completed secondary schooling and for those who have completed a tertiary education are
13.9% and 24.8% respectively.

Level of education plays an equally significant role in determining what
kinds of books people buy and collect as well as their preferences between
different genres. In table 6.5, the different levels of educational attainment

Table 6.4 Newspaper preferences (first choice only) by level of education

	Primary	Some sec.	Comp. sec.	Voc./appr.	Part tert.	Comp. tert.
National daily broadsheets	5.5	6.1	8.9	7.9	21.6	33.5
Metropoli-tan dailies	22.6	17.3	20.8	18.5	27.4	20.1
Daily tabloids	18.1	20.9	23.0	24.3	14.1	14.2
Sunday papers	9.7	6.9	8.8	7.5	4.9	5.4
Provincial city papers	8.8	12.6	10.4	11.7	6.5	4.5
Regional papers	5.9	7.9	4.1	8.8	5.4	3.9
Local papers	16.5	21.4	15.0	18.0	7.6	11.7
Ethnic press	6.7	0.7	0.6	0.0	0.5	0.2

Note: national daily broadsheets comprise the *Australian*, the *Sydney Morning Herald* and the *Age*; metropolitan dailies comprise the *Adelaide Advertiser*, the *West Australian*, the *Mercury*, the *Courier-Mail* and the *Canberra Times*; and daily tabloids the *Telegraph-Mirror* and *Herald-Sun*.

Table 6.5 Ownership of type of book by level of education

	Primary	Some sec.	Comp. sec.	Voc./appr.	Part tert.	Comp. tert.
Literary classics	19.9	35.0	38.4	37.8	61.4	74.8
Art books	15.1	22.7	31.1	31.8	39.1	54.2
History books	34.6	45.2	55.2	50.2	61.2	74.0
Biographies	23.2	37.3	48.0	48.2	62.3	72.1
Poetry	20.6	30.2	39.1	35.7	52.8	59.9
Mean	*22.6*	*34.1*	*42.4*	*40.7*	*55.3*	*67.0*

have been arranged to show how far they are associated with the ownership of aesthetic and documentary books. The final row here shows that, on average, those with tertiary qualifications, with ownership rates of 67%, are about three times as likely to own such books as are those with only primary education (22.6%) and about twice as likely as those with some secondary schooling (34.1%). It is worth noting that, in the case of literary classics, the gradient of difference is somewhat steeper, rising from 19.9% for those with primary schooling to 74.8% for the tertiary-educated.

It is noticeable that here, as in their newspaper reading habits, those with post-secondary vocational education often have lower levels of involvement in aesthetic or educational culture than do those who have completed their secondary schooling but not undertaken any post-secondary study. This becomes particularly clear when, as in figure 6.2, we look more closely at the influence the type of post-secondary educational qualification has on the books people choose to buy and own. Two general tendencies can be noted. The first, not surprisingly, is that those who obtain trade certificates have lower rates of ownership of all of the aesthetic and documentary genres we surveyed than do those with degrees or diplomas. It is also clear that, except for art books, the acquisition of a diploma is more likely to be associated with high rates of ownership of such genres than is the acquisition of a degree. Although, at first sight, somewhat puzzling it is likely that this reflects the role accorded literature and history as generalist elements in teacher-training curricula, whereas those with bachelor degrees also include the graduates of science, business, engineering and other programs unlikely to include literature or history components.

We shall return later to consider the roles that these different kinds of post-secondary schooling play in training personnel for different class positions. While still looking at patterns of ownership, it is important to consider the relative roles of income and education. Some of the differences in ownership patterns considered above can also be related to differences in income: the ownership of literary classics, for example, ranges from 37.9% for those with household incomes of less than $15 000 a year through 50% for those in households with annual incomes of between $20 000 and

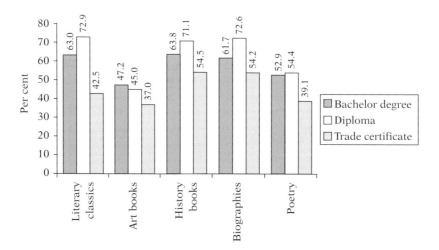

Figure 6.2 Ownership of type of book by tertiary qualification

$40 000 to 68.7% of those with more than $80 000 a year. However, when level of income is controlled, level of education plays a significant differentiating role within each band of household income. For each income group, in fact, level of education affects ownership rates by a minimum of 32 per cent (for households with less than $15 000 per annum, the range is from 35.1% for those with some secondary schooling to 67.3% for the tertiary-educated) and a maximum of 40 per cent (in households in the $40–60 000 per annum income band, those with incomplete secondary schooling logged ownership rates of 26.8% compared with 67.3% for the tertiary-educated).[8]

A similar set of relationships between level of education and official literary hierarchies is evident when genre preferences are taken into account. In table 6.6 genres have been assigned to the educational cohorts with which they have the strongest association: romance fiction, for example, has been assigned to those who have completed their secondary education, on the basis that the members of this educational cohort are, at 19.9%, more likely to read romances than are the members of each of all the other educational cohorts. The figures in the second column then average out the preferences for romance fiction within these other cohorts. The ratio in the final column offers a measure of the strength of the connection between a genre and the educational cohort to which it has been assigned in indicating how likely it is that members of that cohort will include the genre in their favourite reading when compared with the average for all other educational cohorts. Those who have completed their secondary education are thus 172% more likely to read romances than are the members of other cohorts when averaged together. The result is a hierarchy of reading practices arranged by level of education which matches, almost exactly, the ways in which genres are ranked in conventional literary hierarchies. The degree to which the aesthetic and intellectual genres of high culture are most strongly associated with those who have completed a tertiary education is particularly marked. The exception here is poetry which is most strongly associated with those who have incomplete secondary education. The likely explanation for this is that poetry is a more fluid genre description than, say, classical authors or contemporary novels and that positive responses to this option might include a wide range of forms – from the classic works of the poetic canon to bush poetry and religious verse – spanning conventional high/low distinctions. Owning poetry, as we have seen (table 6.5), produces a more expected set of correlations.

Education also plays a role in differentiating responses to the two questions we asked in order to explore attitudes to reading. The first of these asked respondents to indicate what they most enjoy when reading fiction – a good story, interesting characters, literary quality, a complicated plot or experimental writing – in the expectation that the choice of literary quality would correlate strongly with a high degree of involvement in literary and

Table 6.6 Genre preferences by level of education

	Strongest preference by level of education	Average preference of other levels of education	Strongest as % of average preference
Tertiary completed			
Classical authors	12.5	3.1	403
Contemporary novels	23.9	9.6	249
Political	5.6	2.3	243
Historical	19.1	9.9	193
Scientific	6.7	3.8	176
Biographies	24.4	15.2	161
Part tertiary			
Science fiction	16.6	8.9	187
Educational	15.2	10.5	145
Vocational/apprenticeship			
Occult	3.7	1.3	285
Travel, exploration	22.0	11.4	193
Erotica	6.1	3.4	179
Sport & leisure	19.7	11.1	177
Humour/comedy	22.6	15.7	144
Crime/murder/mystery	27.3	23.8	115
Thriller/adventure	32.3	28.3	114
Completed secondary			
Historical romance	11.0	6.4	172
Romance	19.9	11.7	170
Some secondary			
Poetry	6.6	3.1	213
Horror	8.2	4.2	195
Primary			
Cooking	17.2	12.5	138
Garden	15.8	12.1	131
Craft/hobbies	13.1	11.4	115

aesthetic culture. The second question asked respondents whether they prefer stories with a definite ending or open-ended stories, on the supposition that a preference for the latter would indicate a preference for 'modern' forms of writing over traditional realist literary forms and so would also serve as a rough-and-ready index of degree of involvement in literary and aesthetic culture. Patricia, a secretary with largely conservative cultural tastes, illustrates the connection between a preference for stories with a definite ending and traditional literary tastes we had in mind here.

PATRICIA I like, I only like British books. I'm very set in some of my ways. I don't like American novels. I hardly like even Australian novels. I like British books and I like old-fashioned type books and I like, I like murder type things . . .

INTERVIEWER And I'm interested because there's a question here about whether you prefer when stories have a definite ending or an open ending . . . you have actually put that you really do like a 'definite ending'?

PATRICIA Yeah, that would be right. I like something to be tidied up.

These expectations were confirmed by the high degree of correspondence between preferences for these options and other indicators of a high involvement in literary and aesthetic culture – the ownership of literary classics, art books and poetry, for example. Table 6.7 thus tells us that 91.1% of those who look mainly for literary quality in their reading own literary classics while 71.6% of those with similar interests own art books and 79.1% own poetry. Preferences for experimental writing and for open-ended narratives show a similar tendency, with both correlating especially strongly with the ownership of literary classics.

In a famous section in *Distinction*, Pierre Bourdieu, when discussing reactions to a photograph of the gnarled hands of an old woman, interprets the ability to abstract from the emotive and representational aspects of the photograph and to speak, instead, about its formal and symbolic qualities as the manifestation of what he calls an aesthetic disposition – a capacity, understood in its Kantian sense, of being able to take a disinterested pleasure in form for form's sake – whose possession increases with level of education and social position (Bourdieu 1984: 44–5). We can see similar processes at work when we relate the indicators of an aesthetic disposition in the literary field to level of education. In table 6.8, the preferences for open-ended stories, literary quality and experimental writing thus all increase significantly with level of education – from 1.2% of those with primary education looking for literary quality to 8.4% of those with tertiary education, for example – while the preferences for good stories and complicated plots are much more evenly distributed across the different educational cohorts. Education thus plays a significant role in cultivating a capacity to distinguish between the formal aspects of literary texts and their content, as well as a preference for the former over the latter. Perhaps just as important as the positive findings produced by these two questions is the high rate of nil responses they produced and, more important still, their distribution. The high rates of nil response on the part of those with low and medium levels of education – 41 per cent on both questions for those with primary education and 14 per cent for those who had completed secondary education –

Table 6.7   Attitudes to reading according to book ownership

	Good story	Interesting characters	Literary quality	Compli-cated plot	Experi-mental writing	Definite endings	Open-ended stories
Literary classics	47.9	64.3	91.1	55.8	68.1	51.1	61.0
Art books	33.2	48.4	71.6	39.4	48.5	35.7	51.6
Poetry	41.5	61.3	79.1	45.5	56.5	44.5	56.1

Table 6.8   Story type preference and aspects of fiction most enjoyed according to level of education

	Primary	Some sec.	Comp. sec.	Voc./appr.	Part tert.	Comp. tert.
Open-ended stories	3.7	4.9	7.2	11.6	14.5	17.9
Good story	43.6	59.4	62.4	60.8	64.0	57.0
Interesting characters	2.9	7.2	9.6	11.2	16.6	13.6
Literary quality	1.2	1.7	3.4	1.3	3.1	8.4
Complicated plot	7.5	5.5	6.0	4.0	4.8	6.6
Experimen-tal writing	0.0	0.2	0.4	0.0	0.6	1.5

contrasted with the low nil-response rates of between 7 and 9 per cent for the tertiary-educated. These differences highlight the role education plays in cultivating the capacity to understand questions concerned to probe different types of response to literary texts.

Similar tendencies are evident when reading practices are correlated with class, with two important differences. First, the degree of variation in the literary tastes and preferences of different classes is often less pronounced than that between different educational cohorts. Second, while, with the caveats already noted, involvement in high literary culture increases in direct proportion to educational attainment, the pattern is more uneven when it comes to questions of class. The class which is dominant in terms of its economic position – employers – tends to be middle of the range in terms of the aesthetic weighting of its literary preferences. The class which, on all indicators, exhibits the highest levels of literary taste and involvement is that comprised of professionals, with managers usually following a somewhat distant second. These two classes tend to read more than the members of all other classes, except that employers read newspapers more regularly than other classes, and they have the highest rates of overall book ownership. Their newspaper reading also tends strongly towards the quality end of the market. Professionals, at 34.6%, exhibit the highest rate of readership of national daily broadsheets followed by managers at 24.2%, with employers, the self-employed and supervisors all following on with rates in the 15–16 per cent range and falling to 5 per cent for manual workers. The range of variation in the class make-up of the readership of metropolitan dailies is relatively small, ranging from a low of 19.1% for para-professionals to a high of 28.4% for managers. Supervisors are the most avid readers of daily tabloids at 25.7% followed closely by employers at 24.1% and then by sales and clerical and manual workers at 22.1% and 23.1% respectively. These last two classes, at 16 per cent and 20 per cent, are, together with the self-employed at 18 per cent, the most deeply involved in the local press. Professionals, however, have the lowest levels of interest in local papers (8.2%) as well as in regional (2.8%) and provincial city papers (4.7%) and, in this respect, their interests are usually echoed by managers.

There is, then, a clear class pattern here, with the two classes whose members are most reliant on certificated competencies for their social positions and advancement tending clearly – and in marked contrast to the two employing classes – to read papers with a quality and a national focus, while supervisory and working-class readers, both white- and blue-collar, tend most towards the tabloid press and papers with a parochial focus. Professionals and managers also exhibit the highest rates of involvement in literary culture. Table 6.9, comparing rates of ownership of different types of book, offers a measure of the extent to which different classes are involved in literary culture. The high rate of difference – 70 per cent compared with 49 per cent – between the means for professionals and employers here makes clear the lack of a close fit between the distribution of literary forms of cultural capital and the distribution of economic forms of class power.

This is also evident when we consider the class distribution of genre preferences. Table 6.10 assigns genres to classes on the basis of the class with which they are most strongly associated compared with the average for all other classes. It is notable that, except for poetry, which – somewhat puzzlingly, but again probably reflecting the fuzziness of definition which characterises this genre – is most strongly associated with employers, the high literary genres are most clearly associated with professionals, while the genres of popular fiction which enjoy the highest status – crime and science fiction – are most strongly associated with managers and supervisors.

A consideration of choice of favourite authors throws further light on this pattern of class choices (see table 6.11). Employers exhibit an unusually strong interest in the male-centred thriller formula of Wilbur Smith who, along with Stephen King, also rates as the author within this top-ten list who is most preferred by manual workers. The strong preference of professionals for Jeffrey Archer is equally notable. We should add, however, that the pattern of responses to these questions makes it clear that they functioned as much as a test of an ability to name authors as a measure of preference. The overall rate of response was thus low, with less than half the sample nominating a favourite author. Just as important, the inclination or ability to answer this question varies in accordance with both level of educational attainment and class position, with the lowest rates of response coming from those with only a primary education and manual workers. There is also a discernible pattern to the inclusion of literary authors within answers to this question in that classical authors (Brontë, Dickens, Austen, Shakespeare, Hardy, Tolstoy, Lawrence, etc.) are included across a broader spectrum of class choices than are contemporary authors. Margaret Attwood, Peter Carey, Thomas Keneally, Doris Lessing, Ruth Rendell, Patricia Cornwell, David Malouf and P.D. James are thus more likely to be included in the choices of managers, professionals, employers, and the self-employed than in those of the other classes. This is likely to reflect the fact that the names in the first group enjoy a broader social currency than those in the second so that, when a name is needed to answer a question, these are the ones more likely to come to mind.

It is important, when considering figures of this kind, to take account of the gender make-up of these different class categories, especially the marked predominance of men among employers, the self-employed, managers and manual workers, 65 per cent of whom are men, and the predominance of women among supervisors and, in particular, sales and clerical workers, 81 per cent of whom are women. This clearly accounts for the strong preference of sales and clerical workers for the genres of romance fiction, and of manual workers for sport. It also affects the pattern of preferences for individual authors: when manual workers' choice of Wilbur Smith is broken down in gender terms, he emerges as the preferred author for 35% of

Table 6.9 Ownership of type of book by class

	Emp.	Self-emp.	Mgr	Prof.	Para-prof.	Supv.	Sales/cler.	Manual
Literary classics	52.1	46.9	57.0	79.8	47.1	40.3	47.3	28.2
Art books	36.1	38.8	46.1	52.2	33.6	31.5	33.6	22.8
History books	58.3	59.2	75.6	76.1	53.0	56.5	52.8	43.7
Biographies	53.3	55.2	75.3	78.0	50.0	51.7	49.0	35.6
Poetry	45.1	45.1	49.9	65.0	36.3	39.9	43.3	29.7
Mean	*49.0*	*49.1*	*60.8*	*70.2*	*44.0*	*43.9*	*45.2*	*32.0*

Table 6.10   Genre preferences by class

	Strongest class preference by level of education	Average of other class preferences	Strongest as % of average preference
Employers			
Poetry	5.2	3.1	168
Self-employed			
Humour/comedy	18.1	15.3	118
Managers			
Crime/murder/mystery	34.3	25	137
Thriller/adventure	40.6	35.6	114
Professionals			
Classical authors	13.7	4.4	311
Contemporary novels	28.8	12.4	232
Political	5.5	3	183
Historical	19	10.6	179
Craft/hobbies	16	10.6	151
Biographies	26.2	18.4	142
Educational	14.9	10.8	138
Scientific	6.8	5.2	130
Para-professionals			
Occult	3.2	1.7	188
Travel, exploration	19.2	12.8	150
Supervisors			
Science fiction	13.3	9.2	145
Sales/clerical			
Romance	28.8	9.9	291
Historical romance	13.2	7.7	171
Cooking	18.9	11.4	166
Manual			
Horror	7.2	3.4	212
Gardening	17.6	9.2	191
Sport & leisure	19.1	12.1	158
Erotica	4.9	3.4	144

the male manual workers but only 4.9% of the female manual workers comprising this component of the sample. Similarly, among those including these top-ten authors in their first choices, Jeffrey Archer is much more likely to be nominated by male (47.5%) than by female (20.9%) professionals.

Table 6.11 Favourite authors by class, first preferences only (column percentages)†

	Emp.	Self-emp.	Mgr	Prof.	Para-prof.	Supv.	Sales/cler.	Manual
Stephen King	4.1	16.2	11.4	10.4	23.7	16.2	17.9	29.0
Wilbur Smith	56.9	28.0	16.2	10.4	14.3	23.3	8.4	19.9
Agatha Christie	18.9	13.2	4.7	13.8	10.8	7.3	13.0	7.1
Danielle Steel	0.0	9.0	0.0	1.6	7.8	12.0	16.4	5.8
Jeffrey Archer	0.0	6.3	19.6	36.0	15.0	4.1	8.2	0.8
Virginia Andrews	0.0	4.9	16.8	3.3	3.8	6.4	8.4	16.5
Catherine Cookson	0.0	8.0	6.8	2.9	7.1	7.0	5.8	9.7
Sidney Sheldon	5.2	3.4	0.0	6.2	4.6	10.9	8.1	5.1
Bryce Courtenay	15.0	2.7	14.0	8.5	2.6	2.4	10.5	5.8
Tom Clancy	0.0	8.3	10.6	6.9	10.3	10.6	4.3	0.4

† The percentages in this table relate solely to the class members who included these ten authors within their first preferences.

This naturally raises the question, when gender and class are considered together, of their respective roles in determining reading practices. Table 6.12 throws some light on these questions. Its purpose is to identify cases where a specific class effect is strong enough to modify significantly the regular gendered pattern of literary tastes and preferences. The first column expresses the likelihood that men of a particular class will read a particular genre as a percentage of the likelihood that women of the same class will read that genre. Thus, in the case of managers where 32.7% of men read crime fiction and 38.8% of women, the first column tells us that male managers are 84 per cent as likely to read crime fiction as female managers. A plus sign has been appended to the male-to-female ratio of preferences for specific classes given in the first column for those genres where that ratio is significantly higher than the male-to-female ratio of the sample average, given in the second column. Thus, in the case of the self-employed, the high male-to-female ratio of preferences for humour is a more extreme manifestation of the male preference for this genre that is evident at the level of the whole sample. A minus sign (−) indicates where, in the case of a specific class, the ratio of men to women readers is significantly less than that for the sample as a whole. Thus, whereas, in the sample as a whole, men are more likely to include thrillers in their favourite reading than women, this is not true for managers where women's preference for this genre outweighs men's. An equals sign indicates where there is no significant difference between the class-specific and the sample ratios.

It is reasonable to conclude that, in the case of both types of deviation from the sample norm, reading is subject to a specific class effect that is manifested in the distinctive articulation of gendered preferences that it

Table 6.12   Genre preferences by class and gender†

	Male as % of female (class specific)	Male as ratio of female (sample average)
Employers		
Poetry	36 (=)	34
Self-employed		
Humour	188 (+)	132
Managers		
Crime/murder/mystery	84 (=)	79
Thriller/adventure	81 (−)	115
Professionals		
Classical authors	44 (=)	44
Contemporary novels	33 (=)	29
Political	721 (+)	418
Historical	230 (+)	176
Craft/hobbies	78 (+)	55
Biographies	53 (=)	57
Educational	57 (−)	98
Scientific	734 (+)	591
Para-professionals		
Occult	135 (+)	94
Travel, exploration	322 (+)	173
Supervisors		
Science fiction	266 (=)	279
Sales/clerical		
Romances	7 (=)	7
Historical romance	8 (=)	7
Cooking	39 (+)	25
Manual		
Horror	95 (−)	126
Garden	115 (=)	116
Sport & leisure	797 (=)	815
Erotica	228 (−)	414

† (+) = male/female ratio significantly higher than sample average
  (−) = male/female ratio significantly lower than sample average
  (=) = male/female ratio roughly the same as sample average

organises. That said, the meaning and significance of this class effect are sometimes obscure. What aspects of the class situation of working-class women would account for their particularly strong liking for horror stories? Why should occult literature be so popular with male para-professionals? If the answers to these questions are not clear, there are, in other cases, some speculations that might be advanced. It seems likely, for example, that, for women managers, a preference for thrillers forms part of a habitus in which, in order to operate effectively within a predominantly male class milieu, tastes and preferences are regularly masculinised. It is also likely that the patterns of identification associated with thriller reading may relate particularly well to the situation of women exercising senior forms of responsibility in the workplace: a form of 'power reading' which functions as the literary equivalent of power dressing. The most systematic set of class effects, however, is registered in relation to professionals in the unusually strong male bias towards factual and documentary genres – political, historical, and scientific – that this class exhibits. Of course, women professionals retain a marked preference for aesthetic literary genres, but this is no more true of women professionals than it is of women as a whole. It is rather in the unique importance of historical, scientific and political reading to male professionals that the class-specific effect consists.

The calculations in table 6.13 throw a different light on these questions in comparing the male-to-female ratios for different class involvements in aesthetic culture as measured by ownership of works of classical literature, art books and poetry. The pluses and minuses in this table indicate where the male-to-female ratio for a particular class – arrived at in accordance with the same principles applied in table 6.12 – departs significantly from the sample average, while an equals sign denotes that the class and sample ratios are more or less the same. We can see here that male professionals are more likely to own works of classical literature than are men as a whole, but less likely to own art books while just about as likely to own poetry. For professionals, then, as for managers and the self-employed, there are no consistent class effects relating to the ownership of aesthetic genres of a kind that would disturb the gendered patterns of ownership for the sample as a whole. This is not true of employers as the only class in which the male-to-female ratio increases across the board, suggesting that for male employers owning, as distinct from preferring, high-cultural texts has a distinctive value as a symbol of class position. However, the most regular set of class effects evident in this table concerns the almost universal tendency for the male-to-female ownership of such texts to fall significantly below the sample average for para-professionals, supervisory, sales and clerical, and manual workers. Since, among both sales and clerical workers and manual workers, women's ownership of these types of book is below the sample average, this is clear evidence of the degree to which both white- and blue-collar working-class men are radically dissociated from literary culture.

Of course, these are not the only aspects of the relations between class, gender, education and reading that would need to be taken into account in a full discussion. The strong association of science fiction with supervisory workers, for example, resonates well with the findings of other studies – by

Table 6.13 Book ownership by class – male as percentage of female†

	Emp.	Self-emp.	Mgr	Prof.	Para-prof.	Supv.	Sales/cler.	Manual	*Mean*
Literary classics	81 (+)	70 (−)	69 (−)	83 (+)	60 (−)	48 (−)	68 (−)	71 (−)	*75*
Art books	79 (+)	96 (+)	69 (=)	63 (−)	43 (−)	44 (−)	69 (=)	62 (−)	*69*
Poetry	66 (+)	61 (−)	63 (=)	62 (=)	44 (−)	61 (−)	55 (−)	59 (−)	*64*

† (+) = male/female ratio significantly higher than sample average

  (−) = male/female ratio significantly lower than sample average

  (=) = male/female ratio roughly the same as sample average

John Tulloch and Henry Jenkins (1995), for example – which have traced the relationship between an interest in science fiction and the development of modern forms of scientific and technical training connected to the organisation of the workplace and the exercise of authority within it. That horror should be of particular interest to women readers among the manual working classes is also partially explicable in terms of the strong links, examined in convincing detail by Ken Gelder (1994), between the formal and thematic properties of contemporary forms of horror fiction and the female-centred sexual codes of the gothic romance.

The general pattern, however, is reasonably clear. Literary forms of cultural capital are most strongly associated with professionals and managers in a manner which reflects the degree to which both the acquisition and maintenance of their class position is dependent on the certificated intellectual competencies they have acquired through the education system. The chief exception to the strong association between involvement in literary culture, class position and level of education is to be found among those with vocational forms of post-secondary training which, in their diversity, are associated with a more varied range of literary tastes just as they distribute individuals to a more varied range of class destinations. It is also clear, finally, that literary capital within the professional and managerial classes takes different forms for men and women, with the documentary and factual bias of men's reading in these classes being counterbalanced by the stronger interest of women class members in literary and aesthetic genres. Men, it seems, are, in this sense, more likely to 'read by numbers' than women in a pattern which confirms our general argument that the class salience of particular forms of cultural capital is affected by gendered relations and practices that have their own histories, contemporary formations and effects.

Chapter 7

Music Tastes and Music Knowledge

Any assessment of music as an object of cultural choice must recognise that it remains the field in which traditional hierarchies of aesthetic value have been most enduring. Nowell-Smith has observed that if there is any surviving significance in the 'two cultures thesis', then it is in the world of music:

> On the one side stands the classical repertoire of mainly eighteenth- and nineteenth-century music which continues to be performed, in a manner unaffected by changes all around, with twentieth-century music occupying a restricted and uncomfortable place on the fringe; and on the other side is the frenetically innovative world of the pop business. (Nowell-Smith 1987: 86)

Perhaps the most obvious consequence of the dichotomy that Nowell-Smith describes is the obligation for us to engage with, although not necessarily to adopt without question, the genre categorisations – 'highbrow', 'middle-brow' and 'lowbrow', 'elite' versus 'mass or commercial', 'serious' versus 'popular' – which have been deployed by previous researchers. We recognise that there is now a conventional wisdom shared by musicologists, sociologists of popular culture and cultural theorists alike which holds that popular music – at least in its embodiment as rock – has its own aesthetic (e.g. Chester 1990; Frith 1983, 1987); but because our own concerns are descriptive rather than evaluative or prescriptive, the challenge posed to traditional theories of aesthetic value by these debates is of secondary significance for us. Moreover, we shall argue later in the chapter that contrasts between 'high' or 'elite' and 'popular' or 'commercial' are of less use in accounting for participation in the realm of music than the categories 'inclusive' and 'restricted', terms we have introduced in earlier chapters.

It is, however, worth considering at the outset a related issue which stems from the polarity ascribed to music. More than in any other domain, tastes in music have been seen as unusually sensitive barometers of more general cultural dispositions. The canonical exposition of this view is, of course, to be found in Bourdieu, for whom music preferences and musical knowledge can be viewed as the markers of 'legitimate culture' par excellence. It is no accident that he dwells to a considerable extent in *Distinction* on the music tastes of the French. Indeed, his first empirical evidence concerns familiarity with works of classical music and the association between this cultural disposition, and social origin and educational capital. Bourdieu summarises the relationship this way:

> nothing more clearly affirms one's 'class', nothing more infallibly classifies, than tastes in music. This is of course because, by virtue of the rarity of the conditions for acquiring the corresponding dispositions, there is no more 'classificatory' practice than concert-going or playing a noble instrument (activities which, other things being equal, are less widespread than theatre-going, museum-going or even visits to modern-art galleries). But it is also because the flaunting of 'musical culture' is not a cultural display like others: as regards its social definition, 'musical culture' is something other than a quantity of knowledge and experiences combined with a capacity to talk about them. Music is the most 'spiritual' of the arts of the spirit and a love of music is a guarantee of 'spirituality'. (Bourdieu 1984: 18–19)

Bourdieu's reflections on music in this passage are symptomatic of a more general indifference displayed throughout *Distinction* towards popular culture. There is certainly something anomalous about his classification of musical taste into three 'zones',[1] each of which is entirely occupied by classical works and by French singers and performers. In a world in which the global provisioning of popular music has become the most pervasive influence on musical tastes, Bourdieu's zones are of dubious value as a model for replication in a different national context. We shall not dispense with Bourdieu entirely, for there are some aspects of his general thesis linking social background, education and musical knowledge which we propose to consider later in the chapter. But our first priority will be to frame our discussion around the taste cultures of popular music.

Bourdieu's argument that musical tastes stand as a privileged indicator of cultural capital (or its absence) has been mirrored in academic discussions of popular taste. Consider, for example, the following observation from Simon Frith. Bourdieu's interest, Frith argues,

> is in the creation of a taste hierarchy in terms of high and low:
> the possession of cultural capital, he suggests, is what defines
> high culture in the first place. My point is that a similar use of
> accumulated knowledge and discriminatory skill is apparent in low
> cultural forms and has the same hierarchical effect. (Frith 1996: 9)

Low culture, to use Frith's term, has its own forms of capital which are
apparent not only in the more specialised types of dance or club cultures
(see Thornton 1996) but also among the fans – the ones investing the time
and energy in accumulating knowledge – of the most popular musicians and
performers, television shows or sports. 'Popular' music tastes, moreover,
reveal a more heterogeneous ensemble of structural associations than the
world of 'serious' music, where educational background appears the primary
determinant. The point is made again most concisely by Frith:

> Different groups possess different sorts of cultural capital, share
> different cultural expectations and so make music differently – pop
> tastes are shown to correlate with class cultures and subcultures;
> musical styles are linked to specific age groups; we take for granted
> the connections of ethnicity and sound. (Frith 1987: 134–5)

Although these broad connections have frequently been drawn, it is still
the case that we know surprisingly little about the *detailed* structure of
musical tastes – in either their 'serious' or their commercial forms. The
study of popular music has, of course, been a major topic in cultural
studies, but the focus of research has tended to be almost entirely on the
organisation of the music industries or the analysis of music texts: particular genres, performers, music videos.[2] Despite the centrality of music to
everyday life, detailed empirical evidence of musical tastes – the focus of
this chapter – is difficult to come by. What little knowledge we have is
concerned with the tastes and preferences of youth, and as a consequence
refers almost entirely to the consumption of popular formats (Australian
Broadcasting Tribunal 1985; Turner 1993). To date there have been no
studies which have attempted to survey the musical tastes of Australians
in their entirety.[3]

   In what follows, we shall look first at the overall structure of music preferences: which are the most popular genres of music; which are the most
disliked; and what are the most salient demographic variations in this
picture? We then consider the more detailed patterns which the combinations of preferences and dislikes reveal. Our data suggest that musical tastes
are more complex than the conventional genre categorisations allow, and
that we need to think of them as embodying different regimes of value.
Finally, we return to Bourdieu and consider the relevance of his structural
model in relation to knowledge of classical works and composers, as well as

something of the practices of music – the ownership of musical instruments and exposure to musical training – within the home and school.

'If the Music's too Loud you're too Old'

Music is a significant ingredient in the lives of most Australians. As we noted in chapter 3, the overwhelming majority of households contain the appropriate technologies – radios, CD or record players, cassette tape players – for receiving broadcast and playing recorded music. Listening to music is the most common form of domestic recreation, with nearly two-thirds of our sample reporting that this was an activity in which they often engaged. Approximately half of Australian households own at least one musical instrument. But what precisely is being listened to, played and enjoyed?

A recent feature article by the *Sydney Morning Herald*'s rock critic, Bruce Elder, gives us some clues about what to expect. In a passionate defence of its aesthetic form, Elder argued that the appeal of popular music – 'unquestionably one of the 20th century's pre-eminent art forms' – is its ability to resonate with every age group:

> To acknowledge this simple and obvious truth is to marvel at the magic of the medium. Here is a musical form which can have three year olds bouncing around their play group; have angst-ridden adolescents poring over lyrics with all the earnestness of Eng. Lit. academics; have suburban mums getting misty-eyed for a life they can only dream about, and have geriatrics singing along in a soggy orgy of nostalgia for times long past and dimly remembered. (Elder 1997: 8)

Our data confirm Elder's diagnosis of the universal appeal of popular music. Over a fifth of our sample nominated 'easy listening' as their preferred form of music, with almost half giving it their first, second or third preference. 'Rock' and 'top 40 pop' each attracted approximately 15 per cent of first choices, and 'country and western' a further 9 per cent. Collectively these four genres attracted over 60 per cent of first choices, with the top ten accounting for nine out of ten first preferences. Table 7.1 provides the summary figures for the distribution of choices for the complete list of music genres available to our sample, arranged in rank order from most to least popular. The figures in the left-hand column indicate the percentage distribution of first preferences, whereas the right-hand column shows the combined percentage who nominated the genre as one of their three favourites.

Although there are some minor changes to the rank order of the genres when we consider the combined preferences – for example, light classical becomes more favoured than classical; musicals, blues and folk all leap-frog above alternative rock – the picture does not change substantially. Accordingly we

Table 7.1 Favourite music genre – rank order by genre

Music genre	1st choice (column percentages)	Combined choices
Easy listening	22.9	48.4
Rock	15.9	34.4
Top 40 pop	14.6	34.9
Country and western	9.0	24.7
Classical	7.8	15.8
Light classical	7.0	21.8
Alternative rock	4.1	8.3
Musicals	3.7	14.4
Blues	3.2	13.0
Religious	2.6	6.4
Folk	1.9	10.6
Heavy metal	1.6	5.3
Big band	1.5	7.4
Modern jazz	1.3	5.6
Traditional jazz	1.0	6.5
Soul	0.9	5.2
Techno	0.9	4.6
Opera	0.6	4.5
World	0.3	1.4
Avant-garde	0.2	0.5

will generally use the figures for first choice, which allow us more easily to demonstrate the relative attractiveness of each genre.

Before we look at the structure of these tastes in more detail, it is perhaps worth reflecting on the analytical coherence of these genre categories and the degree to which they are tapping mutually exclusive musical experiences. What kind of music does someone have in mind when he or she selects 'easy listening' as their favourite? To what extent is the musical space they inhabit different from others who opt for 'top 40' or 'rock' as their first preference? One way in which this can be explored – although this is by no means a definitive answer to these questions – is to look for evidence that will help pinpoint the musical content of these categories more precisely. The *Australian Everyday Cultures* project questionnaire provided such evidence in the form of an open-ended question which asked our respondents to name their favourite musician, singer or composer.[4] If we examine these data we find that there is, indeed, evidence of overlap between the genre groups. For example the top named favourite for *both* the 'easy listening' and the 'top 40' sub-groups is John Farnham. The same performer, moreover, is ranked fourth in the list of favourites for those who choose 'rock' music as their first preference. The Beatles head the list of named favourites of rock devotees, but they are also in fifth place in the ranking for those who have opted for 'top 40' as their favourite music. Of course, there are many named performers who are unique to each of the sub-group lists of favourites, but they tend to be the less well known or less popular figures. Based on the qualitative evidence from the open-ended questions, we conclude that there is a considerable degree of permeability between the boundaries of these categories, and a musical core which is common to the top three popular genres.[5]

Table 7.2   Preferred music genre by gender (column percentages)

Music genre	Women	Men
Easy listening	25.6	18.2
Rock	12.4	19.8
Top 40 pop	17.5	11.6
Country and western	7.0	11.1
Classical	7.2	8.4
Light classical	9.1	4.6
Musicals	4.0	3.4
Alternative rock	3.1	5.2
Religious	3.3	1.8
Blues	1.2	5.3
Folk	2.3	1.1
Big band	1.3	1.8
Modern jazz	0.9	1.7
Heavy metal	0.1	3.1
Traditional jazz	1.1	0.9
Soul	1.5	0.3
Opera	0.8	0.4
Techno	1.0	0.8
World	0.3	0.3
Avant-garde	0.2	0.1

How does this taste structure vary demographically? We look first at the gendered nature of music preferences. Table 7.2 shows the distribution of first preferences for women and men for each genre. The figures here are again dominated by the popularity of the top six genres, with the result that the gendered character of the less popular musical forms is harder to discern. In table 7.3 we therefore present a more detailed picture of the gendered nature of these choices. This table is derived from the combined preferences for each music type, and has been organised to indicate those

Table 7.3 Combined music genre preferences by gender (column percentages)

Genres with no gender differences	'Female' genres	'Male' genres
Classical	Light classical ***	Heavy metal ***
Avant-garde	Musicals ***	Rock ***
Traditional jazz	Religious ***	Blues **
Modern jazz	Easy listening ***	Alternative rock **
Big band	Top 40 **	Folk **
	Soul *	Techno **
	Opera *	Country & western *

* p <0.1; ** p <0.001; *** p <0.0001

genres for which there is no difference in gender preference, those which are more likely to be favoured by women, and those to which men are more disposed.[6]

Some minor changes can be observed when comparing first preference with the combined first, second and third preferences. 'Classical' and 'modern jazz', which are marginally favoured by men as a first choice, show no gender difference when the combined total of preferences is considered. 'Folk' moves from being a genre favoured by women on the basis of first preference to one which is more masculine in disposition in aggregate terms; 'country' music, strongly marked as masculine on the basis of first preference, gains female support as second or third favourite. Overall, however, the figures confirm the findings of a number of other studies (Christenson & Peterson 1988; Fox & Wince 1975; Gantz et al. 1978) that there is a stronger masculine affinity for 'lowbrow' harder music genres – heavy metal, rock, blues and alternative rock – while women have more eclectic tastes, preferring light classical as well as a mix of 'middlebrow' (musicals, easy listening) and 'lowbrow' (top 40 pop) genres.

It is important not to lose sight of the fact that, despite this masculine affinity for the 'harder' genres, easy-listening music is still the second most popular type of music overall with men, and top 40 pop the third. Despite the more 'feminine' profiles of these genres, a considerable number of men obviously like them; clearly these are not the same men who are opting for genres such as heavy metal, rock and blues. Gender can tell us something about musical tastes, but other demographic factors are at work as well.

We might expect age to make a significant contribution, and the figures confirm that it does. Table 7.4, presenting the breakdown of genre preferences by age, lends support for the findings of previous studies (Australian Broadcasting Tribunal 1985; Hirsch 1971; Denisoff & Levine 1972) which have documented the place of popular music in youth culture. Top 40 pop ranks as the clear favourite of younger Australians, with a third selecting it

Table 7.4   Music genre preferences by age (column percentages)

Music genre	18–25	26–35	36–45	46–59	60+
Easy listening	9.3	23.0	29.2	29.0	25.5
Rock	21.7	25.4	16.9	7.3	0.2
Top 40 pop	33.6	21.4	15.3	5.5	1.0
Country and western	2.6	3.8	7.8	18.3	15.6
Classical	1.6	4.0	7.3	12.4	11.3
Light classical	0.6	0.8	3.8	10.1	20.2
Musicals	0.3	0.8	2.1	2.8	9.4
Alternative rock	13.7	5.0	2.3	0.0	0.0
Religious	1.3	1.8	1.7	4.1	2.9
Blues	1.0	3.4	4.4	2.1	0.4
Folk	1.0	1.4	3.0	2.7	1.9
Big band	0.6	0.4	0.7	1.6	5.4
Modern jazz	1.9	1.2	2.1	1.1	1.5
Heavy metal	4.5	3.8	0.0	0.0	0.0
Traditional jazz	0.0	0.6	0.5	1.2	2.9
Soul	1.3	2.6	1.4	0.4	0.0
Opera	0.0	0.2	0.9	0.9	1.3
Techno	4.8	0.0	0.2	0.0	0.0
World	0.0	0.2	0.1	0.5	0.6
Avant-garde	0.3	0.4	0.4	0.0	0.0

as their first choice. Top 40 and alternative rock both decline uniformly as preferred choice as age increases, but rock music departs from this trend by being more popular with the 'generation X' cohort aged between 26 and 35 than with the young. Indeed, rock music is this cohort's favourite genre. In contrast, several other genres – light classical, musicals and big band music – all increase in popularity as age increases. The 20.2% of older Australians who favour light classical music account for the dip in the otherwise regular trend to favour classical music as age increases. Easy-listening music is the clear favourite with the three oldest age cohorts and the second favourite with the 26–35 group. Among the young it ranks only in fourth position, with less than one in ten giving it their first preference.

A number of genres yield more irregular profiles. Country and western music reaches its maximum popularity with the age cohort in mid to late middle age (46–59), where it ranks as the second favourite before declining marginally. Folk and blues are both more attractive to people in middle age than they are with the young or the old. Traditional jazz (but not modern) is favoured to a greater extent by older people; and 'techno' is entirely the choice of the young, where it rates as the fifth favourite genre, just ahead of heavy metal.

Informative as they are, these figures provide no obvious answers in themselves for *why* we like the music that we do and *why* age seems to matter so much when it comes to music tastes. Is it because these questions seem so self-evident that they are barely considered in depth in the literature? George Lewis' suggestion that 'the central fact is that *we pretty much listen to, and enjoy, the same music that is listened to by other people we like or with whom we identify*' (Lewis 1992: 137, emphasis in original) is no doubt accurate in broad outline but is not particularly informative. And Frith, although more erudite, is not significantly more helpful. For Frith, each of us hears the music that appeals to us the most

> as something special, as something that defies the mundane, takes us 'out of ourselves', puts us somewhere else. 'Our' music is, from this perspective, special not just with reference to other music but, more important, to the rest of life. It is this sense of specialness (the way in which music seems to make possible a new kind of self-recognition, to free us from everyday routines, from the social expectations with which we are encumbered) that is the key to our musical value judgements. (Frith 1996: 275)

Again this is plausible, but it has more than a trace of tautology about it. The issue that these age-related trends raise in its starkest form is this: are we witnessing cohort effects or rather something that is better understood as the changes in taste that come 'naturally' with the process of aging? We deal with this matter in more detail in chapter 8, but it is worth looking briefly at what is at stake here. The issue is whether tastes are relatively durable and are largely formed at a particular point in the life-cycle, or whether tastes in music, and in cultural activities more broadly, are subject to an evolution over the course of the life-cycle.[7] Given that our statistical data cannot resolve this matter, it may be useful to consider our respondents' reflections on their music tastes.

There is certainly evidence from the qualitative interviews we undertook that many of those who were in middle age had retained the music preference of their late teens and early adulthood. Nigel, a residential care officer now in his 40s, had remained a fan of Elvis Costello since encountering him in his early 20s; Grant, a UK migrant in his late 40s, was one of many males of a similar age for whom the Beatles were enduring favourites. Brian, a 39-year-old radiographer, listed David Bowie, Lemonheads and Divinyls as his favourite musical performers. He elaborated on the reasons for this as follows, as well as admitting to still enjoying his participation in the youth music scene:

> **BRIAN** Ah yeah, I'm a big David Bowie fan.
> **INTERVIEWER** So that has remained fairly constant for you?

BRIAN Yeah. I suppose it was one of the things in my last couple of years at high school I sort of discovered David Bowie before he became successful. I think you always link to people like that who subsequently become successful and you feel that somehow, I remember them when. Everyone else likes Bowie now but I liked him before anyone else. It's more than that now . . . I've gotten older and he has pursued different musical things, he has taken me in new musical directions. I have a lot of time for Bowie.

INTERVIEWER And what about some of the other contemporary, alternative music bands?

BRIAN Well, at the moment, certainly in Brisbane bands are fantastic like Regurgitator. Powder Finger are pretty commercial but I quite like Powder Finger, I suppose for someone a bit older. I've been to see a couple of concerts lately. I went to see You Am I and Powder Finger were their support act. I went with my daughter and then I went and saw a concert of Powder Finger and Regurgitator recently. I was standing up the back, of course. The young people thought I was a doorman or something. I still like to go.

Simon, an office administrator also in his mid-30s, although no longer an active concert-goer spoke in rapt terms of his recollections of seeing Bruce Springsteen – his favourite performer – live on stage:

SIMON That guy put on the best concert that I've ever seen in my life. Twelve years ago now it played two nights in a row. Yeah, it was just before Easter and there were five of us. I was living in Adelaide and we had to go across to Melbourne to see it. We just headed off in a car. One of the guys who was there – his friend over in Melbourne got us the tickets, we got the tickets for two nights. We set off on Monday night, drove half way, got there on the Tuesday, the concerts must have been Tuesday and Wednesday and we stayed basically in Melbourne because it was Easter. We drove back on the Sunday so we didn't have to worry about traffic hassles on the Monday. So basically we just spent a week in Melbourne and saw Bruce Springsteen twice and I could have died quite a happy man that night.

For each of these men the music of their young adulthood – essentially 1970s rock – had an enduring appeal. This was not the only example we found. Yvonne, a social worker in late middle age, recalled the influence her mother had on her own music tastes and those of her children:

YVONNE My mother particularly. My father was not so interested. My father was a lovely man but he's an engineer, you see, and I grew up with this sort of stereotype. Whereas my mother, she had all the high culture embedded in her. So, she went to things a lot. But, my dad would never have turned up. She'd meet up with her sister and they'd go to a concert. Even right up to the time she died she would go; she would take my children, little children, to free recitals at the Opera House. She was always doing that sort of thing.

When asked about her children's musical tastes and whether she had maintained this interest in their cultural edification Yvonne was more circumspect:

> **YVONNE** None of them goes to the opera, probably because they can't afford it. But the eldest – she can afford to, she will go to quality music. All of them are interested in a wide range of music I have to say. But one of them – her partner is in a rock band . . .
> **INTERVIEWER** Right ha ha.
> **YVONNE** Hah hah. So you know, I've made it very clear to him and to her that, although I love him dearly, I really am *not* going, I am not going! He had a gig in London actually, when I was there on one occasion, and I was sort of torn and thought, well, maybe I should go and show the family flag but no. No way! I couldn't.

Although we cannot discount the possibility that some people will undergo radical changes in their tastes as they age, on balance the evidence appears to favour the explanation that the tastes acquired in the formative years of a cohort persist into later life. But even if tastes endure in this way, we still need to recognise that not everyone the same age has the same tastes: variations in choice are clearly apparent not only between but within cohorts. To account for these we must consider the contribution of other factors, and the most obvious would seem to be education.

The relationships between educational level and music preferences are shown in Table 7.5. To avoid the repetition of data on genres attracting very few choices we have given only the results for the top six music genres, which between them cover the taste hierarchy. For each genre we present the proportion of our sample, in rank order of level of education, who selected the genre as their first preference.

The first observation we can make about these data is that there is still clear evidence of the effects of age working through these educational cohorts. Those with incomplete tertiary education – who are generally the young – are the *most* likely to select top 40 pop music as their preferred type of music, and the *least* likely to choose easy listening, country and western and light classical. In contrast, the primary-educated – generally older people – are the *least* likely to choose rock and top 40 but *most* likely to favour country and western and light classical. Only two genres – classical, and country and western, conventionally regarded as occupying opposite

Table 7.5 Music genre preferences by highest level of education

Easy listening		Rock		Top 40 pop	
Comp. sec.	25.6	Vocational	21.1	Part tert.	19.5
Primary	24.6	Some sec.	19.9	Vocational	18.0
Some sec.	22.7	Part tert.	15.4	Comp. sec.	17.4
Vocational	20.5	Comp. tert.	15.3	Some sec.	12.7
Comp. tert.	17.5	Comp. sec.	13.4	Comp. tert.	11.5
Part tert.	17.4	Primary	2.4	Primary	2.8
Mean	*21.4*	*Mean*	*16.3*	*Mean*	*14.9*

Country & western		Classical		Light classical	
Primary	32.8	Comp. tert.	16.9	Primary	12.2
Some sec.	12.4	Some sec.	8.6	Comp. sec.	9.7
Vocational	11.1	Comp. sec.	6.1	Comp. tert.	7.3
Comp. sec.	8.7	Primary	5.7	Some sec.	6.6
Comp. tert.	3.8	Part tert.	5.6	Vocational	4.9
Part tert.	1.4	Vocational	1.3	Part tert.	2.8
Mean	*9.0*	*Mean*	*7.9*	*Mean*	*6.9*

poles of the taste hierarchy – come close to mirroring the structure of educational attainment. Classical music is rated most favourably by those who have completed tertiary education, and they are almost twice as likely to choose this genre as the next-highest group, those with some secondary education.[8]

Educational attainment appears, however, to have the greatest effect at the bottom of the taste hierarchy with country and western music. This genre displays the greatest disparity between the cohort which most favours it (primary-educated: 32.8%) and the group for whom it is least likely to be the first preference (incomplete tertiary: 1.4%). Even if we discount this age-affected result, it is still the genre which records the most marked difference between the extremes of the education spectrum: a ratio between the primary- and tertiary-educated of 8.63:1.

Classical and country and western music are again the two genres most strongly marked by class preference, using cultural rather than economic capital as our measure. As Table 7.6 shows, classical music is the genre which records the greatest disparity, with nearly one in five of professionals selecting it as their favourite compared with less than 3 per cent of manual workers. Manual workers, by contrast, head the hierarchies of preference for the two prominent 'lowbrow' genres, country and western and rock music, with professionals at or very close to the bottom of both of these genre hierarchies. As with the education data, however, there are some unanticipated patterns in the class structuring of taste. Managers appear to be

Table 7.6 Music genre preferences – first choice rank order by class

Easy listening		Rock		Top 40 pop	
Managers	26.0	Manual	18.3	Sales & clerical	23.2
Para-professionals	25.0	Para-professionals	15.9	Supervisors	17.6
Supervisors	24.9	Managers	15.6	Manual	15.6
Self-employed	24.5	Self-employed	15.4	Employers	15.2
Sales & clerical	23.2	Sales & clerical	14.0	Para-professionals	11.1
Employers	22.9	Employers	11.6	Professionals	10.7
Professionals	20.8	Professionals	10.8	Managers	8.6
Manual	19.0	Supervisors	10.6	Self-employed	8.4
Mean	*22.8*	*Mean*	*14.3*	*Mean*	*15.3*

Country & western		Classical		Light classical	
Manual	15.6	Professionals	18.5	Managers	14.2
Self-employed	11.0	Managers	10.3	Employers	8.8
Managers	9.6	Employers	8.7	Self-employed	8.2
Supervisors	9.1	Self-employed	8.6	Professionals	7.7
Employers	7.6	Supervisors	5.1	Sales & clerical	7.3
Para-professionals	7.0	Sales & clerical	5.0	Para-professionals	6.8
Sales & clerical	5.0	Para-professionals	4.3	Supervisors	6.5
Professionals	3.2	Manual	2.9	Manual	3.9
Mean	*8.7*	*Mean*	*7.0*	*Mean*	*7.0*

surprisingly heterogeneous in their musical tastes; they are the class fraction most likely to favour light classical music, but they also head the ranking for easy listening music and are closer to the top than the bottom in the preference orders for rock, country and western, and classical music. Manual workers are the least likely to favour not only classical and light classical but also easy listening music, where they are just below professionals at the bottom of the hierarchy.

Finally we note that migrants from northern and southern Europe, as well as those from the UK, are significantly more likely to favour classical and light classical music and, in the case of European immigrants, easy listening music than the Australian-born. In part this no doubt reflects the demographic composition of these migrant populations. Those born in European countries are generally older than the Australian-born and, as we have noted, those in professional occupations are overrepresented among the UK-born. Asian migrants appear less attracted to the highbrow genres and overwhelmingly select easy listening music as their first choice (37.8%). There is also support for country music among the Asian-born, with the proportion favouring this genre (10.9%) slightly higher than that of the Australian-born. Aboriginal people are, however, over twice as likely to choose country music as their first preference (20.8%) compared with non-Aboriginals, and to favour blues (8.3%) and alternative rock (8.4%) disproportionately to about the same level.

Our research also looked at the types of music which Australians say they most *dislike*. Conventional interpretations of the 'elite to mass' cultural hierarchy hold that, in addition to high-status people valuing elite cultural forms and practices, such people are likely to actively disavow or reject the taste cultures of people beneath them in the hierarchy (Gans 1966, 1974). In relation to music preferences we have already seen that there is evidence of considerable heterogeneity of choice. But what of the forms of music which Australians dislike? Is there a corresponding heterogeneity in the pattern of genres that are rejected?

The reverse is in fact the case. There is a stunning uniformity in the pattern of musical dislikes, with almost half of our sample (48.3%) citing heavy metal as the type of music they most dislike, a figure that rises to almost three-quarters (71.3%) when second and third dislikes are included. The almost universal rejection of this genre which other researchers have reported (Bryson 1996) is equally evident among Australians. However, the types of music which are second and third in the list of dislikes – opera and religious music – are conventionally seen as clustering near the top of the hierarchy of genres. Twelve per cent of Australians name opera as their most disliked music, with 37.1% rejecting it overall. Religious music similarly attracted 11 per cent of first nominated dislikes and 34 per cent overall.

To an extent these dislikes are also gendered. Women are far more likely than men to name heavy metal as the music they most dislike (55% to 41%), and men correspondingly outnumber women in their rejection of opera and religious music. There are some differences in this structure of antipathy when class or educational attainment is taken into account, but these are largely attenuated once gender is controlled for. Managers (58%), employers (56%) and professionals (55%) are all more likely to reject heavy metal music than other classes but the difference is only noticeable in relation to manual workers. Even here 38 per cent of manual workers, easily the largest proportion of this category, nominate heavy metal as their most disliked music. But the difference between male and female manual workers is exceptional: 55 per cent of women in manual occupations reject heavy metal music, but the equivalent figure for men is only 29 per cent.

The variation that does exist in the pattern of music dislikes is, again, largely a function of age. Table 7.7 and figure 7.1 show the breakdown of music dislikes for each age cohort.[9] Heavy metal music is the genre most disliked by *all* cohorts, rising from 25 per cent among the 18–25 group to almost three-quarters with the cohort aged 60 and over. But the aggregate figures once again disguise the part that gender is playing: young women are more than twice as likely as young men to reject this genre (33% to 14%).

Table 7.7 Most disliked music genre by age

Music genre	18–25	26–35	36–45	46–59	60+	*Mean*
Heavy metal	24.9	30.4	47.9	65.1	72.5	*50.9*
Opera	21.1	21.3	14.9	8.5	4.4	*13.2*
Religious	22.5	21.1	12.9	7.4	2.6	*12.2*
Techno	11.9	12.6	8.4	5.3	2.6	7.7
Rock	0.7	1.2	2.0	3.7	13.3	*4.5*
Country & western	8.1	6.2	4.0	2.5	0.8	*3.9*

In fact young men are more likely to dislike techno music (16%) than they are heavy metal.[10]

The Structure of Preferences: Omnivores and Univores

So far we have dwelt on the subject of musical likes and dislikes by considering almost entirely the first nominated choice in each case. But our data allow us to look in more detail at relationships in the total pattern of music preferences. Each of the participants in our survey was asked to indicate their first, second and third preference, and then their first, second and third most disliked form of music. By considering all these choices simultaneously we can arrive at a more detailed understanding of how the various music genres are related. The statistical technique most appropriate for exploring common patterns in such ranked data is factor analysis or principal components analysis.[11]

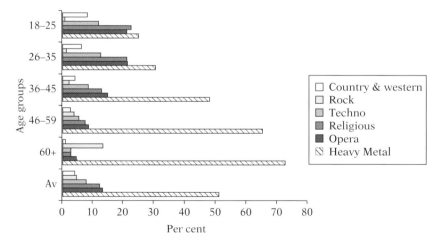

Figure 7.1 Most disliked music genre by age

Table 7.8 shows the results of a principal components analysis undertaken on the combined structure of choices. The first part of the table (A) looks only at the relationships occurring in the three preferences, whereas the second part (B) is based on a combination of all the genres named as likes and dislikes. The factor structures identified by these procedures are broadly similar, but there are some important differences.

In the 'likes only' section we see that the first factor identified is the preference for the highbrow genres, classical and opera. But what is also identified in this first factor is an indifference to 'easy listening' music. This is not the same as a rejection: it simply means that those who are choosing classical and opera music among their three favourite genres are also *not* selecting the easy listening genre as one of their favourites. But easy listening music is also evident as a constituent part of factor 2, which identifies a hardcore youth genre comprising heavy metal, alternative rock and rock. For this sub-group, easy listening music is even more likely not to be included as a preference than was the case with 'highbrow' (factor 1) respondents. This point is worth emphasising: the *most* popular genre overall is the *least* likely to have been chosen as favourite by the two groups who occupy *opposing* ends of the music taste hierarchy.

Factor 3 in the 'likes only' analysis identifies a preference for light classical and musicals and an indifference towards top 40 pop and techno. This factor is in some respects difficult to explain, as these are all 'feminine' genres; significantly, this is the only one not to be retained once the music dislikes are included in the analysis. Factor 4 identifies a shared preference for folk and country and western music and to some extent religious music, and, again, an indifference towards top 40 pop. It appears to invoke a 'rural populist' as opposed to 'commercial urban' ethos. Factor 5 collects people with a shared interest in big band and jazz music; while Factor 6 identifies a preference for 'black' music genres, blues and soul, and an indifference to techno music.

The second part of the table, generated from the combination of likes and dislikes, contains a number of changes. Most importantly, factor 1 now appears to be identifying a more explicit 'elite to mass' taste structure in that it combines a liking for the three highbrow genres and opposes these to rock and top 40. This suggests that although highbrow respondents are indifferent to easy listening music as one of their preferences, they are not actively nominating this as a dispreferred genre. In contrast, factor 2 *does* suggest that those whose preference lies with the hardcore 'lowbrow' genres also actively dislike easy listening music and to a lesser extent country music. The remaining factors are substantially unchanged, although there is some reordering in the factor loading positions.

Clearly, then, we have evidence of music sub-cultures: a preference for elite music combined with an opposition to both commercial pop and rock;

Table 7.8 Factor pattern matrix of music genre tastes†

A: 'Likes only'	Factor 1	Factor 2	Factor 3	Factor 4	Factor 5	Factor 6
Classical	**76***	−7	1	5	7	4
Opera	**67***	−7	10	0	−13	−5
Heavy metal	−10	**64***	10	−4	−13	−8
Alternative rock	−6	**60***	−10	5	11	−1
Rock	−16	**50***	−22	−28	−31	24
Easy listening	**−41***	**−56***	25	−3	−15	−4
Light classical	24	−13	**62***	−1	4	−4
Musicals	−3	6	**57***	−13	6	−15
Avant-garde	14	−2	−23	12	20	−3
Folk	−1	−1	−18	**63***	−3	−2
Country and western	−31	−27	−14	**59***	−16	−5
Religious	17	8	9	**37***	−3	−10
Top 40 pop	−17	−4	**−47***	**−49***	−27	−34
Big band	−20	−5	12	−4	**63***	−15
Modern jazz	4	4	−22	−6	**54***	9
Traditional jazz	4	0	14	−4	**54***	6
Blues	0	13	−13	−12	2	**72***
Soul	4	−17	−29	−20	5	**47***
Techno	9	8	**−35***	−21	6	**−49***

B: 'Likes and dislikes combined'	Factor 1	Factor 2	Factor 3	Factor 4	Factor 5	Factor 6
Opera	**72***	−9	−1	0	−6	−19
Classical	**67***	10	1	9	−2	−15
Light classical	**58***	−14	2	−19	−1	8
Musicals	29	−21	−4	−25	−9	22
Rock	**−47***	**39***	−23	19	−14	**−36***
Alternative rock	−14	**65***	−1	−9	−10	19
Heavy metal	−33	**58***	−21	0	−15	−17
Easy listening	−14	**−67***	−4	−16	−16	−1
Folk	−1	8	**72***	−7	−8	−6
Country & western	−32	**−36***	**55***	−14	−9	0
Religious	28	−30	**42***	−1	−6	1
Top 40 pop	**−48***	−6	**−50***	−10	−19	−6
Soul	−2	−9	−19	**66***	−10	12
Blues	−7	16	2	**65***	15	−7
Traditional jazz	11	0	7	5	**67***	−1
Modern jazz	−2	8	−17	17	**60***	4
Big band	−13	−16	−2	−26	**58***	−12
Avant-garde	−12	6	5	20	−4	**70***
Techno	−7	7	−19	**−39***	−8	**55***

† Factor loadings have been multiplied by 100 and rounded to the nearest integer; the threshold value is set at 0.35.

a strong (masculine?) preference for hardcore rock opposed to (feminine?) easy listening; a rural-versus-commercial musical contrast; and so on. The elite-to-mass factor, in particular, points towards support for one of the traditional hierarchies of music taste, whereas our earlier examination of the structure of first preference suggested there was a good deal of slippage away from such hierarchical rankings, with support for the popular genres among many of the higher-status respondents. How might we extend the analysis further to resolve these potentially conflicting views?

Richard Peterson's suggestion that the taste cultures of contemporary societies have witnessed a historical shift from an elite-to-mass scale to one which is more adequately theorised in terms of a contrast between 'omnivorous' and 'univorous' cultural consumption is helpful in this respect. Peterson and his colleagues (Peterson 1992; Peterson & Simkus 1992; Peterson & Kern 1996) argue that high-status people no longer confine their cultural tastes and practices to the traditional or elite art forms, but rather have a much wider repertoire of cultural interests and, in part, gain their prestige by knowing about and participating in a variety of cultural practices. As a metaphor for capturing this more generalised cultural taste Peterson has coined the term 'omnivore'. In place of the older 'snob to slob' dichotomy, the new model postulates a contrast between high-status people who exhibit 'omnivorous' cultural profiles, and those at the base of the stratification order who, on the basis of their more restricted taste structure, are referred to as 'univores'. We shall adopt Peterson's terminology in the following discussion, but his distinctions can readily be subsumed within the contrast we have drawn in earlier chapters between forms of cultural participation which are 'inclusive' and those which are 'restricted'.

Peterson's point of departure in rethinking the idea of taste structures is provided by Gans' work on mass culture. Although critical of some of the elements of the mass society debate, Gans' (1967, 1974) conception of 'taste cultures' remains one of the most important contributions to it.[12] A taste culture, for Gans,

> consists of the painting and sculpture, music, literature, drama and poetry; the books, magazines, films, television programs; and even the furnishings, architecture, foods, automobiles and so on, that reflect similar aesthetic standards and are chosen by people partly for this reason. People who make similar choices among these products, and for the same aesthetic reasons, will be described as a taste public . . . [taste publics and cultures] are not official bodies or organised groups but aggregates of similar people making similar choices, and aggregates of similar content chosen by the same people who can be identified by sociological research. (1967: 551, 582)

The idea of 'choice' is central to Gans' notion of taste culture. By conceptualising all taste cultures as actively embraced by their constituent audiences and with each having its own specific aesthetic standards, Gans sought to challenge the notion of a homogeneous mass culture which was commercial, derivative and offering only spurious gratification to passive or duped audiences (1967: 551–2). In its place Gans offers a model of a pluralistic society in which active consumers make cultural choices on the basis of aesthetic standards commensurate with the level of education they have achieved. But Gans' ideal was also a society in which people should be given opportunities for cultural mobility through educational improvement which will lead them 'naturally' to prefer the higher taste cultures. Gans thus retains a hierarchical conception of taste cultures, organised primarily along lines of social class and with an assumption of the intrinsic superiority of the 'high' taste cultures.

For Peterson, then, the defining characteristic of 'elite to mass' theory is the clear correlation between the stratification order and cultural taste. Those at the top of the hierarchy favour the elite arts and music genres and reject all others. Those in the middle gravitate towards more derivative or 'midbrow' cultural tastes; and those at the bottom express no interest in the elite forms, favouring the popular or commercial genres.

Looking specifically at the relationship between occupational status and music preference, Peterson argues that the hierarchical model of the taste and stratification relationship would be better conceptualised as a pyramid. According to Peterson and Simkus (1992), there is widespread agreement that classical music is at the top of the music taste hierarchy, but there is much less consensus on the rankings of the genres lower down. Rather than a 'slim column of taste genres one on top of the other' (Peterson & Simkus 1992: 168), they argue that the taste structure has one elite genre (classical) at the top, and then an increasing number of alternative music forms having more or less taste value moving down the pyramid towards the base. Peterson and Simkus propose that 'folk', 'jazz', 'middle-of-the-road', and 'big band' music are located about the middle of the pyramid, with 'rock', 'religious music', 'soul' and 'country and western music' near the base.

Peterson and his co-researchers found it difficult, however, to map their occupational status model to this taste pyramid. Only 28.9% of their highest-ranking occupational status group – 'higher cultural professionals' – said that they liked classical music best. Even more disturbing for the elite-to-mass theory was the fact that more of this group preferred country and western music – a genre at the base of the taste pyramid – than opera. These apparent mismatches led them to suggest that the idea of the taste-exclusive highbrow and the corresponding snob-to-slob taste ranking had become 'obsolete'. Generalising from their study of music taste, Peterson and Simkus found:

> mounting evidence that high-status groups not only participate
> more than do others in high-status activities but also tend to par-
> ticipate more often in most kinds of leisure activities. In effect elite
> taste is no longer defined as an expressed appreciation of the high
> art forms (and a moral disdain or bemused tolerance for all other
> aesthetic expressions). Now it is being redefined as an appreciation
> of the aesthetics of every distinctive form ... Because status is
> gained by knowing about and participating in ... all forms, the term
> omnivore seems appropriate. (Peterson & Simkus 1992: 169)

If those at the top of the status structure are more accurately thought of
as having omnivorous cultural tastes, then those at the base who appear to
be more easily able to choose one genre of music that they like the best or
who are actively involved in only one aesthetic tradition should be designated 'univores'. The linkage between the taste structure and the status structure can thus be likened to two pyramids, one the right side up and the other
inverted:

> In the first representing taste cultures there is at the top one elite
> taste culture constituting the cultural capital of society and below
> it ever more numerous distinct taste cultures as one moves down
> the status pyramid. In the inverted pyramid representing concrete
> individuals or groups, there is at the top the omnivore who com-
> mands status by displaying any one of a range of tastes as the sit-
> uation may require, and at the bottom is the univore who can
> display just one particular taste ... With the data available we have
> been able to glimpse most clearly the workings of these two pyr-
> amidal structures in the case of music taste. Here the elaborated
> musical taste code of the omnivore member of the elite can acclaim
> classical music and yet, in the proper context, show passing knowl-
> edge of a wide range of musical forms. At the same time persons
> near the bottom of the pyramid are more likely to defend their
> restricted taste preference, be it religious music, country music, the
> blues, rap, or some other vernacular music, against persons espous-
> ing other lower status musical forms. (Peterson 1992: 254–5)

What evidence do we have for Peterson's omnivore/univore distinction
within the Australian context? The defining characteristic of a music omnivore for Peterson is someone whose musical tastes embrace quite distinct
genre classifications: that is, someone who likes music genres conventionally
regarded as 'highbrow' as well as genres which are seen as 'middlebrow' or
'lowbrow'. An omnivore, in other words, exists only when these constituent
types are first established. In determining these categories we have drawn,

in part, on Peterson's own criteria as well as taking into account the results of the factor analysis reported above. Elsewhere, Peterson (Peterson & Kern 1996: 900–1) defines a highbrow as someone liking both classical music and opera and who chooses one of them as their preferred musical genre. This would appear to correspond closely to the respondents identified by factor 1 in our analysis. We propose to follow the factor analysis structure based upon likes and dislikes which combines 'opera', 'classical' and 'light classical' genres. In our terms, then, a highbrow is someone whose first, second and third preferences in music are restricted to these three genres (although they can occur in any order).[13]

Middlebrow music genres for Peterson and Kern are 'mood/easy listening, Broadway musicals, and big band music', genres which 'have been in the mainstream of commercial music throughout the twentieth century' (1996: 901). These types of music do not load as a combined factor as was the case for the highbrow genres; indeed, the first two are not part of any of the factor combinations. But the fact that they are absent from the factor structure is a good reason to regard them as ideal middlebrow forms, as it suggests that their appeal is generalised across the sample rather than being a specialised taste grouping. Finally, lowbrow genres for Peterson are 'country music, bluegrass, gospel, rock and blues'. There are obvious national differences in genre categories between the US and Australia which mean that a faithful replication of lowbrow genres is not possible with our data. Instead, we propose to define the lowbrow category as comprising a preference for country and western, rock and top 40 pop, again in any order.[14]

An omnivore, then, is someone whose musical preferences cross these taste boundaries. Seen in these terms there are, in fact, several possible types of omnivore to be found, depending on how these movements are mapped. In the first place there are a number of 'partial' omnivore types. We can use the term 'highbrow' omnivore to refer to someone whose three preferred taste genres consist of any two highbrow genres and any one of the various lowbrow genres. A 'lowbrow' omnivore, by contrast, is someone whose three favourite music types are a mixture of any two lowbrow genres and any one of the highbrow music types. There are, of course, several other logically possible partial types of omnivore: those whose taste structure involves various combinations of highbrow and middlebrow taste, and the various forms of middlebrow and lowbrow hybrids. Finally, there is the complete or 'ideal type' omnivore: someone whose three favourite music genres are drawn from each of the pure taste types. To simplify the following analysis, we shall concentrate upon the ideal type omnivore and the two partial omnivore types who appear to have travelled the greatest distance in cultural space: the highbrow and the lowbrow omnivore.

Our results suggest that the highbrow omnivore type is as unlikely to occur as the pure highbrow. Only 1 per cent of our sample have music tastes which are designated by this category, a figure which is too small for analysis. We will therefore look only at the 'lowbrow omnivore' and the 'ideal type omnivore'. Just over a quarter of Australians (25.5% of our sample) have music tastes which allow them to be categorised as 'lowbrow omnivores'; a further 8.3% are classifiable as ideal type omnivores.

What are the characteristics of the two groups? Is there support for Peterson's proposal that those most culturally credentialled are the main source of omnivorous music taste? We note first that the omnivore types vary significantly in their age profiles. As age increases so the likelihood of having lowbrow omnivorous taste decreases. As figure 7.2 shows, over 40 per cent of the two youngest cohorts are classifiable as 'lowbrow omnivores', but the proportion falls away dramatically with the remaining age cohorts.

An alternative explanation of this trend is to view it as evidence of a broadening of musical taste among young people. To recall: a lowbrow omnivore in our schema is someone who is closer to the more popular commercial genres but who also has a minority interest in the 'higher' genres. We came across this combination of tastes on several occasions in our focus group

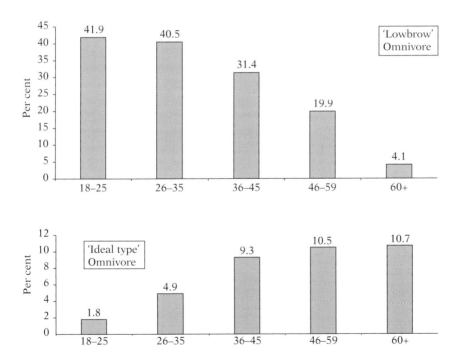

Figure 7.2 Omnivore types by age (percentage of cohort classified as omnivore type)

discussions and interviews. Robert, a 20-year-old clerical worker at an Ipswich abattoir, claimed to listen to most forms of music:

> **ROBERT** All the time really, *really* loud. Varies anything from Def Leppard, Metallica, all the way through to Ice House.
> **INTERVIEWER** That's heavy metal?
> **ROBERT** Yeah, heavy metal to middle-of-the-road Australian rock. Occasionally, I listen to classical every now and then, and jazz. Anything but country. I'll puke if anyone puts country on.

Andrew and Brad, both university students, reconciled their equally catholic tastes as follows:

> **ANDREW** Well, I don't know about Brad but my musical tastes tend to be broad. My two favourite albums are Mozart's *Requiem* and Metallica's *Master of Puppets*. They're a heavy metal band. Other than that, generally the stuff I like to listen to tends to fall into the category of classical, which I just include into basically anything that is even vaguely orchestral ... then general rock which might include bands like the Beatles, David Bowie, Jimmy Hendrix.
> **BRAD** 70s stuff ...
> **ANDREW** Very definitely!
> **BRAD** I tend to shift to more mainstream rock and roll, jazz and rhythm and blues sort of music. But I do like heavy metal – I'm not really interested in the classical music – apart from that we have very similar tastes.
> **INTERVIEWER** Just going back to Andrew – your two favourite albums would be a Mozart album and a heavy metal album?
> **ANDREW** Yes.
> **INTERVIEWER** Do you see anything strange about picking things which are almost – from one point of view – things which are diametrically opposed?
> **ANDREW** Well, I am aware that it is unusual. But I tend to look at music a lot from a technical point of view. Particularly the guitar work in the Metallica songs often seems very reminiscent of the same sort of technicality that you would find in the classical stuff.

Ideal type omnivores, in contrast, are generally older, but there is little difference in the proportion of each cohort who fall into this category after the age of about 40. But of more concern to us is the distribution of the two omnivore types along class lines.

Figure 7.3 shows that the rank order by class location for the lowbrow omnivore is an almost exact inverse match of the categories of our

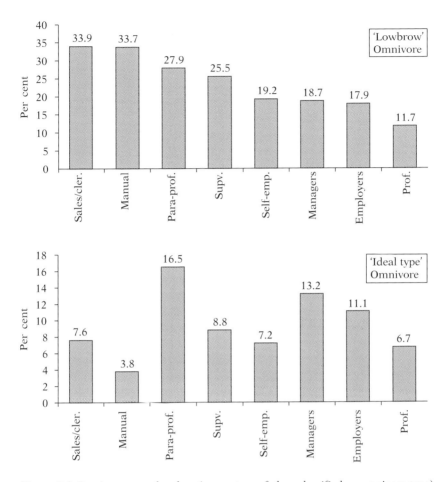

Figure 7.3 Omnivore types by class (percentage of class classified as omnivore type)

model when the possession of credentialled forms of knowledge or expertise (in essence, cultural capital) is used as the yardstick. Significantly, professionals – the category with most similarity to Peterson's 'higher cultural workers' – contain the lowest proportion of this partial omnivore type. A more relevant test of his omnivore hypothesis, however, would be based upon the incidence of the ideal type omnivore. Are these disproportionately recruited from the ranks of professionals as Peterson would predict? Our data suggest otherwise: with the exception of manual workers, professionals contain the lowest number of ideal type omnivores.

How can we account for this apparent inconsistency? Is Peterson incorrect in his suggestion that people with the most cultural capital are the most likely source of omnivorous taste? One way of resolving this question is to deal separately with two categories which are analytically fused in Peterson's work. Recall that for Peterson 'the elaborated musical taste code of the omnivore member of the elite can *acclaim* classical music and yet, in the proper context, show *passing knowledge* of a wide range of musical forms' (Peterson 1992: 255; emphasis added). Peterson appears, in short, to slip between talking about 'preferences' and about 'knowledge'. Omnivores acclaim classical music – this is the form of music they 'really' like best; but they are also knowledgeable about many other genres. However, the question of whether or not they *like* these other genres to the same extent is not really considered. Our data suggest that those most eligible for omnivore status on the basis of their higher credentials do not in fact like the range of genres that Peterson predicts. But are they *knowledgeable* about these musical forms? Two questions from our survey can help us answer this question. Our respondents were asked if they were familiar with a range of musical works and if they could identify the name of the performer, composer or songwriter with whom the work is associated. A list of ten works of classical music and a list of seventeen works which were designed to cover the range of contemporary popular genres were provided; we also asked respondents to name their three favourite works from the classical list.[15] The relevant data from these questions are given in tables 7.9 and 7.10.

From table 7.9 we can see that professionals clearly have the greatest familiarity with the world of classical music. They are the least likely to know none of the works, and three times as likely as the average to be familiar with eight or more. A familiarity with works of popular music (table 7.10) is more widespread, but professionals are again the ones whose knowledge base is most extensive. Fewer professionals than any other group report not knowing any items on the list; they are marginally more

Table 7.9 Knowledge of musical works – 'high culture' (row percentages)

Class category	None	1–2	3–4	5–7	>8
Employers	30.1	19.6	21.8	21.1	7.5
Self-employed	29.2	18.4	24.6	22.2	5.7
Managers	15.4	19.8	20.9	34.1	9.9
Professionals	10.8	14.9	21.3	30.2	22.9
Para-professionals	23.5	15.0	26.6	30.1	4.7
Supervisors	28.0	23.7	24.9	17.1	6.2
Sales & clerical	29.6	20.8	25.6	19.6	4.4
Manual	44.6	25.7	18.3	9.6	1.9
Mean	*28.8*	*20.4*	*23.2*	*20.5*	*7.1*

Table 7.10   Knowledge of musical works – 'popular culture' (row percentages)

Class category	None	1–3	4–6	7–8	9–11	>12
Employers	13.5	20.3	20.3	25.6	19.6	0.8
Self-employed	13.7	22.7	23.0	16.3	18.6	5.7
Managers	7.7	20.9	19.8	27.5	18.7	5.5
Professionals	5.1	13.3	24.1	25.1	24.4	7.9
Para-professionals	7.0	17.4	28.2	22.5	18.3	6.6
Supervisors	8.4	13.7	27.4	24.0	20.3	6.2
Sales & clerical	6.0	17.1	27.5	21.3	21.5	6.5
Manual	15.0	21.7	25.3	16.8	16.6	4.7
Mean	*9.7*	*18.3*	*25.3*	*21.0*	*19.9*	*5.8*

likely than others to be familiar with twelve or more works, and almost a third recognise nine or more.

Music Tastes and Music Knowledge

The strategy we adopted for generating our data on musical knowledge was explicitly modelled on Bourdieu's investigation. In his discussion of the relationship between familiarity with works of 'legitimate' culture and educational capital Bourdieu observes that:

> The strongest correlation between performance and educational capital . . . is observed when, with the question on the composers of a series of musical works the survey takes the form of a very 'scholastic' exercise on knowledge very close to that taught by the educational system and strongly recognised in the academic market. (Bourdieu 1984: 13)

As should be apparent from the findings in relation to professionals, our data confirm the strength of this relationship. We can report that two-thirds (67.2%) of those with primary education could identify only two of the composers from the list of ten music works and less than 2 per cent (1.9%) were familiar with eight or more. In contrast, almost half (48.0%) of those whose educational qualification was a higher degree (MA or PhD) reported knowing eight or more composers, with equivalent figures of 27.3% and 14.7% for holders of graduate diplomas and bachelor degrees respectively.

Without exception, familiarity with the composers of individual works is most strongly related to achieved educational level and class location. Table 7.11 shows the percentage of each class knowing the composers of the musical works. Professionals head the rankings for all but one.

Table 7.11   Knowledge of musical works by class (percentage of each class knowing the composer of the work)

Musical work	Emp.	Self-emp.	Mgr	Prof.	Para-prof.	Supv.	Sales/cler.	Manual	*Mean*
The Four Seasons	31.2	37.0	51.7	55.4	29.0	36.7	35.1	27.6	*36.2*
The Well-tempered Clavier	3.3	3.2	8.7	18.7	1.7	5.8	3.2	1.4	*4.6*
Porgy and Bess	33.8	36.3	49.6	53.7	40.4	35.9	33.1	18.4	*36.0*
Eine Kleine Nachtmusik	19.3	18.9	36.6	37.7	19.6	18.8	16.7	6.2	*19.6*
The Firebird Suite	10.1	10.8	16.5	34.8	10.8	13.5	6.9	2.7	*12.0*
Einstein on the Beach	0.6	1.3	0.0	6.1	0.0	3.1	1.7	0.4	*2.0*
La Traviata	30.0	34.4	49.4	55.0	36.2	29.7	30.8	16.2	*33.0*
The Mikado	39.3	42.3	57.3	69.5	50.6	41.9	43.6	22.3	*44.4*
The Blue Danube	60.6	59.0	72.3	74.3	58.3	60.7	53.8	37.0	*58.2*
The Messiah	40.6	34.5	65.5	62.4	40.3	32.3	30.0	18.3	*36.7*

It is worth noting that *The Blue Danube* is easily the best known of all the works, achieving an average recognition of almost 60%. For Bourdieu this work is emblematic of 'popular' taste, which he understands, in this context, to embrace 'so-called "light" music or classical music devalued by popularization' (1984: 16). It is for him the musical work most likely to be favoured by manual workers and, correspondingly, the least by those he places at the apex of his class schema, higher-education teachers.[16]

It is instructive, therefore, to note that for Australians, *The Blue Danube*, in addition to being the most *recognised*, is also the work which is the most *liked* from the list. As table 7.12, shows there are only two class locations – employers, marginally, and professionals, more conclusively – for whom it is not the most preferred composition. It is difficult to avoid the conclusion that, for the most part, familiarity with a given work is effectively being translated into a liking for that work.

The top five most recognised works are also the five most preferred works, although the rank ordering is different. Vivaldi's *Four Seasons*, one of three compositions to be recognised by 36 per cent of our sample, moves into

Table 7.12 Favourite musical work by class (column percentages)

Musical work	Emp.	Self-emp.	Mgr	Prof.	Para-prof.	Supv.	Sales/cler.	Manual	*Mean*
The Four Seasons	31.1	25.7	22.3	28.5	16.8	25.3	27.5	28.4	*25.0*
The Well-tempered Clavier	0.0	1.0	3.5	2.5	0.5	0.0	0.8	0.4	*1.2*
Porgy and Bess	12.8	10.1	11.9	10.4	9.9	11.3	6.5	10.9	*9.5*
Eine Kleine Nachtmusik	1.3	1.4	8.9	7.6	4.4	7.1	5.2	4.6	*5.2*
The Fire-bird Suite	0.0	0.5	0.0	1.8	0.0	1.9	0.4	0.3	*0.9*
Einstein on the Beach	0.9	0.8	0.0	0.5	0.0	0.5	0.6	0.0	*0.5*
La Traviata	6.3	5.2	2.7	10.5	4.8	9.7	4.5	4.2	*6.2*
The Mikado	8.4	6.8	4.2	8.6	12.8	4.7	10.1	7.5	*8.2*
The Blue Danube	30.8	37.9	31.5	16.0	42.3	33.4	39.1	35.8	*34.2*
The Messiah	8.8	10.6	15.0	13.8	8.4	6.0	5.4	8.0	*9.1*

clear second position in the order of preference, with 25 per cent of Australians selecting it as their favourite work. Professionals' tastes in music are once again marked in relation to all other occupational groups, with less than half the sample average selecting *The Blue Danube* as their favourite work. Even here the effects of class do not go unmediated; fewer than one in ten professionals aged between 46 and 59 choose this as their favourite, and it is also less popular with the younger professional cohorts, for whom the *Four Seasons* ranks significantly. The oldest cohort of professionals appears to have the most heterogeneous tastes, with ratings for *The Messiah*, *Porgy and Bess*, *La Traviata* and *Eine Kleine Nachtmusik* in excess of the already dominant professional average. Do we observe the same relationships between class location and music preferences in the final aspect of musical culture we consider: the ownership of musical instruments, playing music as a pastime, and the extent of formal music training?

Almost half of the homes in Australia contain at least one musical instrument. Regionally, instruments appear to be evenly distributed, although they are marginally more likely to be found in semi-rural (58.3%) and rural households (57.6%). Instrument ownership is slightly higher than average among the youngest cohort, and peaks in the child-rearing 36–45 cohort at over 60 per cent (62.7%) before falling away to just over 30% in the homes of the elderly. However, education and class-related differences in ownership appear to be of most significance. As table 7.13 shows, instruments are most likely to be found in the homes of professional people (71.7%). The same class, moreover, report the highest incidence of multiple ownership, with 30 per cent of the homes of professionals who do possess instruments having three.

Instrument ownership is more evenly distributed among the other classes, although, in a departure from the trends established with respect to music genre preferences, where managers are invariably the class whose cultural profile most resembles that of professionals, we note that managers are, after the working class, the class least likely to own musical instruments. The types of instrument they do own, however, are significant. They are the class most likely to possess a piano – 'the bourgeois instrument par excellence' (Bourdieu 1984: 19) – and the least likely to have a guitar.

Despite their relative abundance, it seems that very few of these instruments are regularly played. Overall, just under 7 per cent of our sample reported that they 'often' play a musical instrument, with a further 10 per cent indicating that this was an activity which they 'sometimes' undertook. Seventy per cent of our sample claimed never to play. Managerial homes appear to be the places where the symbolic value of the instrument most outweighs its purpose, as only 3 per cent of managers report that they often play a musical instrument. A similar situation obtains in the case of employers, who are the class most likely never to play an instrument (85.1%, as

Table 7.13 Ownership of musical instruments by social class (column percentages)

	Emp.	Self-emp.	Mgr	Prof.	Para-prof.	Supv.	Sales/cler.	Manual
Proportion of households with a musical instrument	49.6	54.2	44.1	71.7	45.8	51.2	47.4	42.1
Type of instrument								
Piano or piano accordeon	30.8	28.3	43.7	36.9	26.6	26.3	22.3	11.6
Classical wind, string or brass	7.8	6.7	19.6	18.7	13.3	16.9	22.0	14.9
Guitar	23.1	34.8	10.5	23.2	28.6	33.1	34.1	41.9
Synthesiser, keyboard or electric organ	27.3	22.2	24.0	17.3	24.0	19.0	18.6	24.5
Other	11.0	8.0	2.3	3.9	7.5	5.1	3.0	7.1

opposed to the sample average of just under 70%). Whatever else we might want to say about instrument ownership, it would appear that for a significant proportion of people their instruments are merely decorative.

Professionals stand out as the class with the most active musical life. Fourteen per cent, twice the sample average, are frequent instrument players, and a further 20 per cent sometimes play. The figure of 47 per cent who do not play at all, while it is significant in its own terms, is by far the lowest of all the classes. Finally, we note that an interest in music culture seems to be generationally established in professional families to a greater extent than with other classes. Professionals are the group most likely to have had a mother[17] who played a musical instrument (35% as opposed to the average figure of 24%); to have had formal music training themselves (47.5% compared with the sample average of just under 30%); and to have sent their children to a school which placed a strong emphasis on music as part of its curriculum (56.7% against the average of 37.6%).

In conclusion, does Bourdieu's model of the relationships between cultural competencies, educational capital and class location work for the Australian context? On the basis of the data we have reviewed in this chapter, the relationships, in their broadest outline, largely seem to hold. However – and we suspect this is by no means unique to the Australian case – the entire configuration of relations in our sample appears to have been skewed towards cultural forms which in Bourdieu's terms are 'popular', devalued, or of diminished aesthetic value. Moreover, class judgements of taste seldom display a logic which is separate from the confounding effects of age and gender.

Perhaps the most important finding to emerge from our examination of musical culture is the difference between tastes and knowledge. Never recognised as an issue in Bourdieu, and analytically blurred in Peterson, it is, we suggest, a fundamental point that needs to be recognised when considering the regimes of value that pertain to music. 'Omnivorousness', to employ Peterson and Kern's neologism, should best be understood in terms of a knowledge base rather than of any deep affinity for a range of music genres. In our terms, inclusive music taste – the ideal type omnivore – is not to be found among those closest to the apex of the taste hierarchy. Peterson is partly correct in his view that univorous tastes are more likely to be found among those nearer the base of the socioeconomic order, but we have also found this to be a characteristic of professionals' music tastes as well. Manual workers and professionals may not like the same types of music, but what each has in common is a tendency to make their selections from among aesthetically similar genres: more highbrow in the case of professionals, more lowbrow in the case of manual workers. Both have, in our terms, tastes which are more restricted than other classes. Where they differ is in their command of musical cultures. Manual workers remain more restricted than other classes in the knowledge they have of both classical and popular music; in contrast, professionals have much more inclusive knowledge of both of these realms.

We should not be surprised that professionals appear to have the greatest familiarity with both high and popular music culture. Their training and work environments have disposed them towards the continual accumulation of knowledge, and there is no reason why this disposition should not be extended to their non-work lives. When one adds to this an ethos of involvement in the cultural lives of their children, their expansive musical repertoires are perfectly comprehensible. It may carry just as much kudos at a dinner party to show that you know the current line-up of the Spice Girls as to know the name of Philip Glass' latest composition.

Chapter 8

The United Tastes of Australia?

One of the most puzzling aspects of Bourdieu's inquiry into cultural differentiation is its remarkable insularity. It is difficult to come away from reading *Distinction* without the impression that the tastes of the French in the late 1960s were almost entirely forged within their own national institutions. Apart from the occasional reference to the uptake of 'Californian sports', or an interest in an influential foreign film, the cultural output of the rest of the world was of no apparent interest to Gallic appetites.

Almost thirty years after Bourdieu's original research, it is impossible to imagine that the same indifference to global culture could still prevail even in France, let alone a country like Australia which has traditionally looked outwards for its cultural pleasures. This issue provides the major subtext for this chapter, in which we examine, in some detail, Australians' tastes and preferences in the core domains of media culture: television and film. The chapter draws heavily on the more qualitative components of our survey questionnaire in which we used open-ended questions to identify our respondents' favourite television programs and films. Similar questions were used to record their favourite musicians, singers and composers and the names of their favourite authors. Although, in examining the responses to these questions, we revisit some of the data already touched on in chapters 3 and 7, the theoretical context for this material is rather different. While we are concerned with exploring the social distribution of these preferences, we also extend the investigation to consider an issue not yet broached in any detail, namely the interplay of local and global influences in the formation of our everyday cultures. Our analysis leads us to focus on age differences as the most crucial factor in accounting for popular cultural preferences – in itself a not unsurprising finding in light of the evidence we have presented in the book so far. But the structure of age preferences contains within it a more interesting and, arguably, culturally more significant trend: a generational transformation in taste which dramatically highlights the extent to which American[1] culture has come to occupy an ascendant position in Australian society.

Austerica: The 51st State

One of the most enduring themes in the long debate over the quest for a distinctive Australian identity has been the perceived influence of the United States on our cultural lives. While there are undeniable cultural connections between the two countries, much of the evidence for the 'Americanisation' thesis remains anecdotal and it is still largely the preserve of social commentators or media pundits.[2] Because of these largely impressionistic accounts, it has become almost another national myth through which we strive to understand ourselves. Although there has been some valuable research assessing the impact of American influences on the organisation of the media or entertainment industries, particularly in areas such as sport (McKay, Lawrence, Miller & Rowe 1993; McKay, Miller, & Rowe 1996) and television programming (O'Regan 1993; Cunningham & Jacka 1996), we have surprisingly little knowledge of the impact of these essentially administrative or corporate changes on the everyday lives of Australians. It is one thing to demonstrate that the operation of our cultural institutions has been transformed as a result of such global economic developments; it is quite another to establish that Australians are now turning away from locally produced cultural commodities and actively embracing those from other countries.

In this chapter we look at evidence from our research which suggests that there has been a generational shift towards the consumption of cultural commodities originating from America. In three major areas of cultural consumption – television, music, and literature – younger Australians display a preference for programs, musicians and authors emanating from the United States to a far greater extent than Australians in middle age who, in turn, are more disposed towards American cultural materials than older Australians. A fourth area, film, although overwhelmingly dominated by Hollywood productions, provides a variation in this generational trend and we suggest some possible reasons for this difference.

These data have important implications for current debates about cultural imperialism, Americanisation and national identity. To date most analyses of these phenomena have been preoccupied with economic or political concerns, with the focus being on cultural or media industries and the strategies of the multinational corporations in the expansion of their global institutions (e.g. Schiller 1976, 1991). In this research, as Tomlinson (1991: 40) puts it, 'the moment of the cultural' seems forever deferred. In contrast, the limited number of studies which have sought to explore the reception of cultural or media texts (e.g. Ang 1985; Liebes & Katz 1990) have, by virtue of their ethnographic methodologies, necessarily sacrificed breadth of audience coverage. The data on generational differences in tastes, we suggest, constitute a third and novel way in which claims about cultural dominance might be explored. To the extent that its focus is upon everyday tastes and preferences, 'the cultural' is squarely embraced. Moreover, by making use of data from a large-scale national inquiry, we avoid the limitations of generalisability which traditionally have bedevilled audience ethnographies.

Concern about the viability of a distinctive Australian culture and the perceived threat to it from foreign influences has been a recurring theme for social commentators for most of this century (Boyd 1960; Serle 1967; White 1980, 1983). Long before the 'cultural imperialism' thesis (Mattelart 1979; Nordenstreng & Varis 1974; Schiller 1976, 1991; Varis 1974) was established as a dominant media studies paradigm in the early 1970s, fears of a corrupting Americanisation of Australian society – particularly in relation to film, music, popular literature and design – were being voiced. The Australian case, however, was complicated by the realisation, even if only grudgingly acknowledged in some quarters, that the process of Americanisation was occurring in a society which had already had its character distinctively shaped by its earlier colonial relationship with Britain. Before the twentieth century, as Richard White (1983) observes, Australia could simply and accurately be described as 'a transplanted provincial British culture' (112). According to White, for most of the twentieth century Australia has had two distinct cultures, each with quite different institutional moorings, class identifications and transmission processes. British influence originally stemmed from the

> cultural baggage of Australia's immigrants, always predominantly English or Irish so that up to the second World War the proud boast of the colonials that they were '98 percent British' remained largely true . . . The cultural relationship also reflected the basic economic tie between colony and imperial power. The raw material of the colonies, the sons and daughters of the bunyip aristocracy, were sent off to England to be finished, at Oxford or a London season . . . More important was the deeply felt sense of cultural isolation, the belief that all our vital cultural reference points were to be found on the other side of the globe, so that the first requirement of any budding Australian writer was a ticket to London. (White 1983: 112–13)

By contrast, American culture was arguably more systematically imposed, though no less willingly accepted, as a consequence of exposure to 'the cultural devices of consumer society': films, popular music, and television.[3]

These contrasting influences – on the one hand, a generally more benign English heritage and, on the other, a more insidious American commercial influence – could, however, be further distinguished in terms of the manner of their local adoption. Writing with specific reference to the Americanisation of design and the built environment, Robin Boyd alluded to the creation of a peculiar hybrid condition which was both a distinctive architectural style and 'a way of life':

> the essential thing to be noted about American influence in Australia is that, unlike the English, it never survives the ocean crossing intact. The most mesmerised imitators of America always add a trace of Australian accent and subtract a measure of sophistication, tending continuously to transform Australia into a state which can be called Austerica. (Boyd 1960: 64)

Boyd drew a distinction between what he saw as 'normal international cultural exchange' and the mindless imitation of another country's habits and fashions which he felt characterised Australia's relation to America. Geoffrey Serle was to echo this criticism some years later with his observation that Australia had become a willing accomplice in this process: 'We are happily – or phlegmatically – exchanging one neo-colonial situation for another. Australia has abandoned the prospect of independent nationhood; we are going to become just slightly different sorts of Americans' (Serle, 1967: 240).

It is tempting with hindsight to view the lamentations of Australian intellectuals like Boyd and Serle as early 'first shots' in the cultural imperialism debate; but such a view would be mistaken. Neither Boyd nor Serle nor any of the other Australian commentators held the view that the transplanting of American culture into the Antipodes was part of a larger strategy towards global dominance on the part of the United States. Indeed, as White (1980: 284–5) argues, with the arrival of the cold war the old Anglophile opposition to Americanisation all but evaporated and a 'certain pernicious American influence became acceptable as "the price of freedom"'.

It is, moreover, debatable whether cultural imperialism, with its implied sense of an unwarranted imposition of alien values and practices, makes any sense at all as a description of the Australian experiences, given the apparent willingness with which Australia has embraced its two primary cultural mentors. No doubt this complicitous acceptance, if not active embrace, of American cultural products has been one reason why the Australian case has generally not been seen as an exemplar for the cultural imperialism thesis which has shaped the debate about international cultural flows since the 1970s. As a semi-peripheral country Australia fits uneasily into the world-system model of political relations which framed the debate, and it has been

American cultural domination of peripheral countries traditionally regarded as the third world which has been the focus of critical attention.[4]

A notoriously elusive concept, one whose ideological appeal always outweighed its analytical utility, cultural imperialism has come under increasing scrutiny over the last decade (Claeys 1986; Fejes 1981; Lee 1979; Patterson 1994; Tomlinson 1991). In place of American cultural hegemony, the centrepiece of the thesis, scholarly interest in the explication of cultural relations has turned to embrace a more nuanced set of concerns – a focus on cross- and international cultural flows and processes which have come to be encapsulated in the far more pervasive, although still contested, globalisation paradigm (Ang 1994b; Featherstone 1990; Ferguson 1992; Jacka 1992; Robertson 1992). Continuities between the two paradigms have, nevertheless, been observed. As Cunningham and Jacka (1996: 9) suggest,

> The debate about the cultural effects of globalisation bears similarities to the arguments forwarded by proponents of the cultural imperialism thesis against the earlier modernisation paradigm. On the one hand, an emerging global culture can be celebrated as bringing peoples together in a new cosmopolitanism . . . on the other hand commentators . . . see globalisation as leading to an intensification of cultural imperialism.

We want to stress another continuity between these two approaches: both are largely indifferent to the issue of the formation of everyday cultural choices within specific national contexts. Proponents of the cultural imperialism thesis appear simply to assume that exposure to international audio-visual commodities automatically leads to an uncritical acceptance of this material and a concomitant reshaping of malleable and vulnerable national identities. Those who stress the multi-dimensional nature of cultural flows and the autonomy of local cultures as characteristic features of the more complex global cultural economy, although at times more sensitive to the possibility of idiosyncratic or transformative audience decodings, have little interest in generating more systematic or larger-scale accounts.

The *Australian Everyday Cultures* survey provides us with materials which can help us make an informed contribution to these debates. The information takes the form of the responses we obtained from four open-ended questions inviting our respondents to nominate their favourite television programs, musicians, and authors and the films they most preferred. Unlike the genre preferences we considered in earlier chapters, these data have the added advantage of permitting a more precise contextualisation of these choices. By assigning a country-of-origin category to each of the items nominated, we have available a yardstick by which to assess the extent of foreign cultural influence within Australia's mediascapes. Our strategy is thus to explore cultural dominance by focusing on the topic which both the cultural imperialism and the globalisation theses, with their focus on corporations, industries, and flows, tend to ignore: the structure of everyday cultural tastes and preferences.

In what follows, then, we are less concerned with offering a detailed commentary on the programs, films, musicians and authors which Australians have told us they prefer, and more with the aggregate patterns revealed by these choices. To follow this path is deliberately to down-play the genre categorisations conventionally associated with these cultural domains and their values or significance. Country of origin, in itself, cannot establish the kind of cultural value attached to any particular cultural item. But it remains the best, although by no means perfect, measure of assessing foreign cultural influence.

The data we examine were generated in the following way. For each of the cultural domains the top 30 favourites across our entire sample have been identified and treated as discrete taste groupings. We are less interested in the rankings that are given to them – the staple ingredient of the ratings agencies – although we will draw attention at times to certain items of particular interest. Our primary concern is with the social distribution of these choices, primarily the variations by age, although other demographic variables will be considered in less detail. This method of analysing the data has been adopted in preference to presenting each age cohort's 'top 30' choices separately as it more readily allows for inter-cohort comparisons to be made. One consequence of this approach, however, is that particular programs, musicians or films will be included in the list of a cohort's 'favourites' even when they receive no preference allocations. We feel this strategy is justified since, although there were some important exceptions, particularly in relation to music and film, the top 30 categories for each of the age cohorts comprised substantially the same categories as the overall sample, even where the rank ordering varied greatly. Finally, there is the related issue of the degree of homogeneity of the cultural choices or the extent to which the respondents' choice of favourites fell within these top 30 categories. This varied according to both the cultural domain under consideration and the age cohort in question. Television had the lowest proportion of choices outside of the top 30 categories but in other areas the incidence was much higher. This was particularly the case with the music and film preferences of the youngest cohort. Where relevant the percentage of cohort choices which fell outside the top 30 categories is discussed and its implications considered. For each cultural domain, then, two modes of information have been generated: the first (tables 8.1, 8.2, 8.3 and 8.4) showing the allocation of each age group's choices within the full list of top 30 favourites; the second (figures 8.1, 8.2, 8.3 and 8.4) summarising the aggregate choices according to their country of origin.

Television

Television has, without doubt, received more attention from proponents of the media imperialism thesis and contributors to the debates on media globalisation than any of the other three domains.[5] According to Richard White (1983: 108) the early 1960s represented the peak in the Americanisation of popular culture measured by the proportion of American material transmitted. Most analysts now agree that about half of Australian television schedules is taken up with imports, with US material dominating the commercial channels and British programs comprising the bulk of overseas material broadcast by the ABC. In what is probably the most systematic comparison of international television flows, Tapio Varis (1984) reported that Australia had seen a decline from 57 per cent of imported programming to 40 per cent in 1983, although the proportion of imported programs at prime time was slightly higher at 46 per cent.

Although Australia's proportion of imported television is high by comparison with Western European countries (but significantly lower than New Zealand), commentators have generally claimed that such imports do not attract overwhelming audience attention. Cunningham and Jacka, for example, argue that:

> while US programs lead the world in their transportability, and even manage to dominate schedules in some countries, they are rarely the most popular programs where viewers have a reasonable menu of locally produced material from which to choose. (1996: 12–13)

Writing with specific reference to Australia, O'Regan comments that:

> imports routinely occupy both pivotal and filler spaces in prime-time and off-time alike. Yet those imports as a whole tend to attract less significant viewing from audiences than their half of all broadcast time would suggest. Overall Australian programs are decidedly more popular than the imports. (1993: 12)

The data we present in table 8.1 and figure 8.1 indicate that these claims are only partially correct. It is indeed the case that the majority of the top 30 television programs are locally made. Sixteen programs (53%) are Australian, eleven (36%) originate from the US, while the remaining three programs – all police-related – are from the UK. However, the data in table 8.1 (and figure 8.1) suggest that claims about audience choices which do not differentiate between age cohorts are simply misleading. Although clear majorities of the three oldest cohorts do cite Australian programs as their favourites, this drops to 43 per cent for the 26–35 cohort and then as low as 22 per cent for the youngest age group. The choices of both of these latter

Table 8.1 Top 30 television programs by age (column percentages)

Program	18–25	26–35	36–45	46–59	60+
4 Corners (Aus)	0.0	0.9	0.8	3.2	1.2
60 Minutes (Aus)	0.0	0.6	4.1	3.2	3.0
Between the Lines (UK)	0.5	0.9	4.1	2.1	0.3
The Bill (UK)	0.5	3.4	4.1	4.3	3.9
Blue Heelers (Aus)	2.7	1.2	2.7	4.3	4.9
Burke's Backyard (Aus)	0.5	1.2	1.6	2.1	0.9
A Current Affair (Aus)	0.9	1.5	1.9	4.3	3.3
Days of our Lives (USA)	0.0	1.8	1.1	2.1	1.8
'Films/movies' (Aus)	1.8	2.1	2.7	5.1	2.4
The Footy Show (Aus)	1.8	2.7	1.6	1.1	1.5
GP (Aus)	0.5	3.7	4.4	4.0	4.9
Heartbeat (UK)	0.5	0.9	4.6	2.9	3.3
Home and Away (Aus)	4.6	2.7	0.3	0.8	2.4
Home Improvement (USA)	12.8	13.4	6.8	1.6	1.2
Janus (Aus)	0.0	2.1	1.9	1.1	0.6
Married with Children (USA)	3.2	3.7	1.1	0.5	0.3
Melrose Place (USA)	10.1	3.4	0.5	0.5	0.3
Models Inc (USA)	5.5	2.1	0.5	0.3	0.3
Murphy Brown (USA)	0.9	2.1	1.6	0.8	0.6
NYPD (USA)	0.5	0.6	3.0	1.1	0.0
Neighbours (Aus)	2.3	2.4	0.0	1.1	0.9
'News' (Aus)	5.0	16.2	30.8	39.2	48.5
Our House (Aus)	1.4	3.1	1.6	1.1	0.0
Roseanne (USA)	6.9	2.7	2.7	0.5	1.2
Sale of the Century (Aus)	0.9	1.8	1.4	2.4	7.3
Seinfeld (USA)	21.0	11.3	4.6	2.1	0.0
Simpsons (USA)	7.8	2.4	0.3	0.3	0.0
'Sports' (Aus)	1.4	2.7	4.6	4.5	3.6
Star Trek (USA)	4.1	3.7	2.7	1.9	0.6
Wide World of Sport (Aus)	2.3	2.4	1.6	1.6	0.6
Proportion of cohort's responses accounted for by the top 30 choices	70.4	69.5	68.3	67.1	64.4

cohorts are dominated by US imports. Nearly 78 per cent of the choices of the youngest age group are for programs which originate from the US. For each of the remaining cohorts the proportion favouring programs from the US falls until it is only a tenth of the oldest cohort's choices.

The US sitcom *Seinfeld* is clearly emblematic of this generational shift towards the Americanisation of cultural choice. Twenty-one percent of the entire allocation of the top 30 choices of the youngest cohort are for this program alone; for each of the remaining cohorts this figure drops by about half until the oldest cohort where it goes unacknowledged. Some additional observations are worth making here. The Australian component of the choices of the middle-aged and older cohorts is clearly dominated by the selection of 'news'[6] as their favourite program. Arguably, the dominance of this program could be seen as skewing the results. But this turns out not to be the case: even if this category is dropped from the analysis, the country-of-origin trends remain substantially the same.[7] A second point is that the coding system used to generate these data in fact may well underestimate the degree of Americanisation of television content. Several of the programs which we have categorised as 'Australian' are in fact production clones of US programs (e.g. *60 Minutes*, *Sale of the Century*, *Wide World of Sport*) and from the point of view of the cultural imperialism thesis these programs, although locally produced, can be expected to retain 'American' cultural values if not outright content. This argument can be extended to the category of 'films' which, although included as Australian content, is likely to be dominated by Hollywood releases.

It is also worth recalling the discussion in chapter 3 about the amount of television each group watches. What these data suggest is that, since younger Australians actively target the programs they want to watch, they are therefore more likely to have been viewing almost exclusively US programs rather than selecting these programs as favourites while still exposed to a wider repertoire of local or UK product. Finally, we note that there is a considerable degree of homogeneity of choice of favourite television across the cohorts. The top 30 television programs account for just over 70 per cent of all the nominated favourites of the youngest cohort, and the proportion remains well over 60 per cent for each of the remaining groups. In some

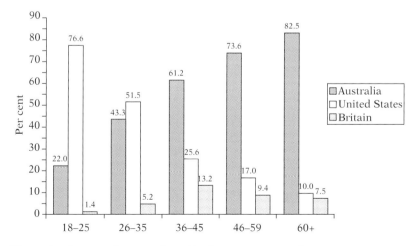

Figure 8.1 Country of origin of top 30 television programs by age

respects this finding is as important as the generational changes which have taken place. It suggests that a good deal of the television that is screened goes unwatched, unacknowledged or at least unappreciated. So young Australians overwhelmingly prefer to watch US television programs. A minor cause for concern, perhaps, but at least defenders of a vibrant local culture can find solace in the knowledge that in relation to music the popularity of Australian performers is secure. Or can they?

Musicians, Singers and Composers

The top 30 musical performers or composers nominated by our respondents are presented in table 8.2 together with the preference scores for each of the age cohorts. Figure 8.2 summarises these choices by allocating them this time to one of four country-of-origin classifications. We appreciate that this may seem like an unwarranted display of taxonomic tidiness and contains within it some debatable assignments. For example, we have classified Pavarotti, a performer whose commercial success goes unquestioned and who sings at the openings of global sports spectacles, as belonging to European 'high culture'. These reservations to one side, however, we focus again on the trends which this classification provides. And once more we observe a similar trend towards US dominance in the music-related preferences of the youngest group, with 55 per cent of their choices allocated for the top 30 categories going to US performers. For the cohorts aged between 26 and 59 the figure drops to just over a third and remains more or less consistent before dropping again by about half to 18 per cent for the oldest cohort. This picture is reversed when Australian musical content is considered, although the trend is not as linear. Australian performers receive 16 per cent of the youngest cohort's choices, and for the remaining cohorts the proportion remains between 20 and 30 per cent.

The most conspicuous trend as far as age is concerned can be seen in the distribution of preferences for European classical music either by virtue of a named composer or a singer. Only 1 per cent of the youngest group's musical preferences fall into this category, compared with 38 per cent of older Australians. Material of European origin – mainly British and Irish popular musical performers (U2, Beatles, Elton John, Phil Collins, etc.) – also features prominently in the choices of most of the cohorts. To a certain extent the aggregate country-of-origin figures disguise some quite specific age-related local inflections, particularly for Australian performers. For example, former Cold Chisel band member Jimmy Barnes ranks favourably with the youngest cohort, accounting for well over half of the Australian component of their choices. There is some support for him in the 26–35 cohort, but their allegiance has squarely shifted towards the more mellow John Farnham who easily rates as this cohort's favourite musician overall

Table 8.2 Top 30 musicians/singers/composers by age (column percentages)

Musician/singer/composer	18–25	26–35	36–45	46–59	60+
3 Tenors (Eur)	0.0	0.5	0.0	1.2	11.4
Abba (Eur)	2.1	1.0	0.8	2.8	5.7
Bach (Eur)	1.0	1.0	0.8	1.6	3.3
Jimmy Barnes (Aus)	10.4	6.2	2.4	0.4	0.0
Beatles (Eur)	3.1	6.7	14.3	4.8	1.0
Beethoven (Eur)	0.0	0.5	1.6	5.2	6.2
Mariah Carey (USA)	16.7	7.2	4.0	1.6	0.0
Phil Collins (Eur)	2.1	4.1	1.6	2.0	0.0
Michael Crawford (Eur)	0.0	0.0	0.8	2.8	4.3
Neil Diamond (USA)	3.1	2.1	4.0	6.0	1.9
Dire Straits (Eur)	2.1	3.6	2.8	0.8	0.0
Slim Dusty (Aus)	0.0	0.5	1.6	2.8	5.2
Eagles (USA)	4.2	5.6	4.4	0.8	0.5
Elton John (Eur)	1.0	6.2	3.2	2.0	0.0
John Farnham (Aus)	3.1	16.4	11.9	5.2	3.3
Whitney Houston (USA)	3.1	1.5	2.8	1.2	0.5
Billy Joel (USA)	7.3	5.1	4.4	3.2	0.0
Madonna (USA)	12.5	3.1	0.8	0.0	0.0
Mozart (Eur)	0.0	2.1	5.6	6.4	7.6
Pavarotti (Eur)	0.0	0.0	1.6	7.6	9.5
Pink Floyd (Eur)	4.2	5.1	2.0	0.8	0.0
Elvis Presley (USA)	6.3	6.7	12.3	12.0	4.3
Cliff Richard (Eur)	0.0	0.0	2.4	4.0	0.5
Rolling Stones (Eur)	2.1	2.6	1.6	1.2	0.5
The Seekers (Aus)	1.0	0.5	2.4	8.4	18.1
Frank Sinatra (USA)	0.0	0.5	0.8	3.2	7.1
Barbra Streisand (USA)	0.0	2.6	4.4	3.2	4.3
U2 (Eur)	12.5	6.2	1.6	0.0	0.0
Andrew Lloyd Webber (Eur)	1.0	2.1	2.0	4.4	2.4
John Williamson (Aus)	1.0	0.5	1.6	4.8	2.4
Proportion of cohort's responses accounted for by the top 30 choices	31.6	42.3	49.1	53.3	54.1

with 16.4% of their top 30 choices; his appeal is significantly female. Farnham also rates well with those in early middle age, but support for him then declines to a level of 3 per cent in the oldest cohort, a figure which, curiously, almost exactly mirrors his appeal with their grandchildren. Finally, we note the popularity which The Seekers enjoy with those aged 60 and over, where the 18 per cent allocation of choices is the highest recorded among any of the cohorts.

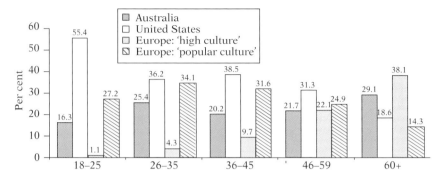

Figure 8.2 Country of origin of top 30 musicians, singers or composers by age

Compared with television there is a much greater dispersion of choices in this domain, with the youngest cohort, as expected, displaying the greatest degree of heterogeneity in their range of nominated favourites. The top 30 music categories account for just under a third of all the nominated favourites of the youngest group, 42 per cent of the 26–35 cohort and about half of the choices of the remaining cohorts. But what is significant here is that US and European performers continue to dominate the choices of the young if the analysis is extended beyond these top 30 categories. More than half (56%) of the remaining unallocated figure for the youngest cohort goes to performers from the United States, 23 per cent are for British or European groups or singers, with the Australian component rising marginally to 21 per cent. In short, the pattern with respect to country of origin established with the most popular performers remains more or less the same over the whole of the youngest cohort's entire list of music preferences.

Authors

There are some obvious difficulties in using an author's country of origin, since it may bear no necessary relation to the genre in which he or she writes. And it is the *content* of reading material – rather than the nationality of the author – which has tended to be of concern here. Next to television, reading material has probably attracted the second-highest amount of attention from the proponents of the cultural imperialism thesis. In particular, the focus has been on the availability of mass-produced comics and other forms of popular magazines which have been widely available in the third world since the 1940s. The most celebrated example of a cultural imperialist case study has been Dorfman and Mattelart's (1975) analysis of the Walt Disney comics which the authors argue are little more than vehicles for the dissemination of American capitalist values.

Clearly, then, there are some difficulties in focusing on the country of origin of our respondents' nominations for favourite author. Moreover, many of the international bestselling authors are truly international in the sense that they reside in more than one country at different times of the year, or they may have moved permanently from their country of origin to reside elsewhere. Of necessity, then, the country-of-origin categorisations for some authors have been pragmatically assigned.[8] With these reservations in mind, the data in table 8.3 and figure 8.3 do, however, confirm the trends established in the first two cultural areas. Eleven of the authors from the top 30 nominated by the full sample are conventionally recognised as American, fifteen are from Britain or Eire, three are Australian and the remaining author, African-born Wilbur Smith, has been allocated a separate category.

Again, the pattern is for the favourite authors of the youngest cohort to be predominantly American. Nearly two-thirds (63.0%) of their allocation of preferences within the top 30 are for US novelists. For the 26–35 cohort the corresponding figure is almost as high at just under 60 per cent. For the middle-aged cohorts American writers receive about 40 per cent of their choices and then the proportion falls sharply, with only 15 per cent of the oldest cohort nominating US authors as their favourites. Stephen King appears to be the literary equivalent of *Seinfeld* as the embodiment of the Americanisation of literary taste, with over a quarter of the youngest cohort's allocation of the top 30 preferences reserved for him alone, a figure which declines to 3 per cent with the oldest cohort. This generational trend is reversed when we consider the allocation of preferences for UK (Britain and Eire) authors, with the latter being the clear favourites of the oldest cohort (68.7%), declining in significance over the middle cohorts and of least

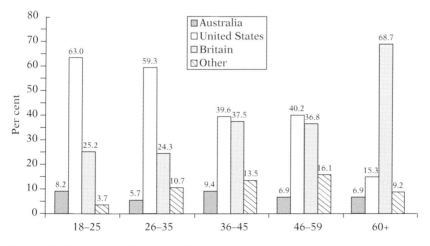

Figure 8.3 Country of origin of top 30 authors by age

Table 8.3 Top 30 authors by age (column percentages)

Author	18–25	26–35	36–45	46–59	60+
Andrews (USA)	11.9	6.8	2.1	0.6	0.0
Archer (UK)	3.7	4.0	2.6	5.8	10.0
Asimov (USA)	0.0	2.8	1.7	2.9	1.5
Binchy (Eire)	1.5	1.1	2.1	1.7	0.8
Bradford (UK)	0.7	2.8	2.1	0.0	3.1
Brontë (UK)	0.7	1.1	0.0	2.9	1.5
Carey (Aus)	0.7	0.0	2.6	0.6	1.5
Christie (UK)	1.5	4.0	10.9	5.2	13.1
Clancy (USA)	2.2	5.7	5.2	4.6	0.0
Clarke (UK)	3.0	0.7	2.6	0.6	2.3
Collins (UK)	7.4	4.0	1.6	1.7	0.8
Cookson (UK)	0.7	1.7	3.1	4.0	19.2
Courtenay (Aus)	7.4	3.4	4.2	4.0	1.5
Dickens (UK)	0.0	0.0	0.0	2.3	6.2
Eddings (USA)	0.7	0.6	1.7	1.7	0.8
Forsyth (UK)	0.0	1.1	1.0	1.7	1.5
Francis (UK)	0.8	0.0	4.7	3.4	4.6
Grisham (USA)	4.4	5.1	0.0	4.0	1.5
Higgins (UK)	0.7	1.1	1.0	1.1	1.5
Heyer (UK)	0.0	0.6	1.0	2.9	1.5
King (USA)	25.9	19.2	9.9	7.5	3.1
Koontz (USA)	3.7	2.3	1.6	1.7	0.0
Ludlum (USA)	0.7	2.8	4.2	8.1	1.5
McCullough (Aus)	0.0	2.3	2.6	2.3	3.9
Maclean (UK)	0.7	0.0	2.1	2.9	3.1
Michener (USA)	0.0	1.1	2.6	2.3	0.8
Sheldon (USA)	3.0	6.2	5.2	3.4	3.1
Smith (Africa)	3.7	10.7	13.5	16.1	9.2
Steel (USA)	10.4	6.8	5.7	3.4	2.3
Tolkien (UK)	3.7	2.3	2.6	0.6	0.0
Proportion of cohort's responses accounted for by the top 30 choices	61.4	57.1	52.3	49.4	46.8

attraction for the youngest cohort (25.2%). Australian authors attract less than 10 per cent from any of the cohorts; the final author, Wilbur Smith, emerges as the clear favourite for those aged between 36 and 59.

It is also interesting to observe the degree of homogeneity in each of the cohort's choices. The pattern for authors mirrors that for television in that the youngest cohort in each of these cases has the largest proportion of their entire list of preferences allocated within the top 30 and the oldest cohort has the smallest. In the case of music this trend is reversed. In essence these figures offer, we suggest, a measure of the degree of cultural relevance and diversity of these different domains for the various age cohorts. That is to say, the *lower* the overall proportion of the cohort's choices which falls within the top 30, the *greater* their entire range of choices must have been. Other things being equal, we could conclude that music is of most cultural significance to the young, with literature (and television) the cultural domains having most appeal to older persons.

Film

The final cultural domain we consider is film. Table 8.4 presents the distribution of preferences for each of the age cohorts for the top 30 films nominated by the full sample, and figure 8.4 shows the distribution by country of origin. The global ascendancy of Hollywood in relation to film production (O'Regan 1992) is clearly evident; 22 of the top 30 films are produced by the major Hollywood film studios, 6 of the films are Australian[9] in origin, and 2 are UK productions. In contrast to the three other cultural domains, overwhelming majorities from each cohort nominate American films as their favourites. Two films out of the top 30 command an extraordinary amount of allegiance from the oldest cohort: MGM's production of *Gone with the Wind* which alone receives nearly 40 per cent of their total preferences, and Twentieth Century Fox's *Sound of Music* which attracts 20 per cent. *Gone with the Wind* is also the most popular film for the two middle-aged cohorts, where it commands 17 and 11 per cent of their top 30 film preference allocation respectively. The significance which the older cohorts attribute to it marks it as the most popular film for the whole sample.

There is, however, one exception to the preference patterns clearly established in two of the first three cultural domains. In the case of television programs and musicians, singers and composers, it was the oldest cohort that was most likely to nominate the Australian items from the top 30 categories as their favourites, followed by the middle cohorts, with the youngest the least likely to opt for local television productions or musical performers. With authors the proportion of each category is generally too small to warrant any inference. In the case of film, however, this dominant trend is reversed: it is the youngest cohort that is the most likely to nominate Australian films as their favourites from within the top 30 categories, to an extent which is about double the other age groups. We note also that, based on the overall proportion measure discussed above, the cinema is of most cultural relevance to the young, an observation which lends additional weight to their Australian film choices. We need to be cautious about this trend. We are not witnessing the wholesale abandonment of Hollywood here, but perhaps something more like a chink in its armour. In contrast to television consumption we know that the young are the group who most

Table 8.4 Top 30 films by age (column percentages)

Film	18–25	26–35	36–45	46–59	60+
Beaches (USA)	6.5	2.2	3.1	1.7	3.1
Blues Brothers (USA)	2.8	4.3	4.6	1.7	1.2
Casablanca (USA)	0.0	1.6	2.1	3.4	5.0
Crocodile Dundee (Aus)	0.9	2.7	2.6	1.7	1.9
Dances with Wolves (USA)	5.6	7.5	7.7	7.9	3.7
Dead Poets Society (USA)	2.9	1.1	1.6	2.3	0.0
Dirty Dancing (USA)	4.6	5.9	6.7	2.8	0.6
Dr Zhivago (USA)	0.0	0.0	2.1	7.3	2.5
Forrest Gump (USA)	3.7	3.2	3.6	0.0	0.6
4 Weddings and a Funeral (UK)	1.9	7.0	3.1	3.4	0.6
Ghost (USA)	4.6	7.5	5.2	5.1	2.5
Gone with the Wind (USA)	2.8	6.5	11.3	17.0	37.9
Indiana Jones (USA)	1.9	2.7	3.6	2.3	0.0
Man from Snowy River (Aus)	1.9	0.0	1.6	4.0	3.1
'Monty Python' films (UK)	0.9	4.3	1.0	1.7	0.0
Mrs Doubtfire (USA)	2.8	5.4	2.6	2.3	1.2
Muriel's Wedding (Aus)	4.6	2.7	2.1	2.8	1.2
My Fair Lady (USA)	0.0	0.5	0.0	5.1	6.2
One Flew over the Cuckoo's Nest (USA)	0.9	3.2	4.6	1.7	0.0
Pretty Woman (USA)	8.3	5.4	1.6	2.8	1.9
The Adventures of Priscilla (Aus)	8.3	3.8	1.6	1.1	0.0
Silence of the Lambs (USA)	4.6	2.7	1.6	1.7	0.0
Sister Act (USA)	0.0	1.1	5.2	1.1	1.9
Sound of Music (USA)	2.9	4.3	5.7	11.9	19.9
Star Wars (USA)	5.6	3.2	3.1	0.0	0.0
Strictly Ballroom (Aus)	0.9	1.1	1.6	1.7	3.1
Terminator 2 (USA)	9.3	3.8	4.6	0.0	0.0
The Piano (Aus/NZ)	3.7	0.5	2.1	2.3	1.2
Top Gun (USA)	3.7	4.3	1.6	2.3	0.0
Speed (USA)	3.7	1.6	2.6	1.1	0.6
Proportion of cohort's responses accounted for by the top 30 choices	36.6	44.4	42.1	40.1	50.5

frequent the cinema, and that this still largely remains an 'American' experience. And yet Australian films are finding popularity among this group. Under the appropriate financial and cultural circumstances the Australian film industry has been able to produce films which have attracted local and international attention. The lessons for cultural policy development implicit in this trend should not be overlooked.[10]

Before considering the implications of these generational changes in taste, we want to comment briefly on some of the other patterns that can be observed in the data. Although there are some notable differences in class, educational and gender tastes for *individual* television programs, films, musicians or composers and so on, these differences largely cancel each other out when the aggregate picture is examined. No other demographic factor accounts for as much of the overall variation in tastes as age. In relation to television, we find that women are overwhelmingly represented among those who nominate the popular soaps (*Melrose Place* (92%),[11] *Models Inc* (86%), *Days of our Lives* (92%)) as well as more 'quality' drama (*GP* (83%), *Heartbeat* (65%)) as their favourite programs. Men, in contrast, opt for local sports programs such as *The Footy Show* (82%) and *Wide World of Sports* (96%), as well as *The Simpsons* (64%) and the sitcom *Married with Children* (92%). Men therefore rate marginally higher on aggregate Australian content in their choice of favourite television, with women more likely to select American programs. Women are also more likely to prefer American musical performers, recording strong support for female vocalists like Madonna (85%), Whitney Houston (82%), Barbra Streisand (82%) and Mariah Carey (75%). Men reciprocate in their preferences for male performers: The Rolling Stones (93%), Slim Dusty (75%), The Beatles (70%) and Frank Sinatra (69%). There are some exceptions: Cliff Richard, Phil Collins and Elton John and, above all, John Farnham appeal more to women, while men – generally older men, we add – appear to like Abba. Men overall are marginally more likely to select their musical favourites from European performers, both 'high' and 'popular'.

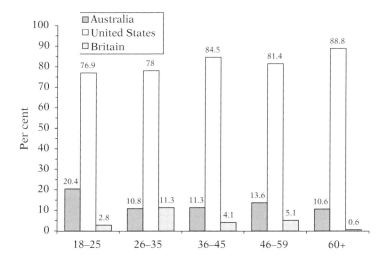

Figure 8.4 Country of origin of top 30 films by age

Tastes in literature are even more gendered, as we observed in our chapter on reading. Here we simply note that three of the authors in the top 30 – Georgette Heyer, Maeve Binchy and Barbara Taylor Bradford – attract exclusively female preferences; and the readership of several others – Danielle Steel, Colleen McCullough, Catherine Cookson and Virginia Andrews – is over 90 per cent female. Men prefer male authors: Dick Francis (100%), Isaac Asimov (93%), Robert Ludlum (83%) and Tom Clancy (81%) are the leading examples here. In aggregate terms, women are more likely to choose British and Australian authors, whereas men are marginally more likely to prefer American authors. Wilbur Smith rates as the most popular author overall among men, attracting nearly 19% of their top 30 preference allocation, about three times as much as he receives from women. Film preferences provide no relief from this by now predictable pattern of gendered taste. Men prefer films about male characters who act tough, shoot, kill, and are heroes or just plain silly: *Blues Brothers* (96%), 'Monty Python' films (93%), *Star Wars* (89%), *Terminator 2* (77%) and *Crocodile Dundee* (71%) stand out as the films which have primarily attracted masculine interest. Women prefer films about relationships and romances of one kind or another: *Beaches* (96%), *Pretty Woman* (93%), *Muriel's Wedding* (91%) and *Dirty Dancing* (89%) are the main examples, but there are several other films which attract almost the same concentration. Within the top 30 there are, in fact, only a handful of films which seem to be equally attractive to men and women: *Silence of the Lambs* (50:50), *Dr Zhivago* (48:52) and *Dances with Wolves* (45:55). But despite these gendered preferences for individual films, the aggregate figures are almost identical. Eighty-two per cent of preferences are for Hollywood productions, 13 per cent are for Australian films and the remainder for UK releases.

Educational attainment appears generally less important than gender for most of these taste domains. Those with only a primary level of education (who are generally older) select the news to a greater extent than any other group, and they are also the most likely to choose local programs such as *Blue Heelers*, *A Current Affair* and *Sale of the Century*. They therefore tend to favour Australian television to a much greater extent than all others – 80 per cent of their top 30 preferences go to local productions compared with an average of about 57 per cent for the other educational groups, with the exception of those with incomplete tertiary education (generally the young) who record a figure of only 36 per cent for Australian content. The primary-educated are the only cohort who record no preferences for several of the popular American programs – *Seinfeld*, *The Simpsons*, *StarTrek*, *NYPD* – but otherwise television program preferences do not vary substantially by level of achieved education. The tertiary-educated are more likely to choose quality local drama – *GP* – than other cohorts but they are also significantly attracted to cult shows like *Seinfeld*. UK police shows such as *The Bill* or

Heartbeat have general appeal across all educational groups. Lower levels of education also seem directly related to a preference for certain Australian musical performers. For example, the country music singer Slim Dusty receives nearly 90 per cent of his preference allocation from those with only primary or some secondary education. There is a similar level of support for The Seekers: over 18 per cent of the former's music preferences are for The Seekers, as are nearly 10 per cent of the latter's, figures which translate into approximately 60 per cent of their total preferences. Overall, these two groups prefer Australian performers more than the remaining educational cohorts (an average figure of 38% compared with the sample average of 26%), with the tertiary-educated being least likely to choose local musicians (13%). But minimal education does not equate with a preference for Australian authors. Rather it is UK novelists who receive the lion's share (56%) of the allocation of the preferences of the primary-educated, a taste in literature they share with the tertiary-educated (48%) to a greater extent than any other group. This literary synergy does not extend to American novelists. The strong support which Tom Clancy, John Grisham, Stephen King and James Michener receive among the ranks of the tertiary-educated goes entirely unmatched with the primary-educated; with the exception of the primary-educated there is a consistent level of support for American novelists. Finally, in relation to film preferences we can observe the dominance that *Gone with the Wind* and, to a lesser extent, *The Sound of Music* exert across almost all the educational groups. These two films alone account for over 50 per cent of the preferences of the primary-educated and nearly 30 per cent of those with incomplete secondary education, but they are still the first and third choices respectively of the tertiary-educated.

Class differences in tastes for specific items are less conspicuous. Apart from the news (most popular with managers, 46%, and employers, 44%, and of least interest to sales and clerical workers at 20%), television program preferences are generally consistent across social class divisions. The two top-rating US programs, *Seinfeld* and *Home Improvement*, are chosen by all classes, although the former is most popular with professionals (12%) and the latter with manual workers (9%). Professionals prefer quality local drama to a greater extent than other groups (*GP* 9%), while managers are attracted to *The Bill* (7%). In aggregate terms, Australian television content is the preferred option for all classes (with the exception of sales and clerical workers who marginally prefer a diet of US television), with an average of 56%. But the proportion of professionals and para-professionals who favour US television programs (33%) is only just below that of the manual working class (39%). Perhaps the most interesting aspect of the distribution of class tastes for musicians, singers and composers is the similarity in the profiles of employers and manual workers. Figure 8.5 records the cultural convergence from within the top 30 categories which these conventionally oppositional social groups display.

Elsewhere we find that a preference for Mozart is conspicuous among managers (14.4%) and professionals (12.5%). Managers are also the group most likely to choose The Beatles (9.3%), whereas professionals are attracted to singer Billy Joel (8.5%) and composer Andrew Lloyd Webber (12.3%) more than members of other social classes.

Employer and manual worker tastes in literature converge in relation to only one writer – Wilbur Smith – who receives 16 per cent of the employers' preferences and 15 per cent of manual workers'. For the other leading authors there is more divergence. Stephen King is the most popular choice of manual workers (18.6%), but he receives only 3.2% of the employer votes. Conversely, Agatha Christie commands a sizeable following with employers (12.9%) but only modest support with manual labourers (5.9%). Managers prefer Jeffrey Archer (13.3%) more than any other class. *Gone with the Wind* is the most popular film with all classes with the sole exception of para-professionals, for whom *The Sound of Music* has more appeal (17.6%).

The birthplace of the respondent appears to be more influential in determining aggregate country-of-origin tastes than any other variable except age, although in ways which are not entirely obvious. Migrants from northern and southern Europe and Asia all prefer Australian television programs to a much greater extent than the Australian-born. About 58 per cent of the Australian-born's top 30 television preferences are for local productions, whereas for both Asian and southern European migrants the figure is 77 per

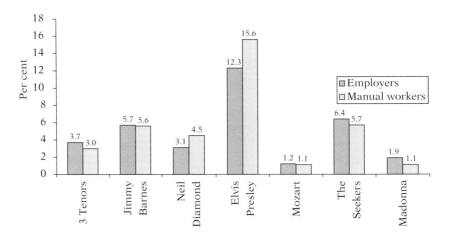

Figure 8.5 Similarities in musical tastes of employers and manual workers

cent and for northern European migrants it is even higher at 85 per cent. For those born in the UK the preference for Australian programs drops to 49 per cent, but this group records the highest percentage for UK television programs – 26 per cent compared with the sample average of just over 7 per cent. The Australian-born, however, favour Australian musical performers to a far greater extent than the other groups. Twenty-six per cent of their top 30 musical preferences are for Australian performers compared with only 9 per cent of the UK-born, and only 6 per cent of the northern European total. Overall the largest allocation of Australian-born musical preferences is for US performers (33%); for the UK-born it is British music (38%); for the two European migrant groups the majority of preferences go to European classical music (NE 44%, SE 35%), while Asian migrants prefer American music to anything else (51%).

It is age, however, which accounts for more of the country-of-origin variations in taste than any other factor. The evidence we have presented would seem conclusively to support arguments in favour of one of the dominant themes of the thesis of cultural or media imperialism, namely that North American cultural products have become the dominant ingredients in the cultural menus of the young. The data suggest not only that young Australians inhabit cultural worlds which are saturated by American materials, but that they are more likely to prefer this material, in some cases to the almost total exclusion of other national products. The data also suggest that the shift towards the embracing of American materials has intensified in that the cultural profiles of the young are more clearly 'Americanised' than their parents', whose own profiles, in turn, are closer to their own parental generation than they are to their children's. But a number of questions need to be considered before these conclusions can be accepted.

In the first place there is the issue we have alluded to in earlier chapters as to whether what is being observed here is real generational shifts in cultural orientations, or rather something which should more accurately be thought of as changes in tastes over the course of the life-cycle. Our survey data cannot conclusively establish the first of these possible explanations. To do this we would need historical data on the tastes of the older cohorts when they were in their late teens and twenties. Moreover, even if such data were available, the fact that the object of inquiry is a moving target, so to speak, would severely curtail systematic comparison. That is, the repertoire of cultural materials from which choices can be made and tastes established has quite obviously changed since members of the oldest cohort were aged between 18 and 25. Not the least of the difficulties here is the sheer increase in the quantity of material in each cultural category, although the fact that so much of this material now comes from foreign sources is in itself evidence for a weaker version of cultural domination or the globalisation of culture.

Despite these reservations, on balance the data do suggest that a generational shift towards preferring American cultural materials has been occurring within Australia.

The second interpretation, however, must also be considered. This alternative explanation holds that what we are witnessing in the data is no more than the natural progression or development of tastes over the course of the life-cycle. It may be the case that respondents in the middle and oldest cohorts had similar dispositions towards American materials when they themselves were the younger cohorts, and that with aging – although this may simply be a convenient description for a far more complex series of social processes – their tastes in television, in music, and in literature have taken on the character they display today. Perhaps there are 'trajectories of taste' which entail a movement from enjoyment of cultural forms which are more active, spectacular, corporeal, of pure entertainment value, to an enjoyment of forms which are more contemplative, informative or cerebral. If such trajectories are in play, then the identification of the young with American popular culture in television, music and fiction could be seen as an affinity which they will eventually abandon. Of course from the point of view of national cultural identity, not to mention the national economy, it would be advantageous if the young assembled their cultural worlds from locally produced commodities. But from this perspective 'Americanisation' is a continuous and continuously overcome state. Clearly, no one would dispute the proposition that young people's tastes are different from those of their parents or grandparents. But we seem less inclined to accept the possibility that cultural dispositions are generationally repeated.

References to American content in the Australian media emerged on a number of occasions during our research. Peter, a 27-year-old engineer from Melbourne, had nominated two leading American soaps – *Melrose Place* and *Beverly Hills 90210* – as his favourite television programs. Alongside these he had volunteered the comment: 'Yes, I am embarrassed!'.[12] We are not sure whether this was meant as a reference to their American origins or a confession on account of their being unusual choices for a male: *Melrose Place* was the program which recorded the greatest gender difference of all the top 30, with women comprising over 90 per cent (92.4%) of those who selected it as their favourite show.

Two of our interviewees, Kenneth and his wife Audrey, who were both in their early 60s, recalled being 'introduced' to *Seinfeld*, a program they enjoyed, by their adult son; but overall they had some reservations about American media content.

> **KENNETH** But just look at G (son). Most of the stuff he watches is American, isn't it?
> **AUDREY** Yes.

KENNETH A lot of American, really awful movies.

INTERVIEWER And how old is G?

AUDREY Twenty-five. And, our daughter, when she was living at home, she's 28, she used to watch, what's that . . . *Days of Our Lives*? Come home from uni and sit and watch this terrible . . . the way they even spoke on the television. I said, 'how can you bear to sit and watch this?' 'Oh, you need to relax, Mum.'

INTERVIEWER Some people say that Australian youth culture is becoming very Americanised, do you think that that's so? You know, like the McDonaldisation of society?

KENNETH Yes. Yes. Well, I guess any small culture is subject to influence by other countries. But, yes I see kids that are dressed with baggy trousers and whatever the latest fashion. But then I think back to when I was a boy in, I think it was about 1938, the older fellows, boys 17, 18, went in for playing Hawaiian guitars and wearing Hawaiian shirts. It was all the thing. And, then later on, when I was a teenager, the Bodgies and Widgies came in. I'm not sure where they started off.

Despite this relativistic perspective on the current situation, Kenneth was concerned by what he saw as the more insidious aspects of American culture:

KENNETH In the – in mannerisms, speech, yes, I've noticed that people, some people including my two children refer to railway stations as train stations. I don't know if that's an American thing. I think I heard on television the other night. Why railway stations have now become train stations, I don't know. And, then, I hear various American pronunciations, even by, say, even by . . .

AUDREY ABC announcers . . .

KENNETH ABC announcers who were once regarded as the paragons of correct English pronunciation once upon a time. So, I suppose that it does creep in and things are pushed more now, I guess, by advertising, this American, what is it, basketball? And they're not content to let it be at that, but, there are shops around, I've seen them sell cards of American basketball players and caps and that sort of thing. When I was a kid, it was cricket with Don Bradman, that was about all.

Both interpretations of the data we have canvassed raise interesting questions for further research. If it is 'cultural imperialism' that best accounts for the trends in the data, can we expect the children of the present youngest cohort to have shifted even further towards American cultural values and commodities? Alternatively, if the patterns revealed here are the outcome of some 'natural' taste trajectory, then what is its shape or contour? At what point in the life-cycle, and for what reasons, do the tastes and dispositions of youth 'mature'? In what sense can we think of aging as being as much a cultural as a biological process?

Regardless of which of these interpretations is correct it seems appropriate at this point to return to the conceptual heart of the cultural imperialism thesis and briefly reassess its core concerns. As we have seen, the thesis entails an implicit assumption of the erosion of cultural sovereignty. Although the mechanisms through which this might occur are seldom explicated, there is an agreement that the sheer presence of the cultural baggage of the dominant source nation will inevitably transform the national character of the receptor country. In its bluntest terms, it entails the view that, in the present context, simply on account of their exposure to or consumption of American cultural products, Australians are turning into Americans. It is precisely the impoverished or unreflexive image of the audience underpinning this position which has been the target of critics of the cultural imperialism thesis. As both Tomlinson and Fejes point out, the inability adequately to conceptualise the nature of audience response remains a serious flaw at the heart of the thesis. As Tomlinson has argued, when faced with 'imperialist texts', 'audiences are more active, complex and critically aware in their readings than the theorists of media imperialism have allowed' (1991: 57).

The nature of the survey data generated by the *Australian Everyday Cultures* survey does not permit any systematic consideration of the readings or meanings our respondents attach to their cultural preferences. But other data from the project do suggest that they are capable of holding complex views as to the importance or salience of their own national cultural identities even in the face of the generally derivative nature of the cultural texts they preferred. In response to the question 'What country has been most important in making you the person you are today?', overwhelming majorities from each of the cohorts gave 'Australia' as their answer. The only other country mentioned to any significant extent was Britain, with 4 per cent for the 46–59 cohort and 6 per cent for the oldest cohort. Perhaps these answers are not surprising, and yet they do strike at the heart of the cultural imperialism thesis. In addition, each of the cohorts was in agreement that a distinctively Australian culture did exist, although there was some variation in the elements deemed to express this culture best.

Table 8.5 shows the relevant percentages of each cohort in response to these questions. Nearly 80 per cent of each of the four oldest cohorts agree with the view that there is a distinctive Australian culture. Although there is a decline evident with the youngest cohort, the difference is not significant. Moreover, some clues as to why this might have occurred can be found in the results concerning the elements which 'best express' this culture. While

Table 8.5   Perceptions of Australian culture by age (column percentages)

	18–25	26–35	36–45	46–59	60+
Proportion believing in a distinctive Australian culture	73.7	77.1	79.2	78.1	77.8
Culture best expressed by					
Novels and films	5.8	5.1	6.6	9.1	7.1
Sport	19.8	21.4	18.1	22.5	27.8
Music	2.1	1.0	0.2	0.4	2.1
Politics	0.4	1.0	0.8	1.3	1.2
Family activities	10.7	12.5	17.0	12.8	20.0
The bush	16.9	23.9	21.7	19.2	16.3
Ethnic diversity	18.6	10.7	13.6	9.5	5.3
The beach	4.5	8.4	4.3	8.0	2.3
Other	21.1	16.0	17.7	17.3	18.1

the oldest cohort is more likely to invoke the traditional image of the sporting Australian, the youngest cohort is more inclined to see Australia as a multicultural nation, one consequence of which may well be a concomitant decline in a belief in a distinctive national identity. In short, although Australians appear to be inhabiting cultural worlds which are more and more likely to be dominated by overseas products, there seems to be very little change in a belief in the importance of Australia in biographical self-awareness or in the view that Australia remains a culturally distinct nation. At one level the findings appear contradictory, but at another level we can find tacit support in them for arguments in favour of the globalisation of culture, particularly those variants which see globalisation not as a process of standardisation and cultural uniformity but rather a more complex situation of intermixing or hybridity (Nederveen Pieterse, 1994). Space does not permit any elaboration of this point and it is one that is tangential to the main thrust of the chapter. Nevertheless, if the case of younger Australians is anything to go by it would seem entirely possible to subsist on a diet of foreign cultural offerings or be increasingly subject to global cultural developments and yet to retain a strong sense of the distinctiveness of one's own national cultural identity.

Chapter 9
Public/Private Culture: Theory and Policy

Our main concern in previous chapters has been to describe and account for the social distribution of cultural tastes in contemporary Australia and the patterns of cultural participation to which they give rise. Here we take a different tack in considering the light our findings throw on current policy debates about how far governments should involve themselves in providing cultural resources for general public use, and why they should do so. This will involve three main areas of discussion. The first concerns the evidence provided by the *Australian Everyday Cultures* survey regarding the sections of the population which make most use of the publicly funded components of Australian culture. Second, we shall look briefly at the different concepts of 'publicness' associated with a range of contemporary traditions of social and cultural theory in order to identify their contrasting implications for the grounds on which government involvement in the sphere of culture might be justified. Our third concern is to place contemporary policy debates in a longer historical perspective for the sake of the critical light this will shed on the tendency, evident throughout the Anglophone world, for governments to reduce the scope of the state's cultural involvements and responsibilities.

We can perhaps best introduce this last concern by quoting a passage from an opponent of the prevailing liberal view that, since 'letting alone' is the chief function of government, this means, among other things, that 'state education goes, as a matter of course, and with it all state-aided museums, libraries, galleries of art, parks, and pleasure grounds'. The sentiments might be those of a contemporary left or social-democratic critic of the new right's ambition to roll the state back as far as possible out of the lives of its citizens and, in the process, to redefine the act of government as one which is properly exercised only when dedicated to its own diminution. In fact, however, it is Thomas Huxley (1890: 859) who speaks here, writing over a hundred years ago in critique of the principles of the laissez-faire liberalism of the Manchester school as they had recently been restated in Auberon Herbert's influential 1885 text *The Right and Wrong of Compulsion by the State*, which had urged that the role of government be kept to an absolute minimum. Huxley, opposing this view, wrote in advocacy of the principles of the new liberalism which, *inter alia*, distinguished itself from its predecessor in stressing the need for government to concern itself with the cultural sphere by being active in providing both public education and – although this was not the term used at the time – public culture: the museums, libraries, art galleries, parks and pleasure grounds Huxley refers to. Although British in its provenance, new liberalism quickly became an influential political philosophy throughout the Anglophone world, including Australia where, in the last two decades of the nineteenth century, it played a significant legitimating role in relation to the development of public schooling, adult education, and state-funded museums and art galleries.[1]

It was during this period that the role of the state in providing for a generally shared public culture first assumed a recognisably contemporary form. There are, however, different ways of describing and accounting for this development. Jürgen Habermas refers to the period as one characterised by a dialectic of the '"societalisation" of the state' and the '"statification" of society', seeing these dual tendencies as working to deprive the institutions of the classical bourgeois public sphere – the press, museums, literary societies, and other sites of cultural assembly – of the conditions of autonomy and separateness that had allowed them, in their earlier formation, to function as the site of a culture mobilised in critique of the state authority (Habermas 1989: 142). The consequence, Habermas argues, was a 'refeudalisation of society' in which the gap between state and society which had previously allowed culture to be mobilised against the state was closed down in the functioning of new forms of public culture, integrated now into the state, as an administered culture directly connected to the tasks of social administration. In Michel Foucault's formulation, by contrast, late nineteenthcentury forms of involvement in the cultural and moral spheres are viewed as an instance of what he calls the governmentalisation of the state, through which numerous initiatives aimed at moralising or culturally managing the poor and working classes which had hitherto been developed in the private sphere were integrated into the state as one of its central functions.[2] Where this account differs most tellingly from Habermas' is in its insistence that these new forms of public culture both depended on and worked to maintain a distinction between state and society, organising the latter – the social as a problematic set of conducts – as the surface on which culture was to act in order to produce the effects of social and moral improvement it was called on to perform.

However, if we leave these differences to one side for the moment, the similarities between the two accounts are compelling. For they are in agreement in underlining the importance of the late nineteenth century as a period in which the relations of public and private in the cultural sphere were reconfigured to provide the basis for the subsequent expansion of governments' involvement in the public provision and regulation of culture as parts of the more general social-welfarist and insurential conceptions in whose name the functions of government were enlarged into and including the aftermath of the Second World War.[3] For it is in the context of these broader historical shifts that the recent tendency to reduce governments' involvement in the sphere of culture needs to be placed as a part of the redefinition of the responsibilities of government associated with what Nikolas Rose (1996) has called advanced liberalism. Developed in the wake of the breakdown of postwar welfarism, advanced liberalism selectively reactivates aspects of classical laissez-faire liberalism in redesignating individuals as, once again, the proper originating source of all social activity, calling on them to be both entrepreneurial and responsible for themselves – for their own health, education, and welfare – in new ways. And, of course, for their culture too, now increasingly seen as a matter for market forces to determine rather than as a responsibility of governments.

The precise form this tendency has taken has, of course, varied between different national contexts. It was initially most vigorously pursued in Britain in the period of Thatcherism and, subsequently, in the United States under the Reagan and Bush administrations, although with long-lasting consequences – because of the Republican right's domination of Congress – into the Clinton era. The so-called 'culture wars' and the cuts in the budgets of the National Endowment for the Humanities and the National Endowment for the Arts have been the most obvious manifestations of a continuing tendency to curtail the role of government, especially at the federal level, in the cultural sphere.[4] While these tendencies were less evident in Australia during the Labor governments which prevailed at the national level from 1983 to 1996, Paul Keating's cultural policy statement *Creative Nation* – in retrospect the swan-song of a decade or so of largely positive cultural policy development – reflected the influence of the international climate in the stress it placed on the need for the public cultural sector to become less reliant on government funding by developing more organised approaches to audience development and the pursuit of corporate sponsorship (Dept of Communications and the Arts 1994). This tendency has been considerably augmented since 1996 when the new coalition government moved relatively quickly to reduce the levels of funding available to the public cultural sector, cutting the budgets of the Australia Council and the ABC, and significantly reducing the funding available for the cultural programs of the Aboriginal and Torres Strait Islander

Commission. At the same time, the role of the Australian Foundation for Culture and the Humanities was changed from that of a direct funding and support agency to that of a facilitator for arts and cultural organisations seeking funding from the private sector. Just as important, the coalition government has supported the increased privatisation of education through a combination of cuts to the secondary and tertiary public education sectors, and unprecedented levels of support for the private education sector. Critical measures at the tertiary level here include the introduction of fee-paying possibilities for Australian undergraduates, differentiated fees for professional degrees and – at the time of writing – proposals for allowing private universities access to the same kinds of government support that private secondary schools enjoy. However, these measures need to be seen in context as parts of a wider range of measures – from a reformed tax system through the promotion of private health insurance to new industrial relations laws – designed to make individuals more self-reliant. These challenges to the public subvention of culture, then, have been envisaged as a means of reviving elements of classical liberalism and inserting them within an enlarged and modified sense of the individual's sphere of responsibility. As such, they have elicited a political response on the part of the Labor opposition which has folded a defence of public culture and of the public culture/public education nexus into a broader defence of the social-welfarist and insurential conceptions against which advanced liberalism pits itself. By 1998, the Labor Party, playing on the coalition's 1996 election slogan 'For all of us', had made 'For the security of all of us' its rallying call as part of an attempt to tar Australia's new right with a return to the pitiless carelessness and socially divisive ethos of classical liberalism.

We can see in these formulations how the terms of contemporary political and policy debates over the relations of public and private in the cultural sphere involve conflicting appeals to different moments of the past. It is in this light that we shall find it helpful, later, to draw on the historical accounts of Habermas and Foucault to distinguish the issues that are at stake in different components of the field of public culture. For the moment, though, we need to add to our remarks on Habermas and Foucault some equally brief ones regarding Bourdieu's perspective on the role of the public cultural sector. From Bourdieu's perspective, the forms of publicly funded culture developed over the late nineteenth and early-to-mid twentieth centuries – art galleries, museums, state-funded theatres, operas, music, etc. – function as components of what he calls the field of restricted culture. This, it is important to note, is a different usage of the term from our own, which refers to those groups whose cultural activities are restricted in the sense of being confined to a limited range of options. For Bourdieu, by contrast, the field of restricted culture refers largely to a range of high-cultural activities to which access is restricted by the operation of a range of barriers. Bourdieu distinguishes this field from the field of large-scale cultural production (culture produced and distributed commercially by the mass media) in terms of their different relations to the education system.[5] In large-scale cultural production, Bourdieu argues, consumption 'is more or less independent of the educational level of consumers' (Bourdieu 1993: 120). By contrast, 'works of restricted art owe their specifically cultural rarity, and thus their function as elements of social distinction, to the rarity of the instruments with which they may be deciphered' (Bourdieu 1993: 120). The means of consuming the cultural goods associated with large-scale cultural production, that is to say, are broadly disseminated by the culture industries in order to produce mass markets and are therefore generally available to all members of society. An ability to consume and appreciate the products of restricted culture, by contrast, depends on the acquisition of interpretative, intellectual and aesthetic skills which, far from being generally available, are selectively distributed via the education system. This leads Bourdieu to suggest that the social logic governing the field of restricted culture consists in the relationship between 'institutions which conserve the capital of symbolic goods, such as museums' and 'institutions (such as the educational system) which ensure the reproduction of agents imbued with the . . . "cultivated disposition"' (Bourdieu 1993: 121) that is necessary for the intellectual and aesthetic appropriation of those goods.

Viewed in this light, the public subsidy of such institutions, far from delivering a general benefit to all, delivers a selective benefit of distinction to those who are equipped, by their social, cultural and educational formation, to make use of them. Their functioning is thus paradoxical. On the one hand, their publicness – their reliance on public funding and administration, and their openness to everyone – places them, at least in theory, in a realm to which access is unimpeded. On the other hand, the actual functioning of these institutions is characterised by varying forms of social closure to the extent that intellectual and cultural access to them depends on cultural skills which are selectively distributed via the education system, and are therefore socially rare. Publicly funded culture thus occupies a particularly important place in Bourdieu's account of the social processes of distinction. For it is through the role that it plays in supporting this range of cultural institutions and activities that the state becomes involved in underwriting class-specific practices of distinction.

How far can this perspective be applied to the Australian context? It is to this issue that we now turn by considering the light our findings throw on the different social patterns of participation that are evident between different components of the public cultural sector when considered, first, in their relations with each other, and, second, in relation to the functioning of private cultural markets.

Public and Private Relations of Distinction

We shall take, as our route into these questions, the results of a principal components factor analysis that identified three different groups of activities – all recruiting their participants mainly from elite social strata of one kind or another – which occupy different positions along a spectrum of public–private relations. The first group comprises a suite of activities that are public in the sense, first, of being located outside the private sphere of the home, and second, of being dependent on some level of government funding while also falling within the official purview of arts or cultural policies. At the same time, most of the activities comprising this first group – which we shall call the realm of subsidised culture – are mainly dependent on user-pays principles for their funding with the result that participation in this set of activities is usually of a hybrid public/private form. The activities in question are attending public musical performances, public lectures, orchestral concerts, chamber music, ballet, musicals, opera, theatre and cultural festivals. The second group of activities, which we shall call the realm of public culture, is also public in the sense of being located in public spaces situated outside the home. Unlike the first, these spaces – art galleries, museums, botanical gardens, public libraries and special exhibits are the ones we focus on here – are, in contemporary Australia, still reliant mostly on government funding, even though some museums now apply entry charges to supplement their support from public sources. By contrast, the third group of activities comprises forms of cultural ownership that are wholly private in the sense of being both centred on the home and privately funded. These include the ownership of art objects, books, and musical instruments of all kinds: here, we focus on a subset of this group – which we call the realm of private culture – in examining the social pattern of ownership of limited-edition prints, sculptures, art posters, large collections of books, literary classics, art books, and pianos. We shall add to these three groups an examination of the make-up of the audiences for public broadcasting, focusing on ABC television and SBS. These involve a different set of relations again since, although both ABC television and (even with sponsorship) SBS are mainly reliant on public funding, their reception takes place in the private sphere of the home. We also include the ABC in view of the requirement that is placed on it to include serious drama, classical music, opera, documentary and current affairs in its programming.[6]

  In summary, our concerns focus on the relations between four groups of cultural activity whose distinguishing characteristics and interrelations are summarised in table 9.1. There are, of course, important variations in the patterns of participation relating to specific activities within each of these groups, and we shall deal with these as we go. Our primary concern,

Table 9.1 Public/private culture

Group 1	Group 2	Group 3	Group 4
Subsidised culture	Public culture	Private culture	Public broadcast-ing (television)
Participation, often or sometimes, in:	*Visiting often or sometimes:*	*Ownership of:*	*Watch mainly or regularly:*
Public musical performances	Art galleries Museums	Signed limited edition prints	ABC SBS
Public lectures	Botanical gardens	Sculpture	
Orchestral concerts	Public libraries	Art posters	
Chamber music concerts	Special exhibits at museums or art	500+ books Literary classics	
Ballet	galleries charging	Art books	
Musicals	entry fees	Piano	
Opera			
Theatre			
Cultural festivals			

however, is with the aggregate patterns of involvement in each of these groups and the differences between them.

We look first at the role of education (table 9.2). It will be worth spending a little time on this table to understand its underlying principles. As we read down each column, it tells us, for each group, the average rate of participation in the activities comprising that group for the educational cohort concerned: that, for example, the average rate of attendance at public musical concerts, public lectures, operas, theatre, ballet, etc. (Group 1), is 12.4% for those with only primary education compared with an average rate of participation of 22.6% in art galleries, museums, public libraries, etc. (Group 2). For each of these two groups, the rates of participation have been arrived at by including those who say they attended the institutions often and those who say they attended sometimes. The figures for Group 3 tell us that the average rate of ownership of signed limited editions, art posters, sculptures, literary classics, etc., is 8.2% for the primary-educated. In the final row, we learn that 30.7% of the primary-educated watch either SBS or the ABC either mainly or regularly.

The most important figures from the point of view of our concerns here are those in the final column, where the relative effects of education are summarised by expressing the rate of participation for those with tertiary education as a percentage of that for those with only primary education. The resulting gradients of participation give us a rough-and-ready measure of the role played by education in mediating access to the cultural activities in

Table 9.2 Public/private culture by education

	Primary	Some sec.	Comp. sec.	Voc./ appr.	Part tert.	Comp. tert.	Tert. as % of primary
Group 1: Subsidised culture	12.4	14.5	16.8	14.7	16.6	24.1	194
Group 2: Public culture	22.6	29.7	33.2	25.9	34.6	46.0	204
Group 3: Private culture	8.2	14.4	18.2	17.6	27.9	36.1	440
Group 4: Public broadcasting	30.7	19.8	25.7	28.1	23.3	38.5	125

question. The steeper the gradient, the more educationally selective the group of activities in question; the lower the gradient, the more open – at least as a general rule.[7] The effects of education are thus most pronounced in relation to the realm of private cultural ownership (Group 3) where the contrast between the highest rate of ownership (36.1% for those with tertiary education) and the lowest (8.2% for the primary-educated) is in the order of 440%. Public broadcasting, by contrast, proves the most open and accessible of all with a tertiary/primary ratio of 125% – although it should be noted that those with incomplete secondary education are the least likely to watch public broadcasting, resulting in a high/low ratio of 194% – with the realm of subsidised culture following a reasonably close second, with participation for the tertiary-educated 194% that of those with only primary schooling. Expressed in terms of a hierarchy of selectiveness, then, the results of this table are as follows:

>   Private culture
>   Public culture
>   Subsidised culture
>   Public broadcasting

The hierarchy is different if we look at the role played by form of schooling (table 9.3) except that private culture still occupies its peak.

There are, however, within all groups, activities which tend to stand out from the general pattern. In the realm of subsidised culture, the rate of participation in public lectures and orchestral concerts on the part of those with a tertiary education is roughly five times the rate exhibited by those with only primary schooling. In the realm of public culture, art galleries and special exhibits are most out of kilter with the patterns for this group as a whole, with participation rate for the tertiary-educated at over three times

Table 9.3 Public/private culture by form of schooling

	State	Catholic	Other denominational	Other private	Other private as % of state
Group 1: Subsidised culture	15.7	18.6	22.9	23.7	151
Group 2: Public culture	32.2	35.2	46.8	36.3	113
Group 3: Private culture	19.8	23.1	35.8	34.3	173
Group 4: Public broadcasting	25.7	27.2	32.4	31.9	124

that for those with only primary education. It is similarly telling that, within the realm of private culture, it is the ownership of signed limited edition prints and art posters that is most strongly associated with level of education, with tertiary participation rates of, respectively, over nine and seven times those for the primary-education cohort.

This pattern of exceptions is somewhat different when we consider the roles of income and class. In the case of income, the realm of private culture is, again, the most highly differentiated, followed by the realm of subsidised culture, and then by public broadcasting, with public culture proving the least stratified in terms of income (see table 9.4). The activities in the realm of subsidised culture which are most sharply differentiated in terms of income are chamber music, with a high/low income ratio of 360%, and opera with a high/low ratio of around 220%. Art galleries and special exhibits are the most sharply differentiated activities in the realm of public culture, with high/low income ratios of around two to one in each case. There is, however, little significant variation in the high/low income ratios for the activities we have grouped as 'private culture': these are consistently high for all the activities comprising this group. On its own, the ABC does rather better, with a high/low income ratio of 134%, than when its figures are combined with those for SBS.

The effects of class are most marked in relation to, first, the realm of private culture, and second, that of subsidised culture. In both cases the highest rates of participation are associated with professionals and the lowest with manual workers (table 9.5). Indeed, this is true for most of the groups. The typical pattern is for managers to come second after professionals, followed by one of the employing classes, while sales and clerical workers usually have closest to the lowest rates of participation which, except in the case of public broadcasting, are exhibited by manual workers.

Table 9.4 Public/private culture by income

	<15K	15–26K	26–40K	40–60K	60–80K	80+K	Highest as % of lowest
Group 1: Subsidised culture	12.1	17.4	16.7	16.4	18.2	21.7	179
Group 2: Public culture	27.7	30.7	32.2	36.7	33.3	37.3	135
Group 3: Private culture	12.7	19.8	22.3	21.6	27.5	36.0	283
Group 4: Public broadcasting	21.6	27.7	26.0	22.9	27.1	35.9	166

Table 9.5 Public/private culture by class

	Emp.	Self-emp.	Mgr	Prof.	Para-prof.	Supv.	Sales/cler.	Manual	Profs as % manual
Group 1: Subsidised culture	18.9	18.4	22.1	25.9	17.4	16.1	16.6	10.0	259
Group 2: Public culture	27.1	33.2	43.2	51.2	39.7	33.1	31.9	22.1	232
Group 3: Private culture	23.5	22.6	28.2	37.5	23.7	19.8	20.8	12.8	293
Group 4: Public broadcasting	32.0	34.3	38.6	43.2	27.0	26.4	21.8	22.1	195

The role of age intersects with considerations of class and level of education in complex ways depending on how generational and life-cycle effects are interpreted. Our interest here, however, is with whether age is significantly different in its effects across the four different groups. Table 9.6 suggests that it is. While, on the whole, involvement increases constantly with each age cohort, this is most dramatically true for public broadcasting. This is mainly attributable to a commonly acknowledged shortcoming of the ABC which does particularly poorly with the under-25s. Involvement in the realm of public culture also increases quite steeply with age, a tendency that is less marked in subsidised culture and complicated in the realm of private culture where the under-25s exhibit higher rates of ownership than both the 26–35 year olds and the over-60s.

The role of gender is not especially marked, particularly in relation to private culture and public broadcasting, reflecting the tendency for choice

Table 9.6 Public/private culture by age

	18–25	26–35	36–45	46–59	60+	18–25s as % of 60+
Group 1: Subsidised culture	14.5	12.8	16.8	20.8	20.8	70
Group 2: Public culture	23.5	27.2	37.2	37.4	40.6	58
Group 3: Private culture	21.8	19.4	26.1	24.1	17.2	127
Group 4: Public broadcasting	9.25	25.5	31.1	32.6	34.7	27

in these areas to be the result of shared decisions within the home. However, women are considerably more likely than men to be involved across the range of activities comprising the realms of subsidised and public culture; female participation in the former is 149% that of men, and 138% in the realm of public culture. In some areas of subsidised culture, the ratios for particular activities depart significantly from the general trend. Women are about twice as likely as men to attend the opera and nearly three times as likely to go to the ballet. It is also notable that there are exceptions to this predominantly female participation in opera on the high rates of participation of male employers and managers.

Aboriginality has few significant general effects, although art galleries and museums do register as being more important for Aboriginal than for non-Aboriginal Australians. This is also true for public musical performances, opera and, most especially, cultural festivals, where Aboriginal participation is just a little under twice that of non-Aboriginal participation. Similarly, while ethnicity has few general consequences, country of birth does have some interesting discriminating effects. As we can see in table 9.7, those born in Britain and other parts of northern Europe are more likely to take part in all four groups of activities than are those born in Australia – and very significantly so in the case of both subsidised culture and public culture. This is also true of the figures for SBS when considered separately from the ABC. These tendencies are in good measure attributable to the class positions – very strongly professional and managerial – of migrants from northern Europe and the UK as well as to their above-average tertiary-education participation rates. Migrants from southern Europe, by contrast, are significantly underrepresented in these classes and contribute disproportionately to the membership of the employer, supervisory and manual working classes. Asian migrants display more divided class characteristics, with very high representation among the self-employed as well as among manual workers accompanying an above-average contribution to the composition of the professional class. The tertiary-education patterns of

Table 9.7 Public/private culture by country of birth

	Australia	United Kingdom	Northern Europe	Southern Europe	Asia	Australia as % NEurope
Group 1: Subsidised culture	10.6	14.4	19.6	14.1	14.7	54
Group 2: Public culture	32.4	43.9	41.3	26.2	33.7	78
Group 3: Private culture	21.4	25.5	24.3	16.2	17.0	88
Group 4: Public broadcasting	24.4	35.9	36.2	33.1	35.1	67

migrants from both southern Europe and Asia are also distinctive. The Australian-born and migrants from northern Europe and the UK all share tertiary-education participation rates – including those still in tertiary education as well as those who have completed tertiary studies – of 29 per cent. Migrants from southern Europe have participation rates of roughly half this level, while Asian migrants come in a little higher at 34.6%.

It's worth taking a brief look at another aspect of geographical location in considering the effect that place of residence has on the patterns of participation across our four groups (table 9.8). As might be expected, participation is greater for all four groups in inner-city areas than all other locations, declining more or less consistently along the urban–rural continuum to reach its lowest point among those living in rural Australia. The notable exception is public broadcasting – mainly because of the ABC's high rates of participation among rural Australians (49.3%), which marginally exceed those of even inner-city Australians.

Table 9.8 Public/private culture by place of residence

	Inner city	Provincial city	Suburban	Semi-rural	Small town	Rural	Inner city as % rural
Group 1: Subsidised culture	24.7	18.6	17.8	13.5	13.9	11.9	208
Group 2: Public culture	47.7	39.7	35.4	31.7	27.5	24.8	192
Group 3: Private culture	30.4	34.1	24.3	24.5	16.8	20.5	148
Group 4: Public broadcasting	34.5	28.7	26.6	28.3	21.6	25.5	135

It is worth noting, finally, as an index of attitudes towards the use of public funds in support of cultural activity, that, of all classes, only professionals think that the arts should receive more rather than less funding (see figure 9.1). When looked at in terms of level of education (figure 9.2), the same is true only for those who have completed a tertiary education, although respondents in the midst of tertiary studies come close to an equal division of opinions on this matter. The view that the arts merit less funding, by contrast, is strongest among manual workers and those with vocational qualifications or only primary education.

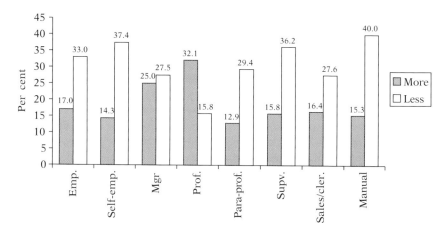

Figure 9.1 Attitudes towards arts funding by class

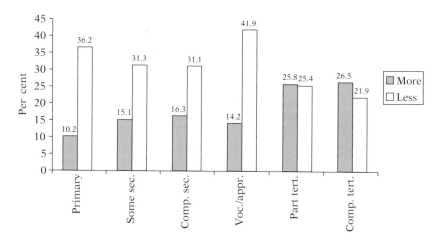

Figure 9.2 Attitudes towards arts funding by level of education

The 'Publicness' of Public Culture

Let us step back, for a moment, from the detail and see what generalisations can be made on the basis of the data presented above (see table 9.9). It seems reasonably clear, first, that the realm of private culture produces the greatest range of variation in relation to the variables of class, education, schooling and income, establishing this as the realm that is most significant from the point of view of practices of distinction. It is also clear that the classes which invest most heavily in these forms of distinction are – as we would expect – professionals and managers. While this is also true of the realms of subsidised culture and public culture, the overall mix of class participation across these three realms differs. The ratio of employers to both professionals and the working classes is highest in the realm of subsidised culture, followed by private and then by public culture. It would seem, then, that the realm of subsidised culture occupies a distinctive niche within the cultural practices of employers – as, incidentally, is also true for women. The realm of public culture, by contrast, has a more even class composition with a higher ratio of manual workers to both employers and professionals and a less sharply differentiated range of income levels, although it is more highly stratified in educational terms.

What might follow from findings of this kind depends on the angle of political and policy vision that is applied in interpreting them. Looked at from one perspective, the predominance of urban, well-educated, mainly female middle-class professionals from a northern European background across this whole field of activities might seem good reasons for reducing the levels of government support for the publicly funded or subsidised components of the field. Indeed, this is far from a hypothetical response. The degree to which such groups derive a disproportionate benefit from Australia's publicly funded cultural infrastructure has been a thorny policy question through the 1980s and 1990s. Discussed in general terms in the 1986 report, *Patronage, Power and the Muse*, by the House of Representatives Standing Committee on Expenditure, the issue was more provocatively broached in the 1989 Department of Finance discussion paper *What Price Heritage?* In seeking to identify how the private benefits accruing to the middle classes from government support for heritage institutions might be distinguished from the public benefits of such support, this paper reflected the increasing influence of the Treasury's economic rationalism and its wish to extend that influence to the arts and culture portfolios.

There are not, we believe, any good grounds for arguing against the need for calculations of this kind, all the more so for the fact that many of the arguments of economic rationalists in this area both echo and owe some debt to the terms of analysis of more left-inclined traditions of social and cultural theory. Indeed, Tim Rowse's (1985) *Arguing the Arts*, enunciating a

Table 9.9   Public/private culture – summary of patterns of participation

	Group 1 Subsidised culture	Group 2 Public culture	Group 3 Private culture	Group 4 Public broadcasting
Female as % of male	149	138	119	99
Tertiary as % of primary-educated	194	204	440	125
Private as % of state schooling	151	113	173	124
Highest as % of lowest income	179	135	283	166
Professionals as % of manual workers	259	232	293	195
Employers as % of professionals	73	53	63	74
Employers as % of manual workers	189	123	184	145
Under-25s as % of over-60s	70	58	127	27
Inner city as % of rural	208	192	148	135
Australia as % of NEurope	54	78	88	67

forthright social-democratic and egalitarian set of policy principles, clearly enjoyed an influence of this kind. Equally, if the social exclusiveness of art galleries, for example, is a cause for complaint on the part of economic rationalists it is no less a concern for Bourdieu, although the conclusions he draws are sharply different in urging an enhanced role for public education in culturally skilling the population so as to make those institutions more democratically accessible. The primary policy consequence flowing from the influence of economic rationalism in Australia, however, has been the increased emphasis on audience development that we referred to earlier. The implications of such policies for the future shape of public/private relations in the cultural field depend on how audience development is interpreted and put into practice. In its theoretical elaboration, it is meant to combine access and marketing concerns harmoniously, developing new audiences through strategies which, working in collaboration with the education system, will disseminate more broadly the skills and interests that might make publicly funded cultural activities intellectually and culturally accessible to an enlarged population. Given the degree to which policy agendas are dependent on short-term political cycles, however, the long-term perspective such a view entails is rarely a luxury that the institutions of either subsidised culture or public culture can afford. More often than not audience development strategies prove to be dominated by marketing imperatives in which it is 'bums on seats' that count, no matter whose bums they are and how many times they might be the same bums. There are countervailing tendencies, most notably in the advisory and research work of the Australia Council, but the tendency for cultural institutions to focus on increasing the rates of participation of existing users rather than attracting new ones is a strong one as it usually represents a better short-term return on the marketing dollar. Where this is so, audience development is likely to reduce rather than increase the social reach of both public and subsidised culture in encouraging them to work increasingly hand in glove with private cultural markets to provide a range of subsidised positional goods for the employing, managerial and professional classes.

That said, perhaps the most notable aspect of the findings summarised above is the confirmation they offer of the role that, to date, public funding has played in equalising access and participation in comparison with the operation of private cultural markets. The interesting questions from this perspective concern the different degrees and kind of publicness exhibited by the three different realms of publicly funded culture we have discussed. What light do Foucault's, Habermas' and Bourdieu's perspectives on the relations of government and culture throw on the different kind of publicness represented by these three realms and the different rationales for government support that they represent?

We have already noted that the participant profile of the realm of public culture is considerably more democratic than that of subsidised culture. There is nothing particularly surprising about this as these differences have their roots in the different histories of the institutions comprising the two groups. Those comprising the realm of subsidised culture derive, in the main, from the courtly and aristocratic practices of distinction which – as the work of Norbert Elias (1994) has shown – were subsequently adapted by the bourgeoisie to their own strategies of distinction and retained this aspect when they were translated to Australia. The high rates of participation of employers in these institutions shows that they continue to retain elements of this earlier function while also providing important sites for cross-class forms of social mingling involving the employing, managerial and professional classes but much less so for forms of cross-class mingling involving the working classes.

It is also notable that, with only one or two exceptions, the institutions comprising the realm of subsidised culture have to do with high-art forms of music of one kind or another. As we have seen, musical tastes remain an unusually sensitive barometer of social distinctions. The conventions governing the performance of high-art musical genres tend to augment such effects to the degree that they usually require special forms of dress and the ability to manifest publicly an aesthetic disposition in exhibiting an appropriately coded and accurately timed appreciation of the performance. These social pressures are much less evident in the realm of public culture where, these days, special dress codes rarely apply.[8] The institutions comprising this realm are also, with the exception of art galleries, more strongly associated with documentary than with aesthetic culture, and they also allow for a greater degree of bodily involvement on the part of the visitor: they are places for walking and seeing rather than for sitting and listening.[9] These differences are tied up with the fact that, historically, these institutions of public culture bear the impress of a different history than that which has shaped subsidised culture. They have their roots in the distinctive kinds of publicness that were created by the late nineteenth century new liberalism in its concern to involve government in the cultural and moral sphere in ways which placed a premium on working-class participation. They were, that is to say, committed to bridging the divide between social classes and, as a consequence, were closely related to other, similar initiatives – to adult education, for example, and, perhaps more important, to the development of public schooling with, from the late nineteenth century through to the present, highly developed and systematic connections with the education system of a kind that are more or less absent from the realm of subsidised culture. The effects of this are evident in the practices of teachers, who are far more involved in the realm of public culture than that of subsidised culture – 50.5% go to museums often or sometimes as do 67.8% to libraries, compared with 16% to orchestral concerts and 36.4% to the theatre – generating benefits whose public effects are multiplied as they are relayed, via the classroom, through the public education system.

The legacies of this history are evident in the demographics of the realm of public culture with its more democratic social profile, and also in the administrative ethos of this sector which places much greater stress on access and equity objectives than does the realm of subsidised culture where such matters are rarely paid even lip-service.[10] There are, it is true, spectacular gestures towards access – the free 'operas in the park' put on by the Australian Opera, for example – but these are very much exceptions which confirm the rule in their failure to connect systematically with the operating routines of the institutions comprising this realm. The differences between these two sectors, however, are due at least as much to the stronger governmental imperatives which have characterised the realm of public culture as they are to the greater stress it has placed on equity considerations. Put another way, the more democratic profile of this realm is due at least as much to the importance that has been attached to its ability to involve the members of lower socioeconomic groups in civilising programs which, historically, have had a variety of aims in view as it has been to the assertion of cultural rights principles. This remains true today, with the important rider that the main targets of this realm are now defined less in class terms, as had been true throughout the history of the new liberalism and the subsequent expansion of the government subvention of culture in later social-welfarist and prudential regimes, than in terms of communities. Within the programs of museums and other collecting institutions, in particular, public culture is increasingly assigned the task of empowering communities: that is, of helping build strong, self-reliant communities that are capable of managing themselves and of producing a strong, but not divisive, sense of identity and belonging for their members. This is not, however, a development restricted to the cultural sphere. The project of 'governing through community' is, in the assessment of Nikolas Rose (1996), part of a significant mutation in the forms of liberal governance in which individuals are increasingly enrolled in the processes of governing themselves not as citizens placed in a direct relationship to the state but indirectly as members of differentiated and often deterritorialised communities.

It is not surprising, then, that relations of culture and community now play an increasingly important role in providing the grounds on which public support for culture is both sought and provided. That said, the meanings that are invested in the term 'community' – one of the loosest and most pliable words in the English language – are highly variable and, depending on how the term is interpreted and operationalised in the policy process, the rationales for public support can be quite different and even diametrically opposed. When its provision is articulated to community empowerment, to the struggles of indigenous Australians, and to the promotion of cultural diversity or to identity politics, government subvention of culture is connected to community as part of a broader program of 'governing differences' through which cultural resources are connected to the task of managing the relationships between the increasingly complex and differentiated ways of life which make up the fabric of Australian civil society. This, however imperfectly it might have been realised in practice, was the aspiration of the multicultural programs developed in the 1983–96 Labor administrations. The coalition government – in disbanding the Office for Multicultural Affairs, in its reluctance to support funding principles that are defined in terms of ethnicity or indigeneity, and in its attacks on 'political correctness' – has sought to redefine the politics of community, construing this mainly in territorial terms in its increased support for cultural funding to flow to the rural and remote areas of Australia as components of regional cultural development programs. At the same time, as arts advocacy and funding agencies look increasingly to American experience to help generate new constituencies of financial support for the arts, there is more than a small risk that the connection that now exists in the United States between philanthropic arts funding and the new right's politics of community will gain an increasing influence here. In this connection, it is not the use of cultural resources to promote *communities* that is at issue but the reinvention of a single and virtuous moral community that will help instil a core, and conservative, set of values which, in turn, will allegedly deliver a series of social benefits of a palliative kind: principally lower rates of crime and drug usage.[11]

From a Foucauldian perspective as well as from the perspective of an economic rationalism committed to principles of distributive justice, the institutions of public culture present a stronger candidacy for government support than do those of subsidised culture. This is because of the ways in which they function, however imperfectly, as parts of capillary systems of cultural distribution through which cultural resources are organised to act on the social in a variety of politically contested ways to bring about a variety of, again politically contested, benefits. Differences of this kind have no particular pertinence in Bourdieu's framework of analysis inasmuch as both realms, albeit to different degrees, involve the use of publicly funded cultural facilities to subsidise as well as to provide a space and setting, a *mise en scène*, for class-based practices of distinction. That said, Bourdieu does attribute a particular importance to the role that the institutions of public culture play in the social processes of distinction when he interprets their openness – that is, the fact that entry to art galleries and museums, for example, is free – as a form of 'false generosity'. Why so? Because, Bourdieu argues, 'free entrance is also optional entrance, reserved for those who, endowed with the ability to appropriate the works, have the privilege of using this freedom and who find themselves consequently legitimised in their privilege' (Bourdieu 1993: 237). The more open and free museums and art galleries are, the more effectively they serve to distinguish between those who, equipped with the cultural resources to understand them, elect to use them and those who, lacking those resources, do not. Their openness in this respect serves only to mask their social closure, and especially as those whom they exclude may not even experience this as a lack. This results, Bourdieu argues, in a paradoxical form of deprivation in which 'the awareness of deprivation decreases in proportion as the deprivation increases, individuals who are most completely dispossessed of the means of appropriating works of art being the most completely dispossessed of the awareness of this dispossession' (Bourdieu 1993: 227).

The different attitudes towards art galleries evident in the conversations of our focus groups provide a telling illustration of Bourdieu's point. Here is how a group of 35–55 year olds with tertiary qualifications and professional, or semi-professional, occupations respond when asked whether they visit art galleries frequently:

DAVID I went back three times – not so much to the art gallery, the museum as well. But there's always something different that you miss the first or second time that you pick up. After the third time, forget it.

GILLIAN I love art galleries.

MAVIS I think maybe a good plan is to just do one section at a time. The State Gallery is so huge. I think that's the way to go.

DAVID It's a whole day's outing – it's that big.

MAVIS But I like Vincent van Gogh's paintings and paintings in that style. But also the one that the Australian government paid a lot of money for. It doesn't have to say a lot to me. But I like sculptures too, especially the one outside the gallery.

Clearly, the degree of involvement in art galleries varies among the members of this group. That said, all of the participants in the discussion are familiar with art galleries and are able to discuss the pros and cons of different ways of using them with a marked degree of cultural confidence. Contrast this with the responses of a group of young working-class adults with no tertiary education:

FACILITATOR I'm wondering if any of you go to art galleries or museums.

JEAN No! Oh, Dad dragged me to one when I was younger. You know, when they had those mud statues. Dad dragged me along to that and that was all right . . .

FACILITATOR And have you been since?

JEAN No!

FACILITATOR Anyone else? Does anyone else go to art galleries or museums?

ALAN Just with the school.

FACILITATOR That was years ago. Tell me why you don't go.

ALAN Boring.

JEAN Boring.

ALAN I went about eight months ago to the Toulouse-Lautrec exhibition. But I only went because my girlfriend dragged me there.

FACILITATOR Did you enjoy it once you were there?

ALAN Oh, just looking at the paintings and seeing what he had done. That was about it.

Of course, the differences between these two patterns of response might be accounted for in many terms. The role of peer-group pressure is evident, particularly in the responses of the young working-class adults where Alan, in order to maintain face within the group, passes himself off as an involuntary art gallery visitor, dragged there against his will by his girlfriend. Even so, something more than an accidental lack of interest is evident here. Rather, and in confirmation of a tendency evident in other studies, what is made manifest in these exchanges is a decided antipathy to art galleries and museums and a determination not to visit them as, more or less, a matter of principle.[12] It might, in this light, seem quixotic or even patronising to view the relatively low levels of participation of the working classes in the institutions of public culture as a matter for concern. If the hierarchy of cultural values that places a special premium on the officially sanctioned culture of art galleries and museums no longer enjoys universal or even widespread acceptance; if those who do not participate in this realm do not experience this as a deprivation – why should these matters be of any general, let alone policy, concern? For it can also be argued that it is not only in relation to high culture that the differential distribution of cultural capital serves to organise relations of distinction between those who possess the cultural skills in question and those who do not. Sarah Thornton (1996) suggests that sub-cultures function in a similar manner, organising relations of cultural inclusion and exclusion between those who can, and those who cannot, exhibit the kinds of *savoir faire* that membership of a sub-culture requires. It is also clear that, in certain circumstances, these and other kinds of cultural capital can be traded in the market for economic advancement: a number of careers in the entertainment and media industries have been based on the successful commercial exploitation of sub-cultural cool.

All of this is true. The major difference, however, is that these forms of cultural capital are not generated in a systematic way in the relations between the education system and the sphere of publicly funded culture. Also, they are not – as yet – associated with long-term and enduring distinctions of class. The reminder is a pertinent one in a political and policy context in which, at the time of writing, those associations may well be strengthened as a result of the increased stress on privatisation and user-pays principles that now characterises both cultural and education policies. It is also important to recall that education serves as a gateway to virtually all forms of cultural participation. Our survey data have thus shown that education increases rates of participation across pretty well the whole field of culture, with only a few exceptions: practising the martial arts and watching sport on television, for example. From this perspective, public investment in education of a kind and level capable of offsetting the effects of different social backgrounds remains crucial to any program of government that is concerned with enhancing the cultural life-chances of its citizens.

The perspectives of distinction and of governmentality, then, provide different vantage points from which to engage critically with the new tendencies in cultural policy associated with advanced liberal forms of government. Habermas' concept of the public sphere has proved somewhat less productive in this regard, partly because of its association with a highly abstract and universalistic set of normative criteria which translate poorly into the terms of public policy debate. In its broader, post-Habermasian interpretation, however, the concept has provided a robust and remarkably fertile point of connection between critical debates and public policy processes and issues.[13] Its pluralisation in the concepts of feminist, black, or indigenous public spheres, for example, has facilitated distinctive and effective interventions in the policy process in establishing forms of cultural entitlement that have gone beyond considerations of access, equity and community empowerment to establish new forms of public, and publicly educative, presence: Sydney's Gay and Lesbian Mardi Gras is a classic example, as is the Aboriginal community-radio sector. Similarly, adaptations of the concept have been significant in debates concerned with the role of government in maintaining conditions that will promote the circulation of varied opinions in face of the oligopolistic tendencies of media markets. It is with these latter concerns in view that we want to draw on the concept, commenting briefly on the significance of the figures relating to public broadcasting. Of all three realms of publicly funded culture, public broadcasting achieves the best social mix in the composition of its audience when measured in terms of level of education, social class, and place of residence, and comes in second in terms of income and form of schooling. Its main shortcoming – but it is a dramatic one – is in its failure to involve young people, although whether this is a generational or a life-cycle effect is hard to determine. Even so, given its programming mix – mainly news, current affairs and quality film and drama in the case of the ABC, and the significantly multicultural content of SBS – our figures suggest that Australia's public broadcasting sector does a passable job of meeting the requirements of a mass-mediated public sphere in regularly involving a heterogeneous public in the major affairs – political, intellectual and cultural – of the day.

There are, of course, other grounds on which government support for particular kinds of culture might be justified: to underpin the development of particular kinds of arts or cultural industries, for example, or as parts of cultural tourism strategies. These are beyond the scope of our concerns in this chapter where, instead, our purpose has been to review our findings in the light of the three main theoretical grammars of publicness available to us in seeking to identify policy rationales for the role of government in the cultural field. Four such rationales have been proposed. The first, taking its cue from Foucault, stresses the importance of bending the inherited apparatuses of public culture to new purposes in the aid of 'governing differences': that is, managing the relationships between the increasingly diverse ways of life that make up civil society. The second, derived from

Bourdieu, concerns the role of the nexus between public culture and public education in enhancing and equalising the cultural life-chances of citizens while, at the same time, reducing its ability to organise, symbolise and thereby legitimise class differences. The third and fourth derive from post-Habermasian debates and have to do, respectively, with the role of government in supporting new forms of public, and publicly educative, presence on the part of groups previously excluded from bourgeois definitions of the public, and with the role of government in organising a public component within the sphere of mass-mediated communication. Little purpose is served by prioritising these rationales one above the other; the challenge for the present is to redefine the discursive ground of public policy in ways that will enhance the effective purchase of these grammars of publicness.

Chapter 10

Conclusion

The Sample as a Whole

To this point in the book our analyses have been comparative, setting the different kinds of groups that make up our sample in relation to each other across a range of cultural domains. The effect of this has been to give glimpses of the general characteristics of our sample, but only in a piecemeal and indirect way. We would now like to take some of the information that we have accumulated about these groups and put it together in a summary biography of three of them. As we shall see, these profiles are not fully adequate as descriptions, but they do allow us to move towards a more general account of the social functions of cultural practices and preferences in Australia.

Age Profiles

Throughout this book we have worked with the fiction of a set of five discrete age cohorts, regularly grouped into clusters of about a fifth of the population each. Of course there are no such cohorts; age is a continuous gradient, and the experience of age at any moment in the life-span is a matter of making intuitive assignments of one's place in relation to peer and non-peer groups which are roughly and variously cut out from that continuum. Rather than trying to map each of these arbitrarily defined cohorts, we shall give here a description of the extreme poles of youth and age, between which the cultural life of the intermediate groups is more or less continuously spread.

At one pole, then, are the under-25s. This group has by far the highest rate of participation in sport, and also the highest rate of smoking. Its members have the strongest preference for American television programs and music, and the weakest preference for Australian television and music.

249

Their favourite authors are American, although they also read more Australian authors than the other age cohorts do. Music is the cultural domain of greatest significance to this group; its strongest preference is for top 40 pop; it does not listen to classical or easy listening music, and strongly dislikes country and western. In general, its tastes are for 'popular' rather than 'high' culture: its attendance at rock concerts, movies, theme parks, night clubs, pubs with live bands and film festivals is very strong; its attendance at high-culture venues is weak. It barely listens to Radio National, and has the lowest rate of watching ABC and SBS television; it has the highest rate for watching commercial television channels and for listening to commercial FM radio. This group does not watch as much television as the older groups; when it does so it watches with friends, and it does not watch news and documentaries; it does watch family sitcoms, sport, films, comedy programs, and soap operas.

At the other pole, the over-60s reverse many of the central cultural values of the young. Lawn bowls is the only sport which its members play frequently; otherwise they play little sport, although they watch more sport at live venues than any other group except the under-25s. This group's strongest preference is for Australian television programs and music, and they have little interest in American materials; their preferred authors are British, and they read substantially more than the young. Literature and television are the most significant cultural domains for them. They mostly watch television alone rather than with friends or family, and they watch a lot of it; they watch the news and documentaries more than other groups, and watch fewer films, comedy programs, sport or sitcoms. They have the highest rate of watching the public broadcasters, and the second-lowest rate of watching commercial television; they listen more to Radio National and less to commercial FM radio than do other groups. When they listen to music their strongest preference is for light classical, musicals, and big band music; there is a steady increase in preference for classical music with age, and an increase in dislike for heavy metal and rock.

Gender Profiles
Gender is perhaps not a fiction in the same way as the concept of an age cohort, but the categories of gender do nevertheless form cultural frameworks, more or less coherent ways of acting and understanding. These frameworks guide choices: women, in our sample, are more strongly involved in dieting and in exercise than men; sport, by contrast, is more strongly coded as a masculine activity, and men play it and watch it more than women. Sports and activities tend to be divided in an exclusive way between the genders, with swimming, walking, netball and aerobics all being coded as 'female', and all either non-competitive or less individually competitive than their 'male' counterparts; golf, squash, touch football

and cricket are coded as 'male', and are competitive at either a team or an individual level. Women dominate the watching of soaps and 'quality' drama on television; men watch sport. The movies that women watch tend to thematise personal relationships and romance, whereas those watched by men tend to involve action. What women look for in a home is a place to be lived in, a place for the family, whereas for men it is, more importantly, a place for the display of class distinctiveness. The kinds of music most listened to by women are light classical, musicals, religious music, easy listening, top 40 pop, soul and opera; the distinctively male genres are heavy metal, rock, blues, alternative rock, techno, and country and western. Women are three times as likely to go to the ballet as men, and twice as likely to go to the opera; they also go more frequently than men to the theatre and to special exhibitions, and in general their rates of attendance at 'high'-culture entertainment venues are greater than men's, and at popular-culture venues they are lower. They also have higher rates of attendance at public 'high'-cultural venues such as museums, botanical gardens, musical performances, public lectures and public libraries. Women read more than men; they have the highest rates of preference for romance fiction, but also for poetry, 'classical' authors and contemporary literature. Men have a preference for factual and documentary genres – scientific, political, historical and travel books, as well as material on sport, erotica and science fiction. Men read newspapers more frequently than women.

Class Profiles
The categories of social class, finally, are very much a construct of our theorisation, the end effect of a long interpretive labour. But although they could have been structured differently, the patterns that they organise are, again, more or less coherent. A schematic profile of the classes is set out below.

Employers have the lowest rate of participation in most sporting and exercise activities, and the highest overall rate of non-participation in sport. Along with the self-employed, they have the highest rate of ownership of fax and answering machines, and the highest rate of ownership of video-cameras. They have high rates of ownership of pottery and of art posters, the highest rate of attendance at the ballet and opera, and high rates of attendance at the theatre, musicals, and shows and expositions. They are the most regular readers of newspapers.

The *self-employed* take fewer holidays than anyone else. Together with employers, they have the highest rate of ownership of faxes and answering machines, but the lowest ownership of CD players. Their ownership of art objects is below the average, and they have the lowest rate of ownership of nature posters. They have average to above-average rates of attendance at most forms of live entertainment, and high rates of attendance at pubs with live bands.

Managers play golf more than any other class (twice the mean rate), as well as lawn bowls and cricket. Together with professionals, they have a high degree of recognition of classical composers, and they have the highest rate of ownership of pianos and other classical musical instruments. Like professionals, they have high rates of ownership of original works of art, high rates of attendance at art galleries, and the highest rates of attendance at museums. They have the strongest interest of any class in photography, and – perhaps correlatively – the highest preference for realist art. They attend musicals, theatre, and special exhibitions more frequently than any other class, and have high rates of attendance at orchestral concerts, chamber music concerts, opera, and movies. Conversely, they have the lowest rates of attendance at rock concerts and pubs with live bands, and rarely go to film festivals and night clubs.

Professionals have the highest rate of holidays of any social class. They attend restaurants more frequently than anybody else. They are the only class with low figures for smoking, and they are active participants in sports (with the highest rates in tennis and swimming), although they watch less sport than any other class. On almost every measure of cultural capital professionals dominate: they have a greater preference than any other class for classical music, and the highest degree of familiarity with classical composers; they own more musical instruments than anyone else, and play them twice as much as any other class; they own more modems than other classes; they have the highest rates of preference for Radio National and ABC Classic FM; and they watch television less than other classes, and have the strongest preference for the public broadcasters and the lowest for commercial television. They have the highest rate of ownership of original works of art, signed limited edition prints, sculptures, nature posters, art posters, and political posters; and of literary classics, art books, history books, biographies and poetry. They have the highest rates of attendance at art galleries, botanical gardens, public musical performances, public lectures and public libraries; at orchestral concerts, chamber music concerts, ballet, movies, shows and expositions, film festivals, and cultural festivals; and the lowest rates of attendance at theme parks and night clubs.

Para-professionals are a culturally ambivalent class, pulling at times towards professionals and at times towards the working classes. They watch more television than any other class, but have the highest rate of preference for abstract art, and the lowest preference for casual family meals. They have the lowest rate of ownership of rock posters, and medium to low ownership of other categories of works of art. Their ownership of books is at the third-lowest overall level, but they have the second-highest rate of use of public libraries. They have average to just above-average rates of attendance at all forms of live entertainment, and they go jogging more than any other class.

Supervisors watch more sport on television than anyone except manual workers. They have below-average rates of ownership of all categories of art object except rock posters and nature posters, and average to below-average attendance at all forms of live entertainment. They constitute the highest readership of tabloid dailies; they have the second-lowest level of overall ownership of books, and the strongest association of any class with science fiction.

The cultural indicators for *sales and clerical workers* intersect strongly with those for women: they have the least interest in news on television, the highest rates of participation in power-walking and aerobics, the highest interest in romance fiction, and they are the most involved in craft activities and clothes making. But their cultural preferences are also those of young people: they have the highest rate of attendance at rock concerts, and high rates of attendance at musicals, movies, theme parks, night clubs, shows and expositions, and pubs with live bands. Gender and age determinations intersect in their scores on the ownership of art objects, where they have the highest rates for pottery and for rock posters.

Manual workers score significantly above the mean in only one sport, touch football, and are only just behind employers in their rate of non-participation in sport. Conversely, they have the highest rates of watching sport at live venues and on television. On virtually all indicators, manual workers represent the pole of least cultural capital, putting them in diametrical opposition to professionals. They have the lowest rate of attendance at restaurants; the strongest preference for country and western and rock, and the least preference for classical and light classical music; they listen least to Radio National and Classic FM, and watch the public broadcasters least while having the highest rate of watching commercial television. They have the highest rate of ownership of guitars but overall the lowest ownership of musical instruments, and the lowest ownership of many domestic technologies (videocameras, computers, answering machines, modems), and are low on all others. They use computers primarily for entertainment rather than for business or education; have a low preference for formal dinners and the strongest preference for casual family meals and barbecues; the lowest ownership of every category of art object except nature posters and rock posters; the lowest ownership of literary classics, art books, history books, biographies, and poetry; and they read newspapers the least of all classes. They have very low attendance at art galleries, orchestral and chamber music concerts, ballet, musicals, opera, theatre, movies, special exhibitions, and film festivals; and they have the highest rates of attendance at theme parks, night clubs and pubs with live bands, and high rates at rock concerts.

Patterns and Probabilities

One of the assumptions underlying the class model that we constructed for this project is that, rather than being an economic structure with effects on other dimensions, class position is formed in each of the economic, the political and the cultural dimensions of social life. There may be homologies or congruences between these dimensions, but equally there may not be; class position is not necessarily unified or non-contradictory.

While the main focus of our survey was on the structure of cultural preference and practice, we also collected quite extensive information on the economic and occupational status of our respondents. The third dimension of class, political orientation, was explored in two sets of questions: one relating to identification with political parties, and another set of questions about attitudes in relation to a range of current social issues.

The question about party-political identification specified four parties (Democrats, Labor, Liberal, National/Country Party) and an 'other' category. We combined Democrat and Labor, on the one hand, and Liberal and National/Country Party, on the other, to produce a broad indicator of 'left' and 'right' orientations, although the large 'other' category (13.7% of respondents) necessarily made this only a rough guide. We made a number of predictable findings: that women are considerably more conservative than men, that conservatism increases with age and with income (especially at the highest level), that suburban and inner-city residents vote less conservatively than residents in rural and semi-rural areas and provincial cities, and that Aborigines vote massively more to the left than the general population. Perhaps the most interesting findings relate to class. We constructed a scale running from 'left' to 'right' on the political spectrum and measured the gap between 'left' and 'right' political orientations within each class. (Thus manual workers, for example, identify strongly with the left of the spectrum, and there is therefore a wide discrepancy between their vote for Labor/Democrats and their vote for Liberal/Nationals.)

Figure 10.1 gives a measure of the extent to which classes are politically cohesive, with the classes at each end of the spectrum being more ideologically unified than those in the middle. 'Left' and 'right' on the political spectrum do not necessarily correspond, however, to 'liberalism' and 'conservatism' in social attitudes. This discrepancy was clearly evident in the answers we received to a standard set of attitudinal questions.[1] We did a principal components factor analysis of these answers and identified three major clusters, as shown in table 10.1. Further analysis gave us information about each factor.

Factor 1 ('conservative welfarist')

Factor 1 brings together a 'welfarist' understanding of the role of government and a suspicion of big business with a conservative attitude towards the role of women in the workforce and the home. It is espoused by the oldest and least-educated members of the community, by men and women equally, and by working-class groups together with the self-employed. Employers and managers are the least favourable to it, with professionals and para-professionals showing ambivalence towards it.

Factor 2 ('progressive feminist')

Factor 2 shares some of the welfarist concerns of factor 1, although it is more open to the role of private enterprise; it differs significantly from factor 1 in its attitude to the role of women. It is espoused by the youngest and best-educated members of the community, by women rather than men, and by working-class groups (especially sales and clerical workers) together with professionals. The strong attitudinal difference between managers (who are strongly opposed to this cluster of values) and professionals – which are, in many other respects, particularly education and income, rather similar groups – is striking, as is perhaps the conservatism of the self-employed on this scale but not on factor 1.

Factor 3 ('conservative pro-market')

Factor 3 is at the other end of the value spectrum: suspicious of the role of government and unions, supportive of private enterprise and of individual responsibility, and conservative in its view of the place of women in the

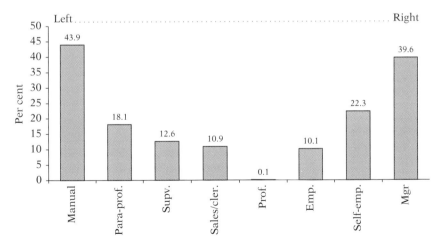

Figure 10.1 Percentage differences between 'left' and 'right' orientations within classes

Table 10.1   Factor pattern matrix of social, political and economic attitudes†

	Factor 1	Factor 2	Factor 3
The government has a responsibility to support the disadvantaged	**61***	24	9
People should be encouraged to take responsibility for providing their own health cover	9	9	**74***
The trade unions in this country have too much power	8	5	**74***
Wages and incomes should be controlled by some government body	**61***	19	24
If both husband and wife work they should share equally in the housework and childcare	24	**64***	25
Big corporations have too much power in Australian society today	**58***	16	17
The government should provide a universal system of health care	**67***	21	−4
It is better for the family if the husband is the principal breadwinner and the wife cares for the home	**53***	**−38***	**45***
If the government was more active in industrial relations industry would run more efficiently	**60***	22	23
Large companies like BHP should always be privately owned	31	6	**60***
There should be satisfactory childcare facilities so women can take jobs outside the home	18	**74***	9
Government instrumentalities such as Telecom should not be privatised	**67***	7	10
The government should provide more chances for children from poor families to go to university	**50***	**50***	5
There should be as many women as men in important positions in government and business	24	**76***	8
The welfare system supports many people who are not genuinely needy	3	18	**66***
The government should move towards the granting of land rights for Aborigines	**51***	**41***	2

† Printed values are multiplied by 100 and rounded to the nearest integer. Values greater than 0.35 have been flagged by an *.

workforce and the home and of Aboriginal rights. These values are espoused by the oldest and least-educated members of the community, and by the two employer classes and managers. Professionals stand alone in their refusal of them, with the working-class groups somewhat more ambivalent but still largely outside of this ethos.

There is thus a neat symmetry between the composition of the three factors, with factors 1 and 3 aligned in being made up of the oldest and least-educated groups, but opposed (by and large) in their class composition; factors 1 and 2 having a similar class composition but diametrically opposed in age and education; and factors 2 and 3 being diametrically opposed both in terms of class and in terms of age and education. If we were to extrapolate from these patterns to consider social class alone, and taking into account some of the ambivalences in these symmetries, we could say that professionals are the most 'progressive' class in their attitudes and that employers and managers are the most conservative in most respects. To this dichotomy we must add, however, that the self-employed share the conservative welfarism of factor 1 (as well as being the most hawkish proponents of the pro-market factor 3); and that the working classes are aligned with professionals on political and economic attitudes, but do not share their progressive views on the role of women in the workplace and the home. Just as significantly, we can see clear evidence here of the demarcation between an older and a younger Australia, and thus of the central place of age in shaping social views.

This concludes our analysis of the configuration of social class in Australia. At this point, however, we must step back for a moment to reflect upon a fundamental deficiency in this profiling of social groups conceived as more or less autonomous social agents. As we argued in an earlier chapter, it is important to avoid a naïve representationalism which would endow the categories of our analysis with an existence outside and prior to the two sets of relations from which they emerge: on the one hand, the multivariate relationality of social life in which lines of force and the shifting crystallisations of structure are complexly interdeterminant; and, on the other, their formation within the frameworks of interest and knowledge that have governed our research. This is not to argue that these categories have nothing to do with reality. But their logic is stochastic rather than representational: they build a reality on the basis of probabilities and statistical trends, rather than reproducing a reality which would in some sense be analogous to that of the material world.

In the 'narrative' modes of presentation that we, like anyone else who attempts to describe and interpret social processes, have necessarily used, we have tended to shift imperceptibly from talking of probabilities to talking of the characteristics of a population: from 'there is about a 10 per cent greater likelihood of men (defined by gender alone without reference to other dimensions of social being) reading newspapers daily than of women (similarly defined) doing so', to 'men read newspapers more frequently than women'. We substantialise a set of statistical variations, thereby producing typifications. And typifications, as Asad (1994: 66) notes, are not a bad abstraction from the specificity of experience; rather, they *inform* that experience, shaping the observation of 'concrete' social processes. They both enable analysis of the detailed distribution of variance, and make possible the reduction of variance to a substantialised sameness. Much of what is most interesting in our data, however, happens non-typically: adolescents who read extensively or listen to classical music; manual workers who watch stockcar races and play the violin; men who do craft activities, women who cannot bear to watch soap operas.

To typify is to reduce complexity; and the problem of all social analysis is to find a way between the overwhelming, disparate, chaotic (or, rather, *overly* meaningful) mass of particulars and the narrative of forces, causes and directions which constitutes the logic of social explanation. We have not assumed that we can avoid this predicament, or that there is a form of explanation which could ultimately allow us to avoid using such a narrative structure; we too have talked of typified social actors, of polarities, of trends and significances. But we have attempted to organise our work around an ideal of multiplicity and complexity of explanation, and to think in terms of open rather than closed systems. We have sought, where possible, to build multi-dimensional matrices to account for the complex configurations that shape and are shaped by social action; the profiles of detached and autonomous groups are reductive of this complexity. Clearly we need to move beyond them, and in the following section we explore some ways of rethinking the relationality of these variables at the level of a more extended analysis of the institutions of cultural value.

Regimes of Value

Between 1559 and 1597 Queen Elizabeth issued ten proclamations seeking to regulate sumptuary practice in England and Wales. These proclamations, aimed in large part at the newly affluent and upwardly mobile class of gentry (Ashelford 1988: 108), defined in great detail the kinds of fabric appropriate to each 'degree, estate and condition', and set in train a series of prohibitions on 'inordinate' display. Thus a law of 1566, for example, ordered:

> that no man under the degree of a baron's eldest son, except that he be of the Order of the Garter or of the Privy Council, or that he may dispend 500 marks by year for term of life in possession above

all charges, shall wear any velvet or satin, or any stuff of like or
greater price, in the upperstocks of his hose or in any part thereof;
or shall garnish the same with any embroidery or any fringe, lace,
or passement of gold, silver, or silk, nor any other garnishing with
any silk, except it be for the stitching only of the upper part to the
lining; nor shall wear any manner of silk netherstocks of hose, nor
any kersey or other thing made out of the Queen's majesty's domin-
ions. (Hughes & Larkin, 1969: 281–2)

The sumptuary code set out in these proclamations is what we have called,
in an earlier chapter, a *regime of value*. It contains explicit instructions about
what is proper or improper, decorous or indecorous in the use of valued
matter by the different degrees of social rank. In fact – as is evidenced by
their continual repetition – these laws, with their petulant denunciation of
'excess', were widely flouted. But this is beside the point: what is of interest
is that they codify, and seek to impose, the values of a set of material objects
and their proper use within the framework of a status system. They legislate,
that is to say, a set of proper relations between cultural goods and a system
of social power.

What is anomalous, from a twentieth-century perspective, about this
codification is just that it is so explicit and so highly ritualised. It is broadly
characteristic of modern social formations that matters of decorum shift
from being governed by religious or civil protocols and become matters of
'personal' taste – that is, a matter of choices made in accordance with no
authority other than personal conscience. (The parallel with the reforma-
tions of religious mediation is clear.) The taxonomic regimes that govern
cultural practice in modern social formations are thus considerably less
inflexible than those governed by strict custom or by the authority of church
and state. They conform to DiMaggio's (1987: 442) description of 'mass
cultures' as being 'weakly differentiated, universal, ritually weak, and
because nondifferentiated, relatively nonhierarchical'. But this is not to say
that there is an absence of codifications, nor that these do not continue to
be overdetermined by 'degree, estate and condition'. Rather, these codifications operate at two discrete levels, such that the appearance of freedom of
personal choice in matters of taste masks the informal but powerful conditions governing choices in all domains of value. Barthes (1990) has plausibly
demonstrated the force of conventions both of combination and of appro-
priateness in the contemporary fashion system; such informal but intense
forms of codification prevail in all of the domains of cultural preference that
we discuss in this book. The templates by which they are structured may
not ever be explicitly set out, but they are expressed and refined at every
level of cultural legislation, from literary and film criticism, to discussions
at work about last night's television programs, to transient comments about

someone's good or bad taste in jewellery or in souped-up cars or in colour schemes for the house.

The name that we have given to these systems of codification is 'regimes of value'. With this term we designate those normative organisations of the proper which specify what counts as a good object of desire or pleasure; a good relation to or use of it; a proper mode of access or entry to it; and an appropriate range of valuations. Such regimes, governing such domains as reading, concert-going, popular music, the watching of sport, or the care of the body, are configurations which, while constantly mutating, have taken on a certain stability over time and which are grounded in a particular crystallisation of administrative, economic, technological and legal infrastructures. They have no given unity, however; nor do they have a literal 'reality'. The concept designates a convergence of lines of force which is discernible in its effects and which can be subsumed within larger conceptual structures or broken down to smaller, more specific levels. They cohere as axiological regularities (regularities of evaluation and judgement), and it is because of this that they are not equivalent to the concept of a culture *industry*. Regimes of value in radio broadcasting, for example, would be posited at the level, not of the industrial organisation of the radio communications system but at that of the historically particular value-laden distinction between commercial and public broadcasters: a distinction which can then always be ramified, according to the context of meaningfulness, into a finer web of differentiations (commercial FM vs commercial AM; talkback vs easy listening stations, and so on). Because regimes are thus a ground, a field of activities and more or less formalised structures, they allow diverse points of entry and diverse uses. They are regulatory but heterogeneous, and this means that they are never simply expressive of, and never simply reflect, a class structure, or the ethos of an age cohort or a gender or a structure of sexual preference. All social groups have, or may have, a place in each of them, but – although no one escapes – they are of different interest to different groups, and attract different kinds of investment of interest. Sites of tension, spaces of dispersion, they are not themselves expressions of power but sites through which power flows.

What a study like ours cannot do (except, to a limited extent, in the interviews and focus groups) is explore the detailed content of these codifications. Each of them is enormously rich and complex, and each would require an intensive and subtle analysis in its own right. That is the task of other, specialised forms of qualitative interpretation. What we can do, however, is analyse the differential relation of social groups to these systems – the patterns of variation which, like a Christo landscape wrapped in cloth, reveal the outlines of those largely invisible taxonomic orders.

The central point that we wish to make – and it is one that is already figured in many of our detailed analyses – is that there is not a single hierarchy organising all regimes of value. In this respect the concept of regime is crucially different from Bourdieu's concept of *field* which in many ways it otherwise resembles. In Bourdieu's argument, the limited domains of cultural practice that he calls fields organise a specific configuration of properties, including a particular relationship between cultural, educational and economic capital and the particular volume and trajectory of these capitals that will prevail in the 'market' that the field constitutes. Ultimately, however, any field is governed by the singular logic of the homology between the hierarchical ordering of cultural domains and the stratified order of social class (Bourdieu 1984: 232). Cultural practice, that is to say, must always be analysed within the specific context of the field in which criteria of judgement are differentially developed and values asserted; but in the last instance this specificity can be reduced to the universality of class domination.

Our analyses do not support this understanding. Let us illustrate our quarrel with Bourdieu by sketching out the configurations of strongest and weakest involvement that correspond to the regimes of value governing theatre, opera and rock concerts (tables 10.2, 10.3 and 10.4).

Some things remain constant across these three configurations: the strong contribution of private schooling, inner-city residence and high income to all these activities; the low participation rates of rural residents. In other respects there are clear patterns of contrast between the two 'high'-cultural regimes and the popular regime of rock: the diametrically opposed participation of manual workers; the opposition of the oldest age cohorts in the former to the youngest cohorts in the latter; the lack of gender differentiation in relation to rock music. But what interests us above all is that there is no single general pattern prevailing either over all three regimes, or even over the two closely associated regimes of theatre and opera. As it happens, employers have high rates of participation in both theatre and opera; but this is not of a piece with their rather low rates of involvement in those forms of high-cultural activity which are not expensive or socially prestigious. Moreover, the different mix of rates of participation as between employers, managers and professionals is not something to be swept beneath the convenient label of 'dominant class': if there is one thing our studies have shown, it is that the commonalities between the two employer classes, managers, and professionals are limited and highly variable. These groups do not form a single class, and neither do they form the 'dominant' and 'dominated' fractions of a single class: they have different and specific interests on each dimension of social life. In many respects employers and, especially, the self-employed have more in common culturally with the manual working class and with supervisors than they do with managers and

Table 10.2 Strongest and weakest levels of involvement in theatre

+	−
managers, professionals, employers	manual
female	male
over 46	under 35
completed tertiary	primary, some sec., voc./appr.
private schools	state schools
highest incomes	lowest incomes
inner city, provincial cities	rural, semi-rural, small town
non-Aboriginal	Aboriginal

Table 10.3 Strongest and weakest levels of involvement in opera

+	−
employers, managers, professionals	manual, supervisors, sales/clerical
female	male
oldest	youngest
completed tertiary	primary, some sec., part tertiary
private schools	state schools
highest incomes	lowest incomes
inner city	rural, semi-rural, small town

Table 10.4 Strongest and weakest levels of involvement in rock concerts

+	−
sales/clerical, manual, para-profs	managers, self-employed
youngest	oldest
part tertiary, voc./appr.	primary
private schools	no formal education
highest incomes	lowest incomes
inner city, small town	rural, provincial city

professionals; and while the latter classes are closer to each other than to any other class, they have diametrically opposed positions on our social attitudes scale.

Certain patterns of cultural difference, it is true, are repeated and consolidated across cultural domains: the constant polarisation of professionals and manual workers is a clear example. But these patterns are differently inflected for each regime by its particular configuration of the lines of social force, by the different weight it assigns to cultural and economic capital, by the different colouring given by the dominance of age or gender or class to the regime as a whole. The shifting rank orders of the mean squares that we have applied in our factor analyses are one way of representing these inflectional variations. It is true, too, that in so far as cultural practice organises relations of distinction, it tends to be organised as a series of dichotomies. But we are unwilling to reduce these diverse dichotomies to a single core structure of which everything else would be the expression. We make three arguments about this. First, unlike the situation that Bourdieu describes for the France of the 1960s, these dichotomisations tend in Australia to be relatively weak and relatively diffuse. Second, the scales of value organising cultural dichotomies are not necessarily shared by all participants – there is, for example, no recognition of the illegitimacy of 'popular' values on the part of those who espouse them. And third, these scales of value are not homologous: different configurations of actors occupy the corresponding positions on them, although the class of professionals tends to be at or near the top of many of them, and manual workers tend to be at or near the bottom. Nor, therefore, are they homologous with an invariant hierarchy of social power. We would want to say that power and prestige flow through these configurations, or are staged in them, rather than conceiving them either as inherently aligned with or against power, or as the secondary manifestation of a structure of power that is defined elsewhere.

Rather than displaying a singular structure of value running from the legitimate and prestigious to the illegitimate and valueless (or – the counter-cultural version of this – from the exclusive to the boldly transgressive), cultural practices in all their heterogeneity are organised by different and often incommensurable scales. Watching the football on Saturday, playing beach cricket, growing giant pumpkins for the show, driving a stock car, walking a bush trail, doing voluntary work for a service club, playing bridge, gardening, working out, going to the movies or to a dance club . . . each of these is diversely configured and specifically valued in ways that do not sustain generalisation. What we can perhaps generalise, however, is the scale that runs from inclusive to restricted forms of involvement in cultural practice, and its almost invariable correlation with level of education. A clear example of this scale can be found in the polarity formed between two sorts of preference for ideal holidays. The right-hand column of table 10.5 corresponds to a measure of high cultural capital and social privilege, the left-hand column to its obverse. What does this opposition mean?

In Bourdieu's frequently reductive account of social interests, the primary (often, it seems, the exclusive) function of possession of cultural capital is that of maintaining and extending social status. While we do not, by any means, wish to reject this argument, we believe that the functions of cultural capital are more complex. Paul DiMaggio wrote recently in a study of museum-goers that, rather than having the function of defining one as a member of a tightly bounded status group, 'taste for the arts may be more

Table 10.5   Preference for holidays

Own state	Overseas
self-employed, para-prof., manual workers	employers, managers, professionals
over-60s	under-25s
primary-educated	tertiary-educated
state and Catholic schools	private schools
Aborigines	non-Aborigines
lowest incomes	highest incomes
provincial cities, rural, small towns	inner city, suburbs

important as a privileged indicator . . . of a more general capacity and inclination to familiarise oneself with whatever cultural currency is valuable in
the contexts in which one functions' (DiMaggio 1996: 163). The significance
of the dominance of professionals on many of our scales is not that it
translates and furthers their social dominance. They are not the dominant
social class, because they do not own and control economic capital; they are
for the most part the employees either of those who do, or of the state. What
it does express is the diversity and scope of their interests, their receptiveness
to the culturally unfamiliar, and the value that they place on information
and learning. These values are not, of course, incompatible with elitism and
exclusiveness, but they do not, in themselves, carry and enact social exclusion. What we might add, however, is that in an information society they
perhaps constitute a form of power in their own right.

Social Reproduction

Let us pursue this question of the functions performed by possession of
cultural capital by looking at the argument – central to Bourdieu's work on
education – that cultural capital is functional not only in differentiating
social groups, but in reproducing over time their internal closure and the
social inequalities that this entails. Our study provides considerable evidence
that 'culturedness' is not particularly salient in the self-definition of the
economically dominant social groups in Australia, with the exception of
certain activities, such as going to the theatre, the ballet and the opera,
which are at once prestigious and expensive. It is likely that conspicuous
consumption, rather than the display of 'good taste', is the primary mode of
status distinction within the Australian social order. Similarly, Crook (1997:
57) provides clear evidence that cultural practices have no bearing on occupational success – although he is naïve in his assumption that the major
determinant of occupational outcomes, educational success, is somehow a
neutral distributive instrument. Bourdieu and Passeron's (1964; 1970: 25)

argument is precisely that the schooling system at once reinforces and inten-
sifies inequalities in the distribution of cultural capital, and thereby reinforces certain kinds of class-based cognitive style which in turn are the
mechanisms for the achievement of academic success.

One of the ways in which our study allows us to test the hypothesis that
possession of cultural capital plays a major role in the reproduction of social
inequalities is by reference to a question asking respondents how much
emphasis their children's school places on art and musical training, on a
scale from 'a great deal' through 'quite a bit' to 'some', 'not much', and 'none
at all' (see figure 10.2).

This question of course allows respondents considerable scope for interpretation, and it may be in part that what the figures indicate is not just
class-based variations in kinds of schooling, but also variations in what
parents expect of their children's schools, or indeed variable understandings
of what would *constitute* a strong emphasis on art and musical training. The
fact that responses by gender give a higher score for female respondents
than for men would support this hypothesis, since men and women do not
send their children to different schools. Nevertheless, it is still striking that
the two classes which arguably have the strongest relation (either of ownership or of administration) to economic capital both score below the mean
on this question. This suggests quite clearly that the acquisition of cultural
capital does not figure high on the list of what they desire or what they get
from their children's education.

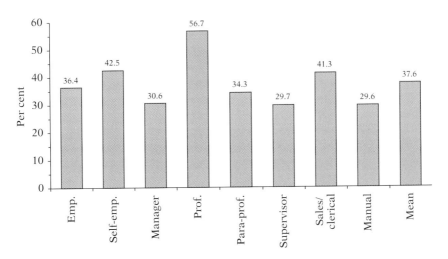

Figure 10.2 Children's school's emphasis on art and musical training by class
(combined responses 'a great deal' and 'quite a bit')

We do, however, have another and much clearer indication of what the different social classes want from their children's schools, and of how it might translate into social advantage. Comparative figures for public and private schooling, both on the part of our respondents and on the part of their children, are shown in tables 10.6 and 10.7.

On the basis of tables 10.6 and 10.7, we made three further sets of calculations. First, we calculated the ratio between the combined rate for all private education, including Catholic schools, in each class and the rate of state school education. The higher the ratio, the higher the degree of private education: thus in table 10.8, under the category 'self', it is clear that professionals and managers have the highest rate of private education, and manual workers and supervisors the lowest. We then made the same calculation for the children of respondents; here it is clear that the children of employers and professionals have the highest rate of private education, and the children of the four 'lower' classes together with the self-employed have the lowest rate. We then calculated the percentage ratio of these two ratios in order to make a cross-generational comparison: the percentage figures give an indication of the increase or decrease in rates of private education from parents to children (see figure 10.3). This is, effectively, an index of the increasing or declining fortunes of each class, or, to put it more precisely, of the extent to which each class values private education as an instrument of class improvement, and has the capacity to invest in it.

The striking figure here, of course, is the one for employers: a group which starts out with a high rate of private education, but which pursues it so vigorously for its children that less than half of them attend public schools. Supervisors have been similarly able to increase upward mobility across the generations, although starting from a low base, and so have professionals from what was already the highest base rate. Managers have remained constant in their cross-generational participation in private schooling, and there

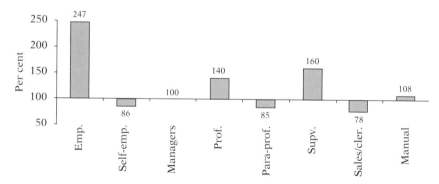

Figure 10.3 Percentage shift to private schooling from respondents' generation to their children's generation

Table 10.6 Rates of public and private schooling by class – self (row percentages)†

	State	Catholic	Combined other private
Employers	65.6	21.6	11.2
Self-employed	69.8	16.9	12.4
Managers	65.4	26.1	8.5
Professionals	64.1	22.9	13.0
Para-professionals	72.6	19.6	7.9
Supervisors	80.5	12.0	7.6
Sales & clerical	69.4	21.4	8.6
Manual	82.3	11.7	3.2

Table 10.7 Rates of public and private schooling by class – children (row percentages)†

	State	Catholic	Combined other private
Employers	44.9	25.9	29.2
Self-employed	73.3	13.5	13.2
Managers	65.5	18.9	15.6
Professionals	56.0	19.5	24.5
Para-professionals	75.7	16.2	8.1
Supervisors	72.0	18.5	9.5
Sales & clerical	74.9	19.8	5.3
Manual	83.6	14.3	2.1

† The category 'no formal education' is not included in these row percentages

Table 10.8 Ratios of all private schooling to state schooling, by class, and percentage shift to private schooling from respondents' generation to their children's generation

	Self	Children	Percentage increase/decrease
Employers	0.50	1.23	247
Self-employed	0.42	0.36	86
Managers	0.53	0.53	100
Professionals	0.56	0.79	140
Para-professionals	0.38	0.32	85
Supervisors	0.24	0.39	160
Sales & clerical	0.43	0.34	78
Manual	0.18	0.20	108

is a slight rise for manual workers – but for both respondents and their children this happens in the context of a strikingly low participation rate in private education. The classes of the self-employed, para-professionals, and sales and clerical workers all show a decline in participation – in effect, a downward mobility across the generations.

The juxtaposition of these figures with those for the emphasis that schools place on art and musical training makes it clear that what parents want for their children from private schooling is not, in the first instance, cultural capital but rather the acquisition of what Bourdieu (Bourdieu & Wacquant 1992: 119) calls 'social capital': that is, 'the sum of the resources, actual or virtual, that accrue to an individual or a group by virtue of possessing a durable network of more or less institutionalised relationships of mutual acquaintance and recognition': a network of 'connections', in short. Erickson (1996), accusing Bourdieu of neglecting social capital, makes a similar argument that social networks play a much stronger role in the maintenance of social position than does the possession of cultural capital. This is not to deny the importance of cultural capital in the formation and differentiation of social classes: clearly 'high'-cultural preferences and practices are important in the formation of the class of professionals, just as rock music is important in the self-definition of the working classes. All we want to argue is that these processes do not take place along a singular scale of cultural value, and that it is not possible to extrapolate effects of dominance from them. They have effects of cohesion in relation to any one class, but they do not necessarily have effects beyond that nexus of class and culture. In general, we hypothesise, it is economic capital and social capital that play the major role in the generation and reproduction of class inequality in Australia.

In this study we have shown, as Bourdieu does, that cultural competence is concentrated in the most-educated classes, the elite social groups of professionals and managers; we have also reproduced his finding of a marked non-coincidence of cultural capital with economic capital. Unlike Bourdieu, however, we do not assume that the employer classes and the classes of professionals and managers are fractions of the same class; we posit that they have different social interests predicated on the difference between the possession and the administration of capital. Managers and professionals, in turn, are differentiated in part by their relation to the division between the private and public sectors. Our analysis shows a clear cultural disadvantage to the working classes, and especially to manual workers; this disadvantage is measured not so much by their exclusion from 'high' culture as by the restrictedness of their cultural practice overall.

We have questioned, however, whether cultural capital is directly tied to the reproduction of class inequality. We posit that the struggle to transmit social advantage to the next generation has more to do with the possession of social capital than with cultural capital. Because of the relatively weak role of cultural capital in this process, we assign it less of an exclusionary role than Bourdieu does – except to the extent that every class, every age cohort, each gender uses *whatever material is to hand* as a tool of differentiation and of exclusion. This can as well be rock music or football or soap operas as ballet or the beaux arts.

The key untested assumption in Bourdieu's work is that there is a single powerful and universally binding scale of cultural legitimacy which produces effects of social legitimation, and which endows those without cultural capital with a sense of their own inferiority. This thesis may have been valid in the France of the 1960s, but we can find little evidence to support it for the Australia of the 1990s. The cultural field that we have investigated is marked by a plurality of scales of value, in many of which age or gender or regional location, rather than social class, play a dominant role. This finding accords with an argument made in much recent work in cultural studies, to the effect that cultural authority and prestige are dispersed across a range of incommensurable regimes of value. Rather than being organised around a polarity of the dominant and the deprived or resistant, the cultural field 'does not have one centre, or no centre, but multiple, simultaneous centres' (Collins 1989: 25; see also Frow 1995: 23–5).

Perhaps our most significant conclusion concerns the importance of the dichotomy between inclusive and restricted forms of cultural practice as the most general form of cultural dichotomisation, cutting across that plurality of value systems. This scale is more strongly linked to education, and the class-forming effects of education, than to other dimensions of social class such as the possession of economic capital; it is also strongly marked by age and gender and urbanity. It expresses a relationship of distinction; but it also marks a more universal set of values (comprehensive rather than limited participation in culture) from which we can derive more positive political and policy conclusions. The advantage of working with this model of cultural dichotomy is that it can move us away from two complementary ways of understanding cultural distinction: as an exercise of power which produces effects of deprivation, or as an exercise of power which produces effects of transgression. Cultural distinction is as complex as social life itself.

Appendix 1: The Sample

The sampling frame for the *Everyday Cultures* survey was based upon the Australian Electoral Roll which had been updated in August 1994. A total of 5000 non-institutionalised adults were obtained by firstly stratifying by state and territory and then applying systematic random sampling within these strata. Fieldwork commenced in late October 1994 and was concluded in March 1995. At this time, of the original 5000 questionnaires a total of 550 had been returned undelivered, a further 450 were returned as refusals, with a total of 2756 useable returns. The response rate calculated as the number of returns as a percentage of the number in-scope is thus 61.9 per cent. The distribution of the sample by state and territory in comparison with 1994 ABS population estimates is shown in table A.1.

A note on weighting
There are some minor discrepancies between the educational level and gender composition of the sample and the adult population as indicated by population estimates obtained from 1994 ABS sample surveys. To correct for this the sample data are post-stratified using a series of weights which brings the age and educational composition of the sample to be representative of the population aged 18 years and older. A further minor corrective was made to make the gender distribution representative. All analyses in the book are based on weighted data.*

---

* We would like to gratefully acknowledge the assistance of Dr Mark Western, School of Sociology and Social Work, University of Tasmania, in the construction of the weight variable.

Table A.1   Distribution of the sample by state and territory in comparison to ABS population estimates

State/territory	1995 Everyday Culture Survey	1994 ABS population estimates
NT (19)	0.7	1.0
ACT (51)	1.9	1.7
Tas. (72)	2.6	2.6
WA (246)	8.9	9.6
SA (253)	9.2	8.2
Qld (529)	19.2	18.0
NSW (867)	31.5	33.9
Vic. (719)	26.1	25.0
N = 2756	100.0	100.0

Appendix 2: The Questionnaire

Section A Your Household

A1   Do you live in a:
     House _____   Flat or unit _____
     Caravan/mobile home _____   Retirement village _____
     Townhouse _____   Rented room _____

A2   Do you:
     Own outright _____   Rent _____
     Have a mortgage _____

A3   If you rent, are you planning to purchase a permanent dwelling at some
     time? _____

A4   Is your place of residence:
     Inner city _____   Semi-rural (acreage) _____
     Suburban _____   Rural _____
     Small town _____

A5   Is your dwelling (house, unit, etc.):
     Less than 10 years old _____   10–20 years old _____
     21–50 years old _____   More than 51 years old _____

A6   Where did you get the *main* items of furniture in your home?
     Department store _____   Furniture warehouse/chain store ____
     Antique dealer _____   Craftshop _____
     Second-hand shop or auction ____   Inherited _____
     Rented _____   Other _____

A7 Thinking for a moment about what would be the ideal home for you, choose the three terms from the list below which come closest to describing your ideal home.

Clean and tidy ——————— Traditional ———————
Comfortable ——————— Distinctive ———————
Well designed ——————— Imaginative ———————
Uncluttered ——————— Elegant ———————
Easy to maintain ——————— Lived in ———————
Modern ——————— Spacious ———————

A8 Looking again at the list, which three terms are of the *least* importance in describing your ideal home?

Least important ——————— Third least important ———————
Next least important ———————

A9 Which of the following items of equipment do you have in your household?

Radio ——————— Television set ———————
Video recorder ——————— Cassette player ———————
Record player ——————— Compact disc player ———————
Camera ——————— Video camera ———————
Personal computer ——————— Fax machine ———————
Telephone ——————— Phone answering machine ———————
Modem ———————

A10 If you own a camera what do you mainly use it for?

Family or holiday snapshots ———— Serious compositions ———————
Portraits ——————— Other ———————

A11 If you have a personal computer what is it mostly used for?

Work or business ——————— Education ———————
Household management ———————— Other ———————
Entertainment or recreation ————

A12 Do you have any of the following in your home?

Original paintings/drawings ———— Pottery or ceramics ———————
Signed limited edition prints ———— Sculpture ———————
Rock music posters ——————— Nature posters ———————
Art posters ——————— Political posters ———————

A13 Do you have a musical instrument(s) in your household? (*Please specify*)

A14 Is there a car in your household? ———————

A15 What make(s)? ———————

A16 What year(s) of manufacture? ———————

A17 Who generally does the servicing on the car(s)? ———————
I do myself ———————
Another household member ———————
A friend or neighbour on an informal basis ———————
A garage or service station ———————

A18 If money was no problem what make of car would you *most* like to own? ————

A19 Do you keep any animals as pets in your household? ———————

A20 Please list up to 3 animals kept as pets including breed or type of animal. ———————

A21   What is your main reason for keeping a pet? _____

A22   Including yourself, how many people normally live in your household? _____

Section B Domestic Leisure

B1   Of the activities listed below, which do you do often, which do you do
     sometimes, which do you hardly ever do, and which do you never do?

	Often	Sometimes	Hardly ever	Never
Home repairs	_____	_____	_____	_____
Do-it-yourself home improvements	_____	_____	_____	_____
Gardening	_____	_____	_____	_____
Drawing or sketching	_____	_____	_____	_____
Photography	_____	_____	_____	_____
Creative writing	_____	_____	_____	_____
Playing a musical instrument	_____	_____	_____	_____
Craft activity	_____	_____	_____	_____
Clothes making	_____	_____	_____	_____
Playing cards or chess	_____	_____	_____	_____
Computer or video games	_____	_____	_____	_____
Board games	_____	_____	_____	_____
Fantasy/role playing games	_____	_____	_____	_____
Listening to music	_____	_____	_____	_____
Reading	_____	_____	_____	_____
Listening to the radio	_____	_____	_____	_____

B2   Which one of the following do you *mostly* look for in your domestic leisure?

Relaxation _____   Intellectual stimulation _____

Escape from work _____   Developing new interests _____

Doing something useful _____   Just passing time _____

B3   If you listen to the radio at home which radio station do you *mostly* listen to?

Commercial FM _____   ABC AM: Radio National _____

Commercial AM _____   ABC AM: Regional _____

ABC FM – JJJ _____   Ethnic radio _____

ABC FM – (Fine Music) _____   Community radio _____

Classical _____   I don't listen to radio _____

Other _____

B4   When you listen to the radio at home how often would you listen to the
     following types of programmes?

	Listen regularly	Listen sometimes	Do not listen
Easy listening	_____	_____	_____

B4 *continued*	Listen regularly	Listen sometimes	Do not listen
Classic hits	_____	_____	_____
Mainstream rock (MOR)	_____	_____	_____
Alternative rock (new music)	_____	_____	_____
Classical music	_____	_____	_____
Sport	_____	_____	_____
News	_____	_____	_____
Current affairs	_____	_____	_____
Talkback	_____	_____	_____
Comedy programmes	_____	_____	_____
Arts programmes	_____	_____	_____
Business programmes	_____	_____	_____
Science programmes	_____	_____	_____
Other	_____	_____	_____

B5   How many hours of TV do you think you watch over the course of a week?

30 hours or more _____   9 hours or fewer _____

Between 20 and 29 hours _____   I don't watch TV at all _____

Between 10 and 19 hours _____

B6   How often would you watch each of the following different stations?

	Mainly watch	Watch regularly	Watch some-times	Do not watch	Not available where I live
ABC	_____	_____	_____	_____	_____
Commercial channels	_____	_____	_____	_____	_____
SBS	_____	_____	_____	_____	_____
Sky channel	_____	_____	_____	_____	_____

B7   Which types of programme do you make a point of trying to see?

News _____	Current affairs _____
Family sitcoms _____	Police/detective _____
Personal issues TV (e.g. Donahue) _____	Documentaries _____
Humour _____	Quiz shows _____
Soap operas _____	Sport _____
Arts programmes _____	Films _____
Chat shows _____	Variety shows _____
Quality drama _____	Children's programmes _____
Open learning _____	Reality TV (e.g. Cops) _____

B8   What are the names of your three favourite television programmes? _____

B9 Do you normally watch television:
    By yourself _____ With family _____
    With friends _____

B10 If you watch with your family, how is programme choice made?
    By mutual agreement _____ Other _____
    I choose _____

B11 How often would you read a newspaper?
    Daily _____ Rarely _____
    Sometimes _____ Never _____

B12 Which newspapers do you read? _____

B13 Which magazines do you read? _____

B14 What is your main source of news? _____
    Newspapers _____ Radio _____
    Television _____

Section C Your Social Activities

C1 When you have guests or visitors to your home, are they mostly:
    Family _____ Work colleagues _____
    Friends _____

C2 When you have guests for a meal, what kind of food do you prefer to serve?
    Your usual cooking _____ Innovative or exotic recipes _____
    Health food _____ Whatever is going _____
    Simple but tasty food _____ Takeaways _____
    Something special _____ I don't entertain _____

C3 How do you generally prefer to present the meal?
    Formal dinner _____ BBQ _____
    Casual family meal _____ Buffet _____
    Brunch _____ Alfresco _____

C4 Which *one* of the following do you prefer to drink socially?
    Wine _____ Juice or softdrink _____
    Beer _____ Cocktails _____
    Mineral water _____ Liqueurs _____
    Spirits _____ Other _____

C5 Do you regularly follow any special diet? _____

C6 Do you regularly use vitamin supplements? _____

C7 Do you smoke? _____

C8 Do you eat at fast food outlets which do not serve alcohol such as *McDonald's* or *KFC*:
    Once a week or more _____ Rarely _____
    A couple of times a month _____ Never _____

C9 Do you eat at fast food outlets which do serve alcohol such as *Pizza Hut* or *Sizzlers*:
    Once a week or more _____ Rarely _____
    A couple of times a month _____ Never _____

C10 Do you eat at restaurants:

Once a week or more _____ Rarely _____

A couple of times a month _____ Never _____

C11 Do you visit or attend:

	Often	Sometimes	Hardly ever	Never	Not available where I live
Art galleries	_____	_____	_____	_____	_____
Museums	_____	_____	_____	_____	_____
Botanical gardens	_____	_____	_____	_____	_____
Public musical perform-ances	_____	_____	_____	_____	_____
Public lectures	_____	_____	_____	_____	_____
Public libraries	_____	_____	_____	_____	_____

C12 If there are any of these activities you would like to attend more than you do at the moment, what is the main reason that prevents you? _____

C13 How long is it since you visited an art gallery? _____

C14 Do you attend:

	Often	Sometimes	Hardly ever	Never	Not available where I live
Rock concerts	_____	_____	_____	_____	_____
Orchestral concerts	_____	_____	_____	_____	_____
Chamber music concerts	_____	_____	_____	_____	_____
Ballet	_____	_____	_____	_____	_____
Musicals	_____	_____	_____	_____	_____
Opera	_____	_____	_____	_____	_____
Theatre	_____	_____	_____	_____	_____
Movies	_____	_____	_____	_____	_____
Special exhibits at museums or galleries (entry fee charged)	_____	_____	_____	_____	_____
Theme parks	_____	_____	_____	_____	_____
Night clubs	_____	_____	_____	_____	_____
Shows, exhibi-tions or fairs	_____	_____	_____	_____	_____

C14 *continued*	Often	Sometimes	Hardly ever	Never	Not available where I live
Pubs with live bands	____	____	____	____	____
Film festivals	____	____	____	____	____
Cultural festivals	____	____	____	____	____

C15 If there are any of these activities you would like to attend more than you do at the moment, what is the main reason that prevents you? _____

C16 Do you participate in any of the following dance activities?

Dance parties _____   Bush dancing _____
Discos _____   Ethnic or folk dancing _____
Ballroom dancing _____   Ballet or contemporary dancing _____
Line dancing _____   Square dancing _____
Slam dancing _____

Section D Tastes and preferences

D1 Which one of the following considerations is *most* important when you buy yourself clothes?

Stylishly cut _____   Flamboyant _____
Practicality _____   Comfortable _____
Casual _____   Designer label _____
Out of the ordinary _____   Fashionable _____
Hard wearing _____   Other _____
What my friends are wearing _____

D2 Would you mostly buy clothes from:

David Jones _____   Other large department stores _____
Myers/Grace Brothers _____   Woolworths _____
Target _____   Small boutiques _____
K-Mart _____   Used clothing shops _____
I make my own/family's clothes _____   Other _____

D3 Which are your three favourites from the following types of music?

Classical _____   Avant-garde _____   Folk _____
Light classical _____   Easy listening _____   Rock _____
Opera _____   Musicals _____   Techno _____
Traditional jazz _____   Blues _____   Alternative rock _____
Modern jazz _____   Soul _____   World _____
Big band _____   Top 40 pop _____   Religious _____
Heavy metal _____   Country & Western _____   Other (*please specify*) ____

D4 Looking at the list again, which 3 types of music would you most *dislike*? ____

D5 Who would be your three favourite singers/groups/composers? _____

D6   Listed below are a number of musical works. Put a tick against those you
know and name the composer if you can.

The Four Seasons _____   Einstein on the Beach _____

The Well-Tempered Clavier _____   La Traviata _____

Porgy and Bess _____   The Mikado _____

Eine Kleine Nachtmusik _____   The Blue Danube _____

The Firebird Suite _____   The Messiah _____

D7   Looking at the list of musical works again please select your three favourites
from those you are familiar with. _____

D8   Here is a further list of musical works. Put a tick against those you know and
name either the composer or the performer with whom you usually associate
these works.

Unchained Melody _____   November Rain _____

Jailhouse Rock _____   Hotel California _____

Dark Side of the Moon _____   Cabaret _____

Tip of my Tongue _____   Stardust _____

Nessun Dorma _____   Stand By Your Man _____

My Fair Lady _____   Predator _____

Piano Man _____   Burning Down the House _____

Smells Like Teen Spirit _____   I'm Your Kind _____

Orinoco Flow ('Sail Away') _____

D9   Which are your three favourites among the following types of books?

Thriller/adventure _____   Science fiction _____   Poetry _____

Crime/murder/mystery __   Romances _____   Scientific _____

Political _____   Travel, exploration _____   Educational _____

Cooking _____   Historical _____   Erotica _____

Historical romances ____   Gardening _____   Horror _____

Biographies _____   Classical authors _____   Occult _____

Craft/hobbies _____   Humour/comedy _____   Sport & leisure _____

Contemporary novels ___   I don't read books _____

D10   Who are your three favourite authors? _____

D11   When reading fiction what do you most enjoy?

A good story _____   A complicated plot _____

Interesting characters _____   Experimental writing _____

Literary quality _____

D12   Do you prefer it when stories:

Have a definite ending _____   Are open ended _____

D13   Where do you mostly obtain your books from?

I purchase them _____   I borrow from friends _____

I borrow from a library _____

D14   About how many books do you have in your house?

Less than 50 _____   200 to 500 _____

50 to 100 _____   500 or more _____

100 to 200 _____

D15   Do you have/own any of the following types of books? _____
       Literary classics _____   Biographies _____
       Art books _____   Poetry _____
       History books _____
D16   How long is it since you read a book?
       A week _____   Three months _____
       A month _____   A year _____
D17   Which are your three favourite types of films?
       Adventure _____   Dramas _____
       War _____   Horror _____
       Westerns _____   Cartoons _____
       Thrillers _____   *Film noir* _____
       Comedies _____   Art films _____
       Spectaculars _____   Independent _____
       Musicals _____   Documentaries _____
       R or X Rated _____   Romances _____
D18   Do you mostly see films:
       by going to the cinema _____
       by going to a drive-in-cinema _____
       by taking out a video _____
       by watching when they are screened on TV _____
D19   We are interested in the films you have seen over the last 3–6 months. Please
       list the three most recent films you have seen. _____
D20   Which are your three favourite films? _____
D21   When deciding to watch a particular film, which of the following is generally
       most important to you?
       The actors _____   The special effects _____
       The director _____   The reviews _____
       The plot _____
D22   Which one of the following kinds of art do you most prefer?
       Abstract art _____   Experimental art _____
       Realistic art _____   Other _____
D23   How would you characterise the following subjects for a photograph?

	Beautiful	Interesting	Clichéd	Unattractive
A landscape	_____	_____	_____	_____
A car crash	_____	_____	_____	_____
A pregnant woman	_____	_____	_____	_____
A vase of flowers	_____	_____	_____	_____
Homeless people fighting	_____	_____	_____	_____
A sunset over the sea	_____	_____	_____	_____
A tackle in a football match	_____	_____	_____	_____
A horse in a field	_____	_____	_____	_____
A demolition site	_____	_____	_____	_____

D23 *continued*	Beautiful	Interesting	Clichéd	Unattractive
Aboriginal dancers	————	————	————	————
The Sydney Opera House	————	————	————	————
A wedding	————	————	————	————
A halved onion	————	————	————	————

D24 Could you indicate in a few words what you think 'good taste' and 'bad taste' entail?

Section E Recreational activities

E1 Do you belong to any of the following?
A choir ————————————————————
A theatre group ————————————————
An RSL club ————————————————
A surf lifesavers club ———————————
A sports club (*please specify*) ————————
Other cultural organisation (*please specify*) ————
Community group (*please specify*) ——————
Other clubs and societies (*please specify*) ————

E2 Do you play a sport? (*please specify*) ————————

E3 What do you *most* enjoy about the sport?

Health ————————	Body contact ————————
Relaxation ————————	Competition ————————
Team spirit ————————	Developing skills ————————
Fitness ————————	Friendship ————————
Discipline ————————	Easing stress ————————
Other ————————	

E4 Do you watch any of the following sports activities at live venues?

	Watch regularly	Watch sometimes
Rugby League	————————	————————
Rugby Union	————————	————————
Australian Rules Football	————————	————————
Soccer	————————	————————
Cricket	————————	————————
Basketball	————————	————————
Netball	————————	————————
Tennis	————————	————————
Golf	————————	————————
Hockey	————————	————————
Volleyball	————————	————————
Swimming	————————	————————
Track and field athletics	————————	————————
Boxing	————————	————————
Wrestling	————————	————————

E4 *continued*   Watch regularly   Watch sometimes
    Motor car racing
    Speedway racing
    Stock car racing
    Motorcycle racing
    Horse racing
    Water polo
    Gymnastics
    Surf carnivals
    Ironman competitions

E5 Do you belong to any health or sporting organisation? _____

E6 Of the activities listed below, which do you do often, which do you do sometimes and which do you never do?

	Often	Sometimes	Hardly ever	Never
Camping				
Visiting the beach				
Bushwalking				
Fishing				
Hunting				
Fossicking				
Sailing				
Swimming				
Surfing				
Body surfing				
Jogging				
Aerobics				
Martial arts				
Weight training				
Cycling				
Walking				
Power walking				

E7 Do you ever gamble on:
    Pokies _____   Bingo _____
    Casinos _____   Lotto _____
    TAB _____   Social gambling with friends or
    On-course (horses) _____   family _____
    On-course (dogs) _____   Scratch-its _____
    Approximately how much would you spend on this activity per week?

E8 Do you have any collections (e.g. stamps, coins, butterflies)? (*Please specify*)

E9 How often do you take a holiday away from home?
    Less than once a year _____   More than once a year _____
    Once a year _____

E10 Which one of the following do you *most* seek when on holidays?
    Adventure _____   Intellectual stimulation _____
    Peace and quiet _____   Experiencing different cultures ____
    Touring _____   Outdoor activities _____

E10 *continued*

        Good entertainment _____   Getting away from the crowd _____

        Meeting new people _____   Lazing around _____

E11   When going on holidays do you prefer to?

        Book organised tour packages _____   Make your own arrangements _____

E12   When on holidays which of the following have you mainly stayed at over the last five years:

        Hotel _____   Motel _____

        Resort _____   Camping or caravan site _____

        Self-catering unit _____   With friends _____

E13   What length of time would you normally spend away from home on each holiday?

_____

E14   If there were no financial constraints, would you prefer to spend your holidays:

        In your own state _____   Overseas _____

        Elsewhere in Australia _____

E15   How often have you travelled overseas?

        5 times or more _____   Once _____

        2 to 4 times _____   Never _____

E16   If you have travelled overseas, was it:

        Usually on business _____   For study _____

        Usually on holiday _____   Other _____

Section F Family and Friends

F1   Were both your parents born in Australia? _____

F2   In which country were your parents born? _____

F3   What was the highest level of education that your parents reached? _____

F4   What was the occupation of the main breadwinner in your family when you were growing up (at age 15)? _____

F5   Did this person own their own business? _____

F6   Was this person a manager or supervisor? _____

F7   Did either of your parents play a musical instrument or paint or draw? _____

F8   Are you currently:

        Living with a partner – married _____   Widowed, divorced, separated _____

        Living with a partner – unmarried __   Single – never married _____

F9   Does your partner currently have a paid job? _____

F10   What kind of work does she/he do? _____

F11   Does she/he own their own business? _____

F12   Does she/he occupy a managerial or supervisor position at the place where she/he works? _____

F13   Do you have any children? _____

F14   Are your children currently living at home with you? _____

F15   What is the age of the youngest child living at home? _____

F16   We are interested in the type of schools your children attend or attended.
      What type of primary schools do/did your children attend?
      All or mostly state schools _____
      All or mostly private schools _____
      All or mostly other private (e.g. Montessori) _____

F17   What type of secondary schools do/did your children attend?
      All or mostly State schools _____
      All or mostly Catholic denominational schools _____
      All or mostly other denominational schools _____
      All or mostly private non-denominational schools _____
      All or mostly special private (e.g. Montessori) _____

F18   What emphasis do/did the school(s) your children attend/ed place on art or
      music?
      A great deal _____   Not much _____
      Quite a bit _____   None at all _____
      Some _____

F19   What are the first names you have given your children? _____

F20   Thinking of your friends, which of the following groups are they mainly
      from?
      Work colleagues _____   Neighbours _____
      Former school friends _____   Other _____
      Sporting or other leisure groups _____

F21   Where do you mostly meet with friends for social occasions?
      At home _____   At a shopping mall _____
      At a pub or club _____   Other _____
      At a restaurant _____

F22   We are interested in the qualities you value in your friends. Which of the
      following would you most like your friends to be?
      Honest _____   Refined _____
      Reliable _____   Responsible _____
      Sociable _____   Conscientious _____
      Amusing _____   Artistic _____
      Educated _____   Loyal _____
      Intelligent _____   Caring _____
      Attractive _____   Witty _____

F23   Looking at the list again, which three items would be of *least* importance as
      qualities you value in your friends? _____

Section G Your personal characteristics

G1   Do you currently have a paid job?
      Yes, full-time _____   Retired _____
      Yes, part-time _____   Never had a paid job _____
      No paid job at present _____

G2   What kind of work do/did you do? _____

G3   What are/were some of your main duties or activities? _____

G4   What business or organisation is/was that? What do/did they make or do? ___

G5   Are/were you employed by *someone else*, are/were you *self-employed*, or do/did you work without pay in a family business or farm? _____

G6   About how many paid employees do/did you have? _____

G7   Do/did you occupy a managerial or supervisory position at the place where you work/worked? _____

G8   Is/was your job a step in the recognised career or promotion ladder within your organisation? _____

G9   What educational qualifications were/are usually required for people to get a job like yours nowadays/when you had this job? _____

G10 Beyond formal education, how much on-the-job training, or job experience is/ was *normally required* for people who do your type of work – nowadays/when you had this job? _____

G11 About how many hours do/did you usually work a week on this job, including paid and unpaid overtime? _____

G12 When did you start working at this job? _____

G13 When did you finish working at this job? _____

G14 Apart from paid employment, have you ever undertaken any voluntary work on a regular basis? _____

G15 Are you?
     Female _____   Male _____

G16 How old are you? _____

G17 What type of school(s) did you mostly attend?
     All or mostly State schools (primary) _____
     All or mostly private schools (primary) _____
     All or mostly State schools (secondary) _____
     All or mostly Catholic denominational schools (secondary) _____
     All or mostly other denominational schools (secondary) _____
     All or mostly private non-denominational schools _____
     All or mostly special private (e.g. Montessori) _____
     No formal education _____

G18 At what stage did you finish your education?
     Still at school _____
     Primary _____
     Some secondary _____
     Secondary completed _____
     Still at vocational training or apprenticeship _____
     Some vocational training or apprenticeship (incomplete) _____
     Vocational training or apprenticeship (completed), NOT COUNTING
        in-service training/seminars _____
     Other (specify) _____
     Still at tertiary _____
     Some tertiary _____
     Tertiary completed _____

G19 Have you attended a College of Advanced Education, Institute of Technology or University? _____

G20   What is the name of the institution you attended? _____

G21   What is the highest qualification you have received? _____

G22   In what field or fields did you specialise? _____

G23   Have you ever had any formal music training? _____

G24   Have you ever had any formal art training? _____

G25   In which country were you born? _____

G26   How old were you when you came to Australia? _____

G27   Are you of Aboriginal or Torres Strait Island origin? _____

G28   Do you consider yourself to belong to an ethnic community? _____

G29   If yes, how important to you is your ethnic culture? _____

G30   Are you a member of an ethnic club (e.g. a Greek club, an Irish
       association)? _____

G31   What country has been most important in making you the person you are
       today? _____

G32   Do you consider yourself as having a religion? _____

G33   What religion is that?

       Church of England (Anglican) _____ Other Christian _____
       Roman Catholic _____ Islam _____
       Lutheran _____ Buddhism _____
       Orthodox Presbyterian _____ Judaism _____
       Uniting Church _____ Hinduism _____
       Baptist _____ Other religion _____
       Other Protestant _____

G34   About how often do you attend religious services?

       More than once a week _____ A few times a year _____
       About once a week _____ Less often _____
       2 or 3 times a month _____

G35   Do you think there is a distinctively Australian culture? _____

G36   Which one of the following do you think *best* expresses this culture?

       Novels and films _____ Sport _____
       Music _____ Politics _____
       Family activities _____ The Bush _____
       Ethnic diversity _____ The Beach _____
       Other _____

G37   Here are some income groups. Would you please indicate which group
       includes your personal gross income before tax or other deductions have
       been taken out for your present job. _____

G38   Looking at the lists again would you please indicate which group includes
       your total combined household gross income before tax or other deductions
       have been taken out. _____

Section H Social and political attitudes

H1   Which of the following statements about Australian society seems true to
you?
Australian society consists of various social classes _____
Australian society is not divided into social classes _____

H2   Do you think of yourself as belonging to a particular social class? Which class
is that?
Working _____   Upper-middle _____
Middle _____   Upper _____
If you had to make a choice, which class would you say you belong to? _____

H3   Which one of the following do you think *most* helps people to get on in life?
Natural ability _____   Who you know _____
Education _____   Ambition _____
Hard work _____   Determination _____
Social background _____   Inherited wealth _____

H4   Do you think there should be more or less public money given to?

	More funding	Less funding	The funding level is about right now
Sport	_____	_____	_____
The Arts	_____	_____	_____
Heritage and environment	_____	_____	_____

H5   Generally speaking, in federal politics do you usually think of yourself as:
Australian Democrats _____   National (Country) Party _____
Labor (ALP) _____   Other _____
Liberal _____

H6   Here are some statements people have made about economic, social and
political issues in Australia. For each statement, please circle the number which
comes closest to how you feel about the issue.

	Strongly agree	Agree	Disagree	Strongly disagree
The government has a responsibility to support the disadvantaged	_____	_____	_____	_____
People should be encouraged to take responsibility for providing their own health coverage	_____	_____	_____	_____
The trade unions in this country have too much power	_____	_____	_____	_____

H6 *continued*	Strongly agree	Agree	Disagree	Strongly disagree
Wages and incomes should be controlled by some government body	_____	_____	_____	_____
If both husband and wife work they should share equally in the housework and child care	_____	_____	_____	_____
Homosexuals should be allowed to serve in the defence forces	_____	_____	_____	_____
The government should provide a universal system of health care	_____	_____	_____	_____
It is better for the family if the husband is the principal bread-winner outside the home and the wife has primary responsibility for the home and children	_____	_____	_____	_____
The logging of native forests should be more strictly controlled	_____	_____	_____	_____
Large companies like BHP should always be privately owned	_____	_____	_____	_____
There should be satisfactory childcare facilities so that women can take jobs outside the home	_____	_____	_____	_____

H6 *continued*	Strongly agree	Agree	Disagree	Strongly disagree
Government instrumentalities such as Telecom should not be privatised	————	————	————	————
The government should provide more chances for children from poor families to go to university	————	————	————	————
Ideally, there should be as many women as men in important positions in government and business	————	————	————	————
The government should spend more on defence	————	————	————	————
Australia should identify more strongly with Asia	————	————	————	————
The Welfare system supports many people who are not genuinely needy	————	————	————	————
The government should move towards the granting of lands rights for Aborigines	————	————	————	————

Notes

1 Theorising Cultures

1 Becker (1974), quoted in Frith (1996: 73).

2 No obvious rationale for these classes is offered other than the fact that they clearly correspond to the 'three zones of taste' (1984: 16) which Bourdieu uses to structure so many of his arguments.

3 For a discussion of the conceptual underpinnings of these class models see M. Emmison, 'Wright and Goldthorpe: constructing the agenda of class analysis', in Baxter, Emmison, M. Western and J. Western (1991).

4 Respondents who were either unemployed or retired at the time of our survey were requested to provide information relating to their last job or the job they held prior to retirement. Just under 9 per cent of our sample overall had either never had a job (2.7%) or failed to provide sufficient information to enable us to determine their class location (6.1%).

3 Media Culture and the Home

1 We refer here to the ABC and the three commercial networks. The Special Broadcasting Service (SBS) was said by just under a fifth of our sample not to be available as a viewing option.

2 Enthusiasm for new electronic technology, apparently, is not just confined to the commercial sector. The Australian Film Commission's 1995 report *Multimedia Developments in Australia* stated that: 'Information technology, and all that it now offers, has crossed the technical Rubicon into the realm of consciousness, to the realm of culture. Multimedia today gives us instruments which will allow us to shape information in so many forms that they can become an integral part of our life's experiences' (quoted in Appleton 1997: 182).

3 Cinema attendances declined throughout the 1980s; however more recent figures for the 1990s suggest that this decline has been reversed. For example, the number of admissions rose from 30 million in 1983 to 54 million in 1993 (Appleton 1997).

4 This is the overall figure for all households. Within capital cities, penetration stands at 33.6 per cent and the figure for the remaining areas is 23.0 per cent (see *Household Use of Information Technology, Australia 1996* (ABS cat. no. 8146.0)).

5 The UK weekly *The Economist* is an example of the former category. In its leader of 17 October 1992, entitled 'The homeless PC', it argued that personal computers had yet to find a significant place in the home and that it was unlikely that they ever would. 'The average consumer', *The Economist* opined, 'does not understand computers . . . the computer industry has yet to sell a PC which can be used by a novice, straight out of the box'. Somewhat less patronisingly, the magazine gave a more sober assessment of the 'multimedia' revolution which computer manufacturers have seen as the catalyst for boosting home usage. The multimedia extravaganza of tomorrow, it suggested, is more likely to be viewed on large high-definition living-room walls than 'the cramped screen of a personal computer'.

6 These figures are somewhat higher than those obtained by the ABS, which estimated the number of computer-owning households in May 1996 at 31.8 per cent, with 9 per cent having access to the internet and other on-line services through a modem (see ABS report *Household Use of Information Technology, Australia* (cat. no. 8128.0)). Our national sample figure is, however, consistent with the number obtained in our pilot survey conducted in the Brisbane metropolitan region in late 1993. The AECP survey data suggest that Australian home computer ownership is very close to that of the US where the national average is 36 per cent. In all other respects the demographic profile for computer ownership which we obtained very closely matches that of the ABS.

7 See for example: Hobson (1982); Seiter et al. (1989).

8 For a more detailed discussion of the concept of the distracted viewer, see Morse 1990.

9 The term 'ontological security' comes from Giddens (1990: 92).

10 For a useful discussion of the problems inherent in such audience measurement research see Ang (1994a).

11 This needs to be borne in mind when considering audience figures. Even more so than watching television, listening to the radio is passive: we seldom undertake the activity as an end in itself; it is much more likely to be an adjunct to another, primary activity. Nevertheless, figures from the Australian Broadcasting Tribunal point to its popularity. The ABT's 1985 inquiry found that some young Australians were listening to the radio for up to 80 hours a week (ABT 1985: 25). Even after the industry shakeout and the decline of 'teen radio' (Turner 1993), ABT research suggests that Australians over the age of 10 listen to nearly 23 hours of radio per week (ABA 1996: 5, quoted in Molnar 1997: 201).

12 At least as far as audience composition is concerned, we can find little evidence in our data which supports Molnar's view that 'the 10–17 and 18–24 age-groups have been largely disenfranchised by commercial radio' (Molnar 1997: 207) as a consequence of its format structure.

13 Certainly in terms of industry organisation there is a considerable blurring with regard to funding, technical and creative personnel, etc. As Elizabeth Jacka has noted 'it hardly makes sense any more to look at Australian film in isolation from Australian television' (Jacka 1997: 227).

4 Leisure and Work

1 See Frith (1983: 262): 'Leisure has become the only setting for the experience of self, for the exploration of one's own skills and capacities, for the development of creative relations with other people' (quoted in Rojek 1985: 173); see also Rojek (1995: 127): 'For many, real life only occurs *outside* the workplace.'
2 On professionalism, see Collins (1979); Jamous & Peloille (1970); Noble (1979); and Perkins (1989).
3 We know from a separate question that RSL clubs, for example, have a clientele in which professionals and managers are underrepresented, men outnumber women by 4 to 3, and membership declines with education, with private schooling, and with income. The largest age group is that of those who are above 60; and membership is very low in the inner city (3.9% against a mean of 13.9%), and very high in provincial cities (25.1%) and small towns (20.4%).
4 The purpose of factor analysis is to explain the correlations among a set of variables in terms of a limited number of underlying, unobservable *factors*. The factor loadings are interpreted as the correlations between the variables and the factors, and often sense can be made of the pattern of the loadings, leading to identification of at least the major factors. The factors are measured by their *factor scores*, whose scale and direction are arbitrary, but which can be analysed meaningfully for differences in terms of explanatory variables such as age and gender. In a factor analysis table, the first factor produced accounts for more of the variation in the entire set of variables than factor 2 which accounts for more than factor 3, and so on. As far as the constituent items within the factors are concerned, the higher the number the more important that item is in defining the factor's content. High negative numbers are also important as these mark items which are significantly *not* associated with the factor. See, for example, Harman (1976), Mulaik (1972), and Kim and Mueller (1978). In table 4.6 the choices which have been identified as comprising each of the factors are marked with an *.
5 Tukey-Cramer is one of many available statistical adjustments to significance levels that take into account the whole range of possible comparisons that could be made.

5 Care of the Body, Care of the Self

1 Foucault's use of this concept owes much to the work of Marcel Mauss (1979) on 'techniques of the body': learned and habitual ways of using the 'primordial technical instrument' of humankind (104).
2 Bordo (1990: 86) distinguishes between the 'practices and "disciplines" . . . which structure the organization of time, space, and the experience of embodiment for subjects', and the system of representations within and in relation to which these practices occur.

3 Defrance and Pociello (1993) document a similar shift in postwar France from a regime of centralised oversight of bodily exercise and training by the state to a decentralised and privatised regime in which entertainment values and commercial sponsorship are prevalent.

4 The mean percentages in the following tables vary slightly in cross-tabulation against different variables, because of different numbers of non-responses, the weighting of the sample, and other complications; these are the absolute percentages of the whole sample.

5 The contents and the scaling of our table of sports played differ from material recently released by the ABS, which lists the order of popularity as follows: aerobics; golf; tennis; netball; lawn bowls; swimming; basketball; cricket; martial arts; tenpin bowling. The difference is accounted for in part by the fact that they ask about sports and activities together; they also included respondents of 15–18 years of age, whom we exclude; and they used an open-ended direct interview method (Australian Bureau of Statistics, *Participation in Sport and Physical Activities, 1996–97*: 3).

6 Our data do not tell us, however, whether men and women play together or separately, or – more importantly – which groups play together and which play separately; nor do they allow us insight into the gendered inequalities that, as we know from other sources, pervade the social organisation of tennis clubs.

7 Bourdieu (1978: 830) argues that it is through 'the division it makes between professionals, the virtuosi of an esoteric technique, and laymen, reduced to the role of mere consumers, a division that tends to become a deep structure of the collective consciousness, that sport produces its most decisive political effects'.

6 Reading by Numbers

1 Modleski (1982) and Radway (1984) are the classic studies.

2 For an account of historical romance and the basis of its appeal to women readers, see Hughes (1993).

3 The importance that women attach to reading in bed is, as Buckridge et al. (1995) have noted, significant here in the opportunity this affords for composing the self in the midst of a domestic space which, for women, is mostly associated with responsibilities for others. Many of the women involved in our focus-group discussions commented on the importance of bedtime reading in their daily routines. In the words of one: 'I could not go to bed without a book. Even if I only read two pages and I'm really tired I read a couple of pages before I go to sleep, otherwise I can't.'

4 The most important source here is the survey of books and reading which the Australia Council conducts from time to time. For the most recent report, see Australia Council for the Arts (1995).

5 See Mercer (1995). It is important to note, however, that this pattern applies mainly in relation to local libraries. Men tend to be more frequent users of state and national libraries.

6 It is clear that the motivations for reading erotica can be quite diverse. Frank, who spoke at length about his reasons for reading soft-porn magazines, couched his

explanation mainly in terms of an anti-statist, libertarian philosophy which he attributed to the independence he had enjoyed in his earlier occupation as a truck driver.

7 Elizabeth's approach to reading contrasts with the conception of reading as a self-improving discipline expressed by Kay, an assistant principal at a primary school, who summarised her orientation to reading in the following terms: 'I've read things like *Les Misérables*. I think that took me six months to read. But I ploughed through it in lots of ways because I still wanted to find out what was going to happen in the end, even though I sort of knew how it was going to end. I'm also a person who reads every word. I'm not a scanner when I read and I suppose I justify it, not that I'm a slow reader, but I pay attention to the language and if there is vocabulary that I don't understand I get the dictionary. I suppose I pay attention to the nuances of how it is actually written.'

8 Figures for those with only primary schooling have not been taken into account here as the relevant cell sizes are too small to allow for valid comparisons.

7 Music Tastes and Music Knowledge

1 Bourdieu's classification runs as follows: 'Within the universe of particular tastes . . . it is thus possible to distinguish three zones of taste which roughly correspond to educational levels and social classes: (1) *Legitimate taste*, i.e. the taste for legitimate works, here represented by the *Well-Tempered Clavier*, the *Art of Fugue*, or the *Concerto for the Left Hand* . . . (2) *"Middle-brow" taste* . . . in this case *Rhapsody in Blue* . . . which is more common in the middle classes or in the "intellectual" fractions of the dominant class. (3) Finally, *"popular" taste*, represented here by the choice of works of so-called "light music" or classical music devalued by popularisation such as the *Blue Danube*, *La Traviata* . . . and especially songs totally devoid of artistic ambition such as those of Luis Mariano, Guétary or Petula Clarke, is most frequent among the working classes and varies in inverse ratio to educational capital'. (Bourdieu 1984: 16)

2 For an example of academic interest in the music video see several of the articles in Dines and Humez (1995). Among individual performers, Madonna has attracted more than her fair share of attention within cultural studies. For a representative discussion see Bradbury (1992).

A limited number of more explicit inquiries into music tastes have been carried out by sociological and communications researchers, but it has generally been an area of lower prestige in these fields up until now. See for example Bryson (1996); Christenson and Peterson (1988); Denisoff and Levine (1972); Deihl, Schneider and Petress (1985); Fox and Wince (1975); Hirsch (1971). Richard Peterson's inquiries (e.g. Peterson 1992; Peterson & Kern 1996) into 'omnivorous' music taste stand as some of the most theoretically innovative on offer and we consider these later in the chapter.

3 Marcus Breen has argued that even the information we have about popular music in Australia is sadly lacking in comparison with other countries. The reasons he offers for this relative paucity of knowledge are worth noting. First he suggests that as a colonial society we have been enthusiastic but, equally, 'uncritical' consumers of material and cultural products of all kinds. But the second reason he

advances takes us closer to some of the theoretical concerns underpinning our inquiry. Breen suggests that: 'class formations in Australia have meant that popular art forms sit uncomfortably with the prevailing middle-class aspirations built, as they are, on the myth of upward mobility within an immigrant community. This myth often requires popular music (and popular arts) to be jettisoned by those making the transition from the lower to the middle classes. The Australian middle classes have always had powerful voices to raise against popular (or what they perceive as "low") culture in their struggle for respectable cultural forms of entertainment'. (Breen 1993: 119–20)

Implicit in Breen's characterisation of the articulation between class and culture in Australia is a surprisingly old-fashioned depiction of an elite- or highbrow-to-mass or popular dichotomy, with the middle class – or at least the upwardly mobile recruits to this stratum – firmly positioned at the elite end of the cultural spectrum. We have little evidence from our research that 'middle-class' taste has the characteristics that Breen associates with it.

4 A more detailed analysis of the open-ended question responses dealing with television, music, literature and film is carried out in chapter 8.

5 Using the same criteria, the next most popular genres would appear to be less 'contaminated'. For example the top five named favourites for the sub-group choosing 'country and western' music as first preference are: Slim Dusty, John Williamson, The Seekers, Elvis Presley, and Garth Brooks. For those selecting 'classical' music as their first preference, the top five favourites are: Mozart, Beethoven, Bach, Pavarotti and Chopin.

6 The latter two groups have been arranged in terms of the degree of feminine or masculine attraction to them as measured by the statistical strength of the gender difference.

7 In one of the few discussions of this issue, Robinson and Fink (1986) appear to favour the view that the preferences which are established in young adulthood will continue to have appeal for that cohort as it ages: 'Thus we see cultural preferences working their way through history like a devoured prey that passes through a snake. As a result cultural change is gradual and there is often resistance to new cultural forms'. (Robinson & Fink 1986: 238)

8 The relationship between educational capital and a preference for this music genre is even more marked once a more nuanced analysis of the type of tertiary qualification is undertaken. Those whose post-secondary educational training is at a university are over twice as likely to favour classical music as those whose tertiary experience has been obtained at a TAFE or business college. Those whose tertiary qualification is a bachelor degree or higher are three times as likely to nominate classical music as are those holding a diploma. Finally, even tertiary field of study appears important. Humanities graduates are over twice as likely to be classical music fans as those in business fields and five times more likely than science graduates. Clearly the experience of higher education is not uniform in its impetus to acquire cultural capital.

9 The table only shows the breakdown for the six most disliked genres, which together account for nearly 90% of choices. The remaining percentages have been omitted.

10 Heavy metal fans might actually take some heart from this mass rejection of their genre. The fact that so many of our respondents selected it as their chief dislike could be seen as a perverse indicator of its cultural availability and presence.

11 In the following analysis, the music genres identified as belonging to one of the factors have been marked with an * and are also in bold type.

12 For a more recent discussion of taste cultures, see Lewis (1981).

13 Operationally speaking, this is close to the sub-group of highbrows whom Peterson and Kern refer to as 'snobs' who do not participate in *any* middlebrow or lowbrow cultural pursuits. Such people, they add, are now extremely rare in the United States; in fact they were only able to identify 10 such people in a national sample of over 11 000. Pure highbrows are also very rare in Australia: only 1% of our sample have tastes in music which are restricted to the three highbrow genres.

14 Based upon the factor analysis which suggests that these three genres are in some respects antithetical, we should not be surprised to discover that 'pure' lowbrows are quite rare; this is in fact the case. Only 2% of our sample have tastes in music comprising combinations of these three genres. However, the existence of these 'pure' types is in some respects irrelevant; what is more important is their contribution to defining the omnivore.

15 The works comprising the two lists can be found in the appendix. The works of classical music are partly based on a list that Bourdieu used in *Distinction*. We are grateful to Dr David Marshall and Professor Graeme Turner from the University of Queensland's Department of English for their advice on compiling the popular music works list.

16 For a discussion of Bourdieu's class hierarchy which raises questions about the apparent correlation between music taste and class structure, in particular the contradictory position of intellectuals, see Frow (1987).

17 Mothers rather than fathers appear generally to be the repository of this form of cultural capital. The working class is the only stratum more likely to have had an instrument-playing father than a mother.

8 The United Tastes of Australia?

1 By 'American' we refer only to the USA; we realise that this metonym is not politically innocent.

2 A useful exception here is Philip and Roger Bell's (1993) account of the involvement of the United States in Australia's political, economic and cultural history. The title of the Bells' book, *Implicated*, nicely captures the essentially ambiguous relationship they see obtaining between the two countries.

3 White argues that Australia was the country which experienced Americanisation 'in its purest form'. Among the reasons he cites for this are the absence of 'natural' filters offered by differences in language and standard of living; and of a protective 'cultural tradition of its own' with the capacity to exert a reciprocal cultural influence on the United States; and second, the historical similarities between the two countries as major destinations for immigrants which lead Australians to see themselves following the American path to progress.

4 To a certain extent this was a consequence of the involvement of UNESCO and the research it sponsored as part of its New World Information and Communication Order.

5 In addition to the references on cultural imperialism already cited, the issue of international television flows has been extensively documented and discussed in particular by Guback (1984); Hoskins and Mirus (1988) and Tracey (1985, 1988).

6 This is an aggregate category covering the news broadcasts on any of the commercial channels or the ABC.

7 The figures for country of origin with the category of 'the news' omitted are as follows:

	18–25	26–35	36–45	46–59	60+
Australia	17.9%	32.2%	43.2%	56.3%	66.5%
USA	80.6%	61.5%	37.4%	28.1%	18.8%
UK	1.4%	6.2%	19.3%	15.6%	14.7%

8 For example, the Australian author Peter Carey has resided in the US for some time although he has been coded as Australian. British-born novelist Jackie Collins is renowned for her sagas of Hollywood stardom although she has been designated as a UK author.

9 The film *The Piano* is, strictly speaking, a joint Australian/New Zealand production, but it has been treated as an Australian film for the purposes of the analysis.

10 These data would also seem to permit us to speculate about the biographical circumstances in which attachments to favoured cultural phenomena are determined. For example, the older cohort would have most likely been in their late teens and twenties when they first encountered *Gone with the Wind*, but for a significant number of them this appears to have been a defining cultural event which they have retained throughout their lives.

11 The percentages figures in the following discussion are based on the proportion of the sample who selected the particular cultural item as their favourite. So, for example, in this case this figure indicates that 92.0% of those people who chose *Melrose Place* as their favourite TV show were female.

12 On this issue, see Alasuutari (1992).

9 Public/Private Culture: Theory and Policy

1 See Collins (1985), Melleuish (1995) and Rowse (1978) for contrasting accounts of the distinctive currency of liberalism in late nineteenth-century Australia.

2 Our reference here is to Foucault's essay 'Governmentality' collected in Burchell, Gordon and Miller (eds) (1991). However, see also the other essays in this collection and those in Barry, Osborn and Rose (eds) (1996), a representative sample of the literature that has developed in the wake of Foucault's essay.

3 See Brown (1995) for a discussion of the implications of insurential and social-welfarist conceptions – allied to eugenic conceptions of population – for the early twentieth-century formation of Australian cultural policies.

4 It is, however, a moot point as to how far the very visible cuts in these areas of federal funding have resulted in an overall reduction in the public funding of culture in the United States owing to increases in the support offered by the state and local levels of government over the same period.

5 The discussion here of Bourdieu's concept of restricted culture has been adapted from Bennett (1997).

6 It should be noted, however, that since SBS was not available in many areas of Australia at the time the *Australian Everyday Cultures* survey was administered (it was not available to 65% of the rural Australians we surveyed), our SBS audience figures are not nationally representative in the same way as are those for the ABC. SBS's brief to serve as a station especially concerned with multicultural issues, to provide programs for non-English-speaking audiences and to serve the needs of Australia's ethnic minorities also means that it is not charged with a responsibility to recruit a nationally representative audience in the same way as is the ABC.

7 The qualification is important as sometimes these figures measure the composite effects of two or more variables. The rates of difference between participation rates for those with different levels of education, for example, also include the effects of age, as those with only primary education tend to be the older members of the sample. This is probably why public broadcasting – which has the oldest age profile of all three groups – includes such a large percentage of those with only primary education in its audience.

8 This, however, is only true of the general public uses of these institutions. The openings of new or special exhibitions, especially in art galleries, often significantly transform the nature of the social relations that are enacted in the institutions of public culture with markedly more selective patterns of participation and, often, distinctive styles of dress and behaviour which – together with the high admission charges that are usually applied – mark the appropriation of the gallery space for the purposes of elite forms of sociability.

9 We are indebted to John Hartley and Toby Miller for drawing this distinction to our attention.

10 Very few of the institutions comprising the institutions of subsidised culture have access policies or conduct visitor surveys to identify the social mix of their audiences. Most major museums, art galleries and libraries, by contrast, have formalised access and equity policies and regularly take soundings regarding the social composition of their users.

11 The American Association for the Arts has been influential in promoting views of this kind as among the rationales that arts lobbyists should use in their search for funding.

12 See Bennett (1994) for a discussion of the social characteristics of 'determined non-goers' of this kind.

13 There is an extensive literature here. For a representative sample of the different ways in which Habermas' concept of the public sphere has been revised and adapted to new purposes in the context of socialist and feminist concerns, debates about media ownership, etc., see Calhoun, Craig (ed.) (1992) *Habermas and the Public Sphere*, Cambridge, Mass.: MIT Press. See also, for a more recent application of the concept to a range of contemporary cultural and media policy debates, McGuigan (1996).

10 Conclusion

1 Respondents were asked to circle a value from 1 to 4 on a scale going from 'strongly agree' through 'agree' and 'disagree' to 'strongly disagree'.

References

Abercrombie, N. (1996) *Television and Society*. Oxford: Polity Press.

Alasuutari, P. (1992) '"I'm Ashamed to Admit it But I Have Watched Dallas": The Moral Hierarchy of Television Programmes'. *Media, Culture and Society* 14, 561–82.

Ang, I. (1985) *Watching Dallas: Soap Opera and the Melodramatic Imagination*. London: Methuen.

—— (1994a) 'Living Room Wars: New Technologies, Audience Measurement and the Tactics of Television Consumption', in R. Silverstone and E. Hirsch (eds) *Consuming Technologies: Media and Information in Domestic Spaces*. London: Routledge.

—— (1994b) 'Globalisation and Culture'. *Continuum* 8: 2, 323–5.

Appadurai, Arjun (1986) 'Introduction: Commodities and the Politics of Value', in Arjun Appadurai (ed.) *The Social Life of Things: Commodities in Cultural Perspective*. Cambridge: Cambridge University Press.

Appleton, G. (1997) 'Converging and Emerging Industries: Video, Pay TV and Multimedia', in S. Cunningham and G. Turner (eds) *The Media in Australia: Industries, Texts, Audiences*, 2nd edn. Sydney: Allen & Unwin.

Asad, Talal (1994) 'Ethnographic Representation, Statistics and Modern Power'. *Social Research* 61: 1, 55–88.

Ashelford, Jane (1988) *Dress in the Age of Elizabeth I*. London: Batsford.

Australia Council for the Arts (1995) *Books: Who's Reading Them Now? A Study of Book Buying and Borrowing in Australia*. Redfern, NSW: Australia Council.

Australian Broadcasting Authority (1996) 'Radio Profits Jump'. *ABA Update* March: 11–12.

Australian Broadcasting Tribunal (1985) *Young Australians and Music*. Melbourne: ABT.

Australian Bureau of Statistics (1998) *Participation in Sport and Physical Activities, 1996–97*. Canberra: ABS.

Barry, Andrew, Thomas Osborn and Nikolas Rose (eds) (1996) *Foucault and Political Reason: Liberalism, Neo-Liberalism and Rationalities of Government*. London: UCL Press.

Barthes, Roland (1990) [1967] *The Fashion System*. Trans. Matthew Ward and Richard Howard. Berkeley: University of California Press.

Barwise, P. and A. Ehrenberg (1988) *Television and its Audience*. London: Sage.

Baxter, J., M. Emmison, M. Western, and J. Western (eds) (1991) *Class Analysis and Contemporary Australia*. Melbourne: Macmillan.

Becker, Howard (1974) 'Art as Collective Action'. *American Sociological Review* 39: 6, 767–76.

Bell, P. and R. Bell (1993) *Implicated: The United States in Australia*. Melbourne: Oxford University Press.

Bennett, Tony (1983) 'Text, Readers, Reading Formations', *Literature and History* 9: 2.

—— (1985) 'Texts in History: The Determinations of Readings and Their Texts'. *Journal of the Midwest Modern Language Association* 18: 1.

—— (1994) *The Reluctant Museum Visitor: A Study of Non-Goers to History Museums and Art Galleries*. Redfern, NSW: Australia Council.

—— (1997) 'Consuming Culture, Measuring Access and Audience Development'. *Culture and Policy* 8: 1, 89–114.

Bordo, Susan (1990) 'Reading the Slender Body', in Mary Jacobus et al. (eds) *Body/Politics: Women and the Discourses of Science*. New York: Routledge, 83–112.

—— (1993) *Unbearable Weight: Feminism, Western Culture, and the Body*. Berkeley: University of California Press.

Bourdieu, Pierre (1977) [1972] *Outline of a Theory of Practice*. Trans. Richard Nice. London: Cambridge University Press.

—— (1978) 'Sport and Social Class'. *Social Science Information* 17: 6, 819–40.

—— (1979) 'Public Opinion Does Not Exist', in A. Mattelart and S. Siegelaub (eds) *Communication and Class Struggle: Capitalism, Imperialism*. New York: International General.

—— (1984) [1979] *Distinction: A Social Critique of the Judgement of Taste*. Trans. Richard Nice. Cambridge, Mass.: Harvard University Press.

—— (1986) 'The Forms of Capital', in John G. Richardson (ed.) *Handbook of Theory and Research for the Sociology of Education*. New York: Greenwood Press, 241–58.

—— (1987) 'What Makes a Social Class? On the Theoretical and Practical Existence of Groups'. *Berkeley Journal of Sociology* 32, 1–17.

—— (1990) 'Programme for a Sociology of Sport', in *In Other Words: Essays Towards a Reflexive Sociology*. Trans. Matthew Adamson. Stanford, Calif.: Stanford University Press.

—— (1993) *The Field of Cultural Production: Essays on Art and Literature*. Cambridge: Polity Press.

—— (1994) *Raisons pratiques: Sur la théorie de l'action*. Paris: Seuil.

Bourdieu, Pierre and Jean-Claude Passeron (1964) *Les Héritiers: Les Etudiants et la culture*. Paris: Ed. de Minuit.

—— (1970) *La Reproduction*. Paris: Ed. de Minuit.

Bourdieu, Pierre and Loïc J.D. Wacquant (1992) *An Invitation to Reflexive Sociology*. Cambridge: Polity Press.

Boyd, R. (1960) *The Australian Ugliness*. Melbourne: Cheshire.

Bradbury, B. (1992) 'Like a Virgin-Mother? Materialism and Maternalism in the Songs of Madonna'. *Cultural Studies* 6: 1, 73–96.

Breen, M. (1993) 'Popular Music', in S. Cunningham and G. Turner (eds) *The Media in Australia: Industries, Texts and Audiences*, 2nd edn. Sydney: Allen & Unwin, 119–33.

Brown, Nicholas (1995) *Governing Prosperity: Social Change and Social Analysis in Australia in the 1950s*. Cambridge: Cambridge University Press.

Brunsdon, C. (1989) 'Text and Audience', in E. Seiter, H. Borchers, G. Kreutzner and E.M. Warth (eds) *Remote Control: Television, Audiences and Cultural Power*. London: Routledge.

Bryson B. (1996) '"Anything but Heavy Metal": Symbolic Exclusion and Musical Dislikes'. *American Sociological Review* 61, October, 884–99.

Buckridge, Pat, Pamela Murray and Jock Macleod (1995) *Reading Professional Identities: The Boomers and Their Books*. Cultural Policy Paper, no. 3. Brisbane: Institute for Cultural Policy Studies.

Burchell, Graham, Colin Gordon and Peter Miller (eds) (1991) *The Foucault Effect: Studies in Governmentality*. London: Harvester/Wheatsheaf.

Chamberlain, C. (1983) *Class Consciousness in Australia*. Sydney: Allen & Unwin.

Chapman, Gwen E. (1997) 'Making Weight: Lightweight Rowing, Technologies of Power, and Technologies of the Self'. *Sociology of Sport Journal* 14: 3, 205–23.

Chester, A. (1990) 'Second Thoughts on a Rock Aesthetic: The Band', in S. Frith and A. Goodwin (eds) *On Record: Rock, Pop and the Written Word*. London: Routledge.

Christenson, P. and J. Peterson (1988) 'Genre and Gender in the Structure of Music Preferences'. *Communication Research* 15: 3, 282–301.

Claeys, G. (1986) 'Mass Culture and World Culture: On "Americanisation" and the Politics of Cultural Protection'. *Diogenes* 136, Winter, 70–97.

Collins, Hugh (1985) 'Political Ideology in Australia: The Distinctiveness of a Benthamite Society'. *Daedalus* 114: 1.

Collins, Jim (1989) *Uncommon Cultures: Popular Culture and Post-Modernism*. New York and London: Routledge.

Collins, Randall (1979) *The Credential Society: An Historical Sociology of Education and Stratification*. New York: Academic Press.

Counihan, M. (1990) 'Radio'. *Metro Magazine* 83, 27–8.

Crook, Christopher J. (1997) 'Occupational Returns to Cultural Participation in Australia'. *ANZJS* 33: 1, 56–74.

Cunningham, S. and E. Jacka (1996) *Australian Television and International Mediascapes*. Cambridge: Cambridge University Press.

Defrance, Jacques and Christian Pociello (1993) 'Structure and Evolution of the Field of Sports in France (1960–1990)'. *International Review for the Sociology of Sport* 28: 1, 1–21.

Deihl, E.R., M.J. Schneider, and K.C. Petress (1985) 'Dimensions of Music Preference: Factor Analytic Study'. *Communications* 11: 3, 51–9.

Denisoff, R. and M. Levine (1972) 'Youth and Popular Music: A Test of the Taste Culture Hypothesis'. *Youth and Society* 4, 237–55.

Department of Communications and the Arts (1994) *Creative Nation: Commonwealth Cultural Policy*. Canberra: Commonwealth of Australia.

Department of Finance (1989) *What Price Heritage? The Museums Review and the Measurement of Museums' Performance*. Canberra: Commonwealth of Australia.

DiMaggio, Paul (1987) 'Classification in Art'. *American Sociological Review* 52, 440–55.

—— (1996) 'Are Art Museum Visitors Different from Other People? The Relationship between Attendance and Social and Political Attitudes in the United States'. *Poetics* 24, 161–80.

Dines, G. and J.M. Humez (eds) (1995) *Gender, Race and Class in the Media*. Thousand Oaks, California: Sage Publications.

Dorfman, A. and A. Mattelart (1975) *How to read Donald Duck: Imperialist Ideology in the Disney Comic*. New York: International General Editions.

Edwards, John (1996) *Keating: The Inside Story*. Ringwood, Vic.: Penguin Books.

Elder, B. (1997) 'Rock of the Ages'. *Sydney Morning Herald*, 30 August: Features, 8.

Elias, Norbert (1994) *The Civilising Process*. Oxford: Blackwell.

Elias, Norbert and Eric Dunning (1986) *Quest for Excitement: Sport and Leisure in the Civilizing Process*. Oxford: Basil Blackwell.

Emmison, M. (1991) 'Wright and Goldthorpe: Constructing the Agenda of Class Analysis', in J. Baxter, M. Emmison, J. Western, and M. Western (eds) *Class Analysis and Contemporary Australia*. Melbourne: Macmillan.

Erickson, Bonnie H. (1996) 'Culture, Class and Connections'. *AJS* 102: 1, 217–51.

Featherstone M. (ed.) (1990) *Global Culture: Nationalism, Globalization and Modernity*. London: Sage.

Fejes, F. (1981) 'Media Imperialism: An Assessment'. *Media, Culture and Society* 3, 281–9.

Ferguson, M. (1992) 'The Mythology about Globalisation'. *European Journal of Communication* 7: 1, 69–93.

Foucault, Michel (1977) [1975] *Discipline and Punish*. Trans. Alan Sheridan. Harmondsworth: Penguin.

—— (1988) 'Technologies of the Self', in Luther H. Martin et al. (eds) *Technologies of the Self: A Seminar with Michel Foucault*. Amherst: University of Massachusetts Press, 16–49.

Fox, W. and M. Wince (1975) 'Musical Taste Cultures and Taste Publics'. *Youth and Society* 15, 13–32.

Frith, Simon (1983) *Sound Effects: Youth, Leisure and the Politics of Rock'n'Roll*. London: Constable.

—— (1987) 'Towards an Aesthetic of Popular Music', in R. Leppert and S. McClary (eds) *Music and Society: the Politics of Composition, Performance and Reception*. Cambridge: Cambridge University Press.

—— (1996) *Performing Rites: On the Value of Popular Music*. Oxford: Oxford University Press.

Frow, John (1983) 'Reading as System and as Practice', in E. Schaffer (ed.) *Comparative Criticism*, vol. 5. Cambridge: Cambridge University Press.

—— (1987) 'Accounting for Tastes: Some Problems in Bourdieu's Sociology of Culture'. *Cultural Studies* 1: 1, 59–73.

—— (1995) *Cultural Studies and Cultural Value*. Oxford: Clarendon Press.

Gans, H. (1966) 'Popular Culture in America: Social Problem in a Mass Society or Social Asset in a Pluralist Society?', in H. Becker (ed.) *Social Problems: a Modern Approach*. New York: John Wiley.

Gans, Herbert (1974) *Popular Culture and High Culture: An Analysis and Evaluation of Taste*. New York: Basic Books.

Gantz, W., H. Gartenberg, M. Pearson, and S. Schiller (1978) 'Gratifications and Expectations Associated with Pop Music among Adolescents'. *Popular Music and Society* 6: 1, 81–9.

Garnham, Nicholas (1986) 'Extended Review: Bourdieu's *Distinction*'. *Sociological Review* 34, 423–33.

Gelder, Ken (1994) *Reading the Vampire*. London and New York: Routledge.

Giddens, A. (1990) *The Consequences of Modernity*. Cambridge: Polity Press.

Glassner, Barry (1989) 'Fitness and the Postmodern Self'. *Journal of Health and Social Behavior* 30, 180–91.

Goffman, E. (1951) 'Symbols of Class Status'. *British Journal of Sociology* 2, 294–304.

Guback, T. (1984) 'International Circulation of US Films and Television Programs', in G. Gerbner and M. Siefert (eds) *World Communications: A Handbook*. New York: Longman.

Habermas, Jürgen (1989) *The Structural Transformation of the Public Sphere – An Inquiry into a Category of Bourgeois Society*. Cambridge: Polity Press.

Haddon, L. (1994) 'Explaining ICT Consumption: The Case of Home Consumption', in R. Silverstone and E. Hirsch (eds) *Consuming Technologies: Media and Information in Domestic Spaces*. London: Routledge.

Harman, H.H. (1976) *Modern Factor Analysis*. Chicago: University of Chicago Press.

Hartley, John (1996) *Popular Reality: Journalism, Modernity, Popular Culture*. London: Edward Arnold.

Herbert, Auberon (1885) *The Right and Wrong of Compulsion by the State*. London.

Hirsch, P. (1971) 'Sociological Approaches to the Pop Music Phenomenon'. *American Behavioural Scientist* 14: 3, 371–88.

Hobson, D. (1982) *Crossroads: The Drama of a Soap Opera*. London: Methuen.

Hoskins, C. and R. Mirus (1988) 'Reasons for the US Dominance of the International Trade in Television Programmes'. *Media, Culture and Society* 10: 4, 499–515.

House of Representatives Standing Committee on Expenditure (1986) *Patronage, Power and the Muse: Inquiry into Commonwealth Assistance to the Arts*. Canberra: Australian Government Printing Service.

Hughes, Helen (1993) *The Historical Romance*. London and New York: Routledge.

Hughes, P.L. and J.F. Larkin (eds) (1969) *Tudor Royal Proclamations, Vol. II: The Later Tudors (1553–1587)*. New Haven, Conn.: Yale University Press.

Huxley, Thomas (1890) 'Government: Anarchy or Regimentation'. *The Nineteenth Century*, May.

Jacka, E. (1997) 'Film', in S. Cunningham and G. Turner (eds) *The Media in Australia: Industries, Texts, Audiences*, 2nd edn. Sydney: Allen & Unwin, 227–44.

Jacka, E. (ed.) (1992) *Continental Shift: Globalisation and Culture*. Sydney: Local Consumption Publications.

Jamous, H. and B. Peloille (1970) 'Changes in the French University-Hospital System', in J.A. Jackson (ed.) *Professions and Professionalization*. Cambridge: Cambridge University Press.

Jarvie, Grant and Joseph Maguire (1994) *Sport and Leisure in Social Thought*. London: Routledge.

Jay, Martin (1973) *The Dialectical Imagination: A History of the Frankfurt School and the Institute of Social Research*. London: Heinemann.

Jenkins, Richard (1992) *Pierre Bourdieu*. London: Routledge.

Kim, J.-O. and C.W. Mueller (1978) *Introduction to Factor Analysis*. California: Sage yPublications.

Kirk, David (1994) 'Physical Education and Regimes of the Body'. *Australian and New Zealand Journal of Sociology* 30: 2, 165–77.

Lawrence, Geoffrey and David Rowe (1986) *Power Play: The Commercialisation of Australian Sport*. Sydney: Hale and Iremonger.

Lee, C.C. (1979) *Media Imperialism Reconsidered: The Homogenising of Television Culture*. London: Sage.

Legge, Kate (1997) 'The Women's Chapter'. *The Australian Weekend Review*, 30–31 August, 1.

Lewis, G. (1981) 'Taste Cultures and their Composition: Towards a New Theoretical Perspective', in E. Katz and T. Szecsko (eds) *Mass Media and Social Change*. Beverly Hills, Calif.: Sage, 201–17.

—— (1992) 'Who Do You Love? The Dimensions of Musical Taste', in J. Lull (ed.) *Popular Music and Communication*. Newbury Park, Calif.: Sage, 134–51.

Liebes, T. and E. Katz (1990) *The Export of Meaning: Cross-Cultural Readings of Dallas*. New York: Oxford University Press.

Linder, Staffan Burenstam (1970) *The Harried Leisure Class*. New York: Columbia University Press.

Lyons, Martyn and Lucy Taksa (1992) '"If Mother Caught us Reading O!" Impressions of the Australian Woman Reader 1890–1933'. *Australian Cultural History* 11, 39–50.

Marghescou, Mircea (1974) *Le Concept de littérarité*. The Hague: Mouton.

Mattelart, A. (1979) *Multinational Corporations and the Control of Culture*. Brighton: Harvester Press.

Mauss, Marcel (1979) 'Body Techniques', in *Sociology and Psychology: Essays*. Trans. Ben Brewster. London: Routledge and Kegan Paul.

McGuigan, Jim (1996) *Culture and the Public Sphere*. London: Routledge.

McKay, Jim (1991) *No Pain, No Gain? Sport and Australian Culture*. Sydney: Prentice Hall.

McKay, J., G. Lawrence, T. Miller, and D. Rowe (1993) 'Globalisation and Australian Sport'. *Sports Science Review* 2: 1, 10–28.

McKay, Jim and Toby Miller (1991) 'From Old Boys to Men and Women of the Corporation: The Americanization and Commodification of Australian Sport'. *Sociology of Sport Journal* 8: 1, 86–94.

McKay, J., T. Miller, and D. Rowe (1996) 'Americanisation, Globalisation and Rugby League', in D. Headon & L. Marinos (eds) *League of a Nation*. Sydney: ABC Books, 215–21.

Melleuish, Gregory (1995) *Cultural Liberalism in Australia: A Study in Intellectual and Cultural History*. Cambridge: Cambridge University Press.

Mercer, Daniel (1995) *Navigating the Economy of Knowledge*. Brisbane: Institute for Cultural Policy Studies.

Miller, Toby (1997) 'Radio', in S. Cunningham and G. Turner (eds) *The Media in Australia: Industries, Texts, Audiences*, 2nd edn. Sydney: Allen & Unwin, 41–58.

Miller, T., N. Lucy, and G. Turner (1990) 'Radio', in S. Cunningham and G. Turner (eds) *The Media in Australia: Industries, Texts, Audiences*. Sydney: Allen & Unwin, 156–70.

Modleski, Tania (1982) *Living with a Vengeance: Mass-produced Fantasies for Women*. New York and London: Methuen.

Molnar, H. (1997) 'Radio', in S. Cunningham and G. Turner (eds) *The Media in Australia: Industries, Texts, Audiences*, 2nd edn. Sydney: Allen & Unwin, 201–26.

Morley, D. (1986) *Family Television: Cultural Power and Domestic Leisure*. London: Comedia.

—— (1992) *Television Audiences and Cultural Studies*. London: Routledge.

Morse, Margaret (1990) 'An Ontology of Everyday Distraction: the Freeway, the Mall, and Television', in P. Mellencamp (ed.) *Logics of Television: Essays in Cultural Criticism*. Bloomington: Indiana University Press, 193–221.

—— (1987/8) 'Artemis Aging: Exercise and the Female Body on Video'. *Discourse* 10: 1, 20–53.

Mulaik, S.A. (1972) *The Foundations of Factor Analysis*. New York: McGraw-Hill.

Murdock, G., P. Hartmann, and P. Gray (1994) 'Contextualizing Home Computing: Resources and Practices', in R. Silverstone and E. Hirsch (eds) *Consuming Technologies: Media and Information in Domestic Spaces*. London: Routledge.

Nederveen Pieterse, J. (1994) 'Globalisation as Hybridisation'. *International Sociology* 9: 2, 161–84.

Noble, D. (1979) *America by Design*. New York: Oxford University Press.

Nordenstreng, K. and T. Varis (1974) *Television Traffic: A One-Way Street*. UNESCO Reports and Papers on Mass Communication, No. 70.

Nowell-Smith, G. (1987) 'Popular Culture'. *New Formations* 2, 79–90.

O'Regan, T. (1992) 'Too Popular by Far: On Hollywood's International Popularity'. *Continuum* 5: 2, 302–51.

—— (1993) *Australian Television Culture*. Sydney: Allen & Unwin.

Patterson, O. (1994) 'Ecumenical America: Global Culture and the American Cosmos'. *World Policy Journal* 11: 2, 103–17.

Perkins, Harold (1989) *The Rise of the Professional Society: England from 1880*. New York: Routledge.

Peterson, R. (1992) 'Understanding Audience Segmentation: From Elite and Mass to Omnivore and Univore'. *Poetics* 21, 243–58.

Peterson, R. and R. Kern (1996) 'Changing Highbrow Taste: from Snob to Omnivore'. *American Sociological Review* 61, October, 900–7.

Peterson, R. and A. Simkus (1992) 'How Musical Tastes Mark Occupational Status Groups', in M. Lamont and M. Fournier (eds) *Cultivating Differences: Symbolic Boundaries and the Making of Inequality*. Chicago: The University of Chicago Press.

Poovey, Mary (1993) 'Figures of Arithmetic, Figures of Speech: The Discourse of Statistics in the 1830s'. *Critical Inquiry* 19: 2, 256–76.

—— (1995) *Making a Social Body: British Cultural Formation, 1830–1864*. Chicago and London: The University of Chicago Press.

Potts, J. (1989) *Radio in Australia*. Sydney: UNSW Press.

Probyn, Elspeth (1993) *Sexing the Self: Gendered Positions in Cultural Studies*. London: Routledge.

Radway, Janice (1984) *Reading the Romance: Women, Patriarchy and Popular Litera-ture*. Chapel Hill: University of North Carolina Press.

Robertson, R. (1992) *Globalization: Social Theory and Global Culture*. London: Sage.

Robinson, J. and E. Fink (1986) 'Beyond Mass Culture and Class Culture: Subcultural Differences in the Structure of Music Preferences', in S. Ball-Rokeach and M. Cantor (eds) *Media, Audience and Social Structure*. Beverly Hills, Calif.: Sage.

Rojek, Chris (1985) *Capitalism and Leisure Theory*. London: Tavistock.

—— (1989) *Leisure for Leisure: Critical Essays*. London: Macmillan.

—— (1995) *Decentring Leisure: Rethinking Leisure Theory*. London: Sage.

Rose, Nikolas (1996) 'The Death of the Social? Re-figuring the Territory of Govern-ment'. *Economy and Society* 25: 3.

Rowse, Tim (1978) *Australian Liberalism and National Character*. Melbourne: Kibble Books.

—— (1985) *Arguing the Arts: The Funding of the Arts in Australia*. Ringwood, Vic.: Penguin Books.

Schiller, H. (1976) *Communication and Cultural Domination*. New York: M.E. Sharpe.

—— (1991) 'Not Yet the Post-Imperialist Era'. *Critical Studies in Mass Communication* 8, 13–28.

Seabrook, Jeremy (1988) *The Leisure Society*. Oxford: Basil Blackwell.

Seiter, E., M. Borchers, G. Kreutzner and E.M. Warth (eds) (1989) *Remote Control: Television, Audiences and Cultural Power*. London: Routledge.

Serle, G. (1967) 'Godzone: Austerica Unlimited?'. *Meanjin* 26, 237–50.

Shilling, Chris (1991) 'Educating the Body: Physical Capital and the Production of Social Inequalities'. *Sociology* 25: 4, 653–72.

—— (1993) *The Body and Social Theory*. London: Sage.

Silverstone, R. (1994) *Television and Everyday Life*. London: Routledge.

Spitzack, C. (1990) *Confessing Excess: Women and the Politics of Body Reduction*. Albany, NY: SUNY Press.

Thornton, Sarah (1996) *Club Cultures: Music, Media and Subcultural Capital*. Cam-bridge: Polity Press.

Tomlinson, J. (1991) *Cultural Imperialism: A Critical Introduction*. Baltimore, MD: Johns Hopkins University Press.

Tracey, M. (1985) 'The Poisoned Chalice? International Television and the Idea of Dominance'. *Daedalus* 114: 4, 17–56.

—— (1988) 'Popular Culture and the Economics of Global Television'. *Intermedia* 16: 2, 9–25.

Tulloch, John and Henry Jenkins III Jr (1995) *Science Fiction Audiences: Watching Dr Who and Star Trek*. London: Routledge.

Turner, Bryan S. (1996) *The Body and Society: Explorations in Social Theory*, 2nd edn. London: Sage.

Turner, G. (1992) 'Australian Popular Music and its Contexts', in P. Hayward (ed.) *From Pop to Punk to Postmodernism: Popular Music and Australian Culture from the 1960s to the 1990s*. Sydney: Allen & Unwin.

—— (1993) 'Who Killed the Radio Star? The Death of Teen Radio in Australia', in T. Bennett, S. Frith, L. Grossberg, J. Shepherd and G. Turner (eds) *Rock and Popular Music: Politics, Policies and Institutions*. London: Routledge.

Varis, T. (1974) 'Global Traffic in Television'. *Journal of Communication* 24: 1, 102–9.

Varis, T. (1984) 'The International Flow of Television Programmes'. *Journal of Communication* 43:1, 143–52.

Veblen, T. (1970) [1889] *The Theory of the Leisure Class: an Economic Study of Institutions*. London: Unwin Books.

Weber, M. (1978) [1968] *Economy and Society: An Outline of Interpretive Sociology*. Eds G. Roch and C. Wittich. New York: Bedminster Press.

White, R. (1980) 'Combating Cultural Aggression: Australian Opposition to Americanisation'. *Meanjin* 39, 275–89.

—— (1983) 'A Backwater Awash: The Australian Experience of Americanisation'. *Theory, Culture & Society* 1: 3, 108–22.

Index